P9-DTI-731

end of tepidarium

Tile&c

opposite Ganymede

opposite Ganymede

candelab

in tepid.

2 ft high

EDITED BY

Victoria C. Gardner Coates and Jon L. Seydl

TEPIDARIVM

Antiquity Recovered

The Legacy *of* Pompeii and Herculaneum

The J. Paul Getty Museum, Los Ang

For Malcolm with love.

© 2007 J. Paul Getty Trust

Published by the J. Paul Getty
Museum, Los Angeles

Getty Publications
1200 Getty Center Drive
Suite 500
Los Angeles, California
90049-1682
www.getty.edu

Mark Greenberg
Editor in Chief

PROJECT STAFF
John Harris
Editor
Kathleen Preciado
Manuscript Editor
Jeffrey Cohen
Designer
Stacy Miyagawa
Production Coordinator

Typesetting by Diane Franco
Printed by Imago, Singapore

Frontispiece: William Gell
(British, 1777–1836),
Tepidarium, ca. 1829–30 (detail).
Pen, ink, and watercolor.
From the sketchbook of
William Gell. Los Angeles,
Research Library, Getty
Research Institute, 2002.M.16.

Library of Congress Cataloging-in-Publication Data

Antiquity recovered : the legacy of Pompeii and Herculaneum /
edited by Victoria C. Gardner Coates and Jon L. Seydl.
    v. cm.
  Includes index.
   ISBN: 978-0-89236-872-3 (hardback)
   1. Pompeii (Extinct city) 2. Herculaneum (Extinct city)
3. Pompeii (Extinct city)—Civilization. 4. Herculaneum (Extinct
city)—Civilization. 5. Excavations (Archaeology) — Italy—
Pompeii (Extinct city) 6. Excavations (Archaeology) — Italy—
Herculaneum (Extinct city) 7. Naples Region (Italy)—Antiquities.
I. Gardner Coates, Victoria C. II. Seydl, Jon L., 1969-
   DG70.P7A73 2007
   937'.7—dc22
                                        2006032188

Contents

Acknowledgments

This collaborative, multifaceted volume could only have come to pass with the help of many willing partners. The most rewarding aspect of this project has been the opportunity to work with such wonderful, capable people over the past several years. Our first thanks go to our fourteen authors, who graciously tolerated our pushing and prodding and who engaged us in such profitable dialogue while they shaped their essays. We are honored to present the work of these imaginative, energetic, and exciting scholars. This book's ultimate success is theirs, not ours.

Our seedling project found welcoming and fertile ground at the J. Paul Getty Museum, where a range of scholars and editors have generously shared their expertise. We must first thank the Department of Antiquities, particularly Marion True and Kenneth Lapatin, whose deep sensitivity to the complex reception of antiquity and warm encouragement helped shape the present volume. We could not be more delighted that the book will be first available at the Getty Villa, a most fitting monument for texts about the reception of the ancient sites of Pompeii and Herculaneum.

We are also grateful to members of the Publications Committee at the J. Paul Getty Museum, led by Michael Brand, for their support.

From the very beginning, it has been a joy to work with our colleagues at Getty Publications. Benedicte Gilman, Christopher Hudson, Kara Kirk, and especially Mark Greenberg astutely helped us position the volume within the impressive series of publications on antiquities from the Getty Museum. John Harris has been a model editor, and his patience, wise counsel, and calm intelligence have been indispensable to two fledgling editors. Our two anonymous reviewers provided helpful perspective and keen commentary. Jeffrey Cohen has designed a beautiful volume, bringing the essays to life through a thoughtful and elegant design, and Stacy Miyagawa organized the production with aplomb. Cecily Gardner and Dominique Loder handled the maddening task of assembling the photographs for so many different authors, and Kathleen Preciado has graciously brought order to the text, notes, and bibliography through her assiduous copyediting.

We would also like to thank Columbia University and Kenyon College for their subventions as well as the Getty Research Institute, which graciously and efficiently handled the lion's share of the photograph requests.

Brian T. Allen has been enormously supportive of this project, and it is because of him that the volume was able to take on such a wide disciplinary and geographical range. For judicious guidance and other pivotal aid at crucial moments, we extend our heartfelt thanks to Peter Bonfitto, William M. Griswold, Ann Harrison, Christopher M. S. Johns, Rose Linke, Claire L. Lyons, Paul Martineau, Katrina Mohn, Betsey Robinson, Audrey Sands, Scott Schaefer, Jennifer Vanim, Julia Wai, Ted Walbye, Lena Watanabe, and Jesse Zwack.

Without the initial generosity of the Samuel H. Kress Foundation, *Antiquity Recovered* would, quite simply, never have left the planning stage. Our thanks go to

Lisa M. Ackerman and Wyman Meers, who provided both sustenance and encouragement through their personal interest in our progress.

Antiquity Recovered began its long journey at the Arthur Ross Gallery of the University of Pennsylvania, and we thank the staff and board of trustees of the gallery, who enabled our 2002 exhibition. We also are indebted to all those who supported the symposium that originally involved us in the material that appears in this volume.

We gratefully acknowledge the assistance of our colleagues in the Department of the History of Art, especially David Brownlee, Renata Holod, and Ann Kuttner, as well as Daniel Richter and the McNeil Center for Early American Studies. Thanks also are due to the University of Pennsylvania Museum of Archaeology and Anthropology, the Center for Ancient Studies, the Center for Italian Studies, the Graduate Group in the Art and Architecture of the Mediterranean World, the Classical Studies Department, the Department of History, the Department of English, and the Comparative Literature and Literary Theory Program. We received additional and timely support from the university administration through the kind auspices of Deputy Provost Peter Conn and (then) Associate Dean for Arts and Letters Rebecca Bushnell and from the Graduate Student Associations Council. Finally, we two Penn alumni would like to extend our thanks to the broader university community, including the staffs of the Department of the History of Art, the Fisher Fine Arts Library and Image Collection, and the Van Pelt–Dietrich Rare Book and Manuscript Collection.

Paul and Carol Collins provided the locus for our Berkshire editorial retreat in the summer of 2004, perhaps the loveliest memory of the entire project. The original Friends of Antiquity helped us make our vision of "Pompeii on the Schuylkill" a reality, and our thanks go to Ronald and Linda Anderson, Cummins and Susan Catherwood, Paul and Carol Collins, Eugene and Anne Gardner, Eugene and Bernadette Gardner, Paul and Beverly Gardner, and Thomas A. and Gina Russo. Our families also deserve to be singled out for their remarkable patience and good cheer throughout the entire enterprise, especially George Coates and Daniel McLean.

We dedicate this volume to our once and future adviser, Professor Malcolm Campbell at the University of Pennsylvania. His intellectual rigor, scholarly generosity, commitment to collaboration, and endless curiosity about the intersection of the classical and modern worlds have been our inspiration for this project.

Victoria C. Gardner Coates and Jon L. Seydl

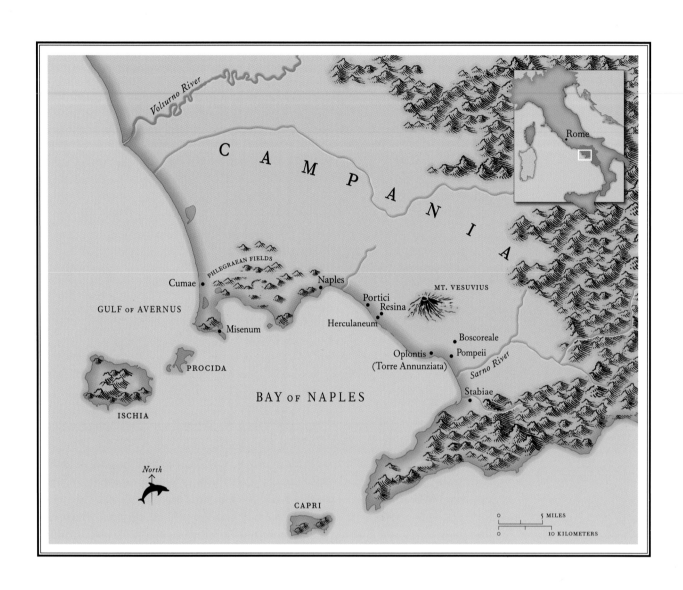

Introduction

Victoria C. Gardner Coates and Jon L. Seydl

*On Sunday we went to Pompeii—there has been much calamity in the world,
but little that has brought posterity so much pleasure.*

Johann Wolfgang Goethe, March 13, 1787[1]

MORE THAN SIXTEEN HUNDRED YEARS after the eruption of Vesuvius physically reshaped the landscape of the Bay of Naples in A.D. 79, the recovery of Herculaneum and Pompeii transformed our understanding of the ancient world. The magnitude of this archaeological event has earned the cities a place among the preeminent sites of classical antiquity, but the wealth of the finds makes their evaluation a herculean task. While their completeness has led to the persistent impression of the recovered cities as a transparent window into the classical past, Herculaneum and Pompeii did not emerge from the earth fully formed like Minerva from the head of Jupiter. On the contrary, the sites have been in constant flux, from the moment in 1709 when the first antiquities were removed from a well shaft in Resina to the present-day excavations. Scholarship on the finds has been equally fluid, as drastic changes in method followed each other in rapid succession and even at times contentiously coexisted. Each layer of interpretation has melded into the next, leaving a complex trail of discovery, response, and exploitation. At the same time the objects and environments have been decontextualized, reshaped, and in some cases lost altogether. Sustained attention to the constantly changing reception of the sites thus tells us not only about antiquity but also about how postclassical mind-sets have shaped interpretations of the past.

Herculaneum and Pompeii have enjoyed almost three hundred years of fame and visibility in the cultural imagination of the West, which has been fascinated alternately by the record of daily life they preserve as well as by the quick and merciless destruction of the cities in A.D. 79. Our volume salutes the afterlife of Herculaneum and Pompeii through case studies illustrating how our perception of the past has changed over the course of excavation. These essays examine how the discoveries were interpreted, reinterpreted, and situated in popular culture and scholarly discourse from 1709 through the mid-twentieth century. How did conditions of their discovery, excavation, publication, fictionalization, and physical accessibility affect understanding of the sites? How did the discoveries alter previously held notions of the classical, and how were new objects, images, and texts incorporated into an expanding classical canon? How did publications (or the absence thereof) condition interpretation of the sites? How did changes in excavation methods and modes of publishing affect reception of the discoveries? How did politics—of the local Neapolitan governments and of the international community—shape perception of the sites? What role did geography play? How did readings of ancient texts shape the interpretation of the discoveries? If the ruins invited a glimpse into the private life of ancient Romans, how did this perspective shape contemporary social norms? Even within the startlingly rich finds, lacunae still exist; how were these gaps of knowledge understood? Reception is thus the primary subject of our volume and not the pursuit of an unattainably pure understanding of the sites, whether through the study of isolated artifacts or of the whole urban or suburban environments. So, just as archaeologists have removed layers of ash and mud to reveal the cities below, we seek to separate strata of interpretation to reveal successive ways of recovering and understanding Herculaneum and Pompeii.

History of the Project

Our prior scholarship on early modern figures such as Poussin, Claude, and David confronted the reconstruction and exploitation of antiquity and eventually led us to the cult of Herculaneum and Pompeii.[2] We had encountered broad assertions that antiquarianism as a field of study was transformed by eighteenth-century discoveries in the Bay of Naples, but the process of transformation was never satisfactorily addressed.[3] Many archaeologists have been quick to criticize the biases and errors of their forerunners who were dealing with a less complete archaeological record. At the same time, they rarely applied such a critical approach to more recent work. Art historians and literary scholars, in contrast, often explored successive interpretations of other antique sites with great sophistication but have regularly taken Pompeii and Herculaneum as a fixed point of tangible and static influence.[4] To some extent this situation was caused by the fortuitous excavation history of the cities. They suddenly appeared in the eighteenth century, heralded by an impeccable classical literary legacy but unburdened by the centuries of interpretation that weighed on the remains in Rome. Pompeii and Herculaneum thus provided not only a window into the past but also a mirror of the present into which modern antiquarians could gaze—and, not seeing their immediate predecessors, they saw themselves.[5] But this process is now nearly three centuries old, and it seemed to us a more sustained exploration of the reception of the sites was in order.

The dual nature of the recovery of Herculaneum and Pompeii as effecting a decisive increase in the knowledge of antiquity and as part of the longer and ongoing history of the classical legacy caught our attention during a discussion inspired by a lecture on the Grand Tour,[6] which for us raised questions about how understanding of the ancient sites was absorbed in specific, local contexts. The Grand Tour is still so often cast as a totalizing phenomenon, but the experience, particularly visits to the sensational digs at Herculaneum and later Pompeii, seemed to have particular resonances for Americans who traveled in Europe.[7] We began to delve into the often asserted but rarely explored notion that the experiences of eighteenth-century Philadelphians in Italy led to a specialized appreciation of classical culture. How did this understanding shape the cultural, intellectual, and political life of the young metropolis, which aspired to the perceived ideals of antiquity? We examined this issue in a 2002 exhibition at the Arthur Ross Gallery at the University of Pennsylvania. *Antiquity Recovered: Pompeii and Herculaneum in Philadelphia Collections* explored how the City of Brotherly Love, with a sense of cultural affinity that bridged gaps of time as well as distance, engaged with the buried cities and drew from their example Philadelphia's own identity from the eighteenth century forward.[8]

Through this exhibition we discovered that the experience of Philadelphians had two distinct but interlaced aspects, which we called Antiquarianism and City of the Dead. The recovery of Herculaneum and Pompeii fortuitously coincided with a broad revival of classical culture in the eighteenth century. The relationship, however, between the recovery of Pompeii and Herculaneum and eighteenth-century classicism is not at all straightforward. Neoclassicism (called the "true style," or *buon gusto*, in the eighteenth century) was already a vibrant international presence by the time the finds were widely published, so the cities cannot be interpreted as its point of origin. Rather, Pompeii and Herculaneum propelled an intellectual and stylistic movement already in full swing, especially since—as many of the authors in this volume underscore—access to the finds remained limited for many decades and the initial response to them was often disappointment rather than rhapsody. The dominance of classicism over eighteenth-century culture ensured that the finds eventually became an international celebrity event, while the new finds endowed neoclassicism with a profound and pervasive aura of archaeological correctness.[9]

For eager antiquarians, these sites represented not only a massive increase in the surviving physical remains of antiquity but also a fusion of the canonical classical civilizations of Greece and Rome. As was well known through ancient authors such as Strabo and Herodotus, southern Italy was a Greek colony from the eighth century until the Roman conquest of Magna Grecia at the end of the fourth century B.C., and the Greek presence in the area remained strong.[10] This combined heritage made the sites particularly compelling. While Winckelmann's studies fueled a growing appreciation for the role of Greece in classical culture,[11] Attica and the rest of the Greek peninsula remained too remote for most travelers. In the Bay of Naples visitors could probe both cultures with relative ease.

Philadelphia was a center for classicizing culture in the United States, and we discovered many individual and collective episodes that brought the finds to the city. Beginning in the second decade of the eighteenth century objects from the sites traveled outside southern Italy by legal and illegal means. Black markets pedaled artifacts of indeterminate origin to Grand Tourists eager to take home a souvenir, while such figures as William Hamilton, the British ambassador to the Neapolitan court, shipped

FIGURE 1
Skyphos, Apulia, Italy,
ca. 340–320 B.C.
Terracotta.
Philadelphia Museum
of Art, 242-1998-175a–b.
Lent by the Commis-
sioners of Fairmount Park,
Philadelphia, PA.

boatloads of objects for sale in London.[12] In Philadelphia James Logan received the first known piece of antique pottery to arrive in America—the fourth-century B.C. skyphos from southern Italy preserved in the collections of Fairmount Park—from his London dealer in 1740 [FIG. 1].[13] In 1765 Samuel Powel, Philadelphia's first mayor after the Revolution, and John Morgan, founder of the University of Pennsylvania Medical School, toured the sites and climbed Vesuvius as the culmination of their tour through Italy. Powel and Morgan recorded their experiences in correspondence and journals, and both men commissioned portraits from Angelica Kauffmann to commemorate their journey [FIG. 2].[14] Despite an abundance of troubling concerns during his post as colonial representative to London (1757–75), Benjamin Franklin found time to respond to the request from the newly established Free Library of Philadelphia for Pierre d'Hancarville's *Antiquités étrusques, grecques, et romaines tirées du cabinet de M. Hamilton* (1766–67), which famously included finds from Pompeii and Herculaneum. This book was considered so precious that it was one of only six volumes in the library not permitted to circulate—and its perpetual presence made the discoveries available to all Philadelphians.[15]

In the nineteenth century archaeology continued to be a vital aspect of the study of Pompeii and Herculaneum, and it is essential to remember that excavations remained active during this century [FIG. 3]. Indeed, some of the best-known discoveries hail from this period. At the same time, as political changes and the escalating ease and relative cheapness of steam and rail travel brought new visitors to the sites, the tragic decimation of the cities moved to the foreground of popular imagination.[16] The encroachment of romantic sensibility onto more detached and abstract antiquarian turf neatly crystallized in 1832, when Sir Walter Scott (himself dying) visited Pompeii and Herculaneum in the company of the eminent archaeologist Sir William Gell. Gell took Scott to see the most important artifacts; he even had a special private excavation arranged for the author's entertainment. According to Gell, his learned discourse fell on deaf ears: "I was sometimes able to call his attention to such objects as were the most worthy of remark. To these observations, however, he seemed in general nearly insensible, viewing the whole and not the parts, with the eye not of an antiquary but a poet, and exclaiming frequently 'The City of the Dead,' without any other remark."[17]

This episode was widely reported, and it demonstrates that a frisson of delight and horror at the prospect of so much death in such an idyllic setting was as valid a response

FIGURE 2
Angelica Kauffmann
(Swiss, 1741–1807),
Portrait of Dr. John Morgan,
1764–65. Oil on canvas.
Washington, D.C., National
Portrait Gallery, Smithsonian
Institution; this acquisition
was made possible by a
generous contribution from
the James Smithson Society.
NPG.78.221.

FIGURE 3
Attributed to
Giorgio Sommer
(Italian, 1834–1914),
Pompeii—Ultimi scavi,
about 1875. Albumen
silver print. Los Angeles,
J. Paul Getty Museum,
2004.51.1.

to the sites as antiquarian reflection. The year A.D. 79 became an allegory for current events in America, with the destruction of the Roman cities interpreted as a precursor of contemporary cataclysms, such as the Civil War.[18] Philadelphians eagerly participated in the creative reconstructions of the eruption that flooded popular culture. In *The Last Night of Pompeii*, Sumner Lincoln Fairfield's poem written in Philadelphia in 1832, the disaster symbolized divine wrath in a classical version of the biblical flood.[19] Fairfield's poem anticipated the British author Sir Edward Bulwer-Lytton's immensely popular *The Last Days of Pompeii*, published in 1834.[20] The craze provoked by this novel in turn inspired Philadelphian George Henry Boker's 1885 *Nydia; A Tragic Play* and especially the runaway sculptural success at the 1876 Philadelphia Centennial Exposition of *Nydia, the Blind Girl of Pompeii* by Randolph Rogers [FIG. 4].[21] During this period an anonymous Philadelphian made the pilgrimage to Pompeii and brought back a relic in the form of a small wooden box filled with the volcanic ash that had buried the ancient city. This treasure was donated to the University of Pennsylvania Museum of Archaeology and Anthropology as an artifact worthy of preservation and display [FIG. 5]. Despite its diminutive size and humble appearance, the box of ash represents the nexus of scientific, romantic, and touristic approaches to Herculaneum and Pompeii at the end of the nineteenth century as well as the desire to appropriate the sites physically to Philadelphia.

Philadelphians could have the sensation of experiencing the excavations without leaving the banks of the Schuylkill River when the Fairmount Park Pompeian Pavilion

FIGURE 4
Randolph Rogers (American, 1825–1892), *Nydia, the Blind Girl of Pompeii*, before 1870s. Marble. Philadelphia, Pennsylvania Academy of the Fine Arts, 1895.5. Gift of Mrs. Bloomfield Moore.

FIGURE 5
Box of ash from Pompeii, collected nineteenth century. Philadelphia, University of Pennsylvania Museum of Archaeology and Anthropology, MS3415.

Photo: University of Pennsylvania Museum (image negative #149026).

FIGURE 6

Chiurazzi Foundry bronze
casts on exhibit in the
Pepper Gallery at the
University Museum, 1904.
Philadelphia, University
of Pennsylvania Museum of
Archaeology and
Anthropology.

Photo: University of Pennsylvania
Museum (image negative
#148681).

opened in 1878. This series of thirty-four massive cabinets—explicitly pitched to
working-class audiences—allowed visitors to witness tableaux narrating the last
days of Pompeii.[22] In a more didactic vein, in 1904 Philadelphia entrepreneur John
Wanamaker purchased from the Chiurazzi Foundry in Naples a fine collection of
bronzes cast from objects found at Herculaneum and Pompeii for the University
Museum. The bronzes were considered so exceptional that they first appeared in the
Italian Pavilion at the Louisiana Exposition in Saint Louis that year. They then were
displayed with the University Museum's Greek and Roman antiquities so that students
could learn about the Bay of Naples discoveries firsthand [FIG. 6].[23] In the late twentieth century changing approaches to museum display relegated most of these objects to
storage as reproductions, but they now are experiencing a contemporary renaissance
as they are appreciated as works of art in their own right as well as representatives of
the past that enhance attempted reconstructions of entire ancient environments. Many
returned to the galleries in 2003 as part of the University Museum's reinstallation of
its Roman collection—a shift in taste reflected in the use of the Chiurazzi bronzes in
the original installation of the J. Paul Getty Museum in Malibu in the 1970s and their
subsequent reinstallation in the Getty Villa.[24]

 The issues raised by the exhibition in Philadelphia were local, so to consider them
in a larger geographical and temporal context, we convened an international symposium at the University of Pennsylvania in October 2002. By concentrating on reception of the site and downplaying focus on individual disciplines, scholars explored
questions traditionally relegated to the periphery of their work and came into long-
overdue contact with one another. The excitement surrounding the conference suggested that a larger volume was in order. For this project, we expanded our purview
to include a broader range of scholars, sought out a wider disciplinary range, and
included new voices to expand the volume's depth and breadth. Ultimately we found

that our understanding of the local impact of Pompeii and Herculaneum has itself been amplified and transformed in the course of forming this collection of essays.

Volume Contents

The following essays are broad in scope. Our goal is a kaleidoscopic view of responses to the excavations, so they range from the sixteenth through the twentieth century and cover disciplines that include archaeology, art history, history, history of science, and literary and film studies. The originality of the material presented enhances the diversity of period and discipline. The authors have incorporated new archival and primary-source material, and while some images discussed are well known, many are published here for the first time. The volume thus provides a more thorough interrogation of the cultural afterlife of Pompeii and Herculaneum than has previously been attempted.

In the broadest strokes the volume confirms the dual response we presented in the Philadelphia exhibition. Interest in the destruction of the city certainly existed from the outset, and archaeological concerns were never abandoned after the eighteenth century, but the essays by Sean Cocco, Alden Gordon, Claire L. Lyons and Marcia Reed, Tina Najbjerg, James I. Porter, and Hérica Valladares reveal that antiquarianism and empirical investigation initially dominated the discoveries and the sites were understood as an opportunity to recover the reality of the ancient world. The drama of destruction came to the fore in the course of the early nineteenth century as knowledge about the cities became more widely disseminated. Pompeii and Herculaneum then became loci for emotional as well as intellectual fulfillment as human sympathy formed a conduit for an immediate and poignant connection with the plight of the ancients, as is demonstrated by the work of Lee Behlman, Chloe Chard, Eugene Dwyer, and Nick Yablon. The essays also expanded our framework, for the sites took on new significance in the twentieth century, with psychoanalytic, modernist, and poststructuralist interpretations emerging as dominant frames; Bettina Bergmann, Elaine K. Gazda, and Jennie Hirsh represent this trend in the volume. This story has led us to wonder how contemporary responses to Herculaneum and Pompeii, such as Robert Harris's 2004 bestselling novel *Pompeii*, the recent Discovery Channel documentary *Pompeii: The Last Day*, the renovation of the Getty Villa (modeled after the Villa dei Papiri), and, indeed, our own volume, subsequently will be judged as evidence of an early-twenty-first-century mind-set.

Geographical concerns have preoccupied many of our authors, who consider how the physical reality of the buried cities has conditioned our perception of them. Sean Cocco begins the volume by considering volcanism in the Campi Flegrei during the sixteenth and seventeenth centuries. Early modern understandings of the violent geographic phenomena were filtered through ancient texts describing similar activity, not only providing scientific evidence but also creating a powerful continuity with the ancient world. Indeed, volcanic activity at Vesuvius in the late seventeenth and eighteenth centuries could only be understood in connection with the Campi Flegrei and the volcanism of antiquity, conditioning the powerful hold that interpretations of ancient texts about the Bay of Naples would have on understanding later events and discoveries.

The legacy of the initial Bourbon excavations and their publication in the massive, nine-volume *Delle antichità di Ercolano* has likewise emerged as a major theme of our volume. These excavations and publications have long been demonized for their decontextualization and exploitation of the ancient sites. Alden Gordon and Tina Najbjerg maintain this sharply critical tradition, but they also provide insight into why the Neapolitan royal family and the Real accademia ercolanese elected to operate in secret and why their excavation methods neglected considerations of context. Although it is well known that Charles-Nicolas Cochin and Jérôme-Charles Bellicard exposed the tightly held secret of the Herculaneum excavations to a waiting international audience, Alden Gordon—by exploring their working methods and placing their acts in a broader context of international antiquarian networks operating in opposition to the Bourbon excavators—has reconstructed, in an eighteenth-century tale of espionage, how these two scholars were able to open the site to serious inquiry.

Tina Najbjerg and Hérica Valladares reexamine the early excavations through individual wall paintings: the works lining the Porticus of Herculaneum and the famous Four Women from Stabiae. These essays explore the crucial issue of the recovery of ancient painting in the course of the Bay of Naples excavations, which substantially altered earlier fragmentary understanding of this lost art. The extraordinary finds in some respects overwhelmed eager scholars and collectors, who treated them according to the aesthetic norms of their own time. Najbjerg explains the frustrating Bourbon approach to wall painting as individual framed works destined for the burgeoning royal museum, sliced without records from their original locations. She then proposes a reconstruction of the original program of the porticus and demonstrates how modern scholars must plumb eighteenth-century sources for archaeological evidence by using, for example, such unexpected objects as the Bourbon ceramic Servizio Ercolano. Valladares closely examines the intellectual aims of the *Antichità* and uses these volumes both to understand the Bourbon reception of some of the best-known ancient paintings, the Four Women from Stabiae, and to seek in the Ercolanesi's multivalent descriptions of the paintings a key to the ancient understanding of them. She presents the Four Women as deliberately elusive, designed to be puzzled over and debated by their original audiences.

The excavations have commonly been presented in a positivist light as revealing a new, empirical understanding of daily life in antiquity and allowing for a more accurate account of Roman wall paintings, domestic architecture, and ancient urban culture than had previously been possible. This approach has proven problematic. Despite mighty efforts to make them conform, many discoveries unearthed in the Bay of Naples flew directly in the face of cherished notions of antique culture and provoked a crisis about the very nature of classicism. James I. Porter's essay on the texts of Philodemus discovered in the Villa dei Papiri places this anxiety in relief. Rather than amplifying venerable ideas about the classical world, the papyri created a rupture in the canon, adding—through the disturbing form of carbonized scrolls—an unfamiliar and apparently dissonant voice to classical literature and philosophy in the work of Philodemus. These scrolls, once painstakingly reconstructed, also emerged as texts that questioned the Platonic, and by extension the Winckelmannian, underpinnings of the entire enterprise of classicism as it had been conceived in the eighteenth century.

Chloe Chard changes the course of these antiquarian lines of inquiry as she explores a more immediate aspect of the challenge of coming to terms with the discoveries. Chard observes that accounts of the ancient sites in travel writing often

FIGURE 7
Giorgio Sommer
(Italian, 1834–1914),
Dog Found at Pompeii, 1863.
Albumen silver print.
Los Angeles, J. Paul Getty
Museum, 84.XP.677.31.

interweave surprisingly discursive descriptions of meals, drinking, and other playful digressions with learned accounts of the ancient sites or sublime encounters with ruins. Rather than working around these interruptions, she makes them the subject of her study, considering them strategies, for example, employed by authors to lend perspective to their commentary, to cope with the overwhelming unfamiliarity of their experiences, or to position the authors' critical distance and, therefore, their authority to interpret their experiences appropriately.

The many publications that have most broadly disseminated the ancient sites in the Bay of Naples to an eager public are the focus of the essay by Claire L. Lyons and Marcia Reed. The rapidly expanding collections of the Getty Research Institute— with many items published here for the first time—provide a case study of how publications and other textual materials (such as prints, maps, sketchbooks, annotated texts, and research notes) developed over two centuries. Lyons and Reed demonstrate how these texts reflect larger developments regarding the reception of Pompeii and Herculaneum as well as how these materials actively shaped the public imagination.

Narratives centering on the trauma of the horrific destruction of the cities became the predominant approach in the nineteenth century as Scott's "City of the Dead" supplanted the antiquarian vision of the sites. Giuseppe Fiorelli's casts of dead bodies played a key role in this change, catalyzing and performing for a broad public the terror of Vesuvius's eruption as they revivified the dead in their final moments [FIG. 7]. Eugene Dwyer explores the ramifications of this shocking physical manifestation of the ghosts of antiquity, whose creation formed a compelling nexus between the subjective and objective aspects of archaeology. Dwyer uses the episode of the casts to consider how death was perceived at Pompeii, ranging from the earliest skeletal discoveries through the perceived narratives of the victims to the decision in the 1860s by Fiorelli to cast and display the contorted bodies.

Lee Behlman has revisited one of the most popular nineteenth-century Pompeian narratives: the tale of the Sentinel of Pompeii, who was reportedly killed as he remained at his post while others fled the city. Behlman examines this motif through some of its best-known representations by Mark Twain, Harriet Hosmer, and Edward Poynter and reveals that the legend became an exemplar for Victorian, rather than classical, Stoicism. The sentinel is disclosed as a modern invention and thus the perfect vehicle to convey images of midcentury masculine identity, alternately celebrated and undermined by its interpreters.

The two interlacing essays by Bettina Bergmann and Elaine K. Gazda consider dimensions of the single best-known Pompeian monument, the fresco cycle in the Villa of the Mysteries. The cycle has been aboveground for only a century, but the paintings immediately gained the canonical status accorded earlier to the paintings of the Porticus of Herculaneum or the Four Women from Stabiae discussed by Najbjerg and Valladares. The frescoes can best be understood, Bergmann argues, by exploring the layers of interpretation that have shaped their modern meaning and by recognizing the unusual prominence of women among the archaeologists, artists, and other scholars presenting and interpreting them. With its analysis shaded from the very beginning by Freudian and Jungian readings, the cycle has been understood as reflecting a twentieth-century psyche that is lent validity by the medium of "scientific" photographic reproduction—a significant parallel to Fiorelli's casting technique as presented in Dwyer's essay.

Elaine K. Gazda examines the enormous replica of the Villa of the Mysteries frescoes made between 1925 and 1927 for the University of Michigan by the Italian artist and archaeologist Maria Barosso. By situating these large-scale watercolors at the intersection of the disparate goals of Barosso and her patron, Francis Kelsey, Gazda sheds light on the complex reception of the frescoes in the 1920s and 1930s, particularly through the initial exhibition of Barosso's paintings at the Villa Borghese in 1926, where the works were alternately appreciated as representing masterpieces of ancient painting, a preservationist project, a sign of two millennia of Italian cultural superiority, and a landmark of Fascist archaeological and cultural policy.

Narratives of decay and destruction preoccupy our final essayists. Nick Yablon examines the theatrical reenactments of the last days of Pompeii presented by the entrepreneur James Pain across the United States from the late nineteenth century through World War I. By situating Pain's pyrotechnical spectacles within the context of theater and film history, Yablon examines the changing representation of Pompeian spectacles within a dynamic of social class rather than a more conventional technological history. Moving away from earlier nineteenth-century plays, which adapted the famous Bulwer-Lytton novel to articulate the superiority of the artisan class, Pain instead provided a mass entertainment appealing to a broader public tied together less by language than by a widespread interest in the tragic decimation of Pompeii and a fascination with spectacular theatrical events.

Jennie Hirsh's essay explores the postwar films *Voyage in Italy* by Roberto Rossellini and *Contempt* by Jean-Luc Godard, which present the ancient sites in modern and postmodern contexts. Hirsh considers the films as a dialogue between these two directors, both profoundly aware of the monumental legacy of the ancient cities. *Voyage in Italy*, part of which takes place amid the ruins of Pompeii, uses the locale to address the protagonists' alienation as well as the dissonance they experience in the ancient city. *Contempt*, in contrast, plays more directly with the language of representation, calling attention to the impossibility of reconstructing a lost past and using the contemporary experiences of antiquity to demonstrate the failure of signifying systems to bridge the divide between past and present.

It is our hope that this volume, like the excavations, will provide insight into specific cases and a panoramic view of the broader history of the recovery of Pompeii and Herculaneum. Each essay is designed to stand alone as a single, coherent argument. At the same time the theme of reception unites the volume, and under its rubric the papers exist as successive windows not just onto the past but also onto our understanding of it and so of ourselves.

Notes

1   Johann Wolfgang von Goethe, *Italian Journey*, ed. Thomas P. Saine and Jeffrey L. Sammons, trans. Robert R. Heitner (New York, 1989), 167.

2   For the authors' prior scholarly investigations, see, for example, Victoria C. Gardner Coates, "A Painting Reserved for 'Nobile diletto': Poussin's Moses and Aaron before Pharaoh for Camillo Massimo," *Gazette des Beaux-Arts* 138 (2001): 185–202.

3   For the effect of the discoveries on eighteenth-century antiquarian culture, see, for example, Ferdinando Bologna, "The Rediscovery of Herculaneum and Pompeii in the Artistic Culture of Europe in the Eighteenth Century," in *Rediscovering Pompeii*, ed. Luisa Franchi Dell'Orto and Antonio Varone (Rome, 1990), 80–91.

4   There are, of course, notable exceptions, chief among them Christopher Charles Parslow, *Rediscovering Antiquity: Karl Weber and the Excavation of Herculaneum, Pompeii, and Stabiae* (Cambridge, 1995); and Carol C. Mattusch with Henry Lie, *The Villa dei Papiri at Herculaneum: Life and Afterlife of a Sculpture Collection* (Los Angeles, 2005). These valuable precedents have been necessarily limited by time frame and topic; our goal is to provide a more comprehensive study of this process.

5   Maxwell Anderson suggests that this "proto-modern" quality could be disconcerting: "The remains of Pompeii have always been felt, in the popular imagination, to show a culture which was oddly close to that of the modern world, and were thus of limited use for those revering the past through a distorted neoclassical prism." See Maxwell L. Anderson, "Pompeii and America," in Franchi Dell'Orto and Varone 1990 (note 3), 95. Anderson concludes that the everyday objects discovered at Pompeii were responsible for this discomfiture; we propose that it may have more to do with the chronology of the excavations.

6   Jon L. Seydl, "The Grand Tour: Tourists and Artists in Eighteenth-Century Italy," lecture, University of Pennsylvania, Philadelphia, March 1998.

7   See Anderson 1990 (note 5), 92–103; and Rolf Winkes, "The Influence of Herculaneum and Pompeii on American Art of the Eighteenth and Nineteenth Centuries," in *Ercolano, 1738–1988: Duocento e cinquanta anni di ricerca archaeologica* (Rome, 1993), 127–32.

8   Victoria C. Gardner Coates and Jon L. Seydl, *Antiquity Recovered: Pompeii and Herculaneum in Philadelphia Collections* (Philadelphia, 2002).

9   Hugh Honour, *Neo-classicism* (Harmondsworth, 1968); and Matthew Craske, *Art in Europe, 1700–1830: A History of the Visual Arts in an Era of Unprecedented Urban Economic Growth* (Oxford, 1997).

10   For discussion of the Greek settlements in southern Italy, see Luca Cerchiai, Lorena Jannelli, and Fausto Longo, *The Greek Cities of Magna Graecia and Sicily* (Los Angeles, 2004).

11 Johann Joachim Winckelmann, *Reflections on the Imitation of Greek Works in Painting and Sculpture*, trans. Elfriede Heyer and Roger C. Norton (LaSalle, Ill., 1987).

12 For William Hamilton, see Ian Jenkins and Kim Sloan, *Vases and Volcanoes: Sir William Hamilton and His Collection* (London, 1996).

13 For James Logan and antiquarian culture in Philadelphia, see Jack L. Lindsey, *Worldly Goods: The Arts of Early Pennsylvania* (Philadelphia, 1999), 86–88.

14 For Samuel Powel and John Morgan, see *A Journal of Samuel Powel*, ed. Sarah Jackson (1764; Florence, 2001). For Morgan's comments on visiting Naples, see the letter from John Morgan to Joseph Shippen, May 12, 1764 (Historical Society of Pennsylvania, ALS, Balch Papers, Shippen, 1:127). For the Kauffmann portraits of Powel and Morgan, see Arthur S. Marks, "Angelica Kauffmann and Some Americans on the Grand Tour," *American Art Journal* 12, no. 2 (Spring 1980): 9–20; and the entry by Jon L. Seydl in *Art in Rome in the Eighteenth Century*, ed. Edgar Peters Bowron and Joseph J. Rishel (Philadelphia and Houston, 2000), 383–84.

15 While in London as the colonial agent not only for Pennsylvania but also for Georgia, New Jersey, and Massachusetts, Benjamin Franklin evolved from a loyalist to a founding father of the new republic and was eventually condemned at Whitehall as a traitor. See David T. Morgan, *The Devious Dr. Franklin, Colonial Agent: Benjamin Franklin's Years in London* (Macon, Ga., 1996); and Cecil B. Currey, *Road to Revolution: Benjamin Franklin in England, 1765–1775* (1968; Garden City, N.Y., 1988). Franklin purchased the copy at the behest of the board of directors of the Library Company of Philadelphia in 1769 (collection number MRC02217960). Many thanks to James Greene for his assistance with this research.

16 Mark Twain, *Innocents Abroad* (Hartford, Conn., 1869). Eric Moormann, "Literary Evocations of Ancient Pompeii," in *Tales from an Eruption: Pompeii, Herculaneum, Oplontis: Guide to the Exhibition*, ed. Pietro Giovanni Guzzo, trans. Jo Wallace-Hadrill (Milan, 2003), 20–25.

17 For Gell and Scott's visit to Pompeii, see William Gell, *Reminiscences of Sir Walter Scott's Residence in Italy, 1832* (London, 1957), 8; and Laurence Goldstein, "The Impact of Pompeii on the Literary Imagination," *Centennial Review* 23 (1979): 227–41.

18 For a related understanding of the temples at Paestum, see Paul A. Manoguerra, " 'Like Going to Greece': American Painters and Paestum," in *Classic Ground: Mid-Nineteenth-Century American Painting and the Italian Encounter* (Athens, Ga., 2004), 89–104.

19 Sumner Lincoln Fairfield, *The Last Night of Pompeii: A Poem* (New York, 1832).

20 The phenomenal success of the now practically unreadable *The Last Days of Pompeii* tells us a great deal about the changing reception of the recovered city. Bulwer-Lytton's novel combined archaeological correctness gleaned from his well-publicized consultations with Sir William Gell with his established formula for a successful nineteenth-century historical novel. For many, the world of the novel became a more real Pompeii than that provided by the archaeological record, and the site was itself adjusted by guides to conform to Bulwer-Lytton's vision. See Curtis Dahl, "Bulwer-Lytton and the School of Catastrophe," *Philological Quarterly* 32 (1953): 428–42; Wolfgang Leppmann, *Pompeii in Fact and Fiction* (London, 1968), 129–36; and James C. Simmons, "Bulwer and Vesuvius: The Topicality of the Last Days of Pompeii," *Nineteenth-Century Fiction* 24 (1969), 103–5.

21 Nydia took on a life of her own. Her blindness acted as a foil for her spiritual acuity, and her slave status made her a sympathetic figure for the abolitionist movement. For Boker, see Edward Scully Bradley, *George Henry Boker: Poet and Patriot* (New York, 1969). The manuscript for *Nydia* is in the Van Pelt Rare Book and Manuscript Library of the University of Pennsylvania (Misc Mss) and is also available as George Henry Boker, *Nydia; A Tragic Play*, ed. Edward Scully Bradley (Philadelphia, 1929). Rogers first modeled *Nydia* in about 1853–54 and received requests for more than one hundred copies in marble over the next three decades. Like Bulwer-Lytton's novel, *Nydia* combines academic references to well-known antiquities with a contemporary Victorian sensibility and was wildly popular. In Philadelphia not only was the statue exhibited at the Centennial, the celebrated author and collector Clara Jessup Moore (Mrs.

Bloomfield Moore) displayed a version in the foyer of her elegant city townhouse. When her collection was auctioned, the *Nydia* was the highest-priced lot, fetching twenty-five hundred dollars. For Rogers's sculpture, see Joyce K. Schiller, "*Nydia*: A Forgotten Icon of the Nineteenth Century," *Bulletin of the Detroit Institute of the Arts* 67 (1993): 36–45.

22   *Description of Pompeian Ruins, Restorations, and Scenes Exhibited at the Pompeiian Museum, Fairmount Park* (Philadelphia, 1890). The top-lit cabinets each had a peephole through which visitors peered at a succession of paintings in three categories: first, images of the present-day ruins; second, imaginative restorations of the same sites; and finally, twelve scenes—enhanced with painted papier-mâché figures—loosely narrating the Bulwer-Lytton novel, culminating in two scenes depicting the wake of the eruption. They were purchased just after the Centennial and installed in Memorial Hall in Fairmount Park in 1878 and remained on regular view until at least 1913. The cabinets were discarded at some point after 1958 (see Jean Barrett, "Park Board Ponders Crumbling Memorial Hall," *Philadelphia Bulletin*, October 26, 1958). Many thanks to Matthew Rader, Ethan Schrum, and Theresa Stuhlman for their help with this research.

23   For a thorough discussion of the history of the Chiurazzi Foundry, see Mattusch and Lie 2005 (note 4), 343–53; for the Wanamaker bronzes for the University Museum, see J. Chiurazzi & Fils., *Reproductions of the Bronzes Found at Pompeii and Herculaneum* (n.p., 1904); and news clippings, 1889–1981, University of Pennsylvania Museum of Archaeology and Anthropology Archives.

24   For the Getty Villa bronzes, see Mattusch and Lie 2005 (note 4), 347–49; and Kenneth Lapatin, personal conversation, January 2005.

Natural Marvels and Ancient Ruins: Volcanism and the Recovery of Antiquity in Early Modern Naples

Sean Cocco

NEAPOLITAN ANTIQUARIANS in the sixteenth century boasted that their city challenged Rome as a site for recovering antiquity. In the spirit of this Italian rivalry, they pointed to a local ring of fire—an active caldera twelve kilometers wide—containing some of the peninsula's finest ancient sites. In the first century A.D. Pliny the Elder had given the name *campi phlegraei*, or "fields of fire," to the calderic depression located on the western rim of the Bay of Naples, a region first settled by the Greeks and home to Cumae, Baiae, and Puteoli in his day.[1] The fire, smoke, and steam described by the Roman naturalist were still salient features of the landscape in the 1500s and 1600s, when volcanic activity intensified considerably. The explosive proximity of volcanoes and ruins greatly enhanced the prestige of Campania in the late Renaissance and baroque periods. This largely uncharted episode in European antiquarianism reveals the intensity of interest that existed two centuries before the unearthing of Pompeii and Herculaneum and offers a window into baroque empiricism and erudition. In the early modern vocabulary of knowledge the word *historia* embraced inquiry into objects of both nature and artifice, situating southern Italy's volcanoes and antiquities in a common field of study [FIG. 1].

Two volcanic events drew unprecedented attention to nature and the recovery of Naples's classical past. The first occurrence was in 1538, when a new cinder cone burst forth in the Campi Flegrei, to the amazement of contemporary observers. Understandably, the emergence of Monte Nuovo provoked speculation on the causes of volcanism, but it also raised the alarm that subterranean forces would obliterate surviving ancient monuments if further unleashed. Fortunately the anxieties of antiquarians never materialized completely—the ruins endured. Volcanism provided, nonetheless, a thrilling urgency to the study of *storia civile* and *storia naturale*—civil history and natural history—that had few parallels elsewhere.

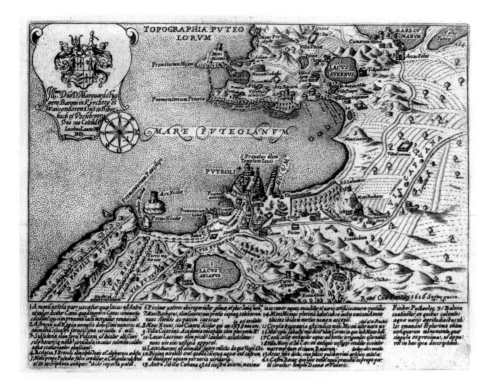

FIGURE 1

Giacomo Lauro (Italian, active 1583–ca. 1645), *Topographia Puteolorum*, 1626. Etching. From Giacomo Lauro, *Heroico splendore delle città del mondo* (1642). Los Angeles, Research Library, Getty Research Institute, G140.L38 1642.

The interest in Neapolitan antiquities that followed the eruption of 1538 was in some measure motivated by patriotic pride. Indeed, this feature was encountered elsewhere in Italy.[2] Benedetto Di Falco wrote the first printed guide to the region in the late 1540s, aiming to give Naples the sort of laudatory description that existed for other Italian cities, such as Rome, Florence, and Venice. To this end, Di Falco's *Descrittione dei luoghi antichi di Napoli e del suo amenissimo distretto* (1549) catalogued and described the principal ancient sites scattered about the caldera but placed considerable attention on its most remarkable natural features, including Monte Nuovo and the region's sulfur fumaroles (open vents that constantly emitted steam and sulfur gas). Thus, even though the *Descrittione* was the work of an antiquarian, the natural effects of volcanism were also a focus of the guide.[3] Similar books combining natural and ancient history were published in the next few decades, including most notably Ferrante Loffredo's *Antichità di Pozzuolo, et luoghi convicini* (1573) and Giulio Cesare Capaccio's *Vera antichità di Pozzuolo* (1607).[4]

Campania's allure extended well beyond the region. The south was already a destination for travelers by the late Renaissance, as it would be for the Grand Tourists of the eighteenth century, many of whom ventured to Naples seeking the thrill of exploring Vesuvius and the cities it had famously destroyed. The region's stature in the European imagination in this later period was due to a second natural occurrence little known to historians, even though it stimulated an unparalleled burst of writing, scientific investigation, and imagery related to volcanism. This event was the paroxysm of Vesuvius in 1631, the most devastating eruption since the classical period.[5]

There are good reasons to identify the unique Neapolitan combination of volcanoes and antiquities—beginning in 1538 and intensifying after 1631—as part of a continuum of mounting interest leading to the development of volcanology and archaeology in the 1700s. Considering the Renaissance origins of these later disciplines helps highlight both the continuities and points of disjuncture between the first efforts to recover antiquity in the sixteenth century and the accomplishments of the eighteenth. In short, this line of inquiry offers a prehistory to the discoveries of Pompeii and Herculaneum in the mid-1700s and the celebrated volcanic investigations of Sir William Hamilton later in the century.[6]

Geology

Long before Renaissance authors wrote of the marvels and dangers of the Campi Flegrei, the Greeks and Romans had believed that the Acheron, or "river of woe," flowed just south of the acropolis of Cuma on the western edge of the caldera. Virgil wrote that Aeneas sought the entrance to the underworld here, somewhere between the gloomy marshes and Lake Avernus, often shrouded in vapor.[7] In a grove near the entrance of a cave, the sibyl instructed Aeneas on how to descend into the nether regions. According to the philosopher Lucretius, the Greeks considered the lake a "bird-less place," because of the deadly gases that purportedly bubbled up from its depths.[8] These ominous ancient narratives set the tone for much of the subsequent exploration of the region beginning in the 1540s.

Renaissance scholars universally agreed that the Solfatara was the region's most thrilling place, an opinion they shared with classical authors. Imagining that Vulcan's forge pumped and bellowed in this active crater, amid steam, boiling mud, and noxious fumes, the Greeks and Romans had dubbed it the "forum Vulcani."[9] Here ancient sources had located a scary passage into the underworld, but there were also references to more pleasant aspects.[10] In his *Natural History*, Pliny the Elder declared that here "the inconvenience of mountains was turned to good." The Roman naturalist argued that the cinders spewed by the Solfatara crater's perpetual combustion contributed to the region's extraordinary fertility. They made the soil porous and spongy, he reasoned, trapping fresh water that would have otherwise flowed into the sea. Mixed with pumice and ash, rainwater created subterranean juices or spirits (*suci*) that made Campania the best agricultural terrain in Roman Italy.[11]

Pliny the Elder's reasoning summarized classical theories on volcanism in general, and, for their part, Renaissance authors almost always sought to confirm what the venerable ancient naturalist had believed. They estimated that the area exhibited the same phenomena it had in the Roman period. They did register surprise, however, when the Bay of Naples's volcanoes began to spew fire more fiercely than previously remembered.

Some understanding of the region's geology helps explain why this fascination flourished in antiquity and intensified in the 1500s [FIG. 2]. Today volcanologists define the Campi Flegrei as a caldera measuring approximately twelve kilometers in diameter (with a significant portion extending beneath the Mediterranean Sea). A caldera is a large crater produced by the deformation and collapse of terrain just above a magma chamber that has been emptied in a massive eruption. Volcanic features of this sort are normally shaped as a ring surrounding a large depression. The Phlegraean caldera was formed by two distinct eruptive cycles, which occurred respectively thirty-seven thousand and twelve thousand years before the present.[12] A magma chamber exists approxi-

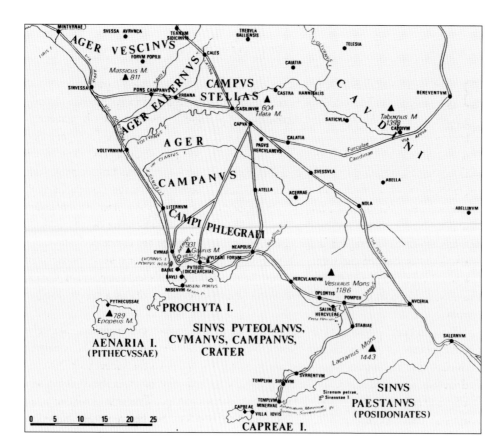

FIGURE 2
Map of ancient Campania
with the Campi Flegrei.
From Paul M. Martin,
*La Campanie antique:
Des origines à l'éruption
du Vesuve* (1984), 1:6.

mately three to four kilometers below the surface and is still very active today. The oldest phase of volcanism covered an area of roughly thirty thousand kilometers with tephra, a layering that created tuff stone—a building material of crucial importance in southern Italy. Between 12,000 and 3800 B.C. frequent and convulsive volcanism characterized the region. This activity resulted in the formation of lava domes, tuff rings, and tuff cones. A long quiescence followed, broken only by sporadic events such as the eruption of Monte Nuovo that attracted so much attention in 1538.[13]

Modern geologists have discovered that different magma chambers fuel Vesuvius and the Campi Flegrei, meaning that eruptions in both places have never been strictly related. Renaissance naturalists and their successors well into the 1700s, however, thought that the volcanoes were interconnected, postulating a common source of underground heat. The Jesuit polymath Athanasius Kircher, author of *Mundus subterraneus* (1678) and a renowned explorer of volcanoes, concluded that a huge subterranean "fire hearth" beneath Naples linked Monte Nuovo and Vesuvius. These two sites were, in turn, a branch of a global network that fed not just the other Mediterranean cones, Stromboli and Etna, but every single cone located around the world. Kircher compared the passage of heat within this system of fire hearths and mines to the flow of blood in the human body. After a daring climb to the active crater in the spring of 1638, he suggested that one courageous enough to peer into Vesuvius would observe the pulse of the earth's lifeblood.[14] In short, fire ran beneath Naples.

Monte Nuovo

Both volcanoes offered a compelling reason to recover the region's past, in two successive phases. The eruption in the Campi Flegrei caldera in 1538 did not initially suggest the "network of fire" later imagined by Kircher in the seventeenth century. It led, however, to the first attempts to explain the volcanoes since Pliny the Elder, creating concurrently an important stimulus to cataloguing the area's ruins. The Neapolitan philosopher Giovanni Battista Della Porta included volcanism in his far-ranging studies, arguing for the attraction of strange telluric phenomena in the Campi Flegrei. These effects, he noted, fueled wonder because they originated in a place no one could really observe—belowground. He declared: "that thing of which the causes are hidden from sight is worthy of marvel, and the more its causes are concealed, the more one holds it as unusual and rare."[15] Monte Nuovo, although it never rose to more than a few hundred meters in elevation between the town of Pozzuoli and the ruins of Cuma, was exactly the sort of wonder Della Porta later intended broadly as a Campi Flegrei *meraviglia*.

Simone Porzio, a natural philosopher who witnessed the 1538 eruption, had written the first specific description of volcanic activity a few decades earlier. His analysis of Monte Nuovo's sudden emergence appeared in a letter to the viceroy of Naples, Pedro Alvarez de Toledo, who had likely solicited an explanation from the philosopher. Porzio offered two important considerations in the missive. The first dealt with the eruption's natural causes, while the second speculated whether future natural disasters were in store—something that would concern antiquarians in the decades to come.[16]

Combining empiricism and authority, Porzio's account compared recent observations of volcanic activity with the theories of ancient natural philosophers. Albeit brief and cautious, his analysis of the eruption began a phase of intensified interest in the Campi Flegrei. Previously medieval balneologists had written extensively about the caldera's hot springs and sulfur fumaroles, but such natural phenomena were much lesser manifestations of nature's marvelous powers than volcanoes—even if it was understood that they presumably originated from the same sources of subterranean heat. Medical treatises on the thermal baths of Pozzuoli had existed for centuries, but the ancients had not watched a volcano rise from level ground in a few short days.[17] An event of this nature and magnitude required considerable explanation.

The novelty of the eruption confronted Porzio with an important epistemological concern. Where should one order such phenomena on the scale of natural, preternatural, or supernatural phenomena? "Many are the things," he declared, "which although they happen due to natural causes, because they present themselves so rarely they seem portents, especially to those who perceive them by hearsay rather than by sight."[18] Portents, in short, were best left alone. Instead, Porzio affirmed that the eruption was a very rare type of subterranean ignition whose causes could be deduced from accepted Aristotelian truths. Natural philosophers, not prophets, were the best predictors of the Campi Flegrei's volcanic future, proceeding in the fashion of Aristotle and Pliny.

Hardly anyone had studied volcanoes since antiquity when Porzio set about writing his short treatise. Inevitably the first authority was Aristotle. In his *Meteorologica* the Greek philosopher argued that earthquakes derived from vapors flowing in and out of the earth; subterranean winds generated heat and moisture. These factors were more pronounced in regions near the seashore and where the terrain was particularly cavernous—a condition that fit nicely, Porzio figured, with the topography of the Bay of Naples.[19]

Reasoning in Aristotelian terms, Porzio concluded that when the sun heated patches of humid terrain in the Campi Flegrei, great quantities of vapor emanated, forming clouds and rain. When the soil was arid, on the other hand, this *fumus* (smoke or vapor) was hot and desiccating. The mechanism triggering earthquakes and subterranean combustion involved the escape of vapors from the earth, a passage that was often obstructed in subterranean caverns—hence the tremors that had preceded the emergence of Monte Nuovo. Porzio found that classical naturalists had suspected that the most violent conflagrations just beneath the earth's crust occurred in spring and autumn, periods that combined moisture and heat. The eruption of Monte Nuovo took place between September 26 and 27, convincing Porzio that Aristotle had been right about the earth's volatility in these periods. Repeated earthquakes had set fire to the "pitchy matter" (*materia bituminosa*) stored in large quantities in the hollow and spongy terrain of the Campi Flegrei, sparking the eruption as one might strike a flint to light a fire.[20]

Porzio consulted sources beyond Aristotle, since the Romans had also formulated their own complex explanations of volcanic activity. The first-century B.C. philosopher Lucretius, for example, compared volcanoes to a vast furnace. Hot vapors running through the fissures of the earth made it tremble and on occasion ignited flammable material—imagined to be alum, bitumen, niter, and sulfur—contained in caverns. These fires then worked their way to the surface.[21] To Porzio, it could only be that the terrifying marvel observed recently in the Campi Flegrei confirmed these classical theories.

Porzio's *De conflagratione* was the most significant attempt since antiquity to explain how volcanoes worked. Even in the early seventeenth century authors cited Porzio as their most trusted contemporary authority on volcanoes.[22] Indeed, that Porzio had also raised the question of Vesuvius a century before its eruption significantly enhanced his reputation among later natural philosophers. So how, then, did Monte Nuovo's eruption compare to that of the much larger volcano in A.D. 79? Porzio argued that it was too early to tell, but he suspected that the vast hollow packed with combustible material that lay beneath Pozzuoli would give ample fodder to future fires on the other side of Naples. It could, in the worst scenario, ignite Vesuvius.

The difficulty of predicting whether there would be further eruptions near Naples led Porzio to warn the viceroy that a portentous interpretation of the eruption could only produce dangerous rumors among an ignorant population. Surely Toledo needed little reminding that he governed a restive city, and he might have suspected that the volcanic events would be read as portending political rebellion.[23] "Some ask me anxiously," Porzio wrote, "what phenomena are prognosticated by these events. In truth, I hold with the Peripatetic school that there is no certain thing in this presage. Even though Cicero attributes much to portents, he also detracts much from them."[24] A convincing natural explanation for this phenomenon, as the philosopher suggested, was the most sensible thing, especially if one considered the detail with which the ancients had described Vesuvius. More recently, in 1300, Mount Epomeo on Ischia had set the island aflame. Porzio closed confidently on scientific terms: "Therefore, my Mecoenas, I felt compelled to write this so that fortune tellers, readers of dreams, and vulgar astrologers not seek to explain those things that otherwise occur by virtue of nature."[25]

The Campi Flegrei eruption of 1538 jolted contemporary scholars into a new consideration of volcanic activity. This awareness now included also the possibility that the little volcano in the caldera was just a lesser example of the great ancient paroxysm of Vesuvius. Porzio worried about the possibility of a new and catastrophic eruption coming from that volcano, but he was also troubled by a more imminent danger. Were the traces of the glorious ancient past of Naples going to be consumed by fire? Many antiquarians expressed this concern with increasing urgency in subsequent years.

Antiquarian Guides to the Campi Flegrei

The first true guides to Naples's natural marvels and antiquities, far more complete than Porzio's hurried description of Monte Nuovo, emerged in the following decade. In 1549 Benedetto Di Falco's *Descrittione dei luoghi antichi di Napoli e del suo amenissimo distretto* inaugurated a type of guidebook focused on the classical and natural sites of the area. Generally speaking, these guides expressed an urgent desire to explore and recover the area before the ravages of time and volcanoes resulted in the irreversible loss of ruins.

One particularly sore point for Neapolitan scholars was the perception that their counterparts in other cities, even outside Italy, had pursued antiquarian studies more vigorously. Di Falco complained that it was not hard to find laudatory descriptions of Marseilles, Venice, Milan, and Rome. Biondo Flavio's *Italia illustrata* (1453), however, was the most inspiring example for Di Falco, as it offered a standard for describing the historical sites of prominent Italian cities. Di Falco's urgency stemmed from what he felt was Naples's obvious deficiency in this field. Even more important, the city's history was, in the antiquarian's opinion, "day by day plunging into the waves of obscure oblivion."[26] As he and other authors now suspected, the rumblings of the earth were rapidly accelerating this unfortunate process.

The Neapolitan concern that its illustrious Greek and Roman past was not fully appreciated or respected reflected contemporary political anxieties, since the *Descrittione* was written during a moment of mounting tension between the Spanish and the subject city. Only two years before, in 1547, Viceroy Toledo had tried to introduce the Spanish Inquisition, igniting a period of serious strife and rebellion.[27] Di Falco's frequent invocation of the Habsburg emperor, Charles V, attempted to heal the rift that had widened between Spaniards and Neapolitans in these years. For Di Falco, nature and antiquity's gifts made a compelling case for Naples, even in the troubled political climate of the mid-sixteenth century. More importantly, however, the city's classical heritage supported claims to long-standing autonomy, first as a Greek and Roman city and then as the capital of a kingdom that had entered into the Spanish imperial system only in 1503. Naples's distinctive combination of natural marvels and ancient ruins could go a long way toward restoring its battered prestige in the eyes of Spain and the rest of Italy.

Di Falco conceded that there were many other beautiful places in the world, but he stressed the uniqueness of his city. He praised the French countryside, the green slopes washed by the Rhine, and the shores of Lake Garda in northern Italy, where lemons grew even in winter. Still, these places lacked the temperance and beauty of the Bay of Naples. "In part for the bounty and fertility of the soil," he wrote, "in part for the clement and temperate air, what's more that it is divided in plain, mount, and fruit laden hills washed by a tranquil sea, it is clear that Naples enjoys for every reason the most beautiful, useful, and salutiferous place in the world."[28] What was behind this unusually wonderful nature? The strange and marvelous fires that burned underneath the Campi Flegrei spewed ash that mingled with thermal waters to create the most fertile soil in Italy. Pliny the Elder's description had once again resurfaced.

The appeal of classical Rome extended beyond references to the ancient naturalist. Di Falco hoped that Charles V would follow the emperors Augustus and Tiberius, and even Galen, the greatest doctor of antiquity, in seeking health and restoration in the thermal baths of Baia. It would be the highest honor, Di Falco proclaimed, to make Campania the site of such *otium*, a state of relaxation free from the burdens of empire. His dream was that "Emperor Charles V will come to reside in his dear Naples, so that after the many travails of his rule he might rest here and enjoy the delightful places, and might be healthy, and have a long life and be happy. Of what common good this would be, for us and the kingdom that constantly mourns having a lord it does not ever see."[29] This sort of flattery was meant to appeal to Charles's sense of continuity and connection with the Roman emperors, but it was, as importantly, also an attempt to repair the damaged prestige of the southern Italian city.

The *Descrittione* was, among other things, a challenge to the cultural superiority of Rome, provoked by the disparagement the Neapolitans claimed to have encountered from other Italians. Di Falco urged his reader to remember that "Pozzuoli is more ancient than any place in Italy. Virgil wrote that Aeneas (whose descendants founded Rome hundreds of years later) came to Cuma, which had been built by the Greeks, who had come to Italy and Pozzuoli long before him." In case any doubt remained, he declared, "Naples is more ancient [than Rome]." Furthermore, the southern city surpassed all others in its natural splendors, and, if Rome was unrivaled in terms of ruins alone, there was nothing comparable to the Campi Flegrei's combined natural and historical significance.[30]

Di Falco's descriptions of the most important antiquities surrounding his city drove home a sense of Neapolitan peculiarity and prestige. The antiquarian asserted, for example, that Cicero had once called Pozzuoli a "little Rome" and, having built a great villa near the Mediterranean littoral between Lake Avernus and the town, here established an academy to rival that of Hellenic Athens. Another important site was the breakwater of Pozzuoli, often referred to as the "bridge of Caligula." Jutting from the shore, Di Falco wrote, "one sees, not without great marvel, great remains of the miraculous dock."[31] The latter example was especially compelling to Di Falco, since it had actually been made more visible by the eruption of Monte Nuovo—when the terrain uplift caused by the volcano's emergence exposed formerly submerged portions of the ruin.[32]

Subsequent authors put varying degrees of emphasis on natural marvels and ancient ruins, some going even further than Di Falco in emphasizing the combination of both that made Naples unique.[33] Ferrante Loffredo, the marquis of Trevico and a man of unusual prestige and importance, merits particular attention. In a long and illustrious career Loffredo served Charles V in the wars of Italy, Germany, and Hungary. He defended the Neapolitan kingdom's coast against Ottoman piracy and shored up its borders when the French threatened. In 1571 he fought at Don Juan of Austria's side at the Battle of Lepanto and subsequently spent years at court in Madrid. When he returned to Naples he sat on the city's chief fiscal council, the Sommaria, and assumed governorship of the Terra d'Otranto, one of the kingdom's provinces. The apex of his career came when he was appointed the Spanish viceroy of Sicily, an immensely prestigious and lucrative posting. Loffredo's book was entitled *Le antichità di Pozzuolo, et luoghi convicini* (1573).[34]

This iter through nature and artifice in the Campi Flegrei was a lasting accomplishment that set a high standard. Even after 1631, when Vesuvius became the primary focus of interest in the Bay of Naples, authors remarked on Loffredo's precision and frequently cited his work. The book's reputation stemmed from a combination of exhaustive field research—including on-site exploration of volcanic features— and the author's rigorous consultation of ancient sources. Loffredo explained the mutual values of fieldwork and humanist study as he proposed a meaningful connection with antiquity:

> By day I would go riding through the countryside, seeking out all things worthy of consideration and marvel, natural as well as artificial, that are present between the promontories of Posillipo and Miseno, then Cuma along the shore, and up along the hills and the surrounding mounts. Then at night, I would confer with the writings of ancient authors that tell of these places. In a similar fashion I would gather the best recollections of local inhabitants, left to them by their fathers and ancestors. Bunching all these together, even if I found many conformities between what I observed riding and the fame of books, I continued to find some discrepancies and differences, and in numerous matters I was greatly challenged by the silence of authors, lost knowledge, the ruins of buildings in complete disrepair, and finally the absence of all things that normally guide conjecture in such matters. I was nevertheless determined to conquer, with as much diligence necessary, all those inconveniences, revisiting many times these places, examining the inhabitants minutely, and diligently reviewing and considering books, so that no labor remained. Unless I am fooling myself, I worked in such a fashion as to shed all the true light possible in such obscurity.[35]

Most of all, the Renaissance naturalist and antiquarian sought to draw parallels with Pliny the Elder, who had spent his final years investigating nature from his villa on Cape Miseno, not far from where the marquis composed his own book. Pliny's insatiable scientific curiosity and sense of duty as officer of the imperial fleet had compelled him to go into the maw of an erupting Vesuvius. Loffredo—naturalist and soldier—surely had the latter gesture in mind as he calculated his own risks, steering his horse gingerly over the hot ground of the Solfatara crater, careful not to plunge into pools of boiling mud.

Loffredo's treatise was an advance in scholarly sophistication distinguished by an elegant blend of natural history and civil history. Loffredo reasoned that his descriptions pertained to two categories, the natural and the artificial—intending by the latter ancient ruins and the study of *storia civile*. Operating with this distinction, he traced an itinerary that moved west from Pozzuoli into the heart of the area, the first significant stop being the city's Flavian amphitheater. He noted that this structure had been remarkably well preserved until it suffered damage in the volcanic eruption of 1538. The ancient Roman dock that protruded from Pozzuoli was also in a sad state but still discernable. It was "a magnificent work, and well liked for its superb and great construction, and the beautiful architecture of its pilings, with arcs from one to the other, built in great stones that are well connected." Cicero's former villa was not far away, and he could still make out the courtyard and the portico.[36]

For all his attempts at precision, Loffredo felt that he was wading through the quagmire of superstition and misinformation that had accrued over long centuries of obscurity. Discordant ancient opinions and contemporary ignorance were further compounded by the difficulties of fieldwork, since the ruins were in great disrepair and in many cases overgrown with vegetation. In a synthesis typical of the tensions among observation, empiricism, and authority experienced in the early modern period, the concerned scholar sought to clear up some of his uncertainties by scouring the relevant classical sources after a day in the field. Even after this exercise, however, Loffredo was frequently befuddled by the contradictions he encountered. On the question of who had built a tunnel between Naples and Pozzuoli, for example, he was exasperated by the differing accounts of Plutarch and Strabo.[37]

The more intense volcanic activity of the previous decades further heightened the sense of urgency that informed Loffredo's work, since subterranean forces threatened ruins already in a poor state. Although it was widely acknowledged that this part of Italy had always been prone to earthquakes, he suspected that this type of telluric activity was only likely to increase.

Such dangerous instability, Loffredo reasoned, had its source in the subterranean heat that fed the little volcano, the fumaroles, and all the other marvels of the Campi Flegrei:

> Since [Pozzuoli] is underneath made up entirely of flammable material, and since its fires are already lit, I am convinced that it will always be in this unhappiness, and that there will always be earthquakes, which will not be lessened by the exhalations. In ancient times it must have been the same, and one can observe many places similar to this [Monte Nuovo], which could not have been made in a different manner than through exhalations, among these the Solfatara, the Astroni, and Campiglione. These exhalations have ruined many magnificent buildings, which one can now see destroyed throughout the area.[38]

Loffredo was thus ambivalent about the precarious state of the Campi Flegrei. On one hand, antiquities were at the mercy of forces that were hard to predict and impossible to control. He could not help, however, marvel at the volcano, and he also had to acknowledge that the area's celebrity status since antiquity depended on the mysterious sources of subterranean heat.

Loffredo lamented that many of the treasures of antiquity—natural and artificial—had been lost due to the region's volatility. Four thermal springs, presumably heated by the Campi Flegrei, had provided healing waters to Naples, while no less than thirty-five had once poured forth near Pozzuoli. The Romans had constructed around these waters baths like those at Baia and on the shore of Avernus, but, though some springs were still active, their associated complexes were totally ruined. Some of the worst destruction had occurred in his own lifetime, when the newly risen Monte Nuovo buried the baths of Tripergole near Avernus.

To the antiquarian, these natural forces presented an intractable problem exemplified best by another of the Campi Flegrei's principal marvels, the Solfatara. "Here," wrote Loffredo, "among other natural things worthy of consideration one sees that the humors in the water preserve the sulfur in such a way that though it burns continuously for a long time, it cannot be consumed completely. And so the fire burns in its tunnels, and the waters pour from the canals."[39] As long as the heat persisted, warm healing waters would spring from the earth, but the antiquarian would also continue to fear the tremors of the earth. Loffredo concluded that he could only hope that the Roman ruins would not be utterly demolished and that his book had made a lasting contribution to recording what remained.[40]

In the early seventeenth century another Campi Flegrei guide expanded upon Loffredo's work. Although it shared similar concerns, it also reflected Europe's growing awareness of the greater world, taking on a more comparative, triumphant, and celebratory tone. This work was Giulio Cesare Capaccio's *Vera antichità di Pozzuolo* (1607), arguably the definitive seventeenth-century guide to the region. Capaccio's first lines described how "nature wished to show herself generous to all places in the world in the distribution of her treasures."[41] He also expressed the antiquarian concern that subterranean forces would obliterate what was left of the Campi Flegrei's ruins, but his primary motivation was to enhance the region's reputation in an expanding world of marvels. Many of his themes continue and enlarge those developed in the preceding decades: effects related to volcanism, ancient natural history, and Naples's superiority to Rome.

Echoing Pliny the Elder's *Natural History*, Capaccio wrote that the marvels of nature were scattered about the world. His list was indeed Plinian—strange beasts and plants, stones with unusual powers, salutiferous springs—but it also reflected a greater geographic distribution and the expansion of knowledge resulting from European exploration. Columbus and Magellan had revealed wonders to the contemporary world "in a new way," confirming how "nature herself wishes to make a display of her greatness." Capaccio stressed, however, a more proximate gaze, focused not on distant and exotic lands but on the marvelous jumble of geology and Roman ruins that filled the Campi Flegrei. "When [nature] came to Pozzuoli," he continued, "gathering herself together, she determined to make herself known so great, so courteous, even so prodigious, that generously she opened her bosom to all goods, and girded [Pozzuoli] not only with a playful and delightful site, but with tranquil and bountiful sea, with benign and happy skies, all laughing and festive."[42]

Like earlier works, Capaccio's *Vera antichità di Pozzuolo* traced an itinerary through the Campi Flegrei. One of the "must-sees" was Lake Avernus. According to the author, Aristotle had commented on the noxious nature of fumes emitted by the lake and on the remarkable clarity and depth of its waters. Regarding the condition of Avernus in his day, Capaccio noted that "the hills around it bear the road to Cuma, where there are many ruins of buildings, that demonstrate with certainty that the area was very well inhabited, on account of the many baths, of which numerous remnants are visible."[43]

Capaccio also reinforced an idea local antiquarians had been edging toward since Di Falco's *Descrittione* in the mid-sixteenth century: the historical and natural superiority of Naples. The claim, which was a none-too veiled comment on the southern city's competition with Rome, emphasized in particular how ruins were situated amid nature's abundant gifts to the region: "If in some regards the edifices of Pozzuolo contend with those of Rome, in the matter of fires, waters, and marvelous things of nature there is no doubt that they are surpassing. What have I said on the Solfatara that does not rouse wonder in the reader? Or what of he who sees it? ... Seeing now vapors exhale and become the cause that level ground rises in mountains of ash, as was the case in the one that covered Tripergole and Lake Lucrino in Pozzuolo, is this not something that surpasses all marvel?"[44] The latter reference was to the volcano Monte Nuovo, the greatest, and most recent, of the Campi Flegrei marvels. Capaccio was undoubtedly boasting, but there was more substance to his claim than merely local hubris. By the beginning of the seventeenth century Naples was already a destination for naturalists, antiquarians, artists, and geographers, who were attracted in no small part by volcanic activity in the Phlegraean caldera.

In fact, the Bay of Naples had its share of illustrious visitors. One of the period's best geographers, Abraham Ortelius, came to the region in the late sixteenth century accompanied by the engraver Joris Hoefnagel. Hoefnagel eventually worked with Georg Braun, coauthor of one of Europe's first comprehensive atlases, the *Civitates orbis terrarum* (1572). His illustrations for this book are well known, and in one Hoefnagel drew himself and Ortelius conversing in the Solfatara [FIG. 3].[45]

In another engraving Hoefnagel portrayed the landscape surrounding the ancient remains of Roman Baiae. Hoefnagel's illustration was crowned by a banner inscribed with the words of the Augustan poet Horace, proclaiming that no bay on earth outshone lovely Baiae—a theme Capaccio had also borrowed in his *Vera antichità di Pozzuolo*.[46] The engraving visually represented numerous themes developed by Di Falco, Loffredo, and Capaccio in roughly the same period. All the major ruins in the Campi Flegrei figured in the image, as did the natural marvels. An accompanying text reinforced, furthermore, what Loffredo had deemed the caldera's natural and artificial treasures [FIG. 4].

Hoefnagel's visual journey though the Campi Flegrei paralleled those of contemporary authors, suggesting that he may well have consulted works such as Di Falco. In any case, its alternating path from ancient ruin to natural marvel must have been familiar by the 1570s. Both didascalia and image identified the ruins of Pozzuoli's Roman dock, the ancient locks that once connected the Mediterranean to Lake Lucrino, the cave of the Cumaean Sibyl, and also Monte Nuovo, the Solfatara, and Lake Avernus. Beyond this cartography, the engraving even hinted at the anxiety expressed in contemporary antiquarian guidebooks. The region's recent volcanism was exciting and dangerous: the texts noted not only the novelty of the young volcano's emergence but also the destruction of ancient temples and bath complexes caused by it. The Flemish engraver's depiction of Baia indicates that the attitudes of Neapolitan scholars resonated elsewhere and that the unusual combination of ancient ruin, marvel, and volcanic instability appealed to European readers.

It would take, however, another extraordinary natural event to transform the recovery of antiquity and the study of volcanoes in this part of Italy into a broader phenomenon. The focus on the Campi Flegrei in the 1500s was superseded by an interest in Vesuvius once that volcano erupted in 1631. Vesuvius confronted naturalists and antiquarians with an overwhelming display of volcanic activity. The eruption of Monte Nuovo suddenly appeared to be a minor, albeit related, sideshow. Seventeenth-century scholars understood the early rumblings of the Campi Flegrei to have been, in hindsight, a signal that the mightiest volcano in Italy was coming to life. The huge power of Vesuvius was a display that only the greatest naturalists of the ancient world had witnessed—suggesting yet another intersection of nature and antiquity.

FIGURE 3
Joris Hoefnagel (Flemish, 1542–1601), *Mirabilium sulphureorum motium apud Puteolos Campos Flegreos*, 1572. Engraving. From Georg Braun and Franz Hogenberg, *Civitates orbis terrarum* (1572). Los Angeles, Research Library, Getty Research Institute, G1028.B7 1966.

FIGURE 4
Joris Hoefnagel (Flemish, 1542–1601), *Nullus in orbe locus Baiis praelucet amoenis*, 1572. Engraving. From Georg Braun and Franz Hogenberg, *Civitates orbis terrarum* (1572). Los Angeles, Research Library, Getty Research Institute, G1028.B7 1966.

The Eruption of Vesuvius

One of the principal chroniclers of the seventeenth-century eruption of Vesuvius, Giulio Braccini, explicitly declared himself a second Pliny for his detailed observations of the volcano's recent paroxysm. Braccini listed, furthermore, all known eruptions of the volcano since antiquity as evidence that the region's volcanism should not have been forgotten. Few authors, he noted, had an accurate understanding of ancient eruptions, one reason most had failed to recognize the mountain's potential to erupt again. "In that time," Braccini wrote, referring to the sixteenth century, "all memory of the fires of Mount Somma [Vesuvius] had been nearly extinguished." Retrospectively, Monte Nuovo had been an important clue. He recalled, "such a great amount of stones and ash was ejected that there was born in that place a little mountain, as all can see. And it was for our day an extremely novel thing, and terrifying, as all memory of the fires of Mount Somma, and of Ischia, that also burned on past occasions, had been almost lost."[47]

When, on December 16, 1631, Vesuvius burst into life, observers of the eruption had good reason to imagine they were witnessing a spectacle identical to the one that occurred in antiquity. Volcanologists today distinguish eruptions by type and power. In 1631 the volcano went through the throes of a "sub-Plinian" eruption only slightly less fierce than the "Plinian" eruption of the first century A.D. Between the first and the seventeenth centuries Vesuvius had erupted with some frequency, at times even dramatically. Between 1159 and 1631, however, the volcano was almost completely silent. The enormous destruction caused by the natural catastrophe was further magnified by the fact that it interrupted five centuries of volcanic dormancy. Approximately four thousand people lost their lives and more than ten towns were destroyed in a volcanic cataclysm that evoked an even deeper past—Roman history [FIGS. 5–6].[48]

Chroniclers of the seventeenth-century eruption emphasized the awe-inspiring parallels with that of the ancient world in a striking fashion and, therefore, abruptly and dramatically refocused onto Vesuvius the recovery of antiquity previously associated with antiquarian explorations of the Campi Flegrei. On the morning of the eruption the Neapolitan nobleman and patron of arts, letters, and sciences Giovanni Battista Manso awoke to the horrifying sight of Vesuvius aflame.[49] Manso's reflex was to assume that he was witnessing exactly what Pliny the Elder and his nephew Pliny the Younger had seen almost sixteen centuries earlier. As Manso looked toward Vesuvius in the predawn darkness, he observed: "On the morning of Tuesday, that which had appeared to be a fiery smoke seemed in new light to be a cloud rising from the earth straight up into the seventh region of the air, and here expanded in such a way that, as the part raised straight up it resembled the large trunk of an extremely tall pine, so the other part...seemed a giant pine cone and more vast than the huge mountain."[50] Manso's reference to Pliny the Younger's letters to the historian Tacitus is unmistakable. The Roman author described how his celebrated uncle had gone to the base of the volcano, never to return. Separated by centuries, the two observers shared a basic impression: for Pliny, echoed by Manso, the eruptive cloud had resembled "nothing so much as a giant pine tree."[51]

Like Manso, other observers fashioned their narratives in imitation of the canonical classical description. Notably, Braccini declared that he read Pliny the Younger during the cataclysm, preferring written text to staring at the monstrous eruptive cloud

FIGURE 5
Nicolas Perrey (Spanish,
d. ca. 1650), *Stato del Monte
Vesuvio dopo l'ultimo
incendio del 16 di Decembre
1631*, 1632. Engraving.
Naples, private collection.

FIGURE 6
Giovanni Battista Passari
(Italian, ca. 1610–1679),
*Disegno dell'incendio
nella montagna di
Somma*, ca. 1631. Engraving.
Naples, private collection.

that threatened Naples. He retreated into his library, drew the shutters, and pulled Pliny's epistles sixteen and twenty from the bookshelf. "Here," he claimed to have announced to his companions during the dire moment, "are described one thousand five hundred and fifty years later what, after all, we are witnessing today." Braccini pored over the letters, noting the similarities between the eruptions of Vesuvius then and now. Calmed by his reading, he decided to compare the height of the past and present eruptive clouds. He then sent a servant onto the roof of his palazzo to make measurements. From the resulting data he derived the height of thirty thousand paces. Not surprisingly, this measurement was very similar to that of the Roman naturalist. Braccini proclaimed himself a "Pliny" for his efforts.[52]

Rather than any substantially novel theories about how volcanoes worked, the seventeenth-century eruption created a large volume of literature that dusted off ancient theories and reconciled them with a flood of new observations. The number of accounts and descriptions of Vesuvius jumped from seven for the period between the fifth and seventeenth centuries to eighty-seven in the final weeks of 1631 and early months of 1632.[53] Capaccio, author of *La vera antichità di Pozzuolo* and authority on the Campi Flegrei, added an urgent appendix to his monumental guide to Naples, *Il Forastiero* (1631), just as the book was going to print. In this hurried addendum Capaccio expressed wonder and dismay at the striking similarities between the eruption of A.D. 79 and the recent destruction caused by Vesuvius. More importantly, Capaccio emphasized how the volcano's eruption required historical reflection, suggesting yet another way inquiry into *storia civile* and *storia naturale* forged vital connections between antiquity and seventeenth-century Naples.[54]

Another author, Vincenzo Bove, summed up the possibilities afforded by the eruption: "The long passage of time makes the thing look new and unusual, even if tradition has transmitted to us knowledge of ancient eruptions of this mountain."[55] For Bove, tradition meant the works of classical authors, confirming the interconnectedness of civil and natural history. The study of both—vividly so when it came to Neapolitan landscapes—relied on shared sources. In 1632 Scipione Falcone, an accomplished natural philosopher and doctor, included a chronology of the volcano's eruptive history in his *Discorso naturale delle cause et effetti causati nell'incendio del Monte Vesuvio*, a work obviously focused on the natural causes and effects of the most recent eruption. Volcanologists today date and sequence eruptions primarily by searching for the various strata of lava and pyroclastic material that correspond to respective occurrences, but Falcone's sequencing and dating did not rely on observation or collected data. They were based instead on the evidence provided by texts such as Pliny the Elder's *Natural History* and Seneca's *Quaestiones naturales*. In his own words he sought to compile "a table of the number of ignitions, their distance one from the other . . . and the authors that describe them."[56] What he faced, therefore, was fundamentally a humanist's and antiquarian's problem.

▣ ▣ ▣

These two centuries of neglected scholarship, first on the Campi Flegrei caldera and then on Vesuvius, gave lasting shape to the subsequent recovery of antiquity in the Bay of Naples. By the mid-eighteenth century efforts centered on the new Bourbon digs at Pompeii and Herculaneum, but the shadow of Vesuvius still loomed large. The unearthing of the lost cities in the 1740s would afford antiquarians a glimpse of the ancient world in nearly intact form, heralding new methods in the process.[57] Important as were Enlightenment advances in archaeology and earth sciences, their foundation in earlier traditions should be remembered, since in some form the process of excavating the classical past had been under way for at least two hundred years.

William Hamilton came to Naples in 1764 for a lengthy stay, during which time he wrote the *Campi Phlegræi* (1776; 1779), a masterpiece based on his volcano exploration. Surely he walked in the footsteps of Di Falco, Loffredo, and Capaccio, who had combined antiquarian study with natural history. At the same time Hamilton heralded the broader Enlightenment effort that saw archaeology, geology, and art history develop as distinct disciplines. As one scholar has noted, what distinguished Hamilton from the curiosi of the sixteenth and seventeenth centuries was a desire to attach a different order to what was observed and collected.[58]

Nevertheless, early modern curiosi transmitted their dedication to both "civil" (as it related to *civiltà* and the course of civilizations) and natural history to their eighteenth-century successors, as the latter continued to search for the objects of nature and artifice. Hamilton collected Vesuvian rocks and Roman antiquities, and in this regard his endeavor was not entirely alien to Loffredo's antiquarianism centuries earlier. A French contemporary to the eighteenth-century Englishman, the great naturalist Georges Louis Leclerc, comte de Buffon, alluded to this fact in his *Des époques de la nature* (1778), where he nodded to his Renaissance and baroque predecessors. "Just as," he proclaimed, "in the history of civilizations, we consult documents, examine medals and decipher ancient inscriptions to determine the sequence of human revolutions or to establish the sequence of events of moral significance, so, in natural history, we should delve in the archives of the earth, [and] bring forth ancient monuments from its bowels."[59] Thanks in part to a period of increased activity, which began in 1538 and culminated in 1631, the volcanoes of Naples helped ignite the effort to recover Campania's ancient past.

Notes

1   Early modern sources used the Italian names—Cuma, Baia, and Pozzuoli—interchangeably. I will use the Italian name for the whole region: Campi Flegrei. For Pliny the Elder's reference to the caldera (a collapsed volcano), see his *Natural History* 3.5.41.

2   Ingrid Rowland's *Scarith of Scornello: A Tale of Renaissance Forgery* (Chicago, 2004), for example, is a delightful portrait of antiquarianism and patriotic interest in seventeenth-century Tuscany.

3   Benedetto Di Falco, *Descrittione dei luoghi antichi di Napoli e del suo amenissimo distretto per Benedetto Falco napolitano* (Naples, 1549). For natural history in the Renaissance, see Paula Findlen's *Possessing Nature: Museums, Collecting, and Scientific Culture in Early Modern Italy* (Berkeley, 1994).

4   Ferrante Loffredo, *Le antichità di Pozzuolo, et luoghi convicini del Sig. Ferrante Loffredo, marchese di Trevico e del consiglio di guerra di sua maestà* (1573; Naples, 1675); Giulio Cesare Capaccio, *La vera antichità di Pozzuolo descritta da Giulio Cesare Capaccio* (Naples, 1607).

5   For the influence of Vesuvius on humanism, science, religion, and politics in early modern Naples, see Sean Cocco, "Vesuvius and Naples: Nature and the City, 1500–1700" (PhD diss., University of Washington, 2004).

6   Histories of the development of volcanology in the early modern period place the greatest emphasis on the later 1600s and the 1700s and unfortunately tend to forget the significant response the eruption of 1631 garnered among contemporary natural philosophers. See, for example, Haraldur Sigurdsson, *Melting the Earth: The History of Ideas on Volcanic Eruptions* (New York, 1999), 100.

7   Virgil *Aeneid* 6.105–9. See A. G. McKay, *Ancient Campania*, 2 vols. (Hamilton, Ontario, 1972), 1:1–7.

8   Lucretius *De rerum natura* 6.739–49; translated in McKay 1972 (note 7), 1:7.

9   The Solfatara crater is part of an active volcanic-hydrothermal system within the Campi Flegrei caldera. Its vents discharge H_2O steam, CO_2, H_2S, and SO_2, with sulfur encrustations forming on the outer portions.

10   Silius Italicus *Punica* 12.133–46; Strabo *Geographica* 5.4.4.

11   Pliny the Elder *Natural History* 18.109–11.

12   Although it has collapsed into a caldera, the volcano that makes up the Campi Flegrei is a strato volcano like Vesuvius. Strato volcanoes are formed from the composite action of lava flows and the buildup of pyroclastic material (volcanic ejecta). The Vesuvius one sees today (and seen by early modern observers as well) is a cone formed by exactly this sort of action inside the caldera left by the huge eruption of A.D. 79. In its early history Vesuvius likely had the nearly perfect conical shape characteristic of this type of volcano. See *Encyclopedia of Volcanoes*, ed. Haraldur Sigurdsson (San Diego, 2000); see also François Girault, *Vulcani* (Novara, 1998).

13   Giovanni Orsi, "Storia geologica e deformativa della caldera dei Campi Flegrei," in *Archeologia e vulcanologia in Campania* (Naples, 1998), 29–37. See John Dvorak and Giuseppe Mastrolorenzo, *The Mechanisms of Recent Vertical Crustal Movements in Campi Flegrei Caldera, Southern Italy* (Boulder, 1991).

14   Athanasius Kircher, *Mundus subterraneus in XII libros digestus* (Amsterdam, 1678), esp. chaps. 3–4, 6. For an analysis of the influence of Vesuvius and the eruption of 1631 on seventeenth-century theories of subterranean heat, see Cocco 2004 (note 5), 203–59.

15   Giovanni Battista Della Porta, *Dei miracoli et maravigliosi effetti dalla natura prodotti. Libri IIII. Di Giovanni Battista Porta Napolitano, novamente tradotti dal Latino in lingua volgare, e con molta fatica illustrati* (Venice, 1560), 3.

16   The letter was subsequently published in Simone Porzio, *De conflagratione agri Puteolani, Simonis Portii Neapolitani epistola* (Florence, 1551). Toledo's interest in the Campi Flegrei is recorded in Capaccio 1607 (note 4), 145.

17   For medieval balneologists in the Campi Flegrei, see C. M. Kaufmann, *The Baths of Pozzuoli: A Study of Medieval Illuminations of Peter of Eboli's Poem* (Oxford, 1959). Recently scholars have stressed the contribution of balneologists in the development of early modern science. See Lorraine Daston and Katherine Park, *Wonders and the Order of Nature, 1150–1750* (New York, 1998).

18   "Multa sunt, quae etsi naturali ratione eveniant, quia tamen raro contigunt, portenta hominibus: atque iis maxime, qui rumore potius ea quamvisu percipiunt, videri solent" (Porzio 1551 [note 16], 2).

19   Aristotle *Meteorologica* 2.8.367. For an introduction to ancient geological theories, see François Ellenberger, *History of Geology* (Rotterdam, 1996), 1:9–57.

20   Porzio 1551 (note 16), 2.

21   Lucretius *De rerum naturae* 6.685–702.

22   Cesare La Galla, *De phoenomenis in orbe lunae novi telescopii usu a D. Gallileo Gallileoque. Nunc iterum suscitatis physica disputatio ad Iulio Caesare La Galla* (Venice, 1612).

23   This connection of geological and political events occurred a century later, when Neapolitan rebels imagined the eruption of 1631 to have been a portent of the 1647 Masaniello revolt, thus transforming Vesuvius into a symbol of an outraged Neapolitan nation suffering under Spanish tyranny (see Cocco 2004 [note 5], 153–202). See also Nicola Badaloni, "Fermenti di vita intellettuale a Napoli dal 1500 alla metà del 1600," in *Storia di Napoli: Il viceregno* (Naples, 1975), 643–89. Della Porta and Tommaso Campanella were part of a tradition of reading natural signs as portending political upheaval, frequently with reference to astrology. There is a vast bibliography on Campanella. A good place to start in English is John M. Headley, *Tommaso*

Campanella and the Transformation of the World (Princeton, 1997). On prophecy in the decades that led up to the Masaniello revolt, see Rosario Villari, *La rivolta antispagnola a Napoli: Le origini (1585–1647)* (Bari, 1967).

24   "Atqui quid haec portendant nonnulli anxie quaerunt ego vero cum Peripateticis dico, nullam praesentionis istius certam esse causam: tametsi Cicero portendis multum tribuat, multum etiam detrahat" (Porzio 1551 [note 16], 5).

25   "Haec igitur mi Mecoenas scribenda duxi; ne Haroli, somniorum interpretes, ac vulgares Astrologi alio trahant, que nature duce proveniunt" (ibid.).

26   Di Falco 1549 (note 3), 9.

27   Villari 1967 (note 23), 33–67.

28   Di Falco 1549 (note 3), 6.

29   Ibid.

30   Ibid., 39.

31   Ibid., 39–41.

32   Dvorak and Mastrolorenzo 1991 (note 13), 1.

33   Pietro di Stefano, *Descrittione de i luoghi sacri della città di Napoli* (Naples, 1560); Antonio Sanfelice, *Campania Antonii Sanfelicii monachi* (Naples, 1562); and Giovanni Tarcagnota, *Del sito et lodi della città di Napoli con una breve historia de gli re suoi* (Naples, 1566).

34   Francesca Ammirante, "Il cinquecento," in *Guide e descrizioni di Napoli* (Naples, 1994), 29. In 1675 the Neapolitan editor Antonio Bulifon republished Loffredo's book, the first edition of which dated to 1573. The later Bulifon reprint is the only one I have been able to view (Loffredo 1675 [note 4]).

35   "Andavo il dì cavalcando per il paese, particolarmente vedendo tutte le cose di consideratione, e di meraviglia; tanto naturali, come artificiali, che sono dal capo di Pausillipo, insino a Miseno, e quindi a Cuma, lungo il lido, e su per i colli e monti d'intorno: e poi la notte conferendoli con li scritti de gli Autori antichi, che ne parlando, e similmente pigliandone quelli rincontri che migliori si poteano da i Paesani per fama, e per memoria lasciata loro da i Padri, e auoli, accozzando tutte queste cose insieme, se ben ritrovai molte conformità di quel che vedea cavalcando, con i libri, e con la fama; nondimeno ritrovai alcune difformita ancora e differenze, e in parecchie cose mi fecero gran difficiolta il silentio de' Scrittori, la fama perduta, le reliquie di fabbriche di tutto disfatte, e finalmente il mancamento de tutti gli aiuti, che sogliono guidare la congiettura di simil cose. Pure determinai di vincere, quanto si bastava, con la diligenza tutte quelle incommodità, e rivedere tante volte i luoghi, essaminare si minutamente i paesani, e diligentemente rivolgere e considerare i libri, che non rimanesse industria da fare. Et travagliai di modo che mi pare di esserne parvenuto, se non m'inganno, a tutta quella vera luce, che si potea in tanta oscurità" (Loffredo 1675 [note 4], 2).

36   Ibid., 6–12.

37   Ibid., 24. Loffredo's reference was presumably to Plutarch's life of Lucullus and Strabo's *Geographica* 4. See also Summonte, *Historia del regno di Napoli* (Naples, 1601), 292.

38   "Et come questo paese di sotto è tutto di materia accomodata ad ardere, già che il suo fuoco vi è tanto acceso, mi persuado, che starà sempre in quest' infelicità, e che vi saranno sempre terremoti, i quali non dimeno mancaranno con le essalationi, e in tutti i tempi antichi debbe essere stato il medesimo, e si vedono molti luoghi simili a questo monte, i quali non potevano farsi altrimenti, che per essalationi, fra quali la Solfatara, li Struni, Campiglione. Et queste essalationi hanno rovinato tante fabriche magnifiche, che per lo paese si vedono distrutte" (Loffredo 1675 [note 4], 15).

39   Ibid., 3.

40 Loffredo was not alone in these concerns. Another local *curioso* expressed the same idea about Baia (see Scipione Mazzella, *Sito et antichità della città di Pozzuolo e del suo amenissimo distretto, con la descrittione di tutti i luoghi notabili* [Naples, 1606]).

41 Capaccio 1607 (note 4), preface.

42 "Ma quando giunse a Pozzuolo, raccogliendo se medesima in se stessa, si determinò farsi conoscere tanto grande, tanto cortese, anzi tanto prodigia, che aprendo largamente il seno di tutti i suoi beni, lasciando ogni altra parte a dietro, l'ornò non solamente di vago, e dilettevol sito; di tranquillo, e copioso mare; di benigno, e allegro Cielo; ma tutta ridente e festevole" (ibid.).

43 Ibid., 169.

44 "Se in alcune opere di fabriche gli edificii di Pozzuolo contendono con le fabriche di Roma, nella materia de i fuoghi, dell'acque, e di cose meravigliose di natura non è dubio che la sopravanzano. Quel che si è detto della Solfatara, non reca stupor grande a chi lege? Hor che sara a chi la vede? Quel che trattiamo della virtù delle terme naturali, non apporta consideratione maggiore, che gli artificiati bagni o publici, o privati che usavano i Romani; ma il veder mo esalare i vapori, e esser cagione, che la piana terra si erga in monti di Cenere qual è quel c'ha coverto Tripergole, e' l Lago Lucrino in Pozzuolo, non è cosa che eccede ogni meraviglia?" (ibid., 163).

45 Georg Braun and Franz Hogenberg, *Civitates orbis terrarum* (1572; Cologne, 1606), 58.

46 Horace *Epistula* I.

47 Somma was the name frequently given. More precisely Somma refers to the lesser peak, the ridge of the caldera formed in A.D. 79, while Vesuvius is the cone proper. Giulio Cesare Braccini, *Dell'incendio fattosi nel Vesuvio a XVI di dicembre M.DC.XXXI e delle sue cause ed effetti* (Naples, 1632), 22.

48 Antonio Nazzaro, *Il Vesuvio: Storia eruttiva e teorie vulcanologiche* (Naples, 2001), 20–32. For a list of all contemporary sources on the eruptions, see Luigi Riccio, "Nuovi documenti sull'incendio vesuviano dell'anno 1631 e bibliografie di quella eruzione," *Archivio storico per le provincie napoletane* 14 (1889): 490–505.

49 Manso was a prominent figure in baroque Naples. He was a patron of artists, a regular correspondent with Galileo, and one of the founding members of the Accademia napoletana degli oziosi. To date, he has not received the attention he deserves. See Aurelio Musi, *L'Italia dei viceré: Integrazione e resistenza nel sistema imperiale spagnolo* (Cava de' Tirreni, 2000), 129–47; and Girolamo De Miranda, *Una quiete operosa: Forma e pratiche dell'Accademia napoletana degli oziosi, 1611–1645* (Naples, 2000).

50 "Il mattino del Martedì quello che di notte tempo era paruto un fumo infocato apparve con la nuova luce a guisa di nube sorgente da terra diritto in alto fino alla settima region dell'aria, e quivi s'allargava per si fatto modo che, come la parte sollevata a dirittura in su rassomigliava un grosso tronco d'un altissimo pino, così l'altra parte superiore dilatata al d'intorno sembrava una smisurata pigna e più vasta d'una grandissima montagna" ("Lettera del Signor Giov. Battista Manzo, Marchese di Villa, in materia del Vesuvio," in Riccio 1889 [note 48], 503–4).

51 The Loeb translation reads: "It was not clear at that distance from which mountain the cloud was rising (it was afterwards known to be Vesuvius); its general appearance can best be expressed as being like a pine rather than any other tree, for it rose to a great height on a sort of trunk and then split off into branches, I imagine because it was thrust upwards by the first blast and then left unsupported as the pressure subsided, or else it was borne down by its own weight so that it spread out and gradually dispersed. Sometimes it looked white, sometimes blotched and dirty, according to the amount of soil and ashes it carried with it." ["Nubes—(incertum procul intuentibus ex quo monte, Vesuuium fuisse postea cognitum est)—oriebatur, cuius similitudinem et formam non alia magis arbor quam pinus expresserit. Nam velut trunco elata in altum quibusdam ramis diffundebatur, crede, quia recenti spiritu evecta, dein senescente eo destituta aut candida interdum, interdum sordida et maculosa, prout terram cineremque sustulerat"] (Pliny the Younger *Epistularum* 6.16).

52   Braccini 1632 (note 47), 31.

53   Iaria Cerbai and Claudia Principe, *Bibliography of Historic Activity on Italian Volcanoes* (Pisa, 1996), 9.

54   Giulio Cesare Capaccio, *Il Forastiero* (Naples, 1631).

55   Vincenzo Bove, *Novissima relatione dell'incendio successo nel monte di Somma a 16 Decembre 1631, con un'avviso di quello è successo nell'istesso dì nella città di Cattaro nelle parti d'Albania* (Naples, 1632), 8.

56   Falcone cited a mix of classical, medieval, and contemporary sources including Dio Cassius, Suetonius, Procopius, Falco Beneventanus, Ambrogio Leone, and even Giulio Cesare Capaccio. He described his table as follows: "Table of volcanic ignitions, with the time between them; of the years of the ignitions after the birth of Our Lord Jesus Christ; of the Authors that record them; leaving untouched the earliest ones, as uncertain, though these ought to be reviewed by someone who has occasion to correct the historical dates." ["Tavola del numero dell'accensioni della distanza fra l'una, e l'altra accensione; dell'anni dell'accensioni dopo la nascita di N.S. Giesù Christo; dell'Autori, ove le scriveno; e si lasciano le precedenti, come non bene accertate ne i tempi, queste anco si sottoponeno a chi ha più tempo per aggiustar li tempi dell'historie"] (Scipione Falcone, *Discorso naturale delle cause et effetti causati nell'incendio del Monte Vesuvio con relatione del tutto di Scipione Falcone spetial di medicina napolitano* [Naples, 1632], 3). Another important scientific treatise on the eruption was Pietro Castelli's *Incendio del Monte Vesuvio di Pietro Castelli Romano* (Rome, 1632).

57   Antonio d'Ambrosio, *Pompei: Gli scavi dal 1748 al 1860* (Milan, 2002), 2–50.

58   Alain Schnapp, "Antiquarian Studies in Naples at the End of the Eighteenth Century: From Comparative Archaeology to Comparative Religion," in *Naples in the Eighteenth Century: The Birth and Death of a Nation State*, ed. Girolamo Imbruglia (Cambridge, 2000), 154–66.

59   Georges Louis Leclerc Buffon, *Des époques de la nature* (Paris, 1778), cited and translated in Imbruglia 2000 (note 58), 159.

Subverting the Secret of Herculaneum: Archaeological Espionage in the Kingdom of Naples

Alden R. Gordon

I N A DARK WELL SHAFT at the foot of Mount Vesuvius, the Secret of Herculaneum was born. The secret—the Bourbon monarchy's restriction of access to
the buried cities—was an assertion of ownership, privilege, and property rights
over archaeological discoveries. As such, it was an intentional restriction on the free
exchange of knowledge and was antithetical to the spirit of the Enlightenment. Thus
the secret led to decades of frustrated international curiosity about the treasures of
antiquity held hostage to Neapolitan political ambition and a misguided pursuit of
national prestige.

The earliest archaeological finds related to the buried cities were made near Portici
in 1709. Unwittingly, a laborer discovered ancient marbles in a well shaft in the courtyard of the Alcantarine monastery at Resina.[1] The peasant took his finds to the nearest
nobleman to turn a quick profit from his discovery. The purchaser was Emmanuel
Maurice de Lorraine, later first prince d'Elbeuf, then duc d'Elbeuf (or d'Elboeuf). He
had come to Naples in the staff of the Austrian Habsburg viceroy and married an Italian, whom he established in a pleasant country house at Portici, southeast of Naples,
where the slopes of Mount Vesuvius touch the shore.[2]

The antiquities so impressed Elbeuf that he purchased the site at Resina and continued to remove sculpture from the well and new radiating tunnels he had dug from
1709 until 1716. The rich find became known through Elbeuf's black-market exportation to his cousin, Prince Eugene of Savoy, of three full-length clothed marble female
figures, known as the Vestal Virgins.[3] In a time-honored tradition of early archaeology
in Italy, Elbeuf smuggled the marble figures in a diplomatically protected military con-
voy through the Papal States to Vienna.[4] Elbeuf also violated bans on unauthorized
sales of antiquities. A bronze bust of Caligula, for example, found its way into Horace
Mann's collection in Florence; Mann in turn gave it to Horace Walpole in 1767.[5] Having

stocked his new villa with his finds, Elbeuf ceased operations in 1716, when he was transferred back to Austria. For twenty years, from 1716 to 1736, no one paid any further attention to Prince Elbeuf's treasure well.

In 1734 the political situation in Naples was completely transformed. In the complex diplomatic settlement of the War of the Polish Succession, Carlo Borbone of Spain displaced the viceroy of the Austrian Habsburg emperor Charles VI in Naples.[6] Significantly Carlo's claim derived from his Farnese lineage on his mother's side and not from his Bourbon descent. As a consequence, many of the officials Carlo brought with him to administer his new government in Naples were Farnese clients from Parma or Tuscany. Carlo Borbone reigned as Charles VII of Naples from 1734 to 1759, when he succeeded his half-brother Ferdinand VI on the throne of Spain.

Four years after he came to Naples, Charles VII married Maria Amalia of Saxony. Only two years before the marriage, Maria Amalia's father, Augustus III, the elector of Saxony and king of Poland, had acquired Elbeuf's three ancient marble Vestal Virgins from the niece of Prince Eugene of Savoy.[7] The new queen, therefore, almost certainly arrived in Naples from Dresden fully aware of the prestigious antiquities that had been found beneath the slopes of Vesuvius.

Charles VII, eager to emphasize that he was the legitimate monarch of an important kingdom, pursued a political and cultural program designed to establish his position.[8] As the first resident king in more than two centuries, he reigned in great state in Naples, undertook ambitious architectural projects, supported the local artistic community, and created a porcelain industry. When Charles VII was twenty-three, his queen, along with his librarian, Niccolò Marcello Venuti, and the military engineer Rocque Joachin Alcubierre, convinced him to search for antiquities, particularly near the house formerly belonging to Elbeuf. The king was an avid hunter already drawn to the Vesuvian slopes by the game, and he duly acquired the former Elbeuf lands from their current owners.[9] He permitted his queen and courtiers to assemble a small work crew, and on October 1, 1738, Charles VII became the patron of regular excavations at Resina.[10] Although Elbeuf and the local residents never suspected, the king's advisers believed they were exploring the destroyed city of Herculaneum, the existence of which was known from ancient authors such as Pliny the Younger, but which had never been recovered.

Antiquities and the Neapolitan Policy of Aggrandizement

The antiquities found by the royal digs at Herculaneum and later at Pompeii and Stabiae became components of Neapolitan statecraft. The discovery of entire buried ancient cities represented a unique and jealously protected endowment of the kingdom of Naples. To secure the full prestige of the discoveries, Charles VII and his advisers decided that Naples must retain exclusive rights to the possession, knowledge, and publication of the finds, thus excluding foreigners from any access to the riches hidden beneath Bourbon soil. Ottavio Baiardi documented this approach in his *Prodromo*, the first official royal publication on Naples's antiquarian patrimony:[11] "The courts of Europe, mired in military and diplomatic war for the control of always more ample territories, must have been stupefied before the spectacle that the King of Naples was able to offer to the entire world of his extensive conquests—as one might say—within the viscera of the earth itself."[12]

The Neapolitan "exaltation of patrimony"—as Fausto Zevi called it—contrasted sharply with the attitude of the more inclusive, learned Enlightenment circles in France, England, and Germany as well as elsewhere in Italy.[13] In 1734 the Museo Capitolino in Rome was founded as the first public museum in Europe, and visitors could freely draw or make notes as they studied the collections. The same was also true in private collections, such as at the Villa Albani in Rome, which was frequented by foreigners and Italians. The Accademia etrusca in Cortona and other learned societies in Florence, Parma, and Venice likewise enrolled foreign members and encouraged the exchange of information on a wide range of subjects. The reputation of the Bourbon monarchy in Naples and the economy of the kingdom would have been better served by a similar policy of openness, but it was not to be. After having been ruthlessly exploited by the Austrian viceroyalty, Naples as an independent kingdom reacted with a paranoid fear of mistreatment by outsiders and instituted a policy of insistence on absolute domestic control.

The Early Excavations

Digging near Portici on the seaward side of the lowest slopes of Vesuvius was extremely difficult owing to the cementlike hardness of the lava (the lava had mixed with sand and shells sucked into the volcano during the eruption through vents in the ocean floor). The finds were deep, some twenty meters from the surface, and, indeed, most of Herculaneum remains buried to this day.[14] The engineers directing the work could not create open-pit excavations from above for three reasons. First, the king was unwilling to pay for more than a dozen workers. Second, a town on privately owned land existed above the site. Finally, Charles wanted to extract individual antiquities as quickly as possible, not to lay bare the entire town.

Workers descended through vertical shafts and then tunneled outward, pursuing their work through narrow tunnels choked with torch smoke and served by baskets dangling from ropes and pulleys.[15] While at first they hoisted excavated debris to the surface, they soon began backfilling explored and plundered tunnels. Because of this method, no two visits to the dig were ever the same, since tunnels that had been in use were subsequently filled in as new ones were opened elsewhere.

At the outset Charles VII was only mildly intrigued by the antiquities, although he subsequently learned to appreciate this extraordinary trove. Each evening his courtiers presented the new archaeological finds as though performing a conjuring trick for the diversion of the king. Charles did not see the site as a historical phenomenon opening a window onto ancient life. Instead he considered the dig a mine from which royal treasure could be extracted.

For this reason—and because of the difficult conditions of the place—Charles fatefully placed the early extraction of objects from the site in the charge of military engineers. These men used tunneling methods designed for sapping fortifications. Such methods were anathema to the emerging group of scholars of ancient culture and professional architects who were beginning to understand the value of recording the relationship between the objects and the setting in which they were found. Niccolò Marcello Venuti provided a lone dissenting voice. A founding member of Cortona's Accademia etrusca, Venuti had come to Naples as the royal librarian at the beginning of Charles VII's reign. He urged the king to acquire the site at Resina and the palace at

Portici and to pursue the excavation of antiquities. Venuti argued for clearing the tunnels to reveal the contours of the buried buildings and to allow for a careful study of the site and the antiquities removed from it. He was opposed by the military engineers, especially Alcubierre and his superior, the architect Giovanni Antonio Medrano, both of whom advocated expeditiously refilling tunnels with the debris of new tunnels. The courtiers, especially Prime Minister José Joachin Montealegre and future prime minister Bernardo Tanucci, placed emphasis on finding the greatest number of valuable artifacts with the fewest number of workers and the least amount of funds expended. The engineers and courtiers won; Venuti resigned and left Naples in 1740.

This focus on efficiently extracting isolated objects remained inured in the thinking of the ministers directing the works and later characterized the nature of the official publications of the Real accademia ercolanese after that body was formed in 1755. It also created a tension between the court officials establishing policy and the architects conducting the work, who came to develop a greater appreciation of the importance of the context in which the works of art were found.[16] Thus began a long, roiling internal dissention, which spilled over to the international community.

The Secret of Herculaneum

The new archaeological sites had a serious problem with theft and illegal exportation. As early as 1740 the king learned that three men from Resina had invaded the site at night and stolen small lamps and other metal objects. These later surfaced in Tuscany with the suggestion that they had been exported with the permission of the king of Naples. Charles VII was so furious at losing any part of his hoard that he declared personal ownership of every object and forbade the export of even the smallest find. Furthermore, he refused permission to disseminate images of his objects. In February 1740 the king discovered that a Roman artist and antiquarian, Camillo Paderni (ironically later to succeed Venuti as librarian of the king of Naples and one of the principal enforcers of royal control), had been allowed to draw a fresco fragment. Charles immediately ordered that no one would henceforth be permitted to sketch on the site or in the impromptu museum of objects at the Portici palace.[17]

The Neapolitan policy was to restrict access to the dig and discourage tourism in order to build an aura of exclusivity around the finds. Permission to see the collections would be by royal dispensation only. This consent was never withheld but was circumscribed by calculated visitor harassment. Guests and scholars thus privileged by the Crown but not associated with the Neapolitan court could see the antiquities but were prevented from publishing them. Charles VII and his government enforced this policy of exclusivity in opposition to the thriving international book trade, unconstrained by copyright laws or issues of academic precedence that supported the Enlightenment Republic of Letters. The publication of the new finds would have been an unprecedented scoop in these scholarly, antiquarian circles, but such publication would have subverted the social and political ambitions of the Bourbon court. Thus was born the Secret of Herculaneum.

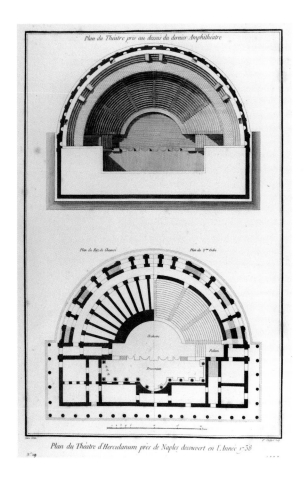

Criticism of the Excavation Method

The earliest serendipitous descents into Herculaneum led into the theater, where a trove of marble sculpture originally had stood in niches on the proscenium or cornice of its semicircular walls [FIG. 1]. The excavators then tunneled into adjacent public buildings, most notably the so-called basilica, a courtyard surrounded by a columned portico within which were walls with niches decorated with fresco paintings of mythological subjects. These places yielded prolific early finds, such as the two equestrian statues of the Balbi and the most famous of the fresco fragments today in the Museo archeologico nazionale in Naples.[18]

In 1740 no one could make out the nature of the buildings, as Camillo Paderni recounts: "I went down into the pit. The part where they are at work must have been a stupendous building; conjectured to have been an amphitheater by the circumference of the walls and the large steps which are still preserved. But it is impossible to see the symmetry of the whole."[19] Horace Walpole, who visited in June 1740, recalled:

> The path is very narrow, just wide enough and high enough for one man to walk upright. They have hollowed as they found it easiest to work, and have carried their streets not exactly where were the ancient ones, but sometimes before houses, sometimes through them. You would imagine that all the fabrics were crushed together; on the contrary, except some columns, they have found all the edifices standing.... They

make out very plainly an amphitheatre: the stairs, of white marble, and the seats are very perfect;...they have found among other things some fine statues, some human bones, some rice, medals and a few paintings extremely fine. These latter...we have not seen them yet, as they are kept in the king's apartment whither all these curiosities are transplanted; and 'tis difficult to see them—but we shall.[20]

Both Paderni and Walpole criticized the conduct of the excavations. Walpole noted: "There might certainly be collected great light from this reservoir of antiquities, if a man of learning had the inspection of it; if he directed the working, and would make a journal of the discoveries. But I believe there is no judicious choice made of directors."[21] Paderni was even more explicit:

The first mistake those men they call intendents [the engineers conducting the dig] have committed is their having dug out the pictures without drawing the situation of the place, that is, the niches where they stood: for they were all adorned with grotesques composed of most elegant masques, figures and animals; which, not being copied, are gone to destruction, and the like will happen to the rest. Then, if they meet with any pieces of painting not so well preserved as the rest, they leave them where they are found. Besides, there are pillars of stucco extremely curious, consisting of many sides, all variously painted, of which they do not preserve the memory.[22]

The theater at Herculaneum is closed to tourists today because of its condition. The appearance, however, of the tunnels as I photographed them in 1991 [FIG. 2] corresponds closely with Walpole's description of more than 250 years ago. The damp and narrow tunnels have the feel of a mine rather than an archaeological dig. The chisel and drill marks of eighteenth-century diggers appear clearly on the walls and are easily distinguishable from the smooth Roman ashlar masonry, some of which still bears fragments of red fresco decoration. Carbonized wood from ancient beams remains atop some of the piers. But almost every fragment of marble and every portable artifact has long since been removed.

FIGURE 2
Inside the excavation of the theater at Herculaneum, 1991.

Photo: Alden R. Gordon.

Enforcing the Secret

The Secret of Herculaneum was in place from before Walpole's sojourn in 1740 until after Johann Wolfgang von Goethe's visit in 1787. Visitors to both Portici and Herculaneum were rushed and strictly supervised. The descent into the narrow tunnels at Herculaneum was disorienting, claustrophobic, suffocating, and brief, while the guided tour to see the objects removed to the palace at Portici was closely surveyed by the king's servants. Most tourists, however, did not publicly complain since they did not want to jeopardize the privilege of seeing the king's private collection.

Some foreigners, however, with direct knowledge of the dig quietly began to challenge the secret. The English artist and cicerone James Russel published a series of letters in 1748 that eloquently expressed the frustration of the learned community in the face of the restrictive Neapolitan policies.[23] Although desirous of acquainting the public with the "great discoveries made among the ruins of Herculaneum," Russel warned that he could not deliver on that desire and that readers would have to wait years for the promised official publications. Russel circumspectly wrote:

The Reader…may not expect, either to receive more satisfaction from the present account than it will yield him, or to see any other more satisfactory in a little time. His Sicilian Majesty is building a Palace, and in it a fine Gallery, for the reception of all the Curiosities, which have already been, or may hereafter be, discovered, in this wonderful place;…all these he designs to have ingraved, described, and explained, in the same manner, as in the *Musaeum Florentinum*. A Work of this nature can not be completely executed, 'till all these things have been ranged in their proper order in the intended Gallery; and consequently will not probably see the light; 'till some years hence. In the mean time, to prevent any anticipation, no one, who is admitted to the sight of these Antiquities, is permitted to make use of a pencil, either in the subterraneous City, or in the palace at Portici. Which precaution, as it takes away all reasonable hopes of our having any very exact and perfect Account of them 'till that authentic one shall appear; so it may serve to induce the Public to be the better satisfied, in the mean while, with that which is given in these Letters.[24]

Visits of knowledgeable scholars were especially suspect and often charged with tension. Johann Joachim Winckelmann, the papal librarian whose first tour occurred in February 1758, was subjected to the note-taking restrictions and was not given free access to the collections.[25] He posed a particularly serious threat to the secret because of his connections to the Accademia etrusca in Cortona and the Society of Antiquaries in London, not to mention links to virtually all serious antiquarians and tourists who visited Rome and the papal collections. Winckelmann wrote bitterly: "I cannot take a step without having an overseer next to me, whom I have given plenty of trouble."[26]

When Goethe visited in March 1787 he was never unattended, nor could he linger at Herculaneum or Portici: "We had good letters of recommendation to the museum and were well received, but we were not allowed to make any drawings….We followed the custodians from room to room, trying to enjoy and learn as much as possible in the little time we had." He described the escorted visit to the site thus: "We descended a flight of sixty steps to a vault, where we admired by torchlight the former open-air theater, while the guard told us about the things which were found there and brought to the light of day." Like Walpole and Winckelmann, Goethe was dismayed at how the Neapolitans had excavated: "It is a thousand pities that the site was not excavated methodically by German miners, instead of being casually ransacked as if by brigands, for many noble works of antiquity must have been thereby lost or ruined."[27]

Subversion of the Secret, 1740–56

The Neapolitan monarchy intended to exploit the propaganda value of the archaeological finds through their controlled publication. A luxurious, limited edition was to be written by a single distinguished scholar, and the books were to be given exclusively as royal gifts, primarily to other princes, rather than offered for sale. In 1746 Prime Minister Giovanni Fogliani d'Aragona convinced the king to summon from Rome Fogliani's cousin, Ottavio Antonio Baiardi, to undertake the catalogue.[28] The slow, arrogant, and exclusivist Baiardi was as unfortunate a candidate for the publishing enterprise as Alcubierre was for the excavation. Baiardi was selected over several competent Neapolitan scholars, notably the epigrapher Alessio Simmaco Mazzocchi and Giacomo Martorelli, a professor of Greek at the university. Baiardi used his relationship with Fogliani to ban his competitors' publications, while he jealously guarded his exclusive access to the objects. Baiardi also received ten times the salary of Karl Weber, the director of the excavation from 1750 to 1764, creating another source of frustration and indignation between the archaeological and academic professionals engaged in the excavations.[29] All the excavation directors had been foreign military engineers serving in the Neapolitan army and were looked down upon by the Neapolitan academicians and government authorities. The nepotistic appointment of Baiardi added bile to the already corrosive distrust and jealousy among the insiders supposedly working collaboratively as part of the official Neapolitan team.

The exclusion of foreigners, the obstruction of scholarly interchange, and the failure to produce the promised publications created a climate in which respectable members of the learned community willfully engaged in a black-market exchange of information on Neapolitan antiquities.[30] Resentful Neapolitan scholars passed over for Baiardi, such as Martorelli and Mazzocchi, became domestic agents of the foreigners who sought to subvert the secret.

International indignation at the restrictive Bourbon policy had existed since Venuti's resignation in 1740. Curiosity about the finds was intense among the small but growing community of Enlightenment intellectuals—a nascent core of art and architectural historians—as well as among professionals whose appetites were stirred by the specific reports on Naples from Italian insiders and foreign travelers. Leaked information began to appear in print as early as 1740, when Allan Ramsay conveyed Camillo Paderni's letters to the Royal Academy.[31] George Turnbull also cited Paderni as a firsthand authority in his 1740 *Treatise on Ancient Painting*.[32] Anton Francesco Gori, a Florentine correspondent of Venuti's, was another early conduit of information from Naples. He announced the finds in a brief letter of February 26, 1740, and followed with a treatise in 1748, both of which infuriated the keepers of the secret.[33] Eighteenth-century authors identified Gori's source as Martorelli, who had been slighted by Baiardi's hire in 1746.[34] Using a drawing illicitly smuggled to him by Martorelli, Gori published the first image of the finds, an engraving of two views of the marble equestrian figures of Marcus Nonio Balbo discovered in 1738.[35] The engraving was labeled as having been made *a memoria*, probably to protect Gori's source. A wave of Italian publications in Florence, Venice, Rome, Brescia, and Verona followed in 1748.[36] Venuti also published his earlier groundbreaking research that year.[37] Baiardi was outraged and used all his influence at court to have the publications banned and their authors denounced in Naples, but he could do nothing to stop the distribution of these pamphlets in northern Italy or across the rest of Europe.

Foreign authors quickly joined those providing accounts of the discoveries. Charles de Brosses was among the few foreign visitors to Herculaneum immediately after the excavations resumed under royal aegis in 1738.[38] As a French government official, president of the court at Dijon, and an officer of the law who had been received by the king of Naples, it would have been unthinkable for Brosses to openly defy the wishes of a foreign ruler, and he did not publicly reveal the discoveries for another ten years, when he did so anonymously in a 1750 unillustrated report. He did, however, write private letters describing his experience.[39]

Brosses's countryman Guillaume-Marie d'Arthenay (or Darthenay), secretary to the French ambassador in Naples in the 1740s and an associate member of the Neapolitan academy of sciences, as well as a volcanologist and amateur antiquarian, submitted his *Mémoire sur la ville souterraine découverte au pied du Mont Vésuve* to the academy in Avignon in December 1747 and published it in Paris in 1748.[40] While there is no documentary proof, d'Arthenay was probably significantly involved in the Neapolitan information underground linking foreigners with local scholars and the professional employees of the excavations.

The early unauthorized accounts of the discoveries near the Bay of Naples were sought avidly throughout Europe. All these reports, however, depended on recounting leaked information and were by and large unillustrated. Fueled by an escalating desire for more precise information and, above all, for pictures to amplify the descriptions, a group of French travelers were the first to engage in conscious archaeological espionage. In a premeditated campaign they made drawings and detailed descriptions for the first illustrated publications of the buildings and artifacts found at Herculaneum.

These men came in the entourage of Abel-François Poisson de Vandières, future marquis de Marigny and already named in 1746 to the reversion of *directeur-général des bâtiments, jardins, arts, académies et manufactures du roi*. Marigny had left France in December 1749 for a three-year sojourn in Italy to prepare himself for his future administrative role.[41] He traveled with a party of tutor-advisers, chosen to assist the formation of an ideal enlightened government official. His entourage originally consisted of Jacques-Germain Soufflot, a young architect from Lyon who had traveled previously in Italy; Abbé Jean-Bernard Le Blanc, a critic, philosopher, and playwright; and Charles-Nicolas Cochin, an engraver, art theorist, and adjunct member of the Royal Academy of Painting and Sculpture. After Soufflot became ill during a visit to Paestum in June 1750, he was replaced by Gabriel-Martin Dumont, an architect, author, and engraver. For journeys outside Rome, the role of architectural draftsman and adviser to Marigny was filled by Jérôme-Charles Bellicard. An architecture student at the French Academy in Rome and one of the French engravers collaborating with Giovanni Battista Piranesi and others in Rome to publish views of ancient buildings, Bellicard had also contributed engravings to Venuti's *Roma* and to Louis-Jean Duflos's *Varie vedute di Roma*.[42]

Marigny spent November and December 1750 in Naples.[43] Because of his privileged status—as a royal official and the younger brother of Madame de Pompadour—his party operated from the French ambassador's residence in Naples.[44] The ambassador's secretary, d'Arthenay, was the acting French chargé d'affaires and host for this important visitor. Marigny was received courteously by Neapolitan court society and honored with invitations to hunt with the king. Marigny's companions, thanks to his status and to d'Arthenay's established connections, quickly formed a network of friendships and became familiars in Neapolitan intellectual circles.

For two months Marigny and his companions visited churches and royal palaces, the private palazzi of the della Rocca and Francavilla princes, and discussed the merits and defects of pictures and buildings.[45] They also made the now-obligatory pilgrimage to Herculaneum and Portici. But while Marigny attended the court and the opera in the evenings, Bellicard and Cochin used their time at their lodgings to compile the notes and drawings in secret for an illustrated book on the antiquities of Herculaneum and the Bay of Naples. The idea for this publication was certainly not planned in Paris. Before Cochin left France, he could not have known that Bellicard would replace Soufflot. Moreover, Cochin did not know what he would encounter in Naples or what sort of assistance might be found to provide access to internal documents. Bellicard, however, in conversation with his Roman colleagues Duflos, Dumont, and Piranesi, may well have discussed an illustrated publication on Herculaneum. These Rome-based architects of French and north Italian ancestry would have read the publications of Venuti and Gori and would have resented the xenophobic Neapolitan policy. Furthermore, the young and ambitious Bellicard could not have been immune to the promise of fame and fortune represented by such an enterprise.

The scheme to thwart the secret must have been hatched once Cochin and Bellicard had made contact with the people involved in the archaeological enterprise. After they discovered those willing to give them access to the records of the finds and to individuals with firsthand knowledge, they could combine this information with their own limited impressions of the collections and site. The secret composite drawings of the buried buildings made by the architects directing the excavation, for example, would have required lengthy investigation and the time to make detailed copies.

Cochin, the more theoretical of the conspirators, concentrated on describing the paintings and rushed this text back to Paris for publication before his return from Italy. It appeared in the *Mercure de France* in September 1751.[46] Cochin's "Lettre sur les peintures d'Herculanum" was reworked as his contribution to the book he coauthored with Bellicard and first published in 1753. His original notes also served for the account of Portici in his 1758 publication of a guidebook, *Voyage d'Italie*.[47]

The publications by Cochin and Bellicard were probably based on drawings made from memory. Bellicard's surviving notebook, today in the Metropolitan Museum of Art in New York, is the crucial document of this archaeological espionage.[48] Its structure reveals its creation as a diary with thumbnail sketches made from memory often within hours after leaving the site. Bellicard's notebook also includes sheets with numerous tiny designs after the paintings and objects in the palace at Portici [FIG. 3]. Both Cochin and Bellicard drew the fresco paintings from memory and corroborated each other's impressions. Even so, these artists would have needed superhuman memories to draw so many different objects with sufficient detail to be used as models for etchings. Their thoroughness is either a testimony to the memory training of the French school or, more likely, further evidence that inside sources in Naples provided substantial assistance.

In addition to the memory sketches of paintings, lamps, and utilitarian objects, Bellicard made reconstruction drawings of the unexcavated buildings—the theater [FIG. 4], the so-called basilica, and some tombs. Bellicard could not have conceived of the entirety of any building from the claustrophobic and random experience of the tunnels. Instead he needed access to the plans compiled by the architect-engineers directing the excavations over a span of years well before Bellicard's trip to Naples. Some of Bellicard's published plans show only the excavated parts of the theater, while others reconstruct the entire theater, including sections that had not yet been excavated and could only have been based on interpolation and guesswork.

In every likelihood, d'Arthenay had found someone willing to smuggle drawings of the building plans to Bellicard for copying. According to Christopher Parslow, Bellicard almost certainly used drawings made between 1741 and 1743 by the French architect-engineer Pierre Bardet de Villeneuve, and Bardet himself may well have been the intelligence leak.[49] Bardet's appointment to direct the excavations had been negotiated by the French ambassador, Paul-François de Gallucci, marquis de L'Hôpital, in 1741.[50] Bardet was forced from his appointment by Prime Minister Montealegre in 1745 and retaliated by refusing to turn over his daybooks and plans.[51] In late 1750 Bardet was still living in Naples and possessed at least some of his original drawings, so d'Arthenay probably brought the two Frenchmen together. D'Arthenay, after all,

FIGURE 3

Jérôme-Charles Bellicard
(French, 1726–1786),
*Sketches of Fresco
Fragments*, 1750. Page 9
from Jérôme-Charles
Bellicard, manuscript
notebook (1750–51).
New York, Metropolitan
Museum of Art, Department
of Prints and Drawings,
Harris Brisbane Dick
Fund, 1940, Inv. 40.59.6.

FIGURE 4

Jérôme-Charles Bellicard
(French, 1726–1786),
*Notes and Drawing of the
Theater of Herculaneum*,
1750. Page 3 from Jérôme-
Charles Bellicard, manu-
script notebook (1750–51).
New York, Metropolitan
Museum of Art, Department
of Prints and Drawings,
Harris Brisbane Dick
Fund, 1940, Inv. 40.59.6.

would have commiserated with Bardet's treatment, having been L'Hôpital's secretary during the effort to place Bardet at the head of the excavation team back in 1741.

Bellicard himself attests: "The plan which I represent is that which I received in the country, for I would not too much depend upon my own original sketch. But I scrupulously examined all that was discovered of it, going through all the paths that were then formed at random, in the extent of the Theater."[52] Moreover, Bellicard makes clear that he had consulted the plans before he visited the tunnels.[53] He was, therefore, able to draw precise plans of the theater and basilica even though these buildings remain buried.

Bellicard's notebook contains no images of the bronze or marble sculpture, and his books include etchings of only the two bronze equestrian figures of the Balbi, which were the most publicly visible of all the works at Portici. They were set up inside iron railings at the entrance to the complex and could be seen without entering the palace grounds, the domain of the secret.[54] Presumably Bellicard failed to gain sufficient access to the sculpture. In any event, some of the most important discoveries of sculpture at Herculaneum occurred just after the departure of Bellicard and Cochin, notably the exploration of the Villa dei Papiri, beginning in June 1751.

Cochin and Bellicard used their illicit drawings, such as those in the Metropolitan notebook and others that are probably lost, for a sequence of unauthorized publications. The small sketches were translated into free etchings to illustrate books published in London and Paris in 1753 and 1754. For example, a small thumbnail sketch records the fresco fragment of *Theseus Triumphing over the Minotaur* [upper right,

FIG. 3], which appeared in the Paris edition of Cochin and Bellicard's *Observations* as plate 15 [see p. 136, FIG. 3]. The artists probably made the etchings within weeks of first seeing the objects, most likely on the return of Marigny's traveling party to Rome in January 1751.

These precise and novel illustrations were the highlight of a stupendously successful publication that appeared in three English- and three French-language editions. In an echo of the flurry of publications in 1748, the nearly simultaneous publications demonstrate the urgent desire of amateurs, artists, and scholars for information on the sites as well as the almost frictionless nature of the illicit international book trade. The 1753 *Observations upon the Antiquities of the Town of Herculaneum, Discovered at the Foot of Mount Vesuvius* appeared first. This edition was published without Cochin's name, but the subsequent London editions of 1756 and 1758 bear the names of both Bellicard and Cochin. The 1754 French edition and all subsequent French editions bear both Cochin's and Bellicard's names.[55]

Official Publication of the Royal Collections after 1756

The success of the Cochin and Bellicard conspiracy and the enthusiastic reception of their books increased pressure on the Neapolitan authorities to produce their own publications. Frustrated by the appearance of Cochin and Bellicard's volumes and the criticism they implied of the Neapolitan policy, the king and his new prime minister, Bernardo Tanucci, reviewed the prospects for the official royal publications. Tanucci found Baiardi's approach tediously pedantic and philological. Because he became asthmatic, Baiardi could no longer tolerate the smoky tunnels and so could not sustain firsthand knowledge of the site. He devoted himself instead to literary research on historic allusions to Hercules and his namesake, the city of Herculaneum.[56] After seven years Baiardi published the first volume of his promised catalogue in 1755, to universal disappointment. His *Catalogo degli antichi monumenti dissotterrati dalla discoperta città di Ercolano* was an unillustrated list of the objects that had been exhumed and transported to Portici, preceded by a turgid twenty-two-page preface on the mythology of Hercules and his association with the buried city.[57] His philological—rather than historical or artistic—methodology meant that there was no discussion of the style or quality of the objects, nor were they treated as evidence of a lost culture.

The king dismissed Baiardi in 1755 and permitted Tanucci to found the Real accademia ercolanese to take over the publication project.[58] Unlike its Enlightenment counterparts, this academy excluded foreigners and correspondent members. Fifteen members appointed by Tanucci convened in his offices once every fortnight to consider a topic proposed by him. Virtually a branch of government, the academy acted collectively and did not permit its members to publish under their own names. Tanucci summarized the findings and conclusions of these discussions and articulated the academy's official position. The Real accademia ercolanese excluded the architects and artists who conducted the excavations or curated the collections, though it did include some numismatists and antiquarians along with members of the court. Petty intrigue, jealousy, and parochialism dominated the selection of members and the direction of their efforts.

The academy maintained that the royal collections should be published by material category—paintings, marble sculpture, bronze sculpture, metalwork, mosaics—

rather than in an architectural context presenting the objects together depending on where they were found.[59] As Hérica Valladares and Tina Najbjerg discuss in this volume, this decision was in large part governed by the view that the antiquities were valuable as collectibles rather than as cultural artifacts. Such choices were motivated partly by a desire to keep the professional employees—the architects and artists—in their social place, excluded from the academy and without a voice in larger decisions. The decision to reject contextual study of the sites or any discussion of the style and quality of the paintings and sculptures also explicitly rejected the approaches of such northern European scholars as the comte de Caylus, Abbé Jean-Jacques Barthélémy, Pierre-Jean Mariette, and Cochin as well as Winckelmann. These authors in turn became open critics of Tanucci's publications and methodology.[60] It is certainly possible to see the Tanucci approach as legitimate, based strictly on the typology of the objects by material and category and in opposition to alternative positions incorporating the architectural setting and mixture of objects in the context in which they were found. Most scholars, however, have interpreted the methodology of the Tanucci circle as motivated by petty concerns and expediency and lacking in a real sensitivity or learned approach to the material.

Karl Weber, the most progressive architect-engineer to direct the excavations, proposed a treatise in 1759–60 on the architecture of Herculaneum, to be illustrated with architectural plans. His petition, however, was tied up in discussion among the academicians and was never acted on. Christopher Parslow has argued that the effective rejection of Weber's project stemmed from jealousy among his fellow architects and a suspicion that Weber sought membership in the Real accademia ercolanese by becoming one of its authors.[61]

Despite the criticisms leveled against the academy publications, the volumes were precious and widely sought by amateurs and scholars. In rare cases, as for Winckelmann and Abbé Barthélémy, certain volumes were given as gifts to commemorate visits to Portici. Otherwise, the authorities in Naples hoarded the books, which incited frustrated scholars to challenge Neapolitan authority openly. For example, the comte de Caylus attempted to draw his principal Italian agent, the scholar-monk Paolo Maria Paciaudi, into a scheme to steal a papyrus from Herculaneum just to *faire fumer les Napolitains* and above all *le vilain Tanucci*.[62]

⬚ ⬚ ⬚

The open nature of northern European academic circles from the 1730s onward brought great benefits to the intellectual and artistic life of England and France.[63] In contrast, the Secret of Herculaneum poorly served the kingdom of Naples and archaeology in general. The knowledge generated in the circle of Sir William Hamilton during his long tenure as British ambassador to Naples (1764–1800) suggests the role the king could have played had he welcomed the active participation of foreign scholars, amateurs, and architects in the excavations.[64] Hamilton was hardly a disinterested idealist and, like Charles, sought to enrich himself and enhance his reputation through association with these prestigious antiquities. But rather than trying to exclude others, when Hamilton arrived in 1764 he enlisted the adventurer-scholar Pierre François Hugues—who styled himself Baron d'Hancarville—in the formation and publication of his first collection in the volumes entitled *Antiquités étrusques, grecques, et romaines tirées du cabinet de M. Hamilton* (1766–67). Hamilton also played a role in the formation of a new, informal but more accessible and transparent gathering of antiquarians who met in the shops of antique dealers or in homes, which encouraged his plunge into studies of the relationship of ethnography and archaeology.[65]

Hamilton's public success in Naples may have made the failure of the secret unavoidably apparent. While the secret of the Vesuvian finds was never lifted and had, in fact, been extended since 1751 to cover the Villa dei Papiri and the finds excavated from Pompeii in the 1770s and 1780s, Naples began to place fewer restrictions on the activities of foreign artists and scholars. Ferdinand IV's Austrian wife, Maria Carolina, forced the retirement of Tanucci in 1776 and non-Neapolitans began to have a prominent voice in the kingdom's cultural policy. John Acton, an English Catholic born in France and with long naval service under the Austrian duke of Tuscany, assumed most of Tanucci's responsibilities. The Prussian Jacob Philipp Hackert became first painter to Ferdinand and an important adviser on his collections.

Other forces made foreigners more welcome in the Naples of King Ferdinand IV. Queen Maria Carolina, daughter of the Austrian empress Maria Theresa and sister to Marie Antoinette, was pro-France, and French artists became welcome in the kingdom. In 1777 an ambitious project was launched in France to create the greatest illustrated travel publication on the kingdom of Naples and Sicily. Abbé Jean Claude Richard de Saint-Non, an editor of lavishly illustrated volumes on modern artists and travel literature, engaged French artists, architects, engravers, and writers to create the *Voyage pittoresque, ou, description des royaumes de Naples et de Sicile*. Saint-Non directed the project from Paris but deputized Dominique-Vivant Denon, future director of museums to Napoleon, to visit and detail all the important sites in southern Italy and Sicily. Denon wrote descriptions while the architect-artists Pierre-Philippe Choffard, Louis Jean Desprez, and Pierre-Adrien Pâris measured and drew the monuments and landscapes, and the brilliant young painters Jean-Honoré Fragonard and Hubert Robert engraved the original plates to illustrate the volumes. The resulting publication is a magnificent four-part, five-volume grand folio, printed in Paris between 1781 and 1786.[66]

Because the *Voyage pittoresque* began to appear in 1781 — only after the Real accademia ercolanese's official volumes had already been published (seven were in print by 1779) — Saint-Non was permitted to prepare engravings for a selection of antiquities covered by the secret. Saint-Non's second volume, in preparation since 1777, contained "Une description des antiquités d'Herculanum, des plans & des détails de son théâtre, avec une notice abrégée des différens spectacles des anciens."[67]

Among the most impressive reconstructions of ancient architecture are Pierre-Philippe Choffard's engravings after the drawings of Pierre-Adrien Pâris of the section and plan views of the theater at Herculaneum.[68] Pâris and Choffard's cross section and elevation of the theater [see FIG. 1] shows a hypothetical reconstruction. Notably, it depicts the placement of the sculptural decoration, in particular the sculptures in niches atop the amphitheater, riderless horses on pedestals above and flanking the main entrances to the seating area, and carved decorations and sculptures on the proscenium. This engraving, among many contemporary efforts, is the most elaborate design derived from the same group of unpublished and secret drawings made by the various architect-directors of the Herculaneum excavations dating back to the 1740s, which either are lost or lay unknown in Neapolitan archives until recently.[69]

Transport des Antiquités d'Herculanum, du Museum de Portici au Palais des Etudes à Naples.

Composé par Des Prés Arch.te Pension.re du Roi à l'Académie de France à Rome.

FIGURE 5

Louis Jean Desprez
(French, 1743–1804),
engraved by Robert Daudet
(French, 1737–1824), with
figures engraved by Jean
Duplessis-Berteaux (French,
1747–1819), *The Transfer
of the Antiquities from
Portici to Naples.* Plate 98
from Jean Claude Richard
de Saint-Non, *Voyage
pittoresque, ou, description
des royaumes de Naples
et de Sicile* (1782), vol. 2.
Hartford, Conn., Watkinson
Library, Trinity College,
Fol DG 821.S14.

Circulated images of the theater at Herculaneum can stand for many other examples of the repeated violations of the secret. Bellicard's 1750 engraving is the first, followed by Gabriel-Martin Dumont's 1765 reconstruction of the theater based on a lost drawing by Weber, known today from an engraving by Camillo Paderni.[70] The Choffard-Pâris reconstruction comes next, almost simultaneous with Francesco Piranesi's 1783 reconstruction based largely on recent work by the current director of Neapolitan excavations, Francesco La Vega. Piranesi's print is the clearest of all and benefited most from the cumulative knowledge of the excavation directors.[71] The number of unauthorized plans by foreign architects working from drawings that were supposed to be closely guarded demonstrates that the secret was repeatedly flaunted and untenable within the corps of professionals in Naples. The only real losers were among the Neapolitan excavation team, caught between the secret and the exclusivity on publication reserved for the Real accademia ercolanese.

In his *Voyage pittoresque* Saint-Non flattered Ferdinand IV's project to convert the old Austrian viceroy's stables in Naples into a museum to be called the Palazzo dei vecchi studi that would house the combined Bourbon and Farnese collections of antiquities.[72] Saint-Non had Louis Jean Desprez invent a fanciful image anticipating the splendor of a procession of the great Herculaneum treasures moving from the palace at Portici to the Palace of Ancient Studies [FIG. 5]. The engraving embodied the foreign dream of a public museum of the king of Naples's antiquities, but the reality of the situation was far removed from this image, as was so often the case with the Bourbon approach toward the finds from Herculaneum. The transfer of the collections would not be complete before 1822, when, after more than eight decades, the Bourbon monarchy agreed to share its collections with the world.[73]

Notes

[1] The story of the early discoveries has variations in different sources, some identifying the well at the church of San Giacomo Apostoli in Resina and others stating that the site belonged to the Nocerini family. The earliest accounts were published in 1748: Anton Francesco Gori, *Notizie del memorabile scoprimento dell'antica città Ercolano* (Florence, 1748); Scipione Maffei, *Tre lettere del Signor Scipione Maffei* (Verona, 1748); Niccolò Marcello Venuti, *Descrizione delle prime scoperte dell'antica città d'Ercolano* (Rome, 1748). The history is retold in Amedeo Maiuri, *Herculaneum*, trans. V. Priestley (Rome, 1937), 8–9; and summarized in Joseph Jay Deiss, *Herculaneum: Italy's Buried Treasure*, rev. ed. (New York, 1985), 26–27; and in *The Grove Dictionary of Art* 14:22.

[2] That a foreign princeling should be involved in Neapolitan affairs was the norm rather than the exception, since the kingdom of Naples had not had a resident monarch for two hundred years. Naples lost its independence to the Spanish Habsburgs in 1503. In 1707, during the War of the Spanish Succession, Naples passed to the Austrian Habsburgs, who sent a stream of viceroys until they were expelled by the Spanish Bourbons in 1734, thereby ushering in the return of a resident monarchy under Charles VII. *Naples in the Eighteenth Century: The Birth and Death of a Nation State*, ed. Girolamo Imbruglia (Cambridge, 2000), 1.

[3] Francis Haskell and Nicholas Penny, *Taste and the Antique: The Lure of Classical Sculpture, 1500–1900* (New Haven, 1981), 74.

[4] Egon Caesar Conte Corti, *The Destruction and Resurrection of Pompeii and Herculaneum* (London, 1951), 104n. 1.

[5] Haskell and Penny 1981 (note 3), 75.

[6] Harold Acton, *The Bourbons of Naples (1734–1825)* (London, 1956), 11–24. Carlo's mother was Elizabeth Farnese, second queen of Philip V of Spain. Although he was raised by his mother at San Ildefonso in Spain, Carlo was sent at the age of eighteen to assert the Farnese claims in Italy.

[7] The three figures are today in the Staatliche Kunstsammlungen Dresden, where they are recognized as not being a coherent group. Two of the three are today referred to as the Large Ercolanese and the Smaller Ercolanese. They were moved to Dresden after they were purchased in 1736 by the elector of Saxony from the niece of Prince Eugene. See Peter Holliday, "Herculaneum, III, Sculpture," in *The Grove Dictionary of Art* 14:442; and Haskell and Penny 1981 (note 3), 74.

[8] For Charles VII and Ferdinand IV, see *Civiltà del '700 a Napoli: 1734–1799*, 2 vols. (Florence, 1979); and *The Golden Age of Naples: Art and Civilization under the Bourbons, 1734–1805*, 2 vols. (Detroit, 1981). For the political, economic, and social history of Bourbon Naples, see Imbruglia 2000 (note 2).

[9] Corti 1951 (note 4), 105.

[10] The excavations were pursued sporadically until 1765 with crews of between six and twenty men. From 1738 into the 1760s the small crews of workmen avoided the effort of hoisting the excavated material to the surface and the expense of shoring up the tunnels with timber. Rather, previously explored tunnels were filled in with the material from subsequent tunnels. Christopher Charles Parslow, *Rediscovering Antiquity: Karl Weber and the Excavation of Herculaneum,*

Pompeii, and Stabiae (Cambridge, 1995); Fausto Zevi, "Gli scavi di Ercolano," in *Civiltà* 1979 (note 8), 2:58–68.

11　Ottavio Antonio Baiardi, *Prodromo delle antichità d'Ercolano*, 5 vols. (Naples, 1752).

12　Elvira Chiosi, "La Reale accademia ercolanense," in *Bernardo Tanucci: Statista letterator giurista*, ed. Raffaele Ajello and Mario D'Addio (Naples, 1986), 2:504, citing Baiardi 1752 (note 11): "Le corti d'Europa, impegnate in guerre militari e diplomatiche per il controllo di sempre più ampi territori, dovevano stupire di fronte allo spettacolo che il re di Napoli poteva offrire al mondo intero delle sue conquiste estese—come si disse—sin 'nelle viscere della terra'" (my translation).

13　Zevi 1979 (note 10), 60; and Agnes Allroggen-Bedel, "Tanucci e la cultura antiquaria," in Ajello and D'Addio 1986 (note 12), 2:531–35.

14　Only a portion of the site has ever been excavated from above, in two campaigns in the nineteenth century and then as a nationalist priority of the Fascist Party in the 1920s.

15　Attention shifted dramatically to Pompeii because, lying to the landward and southern side of the volcano, the city had not been in the direct lava flow. Pompeii was burned by fire from the cinders and buried with relatively light ash at no great depth and proved vastly easier to explore as an open-air excavation.

16　This intriguing tension in the early history of archaeological method is the subject of Parslow 1995 (note 10).

17　Ibid., 33. Camillo Paderni was conducted to the site by Joseph Canart, a Roman sculptor, employed on the excavation to assist with the extraction of the bronze and marble sculpture as well as sections of wall painting. Paderni made a sketch of a fresco and communicated a description of his visits to the dig in letters to the English painter Allan Ramsay, who in turn read them to the Royal Society of London. Paderni, however, did not publish his drawing.

18　The equestrian statues of the Balbi are thought today to have been found in a complex adjacent to the theater that has to this day not been precisely identified (Parslow 1995 [note 10], 42). The sense of the location of the finds in terms of their architectural setting was so poor during the early digging that scholars debated the ancient placement of even monumental sculpture. It was speculated, for example, that the equestrian statues of the Balbi could have been on pedestals high atop the theater, as in the drawing by Bellicard in figure 4.

19　Camillo Paderni, "Extracts of two letters from Sign. Camillo Paderni at Rome to Mr. Allan Ramsay, Painter, Covent-Garden, concerning some ancient statues, pictures and other curiosities found in a subterraneous town lately discovered near Naples; dated Rome, November 20, 1739, and February 20, 1740," *Philosophical Transactions of the Royal Society of London* 41, no. 2 (1740): 484.

20　Walpole to West, June 14, 1740. Transcribed in Horace Walpole, *Correspondence*, ed. Wilmarth S. Lewis (New Haven, 1937–83), 13:222, and as cited in *Pompeii as Source and Inspiration: Reflections in Eighteenth- and Nineteenth-Century Art* (Ann Arbor, 1977), 13–14.

21　Ibid.

22　Paderni 1740 (note 19), 484.

23　[James Russel], *Letters from a Young Painter Abroad to His Friends in England* (London, 1748). Russel's 1748 publication was illustrated, but the images were of the antique structures found above ground around the Gulf of Baia, an area not covered by the ban on the Vesuvian sites east and south of Naples. Russel served as cicerone to George Pitt of Stratfieldsea, William Drake of Shardloes, John Bouverie, and Nathaniel Castleton. See also John Ingamells, *A Dictionary of British and Irish Travellers in Italy, 1701–1800* (London, 1997).

24　[Russel] 1748 (note 23), vi–vii.

25　Parslow 1995 (note 10), 217.

26   Winckelmann to Bunau, April 26, 1758, ibid., 361n. 52.

27   Johann Wolfgang von Goethe, *Italian Journey, 1786–1788*, trans. W. H. Auden and Elizabeth Mayer (San Francisco, 1982), 202–3, letter of March 18, 1787.

28   Acton 1956 (note 6), 88–89; Zevi 1979 (note 10), 66; Parslow 1995 (note 10), 80.

29   There were four principal directors of the excavations in the period under consideration: the Spanish military engineer Rocque Joachin Alcubierre, from 1738 to 1741, when poor health forced him to take leave; the French engineer Pierre Bardet de Villeneuve, from 1741 to 1745; Alcubierre, from 1745 to 1750; the Swiss military engineer Karl Weber, from 1750 to 1764; and Francesco La Vega, from 1764 until the suspension of activity at Herculaneum in 1780.

30   Maria Pia Rossignani, "Saggio sui restauri settecenteschi ai dipinti di Ercolano e Pompei," *Contributi dell' Instituto di archeologia* 1 (1967): 8–9, cited in Parslow 1995 (note 10), 361n. 51.

31   For Paderni's letters, see Paderni 1740 (note 19).

32   George Turnbull, *A Treatise on Ancient Painting* (London, 1740).

33   Gori 1748 (note 1). See also Zevi 1979 (note 10), 64.

34   Francesco Soria, *Memorie storico-critiche degli storici napolitani* (Naples, 1781), 1:234, cited by Franco Strazzullo in his introduction to J. J. Winckelmann, *Le scoperte di Ercolano* (Naples, 1981), 33n. 42, 61n. 96.

35   Fernando Galliani, "Ragguaglio di Parnaso sotti i 13 Maggio 1765" to M. Zarrilli, published as an appendix to Winckelmann 1981 (note 34) and cited in Zevi 1979 (note 10), 68n. 20.

36   Gori 1748 (note 1); and Scipione Maffei, *Tre lettere* (Verona, 1748). Also M. Quirini, *Epistola ad Joan Math. Gesnerum de Herculano* (Brescia, 1748); J. Belgrado, *Ad Scipionem Mapheium epistolae IV de physicis et antiquis monumentis sub Resina recens inventis* (Venice, 1749). See Georges Vallet and Fausto Zevi, eds., "Architectes antiquaires et voyageurs français à Pompéi: Milieu XVIIIe siècle–fin XIXe siècle," in *Pompéi, travaux et envois des architectes français au XIXe siècle: École nationale supérieure des beaux-arts* (Paris, 1980), 20n. 45.

37   Venuti 1748 (note 1).

38   Charles de Brosses, *Lettres d'Italie* (reprinted as *Voyages en Italie* [Paris, 1964], 129), letter to Jacques-Philippe Fyot de Neuilly, written from Rome after Brosses's return from Naples, November 24, 1739. "Quand nous arrivâmes, le roi était à Portici, petite maison au pied du Vésuve: c'est son Fontainebleau; il en revint le 3 au soir et le lendemain nous lui fûmes présentés. Ce même jour il y eut grand gala à la Cour, à cause de la fête du roi, qui donne sa main à baiser à tous les gentilshommes. Tous les seigneurs étaient vêtus avec beaucoup de magnificence, et sa majesté s'était ornée d'un vieux habit de droguet brun à boutons jaunes. Il a le visage long et étroit, le nez fort saillant, la physionomie triste et timide, la taille médiocre et qui n'est pas sans reproche." English translation by the author: "When we arrived, the king was at Portici, a small house at the foot of Vesuvius—it is his Fontainebleau. He had come back at 3 in the afternoon and the following day we were presented to him. This same day there was a great celebration at the court because it was the king's birthday and he gave his hand to be kissed by all the gentlemen. All the nobility were dressed with great magnificence, but his majesty was ornamented in an old suit of brown druget with yellow buttons. He has a long, narrow face with a very big nose, a sad and timid facial expression and has a figure both mediocre in size and not above reproach in form."

39   Charles de Brosses, *Lettres sur l'état actuel de la ville souterraine d'Herculée et sur les causes de son ensevelissement sous les ruines du Vésuve* (1750; Dijon, 1927), cited by Elisabeth Chevallier, *Iter Italicum* (Geneva, 1984), 25nn. 6, 32.

40   [Guillaume-Marie d'Arthenay], *Mémoire sur la ville souterraine découverte au pied du Mont Vésuve* (Paris, 1748). The edition in the Houghton Library, Harvard University, contains a dedication addressed to the marquis de L'Hôpital from the vice legate of Avignon, which confirms

d'Arthenay as the author and apologizes for an unauthorized 1747 Avignon edition printed by the press of one Giroud. I know of no surviving copy of the 1747 Avignon bootleg edition. An Italian edition of d'Arthenay's essay was published as *Notizie intorno alla città sotterranea discoperta alle falde del Monte Vesuvio* (Florence, 1749). This slim volume has for many years been mistakenly associated with a certain Abbé Moussinot by the error of Antoine-Alexandre Barbier, *Dictionnaire des ouvrages anonymes* (Paris, 1872–79).

[41]   For the larger context of the Italian journey of Marigny and a full discussion of Bellicard's notebook, see Alden R. Gordon, "Jérôme-Charles Bellicard's Italian Notebook of 1750–51: The Discoveries at Herculaneum and Observations on Ancient and Modern Architecture," *Metropolitan Museum Journal* 25 (1990): 49–142.

[42]   Ibid., 51.

[43]   The season proved so rainy and stormy that the sea-lanes were closed and the group gave up the voyages to Sicily and Malta and returned to Rome just after Christmas 1750.

[44]   The marquis de L'Hôpital, French ambassador to Naples, was not in residence but en route to Paris for reassignment. The ambassador's house was small, so Marigny and Le Blanc resided there, while Cochin and Bellicard took lodging at a nearby inn.

[45]   Charles-Nicolas Cochin, *Voyage d'Italie* (Paris, 1758), 2:129–202; Venuti 1748 (note 1), 203–11. See the annotated edition, *Le voyage d'Italie de Charles-Nicolas Cochin, 1758*, ed. Christian Michel (Rome, 1991), 142–83. Cochin was keeping notes for a guidebook and recorded, with commentary, the impressive list of sites—modern and ancient, royal and private—that they saw.

[46]   Charles-Nicolas Cochin, "Lettre sur les peintures d'Herculanum, aujourd'hui Portici," *Mercure de France*, September 1751, 171–83 (fictitiously dated Brussels, January 20, 1751).

[47]   Cochin 1758 (note 45), 2:208. Cochin was characteristically blunt in his assessments of works of art and architecture. After describing the fresco fragments from Herculaneum at the Portici palace, he declared: "In general these paintings are very mediocre, without finesse in drawing, and with very weak color: furthermore, they are barely finished and treated approximately like our theater sets" (my translation). He declares the sculptures found at Herculaneum vastly superior to the paintings. Cochin does not mention his visit to the underground site or anything to do with the architecture.

[48]   A full transcription of Jérôme-Charles Bellicard's Italian notebook was made in 1990 by Alden Gordon and Christopher Riopelle and is available by application to the editorial office of the *Metropolitan Museum Journal*.

[49]   Parslow 1995 (note 10), 57, 235, 241.

[50]   Ibid., 38. For the list of principal directors of the excavations, see note 29. L'Hôpital was French ambassador to the Kingdom of the Two Sicilies from 1740 to 1750.

[51]   Ibid., 41.

[52]   Jérôme-Charles Bellicard, *Observations upon the Antiquities of the Town of Herculaneum, Discovered at the Foot of Mount Vesuvius* (London, 1753), 17–18.

[53]   The French edition is more explicit than the English-language version in delineating the sequence of Bellicard studying the plan and then visiting the tunnels afterward to verify the facts of the plan: "Pour vérifier autant que je le pouvois le plan qui m'avoit été donné, . . . je parcourus les sentiers qu'on avait alors pratiqués, assez au hasard, dans l'étendue du théâtre, et j'examinai tout ce qui en était découvert" (Charles-Nicolas Cochin and Jérôme Bellicard, *Observations sur les antiquités d'Herculanum* [Paris, 1755], 12). English translation by the author: "In order to verify as much as possible the plan that had been given to me, I traveled through the paths that had been previously worked, rather haphazardly, throughout the extent of the theater, and I examined everything that had been discovered."

[54]   Haskell and Penny 1981 (note 3), 158–61.

[55]   The full titles of the London and Paris first editions gave lengthy credentials for the authors. The 1753 London edition published by D. Wilson and T. Durham, at Plato's Head in the Strand, described Bellicard alone as author: "Mr. Bellicard, Architect, Member of the Academies of Bologna and Florence, enriched with forty-two plates designed and engraved by the author." In the 1756 edition by the same publishers the credits listed the book as "By Mr. Cochin the Younger . . . and Mr. Bellicard." The title page of the first Paris edition of 1754 read as follows: *Observations sur les antiquités de la ville d'Herculanum avec quelques réflexions sur la peinture et la sculpture des anciens & une courte description de quelques antiquités des environs de Naples par Messieurs Cochin le fils & Bellicard. A Paris, chez Ant. Jombert, rue Dauphine, à l'image Notre-Dame, 1754.* A facsimile edition with introduction and notes by Edith Flamarion and Catherine Volpilhac-Auger was published by the press of the Université de Saint-Étienne in 1996. The 1754 Paris edition is made with a different set of etching plates than those used in the 1753 London edition, suggesting that the two were in press simultaneously. The 1755 Paris edition reuses some of the plates of the 1754 Paris edition but with significant changes. The 1757 Paris edition uses an entirely different and quite inferior set of etching plates.

[56]   Acton 1956 (note 6), 88–89. Tanucci took over from Fogliani on June 9, 1755. Without Fogliani there to sustain him, Baiardi was forced into retirement. By 1752 Baiardi had compiled his *Prodromo*, dealing with the literary evidence for the existence of Herculaneum and discoursing on the mythology of Hercules and his associations with the city.

[57]   Ottavio Antonio Baiardi, *Catalogo degli antichi monumenti dissotterrati dalla discoperta città di Ercolano* (Naples, 1755).

[58]   Chiosi 1986 (note 12), 2:490–517.

[59]   The Real accademia ercolanese's first volume—of a projected forty volumes—appeared in 1757. They never got past volume 8 and that took them until 1792. The volumes were heavily illustrated with engravings reproducing the objects in the Portici museum: the paintings—volumes 1 (1757), 2 (1760), 3 (1762), 4 (1765), 7 (1779); bronze sculptures—volumes 5 (1767), 6 (1771); lamps and candelabra—volume 8 (1792).

[60]   On Mariette's criticism and Tanucci's rejection of the French emphasis on architecture, see Allroggen-Bedel 1986 (note 13), 2:519–36, esp. 528–29.

[61]   Parslow 1995 (note 10), chap. 6, "Weber's Application to the Accademia ercolanese," 153–98.

[62]   Zevi 1979 (note 10), 66, citing Anne Claude Philippe, comte de Caylus, *Correspondance inédite du comte de Caylus avec le P. Paciaudi Théatin, 1757–1767,* ed. C. Nisard (Paris, 1877), 1:262–63, 281, 320. For more on Caylus, see Irène Aghion, *Caylus, mécène du roi: Collectionner les antiquités au XVIIIe siècle* (Paris, 2002).

[63]   Shearer West, "Xenophobia and Xenomania: Italians and the English Royal Academy," in *Italian Culture in Northern Europe in the Eighteenth Century,* ed. Shearer West (Cambridge, 1999), 116–39.

[64]   Ian Jenkins, "'Contemporary Minds': Sir William Hamilton's Affair with Antiquity," in Ian Jenkins and Kim Sloan, *Vases and Volcanoes: Sir William Hamilton and His Collection* (London, 1996), 40–64.

[65]   Ibid., 52–53; Alain Schnapp, "Antiquarian Studies in Naples at the End of the Eighteenth Century: From Comparative Archaeology to Comparative Religion," in Imbruglia 2000 (note 2), 154–66.

[66]   Saint-Non used several teams of artists to compile the illustrations. Denon directed four architects doing the surveys and measurements, while draftsmen and engravers made views and translated the designs into engravings. Independent artists including the younger talents Robert and Fragonard also contributed inventive original plates to the publication. Petra Lamers, *Il viaggio nel sud dell'Abbé de Saint-Non* (Naples, 1995).

67 Jean Claude Richard de Saint-Non, *Voyage pittoresque, ou, description des royaumes de Naples et de Sicile, seconde partie du premier voyage, tome second, contenant une description des antiquités d'Herculanum* (Paris, 1782).

68 Reproduced in Gordon 1990 (note 41), 63, figs. 14–15.

69 Parslow 1995 (note 10), 233–63, and esp. fig. 71.

70 Paris, Bibliothèque nationale (5692 v. 69), published in Gordon 1990 (note 41), 62, fig. 13; Parslow 1995 (note 10), 247, fig. 70.

71 Parslow 1995 (note 10), 261–63, figs. 72–73.

72 The Bourbon collection had been augmented by the inheritance of the Farnese collections following the death in 1766 of Elizabeth Farnese, mother of Carlo Borbone (Charles VII) and grandmother of his son and successor on the throne in Naples, Ferdinand IV.

73 Haskell and Penny 1981 (note 3), 76–77.

From Art to Archaeology: Recontextualizing the Images from the Porticus of Herculaneum

Tina Najbjerg

T HE OFFICIAL EXCAVATION of Herculaneum, sponsored by the Bourbon king of the Two Sicilies, Charles VII, began in 1738. The military engineers in charge of the excavations explored the ancient town by digging tunnels through the twenty meters of volcanic material that supported the modern village of Resina. The monarch, however, rarely entered these narrow, muddy tunnels. Instead, the excavated objects, including painted wall fragments, were removed from the site and brought to the king. When choosing which painted sections to cut from the wall of a building, the excavators favored images they considered aesthetically pleasing and works that were easy to isolate and frame, such as panel pictures of mythological scenes and figures. For decades hundreds of such fragments were removed from the ancient buildings of Herculaneum and stored in the king's palace in neighboring Portici with little regard of their original first-century context.

The Bourbon interest in the aesthetic and framable qualities of the ancient images—mirrored in late-eighteenth-century travel accounts and in subsequent Bourbon publications and souvenirs—effectively transformed the painted fragments into objets d'art. Building on these sources, artists and scholars of the nineteenth and twentieth centuries continued to consider the painted fragments as individual works of art and to disregard their Roman context. At the end of the twentieth century, however, renewed interest in Roman art gave birth to a new type of contextual archaeology that focuses on the relationship between the art and the ancient viewer. At the end of this essay my reconstruction of the original context of the images from the Porticus of Herculaneum will represent this new methodology. The underlying premise of my thesis is that the images painted on the walls of a given building belonged to a narrative or thematic program that expressed the particular interests of the Roman patron(s) responsible for the selection. Thus, only by re-creating the original Roman context of the painted fragments can we hope to understand what the images meant to the ancient viewer. This process of recontextualization involves reconstructing the relationship between the images themselves and investigating their association with other objects and with the building in which they once existed. For this methodology, the eighteenth-century sources, despite their decontextualization of ancient paintings, are on occasion helpful resources for determining aspects of the original context.

To demonstrate the effect of the Bourbon excavations and publications on nineteenth- and twentieth-century art and archaeology, I shall trace the modern history of painted images from a specific building in Herculaneum. Formerly known as the basilica, the porticus was among the first structures to be excavated in Herculaneum in 1738.[1] Between 1738 and 1761, when the building was reburied for safety reasons, the military engineers leading the excavations removed numerous painted sections from its walls. Some depicted mythological scenes or figures within a fictional frame or panel: Theseus being thanked by the Athenian children after having slain the Minotaur [see p. 47, FIG. 3, upper right], Hercules finding his son Telephus, Medea contemplating the murder of her children, and Baby Hercules strangling the serpents. Many were part of the frieze that ran along the top of the interior walls of the building: The boy Hylas being raped by water nymphs, the young hero Bellerophon meeting King Iobates, Minerva and Hercules overseeing the construction of the ship *Argo*, and the three labors of Hercules. Others belonged to a now-lost decorative schema of architectural and vegetal features, which remains buried on the walls of the building: Marsyas teaching the boy Olympus to play the double flute, Chiron instructing young Achilles to play the lyre [FIG. 1], and young male and female attendants holding ritual objects.[2]

The sculptor and royal conservator Giuseppe Canart initiated the practice of cutting such images from the walls, noting that these "pictures are much appreciated in Rome and in England."[3] The remark highlights the court's interest in turning decorated wall sections into individual pictures consistent with international classicizing fashion. While the excavators oversaw the initial selection process, the ultimate fate of the fragments lay in the hands of the curator of the royal collection, Camillo Paderni, who selected which fragments to present to the monarch.[4] At least three images from the porticus did not pass muster and were destroyed by Paderni's direct order.[5] This demolition, however distressing to us now, was not entirely willful; it took place to prevent images left in situ from falling into the hands of thieves. Once removed from the ancient walls, the fragments were placed in wooden frames; those considered most precious received gilded frames.[6] The freshly framed images were then transported to the royal palace in Portici, which by 1758 had become the Museo ercolanese. Here, they went either into storage or on exhibition in the fifteen rooms devoted to paintings.[7] Their organization within these rooms is not known, as no visitor was allowed to sketch in the museum. Since, however, the authors of the official Bourbon publication, *Delle antichità di Ercolano*, divided the fragments into three groups, based on their formal qualities, they were probably exhibited in the museum according to a similar principle. While some attempt possibly was made to exhibit pendants together (as in the publication), the original context of the fragments was not the directing principle of the display.

The excitement of European elite and scholarly societies on hearing about the discoveries at Herculaneum reached a fever pitch in the 1740s, and the underground site and the king's collection in Portici became popular stops on the Grand Tour.

FIGURE 1

Achilles and Chiron,
Herculaneum, third quarter
first century. Wall frag-
ment from the Porticus
of Herculaneum. Naples,
Museo archeologico
nazionale, Inv. 9109.

Photo: Erich Lessing / Art
Resource, NY.

FIGURE 2
Charles-Nicolas Cochin
(French, 1715–1790),
Achilles and Chiron,
1750–51. Etching.
Plate 17 from Charles-Nicolas
Cochin, *Lettre sur les
peintures d'Herculanum,
aujourd'hui Portici* (1751).
Los Angeles, Research Library,
Getty Research Institute,
93-B3355.

FIGURE 3
Francisco La Vega (Spanish,
1737–1804) and Rocco
Puteo (life dates unknown),
Achilles and Chiron,
ca. 1739–57. Engraving.
Plate 43 from *Delle antichità
di Ercolano* (1757), vol. 1.

Photo: Tina Najbjerg with
permission of the Library of the
American Academy in Rome.

Charles VII saw the discovery as his crowning glory and as an opportunity to place his kingdom at the center of Europe's cultural and political scene. He, therefore, fiercely guarded his ownership of and publication rights to the Herculanean antiquities. Visitors were rushed through the tunnels and the collections by sullen guards, and even the most illustrious scholars, artists, and architects were prohibited from drawing anything they saw on the tours.[8] Despite these precautions, the king could not prevent the spread of unauthorized travel accounts in the 1740s and 1750s, through which the news-starved European audience learned about the antiquities from Herculaneum. Notable among these were publications by Anton Francesco Gori, Niccolò Marcello Venuti, Moussinot d'Arthenay, and Charles-Nicolas Cochin.[9]

All these accounts largely ignored the original Roman context of the painted images from Herculaneum. The publications by the French artist and engraver Cochin, however, were especially instrumental in publicizing the fragments as individual works of art, devoid of larger meaning. In the company of the architect Jérôme-Charles Bellicard, Cochin had made several visits to the underground excavations of Herculaneum and the royal palace in Portici as part of an Italian tour in 1750–51.[10] Despite the royal restrictions, he managed to copy several images in the king's collection [see p. 47, FIGS. 3–4], among them the Theseus, the Achilles and Chiron [FIG. 2], and the Hercules and Telephus fragments from the porticus.[11] The drawings and essays in his publications presented these three fragments as individual works of art. Each appeared in the center of a blank page, which highlighted the artful isolation of the original image. In a style highly admired at the time Cochin romanticized the antiquity of the pieces by omitting the modern frames that surrounded the fragments and by rendering the works as thick pieces of plaster with rough, uneven edges that cast shadows along their sides.[12] Thus, he effectively transformed the two-dimensional representations into three-dimensional objects. In the essays that accompanied the drawings Cochin focused on the aesthetic merits of the ancient depictions (which he deemed inferior to Greek and to modern painting) and chose to ignore their original Roman context. In doing so he became the first of a long line of eighteenth-, nineteenth-, and even twentieth-century scholars to employ the images as individual examples of Roman wall painting in a scholarly discourse on the merits of Greek versus Roman and ancient versus modern painting.

The second vehicle by which knowledge of the painted images from the porticus was spread throughout Europe in the latter half of the eighteenth century was Charles VII's official publication of the antiquities from Herculaneum, *Delle antichità di Ercolano*.[13] Five volumes were devoted to painted wall fragments from Herculaneum, including those removed from the porticus [FIG. 3].[14] It was a model publication of art-historical scholarship for its time: the engravings were of high quality; they included the original painted framework, if known; Roman and Neapolitan measurement scales appeared below each image; and scholarly entries accompanied each etching. The publication, however, was clearly organized along the same principles that had guided the excavations and the installation in Portici: the formal quality of the pieces (state of preservation, size, style, and composition) was favored over their original Roman context. For example, as part of their mission to dazzle the European audience, the court-appointed editors grouped the largest and most beautiful images together in volume 1.[15] Since the first batch of fragments from the porticus was discovered in 1738 and the second in 1761, when the first two volumes had already been published, they were split up and distributed across all five volumes.[16] Within each volume, the authors grouped certain images according to provenance—less an effort to preserve the original Roman setting of the images than to create an overall stylistic coherence in the presentation.[17] For the same reason stylistically similar images were assigned to one engraver, with the master engravers commissioned to do the best pieces. What especially demonstrated the neglect of the original setting of the fragments, however, was the fact that the written entries rarely yielded basic information about the exact findspot and date of discovery of the fragments. The engravers of the four largest images from the porticus, representing Theseus, Hercules and Telephus, Achilles and Chiron, and Marsyas and Olympus, also ignored the concavity of these paintings and rendered them as if they were flat pictures, although the concave shape is crucial to the identification of their original setting in the building. While the engravings in the *Antichità* can be extremely helpful today in clarifying certain details of the now-faded originals and, as in the case of the Bellerophon image from the porticus, even help identify their iconography, the royal publication was clearly designed to promote the collections in Portici rather than to function as an archaeological research tool by today's standards.[18] Ultimately, at the time, it only added more fuel to the scholarly debates about the merits of Roman wall painting—a debate in which each image was judged individually and in which style was all-important and the original context was secondary at best.

The tradition of promoting the painted wall fragments from Pompeii, Stabiae, and Herculaneum as isolated, framable images extended beyond their reproduction in books. The souvenirs produced by the royal Bourbon porcelain factory in Naples, the Real fabbrica ferdinandea, provide a dramatic example of this practice. With the discovery of kaolin in 1709 porcelain production had become a favorite endeavor among European monarchs. Eager to join them, Charles VII began in 1739 to experiment with the production of porcelain.[19] In this undertaking he was undoubtedly encouraged by his young wife, Maria Amalia of Saxony, whose father, Augustus III, king of Poland and elector of Saxony, had sponsored Johann Friedrich Böttger in his discovery of white porcelain and who had built Europe's first porcelain factory, Meissen, in 1710. In

1743 Charles constructed his own porcelain factory on the Capodimonte. In function until 1759, the factory became one of the leading porcelain producers in Europe, on a par with Meissen in Saxony and Vincennes in France. When Charles VII assumed the Spanish throne, his son Ferdinand constructed a second factory in Naples, in operation from 1771 to 1806.[20]

In 1782 Domenico Venuti was appointed to direct the production of the Real fabbrica ferdinandea. As the son of Marcello Venuti, the antiquarian who had been in charge of the collection in Portici and who was credited with the discovery of the identity of Herculaneum, Venuti was a great admirer of classical antiquities. Where the sculptors and painters of Charles VII's factory had produced baroque and rococo objects, borrowing subjects from real life and motifs from local Neapolitan paintings, the artists working under Venuti used classicizing themes inspired by the ancient objects discovered in the Bourbon excavations.[21] Under Venuti's direction, Ferdinand's factory began the production of large dining services as diplomatic gifts to other European courts. First in this series was the impressive Servizio ercolanese, consisting of eighty-eight pieces, which was designed as a gift that would convey the Herculanean treasures in reproduction to Charles VII, now King Charles III of Spain.[22] The images on the plates and cups of the Servizio ercolanese were inspired by the wall fragments from Herculaneum, including some from the porticus. The painters of the service, Giacomo Milani and Antonio Cioffi, favored uncomplicated and easily contained compositions of one or two figures. They copied the ancient figures into new settings and surrounded them with gilded borders designed to fit the cups or plates and bearing little resemblance to the original painted frames. Thus Hercules wrestles with the Nemean Lion on the side of a creamer against the background of a lush, green countryside quite unlike the dark, foreboding landscape of the original. The woman with the drinking horn magically reclines in a white, empty space within an octagonal cameo on the side of a cup—a pale, thin version of the sensuous, red background and thick, gilded frame that surrounded her in the original image. And Achilles and Olympus receive their musical training against a plain blue wall and in a wooded grove, rather than the ornate interior setting of the original images [FIG. 4].[23] Presumably the Servizio ercolanese was never reproduced in multiple copies for sale as souvenirs to the general public, as it was a very personal, albeit grand, gift from son to father. Venuti, however, published his illustrations of the pieces in 1782—the same year that Milani and Cioffi presented the service to the king in Spain.[24]

Under the master *plasticatore*, Filippo Tagliolini, the royal porcelain factory began in the last years of the eighteenth century to produce miniature copies of ancient sculpture in biscuit, a material whose matted white surface highlighted the subtleties of the modeling and details of the execution. The factory artists drew inspiration from some of the Farnese statues from the Bourbon collection, which Venuti had transferred to the Real fabbrica to serve as models.[25] Presumably searching for additional subjects, the sculptors also began experimenting with transforming two-dimensional figures depicted in the images from Pompeii, Stabiae, and Herculaneum into three-dimensional miniature sculpture. The Achilles and Chiron [FIG. 5] and Marsyas and Olympus groups from the porticus were among the favorites. In 1804 the sculptors Camillo Celebrano and Antonio Sorrentino copied the colorful renderings of the two young heroes with their tutors and produced miniature sculptures, whose three-dimensionality was emphasized by the whiteness of the biscuit.[26] The experiment embodies the eighteenth-century detachment of the ancient images from their origi-

nal Roman context: they had truly become objets d'art. In an interesting twist it also represents a case in which the eighteenth-century aesthetic reflected a Roman tradition: the Achilles and Chiron and Marsyas and Olympus images in the porticus copied actual three-dimensional statues that stood in the Saepta Iulia in Rome in the first century.[27] The frequent appearance of the Achilles and Chiron composition in Roman art demonstrates that the Romans also thought it suitable as both a two- and a three-dimensional subject.[28]

The images copied onto the Servizio ercolanese were all from different contexts in Herculaneum; the value of the dining service as an archaeological research tool for reconstructing their original settings is therefore limited. Nevertheless, in one instance it may actually help re-create the identity of a now-missing image from the porticus. The creamer with the image of Hercules and the Nemean Lion on the front illustrates another of the hero's labors on the back: his fight with the Hydra.[29] As the porticus contained documented representations of three of Hercules' labors (the Stymphalian Birds, the Erymanthean Boar, and the Nemean Lion), the picture on the back of the sugar bowl possibly copied the image of yet another Herculean labor from the building.

The Bourbon propensity to select, isolate, frame, and recontextualize the painted images from the Campanian excavations into new settings influenced not only scholars but also artists of the time. A passage from Goethe's *Italian Journey* (1786–88), for example, vividly illustrates the impact on the eighteenth-century performance artist Emma Hart (born Amy Lyon), mistress and later wife of England's ambassador to Naples, William Hamilton. On a visit to the Hamilton estate in Naples, Goethe was invited to explore the host's chaotic collection of curiosities and antiquities. He relates:

> A box standing upright caught my eye, open in front, painted black inside, and surrounded by the most splendid golden frame. The space was large enough to hold a

standing human figure, and we learned that indeed such was its purpose. This admirer of art and girls [Hamilton], not satisfied with seeing the lovely creature [Emma] as a moving statue, also wanted to enjoy her as a colorful, inimitable painting. And so, inside this golden frame, dressed in many colors against the black ground, she had sometimes imitated the ancient paintings of Pompeii.[30]

Ambassador to the Neapolitan court and a fervent collector of ancient art, Hamilton was intimately familiar with the Campanian fragments in the Bourbon collections, and Goethe's description suggests that he shared the court's appreciation of their formal qualities. Like the painters and sculptors in the Real fabbrica ferdinandea, Hamilton and Hart imitated the ancient figures against a plain background, which obliterated their original setting and enclosed them, if only for a moment, within a thick, golden frame as if they were individual pieces of art.

By the end of the eighteenth century the Bourbon excavations had made available to the world a huge corpus of painted fragments from Pompeii, Herculaneum, and Stabiae. Subsequent publications had transformed images that originally decorated the interior walls of buildings into individual works of art and paved the way for them to be copied into new settings. Artists such as Jean-Auguste-Dominique Ingres and Lawrence Alma-Tadema borrowed subjects and compositions from the architecture, statuary, and painted wall fragments that had emerged in the excavations, and they copied entire images, including some from the Porticus of Herculaneum, into new contexts for their own paintings. Ingres modeled his famous portrait of Madame Moitessier (1856) on the so-called Arcadia figure from the Hercules and Telephus fragment,[31] and he decorated the walls of the bedroom featured in his many versions of Antiochus and Stratonice with images of Theseus and of Baby Hercules.[32] The Medea fragment from the porticus appeared in two different paintings by the British painter Alma-Tadema: *The Collector of Pictures in the Time of Augustus* (1867) and *The Picture Gallery* (1874).[33] In both cases Alma-Tadema cast the Medea fragment in the role of a panel painting—more specifically as a Roman copy of a Greek masterpiece, one among many for sale in a Roman painting gallery. For both Ingres and Alma-Tadema the original context of the ancient images was irrelevant; what mattered to these artists was that the antiquity of the pieces be immediately recognizable to the nineteenth-century audience.

The excavations of the buried cities initially prompted a deluge of antiquarian interest in the painted images. By the end of the eighteenth century, however, scholarly activity had come to a standstill, and Roman wall painting did not emerge as a field of study until the end of the following century. The trailblazers were Wolfgang Helbig's comprehensive catalogue of fragments exhibited in the Museo nazionale in Naples, *Wandgemälde der vom Vesuv verschütteten Städte Campaniens* (1868), and August Mau's *Geschichte der decorativen Wandmalerei in Pompeji* (1882), in which the author established a famous and still-used classification system of four Pompeian painting styles.[34] Following eighteenth-century tradition, however, both men disregarded the primary context and meaning of the fragments. In the century that followed scholars continued to concentrate on the aesthetic quality of the painted images and their relationship to Greek painting, or they focused on fine-tuning Mau's classification and dating system. Only a few publications, such as "The Imagines of Philostratus the Elder" (1941) by Karl Lehmann, *Pompejanische Malerei: Sinn und Ideengeschichte* (1952) by Karl Schefold,[35] and "The Monumental and Literary Evidence for Programmatic Painting in

Antiquity" (1960 and 1961) by Mary Lee Thompson, acknowledged that the Campanian images might have served more than a decorative function in antiquity.[36] Only at the end of the twentieth century did scholars such as Eleanor Leach, Andrew Wallace-Hadrill, Bettina Bergmann, and John Clarke seriously consider the possibility that Roman patrons carefully designed and conceived the themes, styles, colors, sizes, placements, and combinations of painted images within a building.[37] Consequently a new archaeological methodology emerged—one that requires the reconstruction of the original Roman setting of the images to determine their relationship to the ancient viewer. Formal analysis of individual fragments—a process that began with the Bourbon excavations and was furthered by the subsequent eighteenth-century sources—is now considered a methodology of the past, one that reflects neoclassical ideology and taste more than classicism proper.

To demonstrate the archaeological value of reconstructing the original context of the Campanian images, I return to the Porticus of Herculaneum. With the help of the eighteenth-century excavation reports, the engravings in the *Pitture d'Ercolano* volumes, and one of the images on the Servizio ercolanese, it is possible to identify many painted segments that were removed from the walls of the porticus, a majority of which are now kept in the Museo archeologico nazionale in Naples. At first glance the subjects depicted on the fragments seem random and unrelated. A closer look reveals at least three uniting themes: one celebrates the physical strength and moral virtue of Hercules, one highlights the trials and triumphs of virtuous young heroes, and one centers on the nurture and education of children. The combination of these particular themes indicates that, among other functions, the porticus served as a school for the *iuvenes*, the elite and freedmen youth of Herculaneum.[38] The patrons of the building deliberately selected these particular images as exempla of heroic virtue and strength for the civic and religious education of the town's youth.

While representations of Hercules abound in Herculaneum—not surprisingly, as the town claimed him as its mythical founder (*Dionysius of Halicarnassus* 1.35)—only in the porticus have we found depictions of the heroic semigod with children and young, mythological heroes. This unusual juxtaposition reflects a trend in the first and second centuries, when Roman youth especially revered Hercules for his physical strength and moral virtue. Youth organizations flourished in towns throughout Italy, many of them worshiping Hercules as their patron god.[39] Like the youth in neighboring Pompeii, the *iuvenes* of Herculaneum would have received their physical and perhaps even military training in the nearby palaestra. The porticus, however, might have been the space where the young men and women were educated in gentility and civic virtue. Between 49 and 79, when the building was destroyed, the local elite and the freedmen organization of the Augustales decorated the porticus with sculptural cycles depicting Julio-Claudian and Flavian imperial family members. These patrons were probably also responsible for the building's painted decoration and for selecting subjects to serve as didactic tools in the cultural and civic education of their sons and daughters.

If we study the painted images from the porticus as simple, didactic exempla in the literary and moral education of Herculaneum's youth, the paintings suddenly come to life. The depictions of beautiful nymphs emerging from the lake, seducing and drowning Hercules' shipmate, the young boy Hylas, and of Medea contemplating the murder of her children exemplified the dangers that await youngsters in seemingly trustworthy and nurturing environments. The representations of Baby Hercules strangling the two serpents sent by Juno to kill him and of the young hero Bellerophon unknowingly handing King Iobates the sealed letter that demands Bellerophon's own death demonstrate how moral strength and virtue can overcome treachery. Images depicting the labors of Hercules and the two young athletes bathing after their exercise emphasized the value of physical power. The depictions of young men and women in sacrificial garb reminded youngsters of their religious duties to the gods, in particular to Hercules, their patron god (and perhaps reflected the use of the porticus as a space in which they performed the rituals associated with the worship of Hercules). The fragments showing an aging Chiron teaching the young hero Achilles to play the lyre and old Marsyas instructing young Olympus how to play the double flute promoted mutual obligations between young and old and delineated the importance of educa-tion and patronage. The figures of Theseus and Hercules in the two largest images from the porticus also advocated heroic virtue and strength—traits highlighted by their nudity. These images, however, depict the two popular heroes in a slightly different context than what was usual at the time, which suggests that the patron(s) of the building wanted to emphasize more than those particular qualities. The Athenian hero and founding father, Theseus, appears here not in his typical role as the slayer of the Minotaur (the beast is hidden and barely visible in the corner) but in the role of the savior of the Athenian children (who crowd the composition—unlike most other ancient representations of this scene). This image thus focuses on Theseus not as the powerful hero but as the savior of the young and the weak, the protective ruler, and the father of his people. Similarly, Hercules appears not in his usual role as the invin-cible hero performing some extraordinary labor through which he receives immortal-ity but in a unique composition in which he searches for his lost child, Telephus, and rescues him from an uncertain fate in the wilderness. Like Theseus, Hercules figures in this image as an example of the protecting father and ruler.

Examining the images of Theseus and Hercules in the context of the architecture and sculptural decoration of the porticus enhances our understanding of their function within the building and explains why the patrons chose to emphasize these heroes as strong, protective rulers and father figures. Having suffered damage in the earthquake of A.D. 62, the porticus was repaired during the reign of Vespasian (A.D. 69–79)—perhaps financed by the emperor himself in A.D. 76.[40] In gratitude, the patrons of the building had its walls, niches, and top frieze decorated with the many images here dis-cussed. The depictions of Theseus and Hercules occupied the tall and highly promi-nent, semicircular exedrae at the end of the two lateral porticoes, flanking the central sacellum. At the same time the patrons replaced some of the Julio-Claudian sculptural groups with statues of Vespasian and his extended family, granting Vespasian the place of honor in the sacellum.[41] The new statues celebrated the Flavian dynasty that would bring stability and peace to Rome just as Augustus had done—a common theme in Vespasianic propaganda.[42] Underscoring the continuity between Vespasian and the Julio-Claudian rulers, especially the two deified emperors Augustus and Claudius, over-life-sized statues of Augustus and Claudius stood in front of the semicircular exedrae with their images of Theseus and Hercules, and seated statues of the two gods flanked the statue of Vespasian in the central niche.[43] The placement of Vespasian's statue between representations of Theseus and Hercules and Augustus and Claudius recalled the vision of the deified Augustus seated between Hercules and the Dioscuri in an ode by Horace (3.3.9–12) and extolled Vespasian's moral strength and virtue, through which he was certain to win immortality like Hercules and Augustus before him.[44] The juxtaposition of the Flavian and Julio-Claudian statues with the Theseus and Hercules images also celebrated the peace, stability, and prospects of a new Golden Age that Vespasian, like Theseus, Hercules, and Augustus, would bring to his people through his family dynasty — a peaceful age perhaps personified by the seated, female figure in the Hercules image. The particular emphasis in these representations of Theseus and Hercules in addition assimilated Vespasian with the just and protective ruler and promoted him in his role as *pater patriae*. Thus the two most prominent images from the porticus not only promoted physical strength and moral virtue but also reminded the local youth of the *potestas*, or power, of Roman fathers and encouraged them to observe filial duty.

This relationship between the architecture and the sculptural and painted programs of the porticus demonstrates that the patrons decorated the building in a manner that not only celebrated and honored the emperor Vespasian but also endorsed his dynastic ideology. Titus and Domitian, his sons, were, of course, fundamental to the continuation of the Flavian dynasty and the stability of the empire, and Vespasian advanced them as his heirs by promoting them as princes of the youth, *principes iuventutis*, just as Augustus had promoted his grandsons, Lucius and Gaius.[45] That Vespasian concerned himself with educating his children and Roman youth in the liberal as well as the martial arts is suggested by Suetonius's descriptions of the young Titus as a master of weaponry, horsemanship, Greek and Latin composition, poetry, and music and by Vespasian's generosity toward teachers of Greek and Latin rhetoric.[46] It is possible that Vespasian chose to finance the repair of the porticus because this particular building served a purpose of interest to him: the civic education of Roman youth.

▣ ▣ ▣

The eighteenth-century excavations of Herculaneum and subsequent Bourbon sources both accelerated and impeded the progress of modern Campanian archaeology. On the one hand, the Bourbon agenda made available to the world a great corpus of ancient images that inspired artists and students of Roman painting for centuries. On the other hand, it transformed the painted fragments into individual works of art and initiated a 250-year-long trend that focused on the formal qualities of the depictions while ignoring their Roman context. The example of modern Herculanean archaeology here presented demonstrates the benefits of studying ancient objects such as wall fragments in the context of their original surroundings. The premise is that only by doing so can we begin to understand what they meant to the Roman viewer — only then do they become more than pretty pictures.

Notes

I am extremely grateful to the editors, Victoria Coates and Jon Seydl, for their many insightful and helpful suggestions.

[1]   For the most recent work on this building, see Tina Najbjerg, "A Reconstruction and Reconsideration of the So-Called Basilica in Herculaneum," *Journal of Roman Archaeology*, suppl. 47 (2002): 122–65.

2   In addition, the following images were discovered: Leda embracing the swan, Jupiter residing in the clouds, a woman reclining with a drinking horn, a woman playing the lyre, a servant pouring water for two athletes, a veiled priestess, a fountain with birds, architectural landscapes, majestic eagles, and several theatrical masks. For a discussion, catalogue, and reproductions of all the images, see Tina Najbjerg, "Public Painted and Sculptural Programs of the Early Roman Empire: A Case-Study of the So-Called Basilica in Herculaneum" (PhD diss., Princeton University, 1997), 254–348, 370, figs. 153–205.

3   Michele Ruggiero, *Scavi di Ercolano* (Naples, 1885), 33: "Y el dho estatuario dize que en Roma y mas en Inglaterra se aprecian muchisimo estas pinturas, las quales se quitan de semejantes parajes." Reference from Agnes Allrogen-Bedel and Helke Kammerer-Grothaus, "Das Museo ercolanese in Portici," *Cronache ercolanesi* 10 (1980): 188.

4   Allrogen-Bedel and Kammerer-Grothaus 1980 (note 3), 188.

5   The destruction of three painted sections, depicting a fountain with a bird, a mask, and a naked youth with flowers, is recorded in the excavation report on August 22, 1738, as transcribed in Ruggiero 1885 (note 3), 364.

6   Allrogen-Bedel and Kammerer-Grothaus 1980 (note 3), 188.

7   Ibid., 182, 185.

8   Alden R. Gordon, "Jérôme-Charles Bellicard's Italian Notebook of 1750–51: The Discoveries at Herculaneum and Observations on Ancient and Modern Architecture," *Metropolitan Museum Journal* 25 (1990): 58.

9   Anton Francesco Gori, *Notizie del memorabile scoprimento dell'antica città Ercolano* (Florence, 1748); idem, *Symbolae litterariae: Opuscula varia philologica, scientifica, antiquaria, . . . Decas I and II* (Florence, 1748–53; and Rome, 1751–54); and idem, *Admiranda antiquitatum herculanensium descripta et illustrate ad annum MDCCL*, 2 vols. (Padua, 1752); Niccolò Marcello Venuti, *Descrizione delle prime scoperte dell'antica città d'Ercolano* (Rome, 1748); [Moussinot d'Arthenay], *Notizie intorno alla città sotterranea discoperta alle falde del Monte Vesuvio* (Florence, 1749); Charles-Nicolas Cochin, *Lettre sur les peintures d'Herculanum, aujourd'hui Portici* (Paris, 1751); Charles-Nicolas Cochin and Jérôme-Charles Bellicard, *Observations sur les antiquités d'Herculanum* (Paris, 1755); and Charles-Nicolas Cochin, *Voyage d'Italie* (Paris, 1758).

10 Gordon 1990 (note 8), 50–52; also his essay in this volume.

11 In the second French edition of Cochin and Bellicard's *Observations* of 1755 (note 9), the three images from the porticus appeared as plates 15–17, on pages 38–39, 41.

12 As highlighted by this author and Jennifer Trimble in "The Forma urbis romae since 1980," *Bullettino della Commissione archeologica comunale di Roma* (forthcoming), Giovanni Battista Piranesi treated the fragments of the third-century Severan Marble Plan in a similar, highly romantic manner in his *Antichità romane* (Rome, 1756). Here, Piranesi depicted the marble pieces as individual, three-dimensional objects surrounding a great map of Rome. He drew them as seen from above, with rough and broken edges that were shaded to indicate the thickness of the marble and that cast shadows on the surface below.

13 Of the eight volumes, volumes 1 to 4 and 7 were devoted to painted images from Herculaneum and were published under the name *Le pitture antiche d'Ercolano e contorni incise con qualche spiegazione* (Naples, 1757, 1760, 1762, 1765, and 1779). Volumes 5 and 6, *Bronzi di Ercolano* (Naples, 1767 and 1771), focused on bronzes; and volume 8, *Lucerne e candelabra* (Naples, 1792), was a publication of lamps and candelabra from the site.

14 For a complete listing of the painted images from the porticus in the *Delle antichità di Ercolano*, 8 vols. (Naples, 1757–92), see the catalogue in Najbjerg 1997 (note 2), 316–45.

15 Allrogen-Bedel and Kammerer-Grothaus 1980 (note 3), 190.

16 Among the most impressive compositions appearing in volume 1 of *Delle antichità di Ercolano* (Naples, 1757) are Theseus, Hercules and Telephus, Achilles and Chiron, Baby Hercules and the Serpents, and Medea. See the catalogue in Najbjerg 1997 (note 2), 316–45.

17 For example, Leda, Reclining Woman with a Drinking Horn, and Citharista all appeared in volume 3, plate 4; Jupiter in the Clouds, Priestess, and Male Attendant were engraved in volume 4, plate 1.

18 The Bellerophon image from the Porticus of Herculaneum is missing but can be identified thanks to its depiction in *Delle antichità di Ercolano*, vol. 3 (Naples, 1762), pl. 48.

19 Teresa Elena Romano, *La porcellana di Capodimonte: Storia della manifattura borbonica* (Naples, 1959), 28.

20 Ibid., 25–26.

21 Ibid., 12.

22 Ibid., 146–48.

23 Ibid., figs. 105, 118, 120.

24 Domenico Venuti, *Spiegazione d'un servizio da tavola dipinto e modellato in porcellana nella Real fabbrica di sua maestà il re delle Due Sicilie sopra la serie dei sasi e pitture esistenti nel Real museo ercolanese per uso di sua maestà cattolica* (Naples, 1782).

25 Romano 1959 (note 19), 148–51.

26 Ibid., figs. 132, 141.

27 That the Achilles and Chiron and Marsyas and Olympus images in the porticus perhaps copied sculptural groups in the Saepta Iulia has long been speculated; see, for example, Karl Schefold, *La peinture pompéienne: Essai sur l'évolution de sa signification*, trans. Jean-Michel Croisille (Brussels, 1972), 201–2. The theory is based on a statement by Pliny the Elder (*Natural History* 36.29), according to whom the Saepta contained statues of Olympus and Pan and of Achilles and Chiron.

28 For a list of all known occurrences of the Achilles and Chiron group in ancient art, see "Achilleus," in *Lexicon iconographicum mythologiae classicae* 1:51.

29 See Romano 1959 (note 19), fig. 115.

30 Johann Wolfgang von Goethe, *Italian Journey*, ed. Thomas P. Saine and Jeffrey L. Sammons, trans. Robert R. Heitner (Princeton, 1994), 261–62.

31 Robert Rosenblum, *Jean-Auguste-Dominique Ingres* (New York, 1967), 164, fig. 137, pl. 46. See also *Portraits by Ingres: Images of an Epoch*, ed. Gary Tinterow and Philip Conisbee (New York, 1999), 429.

32 The Baby Hercules image appeared as a backdrop in two versions of the Antiochus and Stratonice painting, one in the Musée Condé, Chantilly, the other in the Musée Fabre, Montpellier (see Georges Vigne, *Ingres* [Paris, 1995], figs. 184, 276).

33 R. J. Barrow, *Lawrence Alma-Tadema* (London, 2001), figs. 32, 69.

34 Wolfgang Helbig, *Wandgemälde der vom Vesuv verschütteten Städte Campaniens* (Leipzig, 1868); August Mau, *Geschichte der decorativen Wandmalerei in Pompeji* (Berlin, 1882).

35 Karl Lehmann, "The Imagines of Philostratus the Elder," *Art Bulletin* 23, no. 1 (1941): 16–44; Karl Schefold, *Pompejanische Malerei: Sinn und Ideengeschichte* (Basel, 1952).

36 Mary Lee Thompson, "The Monumental and Literary Evidence for Programmatic Painting in Antiquity," *Marsyas* 9 (1961): 36–77. The article was a synthesis of Thompson's dissertation, "Programmatic Painting in Pompeii: The Meaningful Combination of Mythological Pictures in Roman Decoration" (PhD diss., New York University, 1960).

37   Eleanor Leach, *The Rhetoric of Space* (Princeton, 1988); Andrew Wallace-Hadrill, "The Social Structure of the Roman House," in *Papers of the British School in Rome*, vol. 56 (London, 1988), 43–97; Bettina Bergmann, "The Roman House as Memory Theater: The House of the Tragic Poet in Pompeii," *Art Bulletin* 76, no. 2 (1994): 225–56; John Clarke, *The Houses of Roman Italy, 100 B.C.–A.D. 250: Ritual, Space, and Decoration* (Berkeley, 1991).

38   For my suggestion that the porticus served a variety of functions, among them as the headquarters for the Augustales in Herculaneum and as a market, see Najbjerg 2002 (note 1), 122–65.

39   On the special reverence of Hercules by the *iuvenes*, see Maria Jaczynowska, "Les collegia iuvenum et leurs liaisons avec les cultes religieux au temps du haut-empire romain," *Zeszyty naukowe Uniwersytetu Mikołaja Kopernika w Toruniu* (Toruń, 1968), 28–32; and Pierre Ginestet, *Les organisations de la jeunesse dans l'Occident romain* (Brussels, 1991), 172.

40   An incomplete inscription (*L'Année épigraphique* 1979, 170) discovered in the intersection between the Cardo III and the Decumanus Maximus in Herculaneum (in front of the porticus) refers to the repair of a building by Vespasian (Giuseppe Guadagno, "Supplemento epigrafico ercolanese," *Cronache ercolanesi* 8 [1978]: 134–36). The inscription probably referred to the porticus. Mario Pagano, "Il foro," in *Gli antichi ercolanesi: Antropologia, società, economia* (Naples, 2000), 86, also suggests (without citing evidence or explaining his reasons for this assumption) that Vespasian financed the post-A.D. 62 repair of the porticus.

41   Although no statue of Vespasian was ever discovered inside the porticus, the original Flavian group in the building almost certainly included a statue of him, the founder of the dynasty. It was probably replaced after his death in A.D. 79 (a few months before the porticus was destroyed in the eruption) with the statue of Titus that was discovered by eighteenth-century excavators in the central sacellum of the building. On the identification of the Titus statue, see Agnes Allroggen-Bedel, "Dokumente des 18. Jahrhunderts zur Topographie von Herculaneum," *Cronache ercolanesi* 13 (1983): 148. For a complete discussion and catalogue of the sculptural groups in the porticus, see Najbjerg 1997 (note 2), 138–251.

42   Kenneth Scott, *The Imperial Cult under the Flavians* (Stuttgart, Berlin, 1936), 25–39, demonstrated that Vespasian's propaganda to a great extent was based on the ideological programs of Augustus.

43   The seated statues in the central sacellum were discovered without heads and were restored by the sculptor Filippo Tagliolini in the nineteenth century as Augustus and Claudius (Allroggen-Bedel 1983 [note 41], 148n. 46). Their identity, however, is disputed by some scholars. R. Gall ("Herculaneum," in *Paulys Realencyclopädie der classischen Altertumswissenschaft* 8, no. 1 [1912]: 542) and A. M. G. Little ("A Series of Notes in Four Parts on Campanian Megalography," *American Journal of Archaeology* 67 [1963]: 393) believed that they represented Titus and Domitian. Mario Pagano ("La nuova pianta della città e di alcuni edifici pubblici di Ercolano," *Cronache ercolanesi* 26 [1996]: 241) suggested that one depicted Vespasian, the other Augustus or Claudius.

44   Karl Schefold (1972 [note 27], 201) was the first to note the meaningful juxtaposition of Vespasian and the Theseus and Hercules images, which he saw as a celebration of Vespasian's moral virtue and future apotheosis.

45   Harold Mattingly, *Coins of the Roman Empire in the British Museum* (London, 1930), 2:32–33; Scott 1936 (note 42), 23–25. For examples of Vespasianic coins on which Titus and Domitian appear as *principes iuventutis* and on horseback, see *Le collezioni del Museo nazionale di Napoli* (Rome, 1989), 1: nos. 153, 155.

46   Suet. 11.3 (Titus); 10.18 (Vespasian).

Four Women from Stabiae: Eighteenth-Century Antiquarian Practice and the History of Ancient Roman Painting

Hérica Valladares

THE SO-CALLED *FLORA* from the Villa Arianna in Stabiae [FIG. 1] is one of the best-known Campanian frescoes and an icon of ancient Roman painting. In a visit to the Museo archeologico nazionale in Naples, this work is the first image one sees: reproduced on a panel, Flora points the way to the ticket booth. In the bookshop, strategically located before the entrance to the museum proper, reproductions proliferate: posters, postcards, mouse pads, bookmarks, tote bags, and magnets all encourage visitors to take this image with them as a token of their experience in the galleries. Emblazoned on the cover of the official guide to the collection, Flora also appears as a seductive vade mecum, who, with her back turned and a hint of a profile, invites the reader to follow along and discover the treasures that lie within. But despite its beauty, fame, and prominent role in shaping contemporary perceptions of Roman art, *Flora* is rarely discussed in current academic debates on ancient painting. The discrepancy between the general public's interest in this image and the scholarly silence around it is in itself intriguing. Why should a work of art so alluring to lay viewers elicit so little interest among specialists?

Part of the problem lies in the painting's loveliness. *Flora* and its three companions, *Leda*, *Medea*, and *Diana* [FIGS. 2–4], belong to that category of images described by Johann Joachim Winckelmann as "fleeting as thought and as beautiful as if drawn by the hand of the Graces."[1] Small, elegantly rendered, and often unframed, such vignettes or floating figures, representing gods, goddesses, satyrs, maenads, cupids, and other mythical beings, were, from the moment of their discovery, among the most beloved genres of ancient painting. Their graceful form and whimsical abstraction easily suggested their transformation into *quadretti*, small, framed panels intended to be admired as individual works of art. As Agnes Allroggen-Bedel noted, the holes on third- and fourth-style Campanian walls indicate not only where the frescoes were detached in

FIGURE 1
Flora, Stabiae, A.D. 10–20.
Wall fragment from room 26,
Villa Arianna. Naples,
Museo archeologico
nazionale, Inv. 8834.

Photo: Scala/Art Resource, NY.

FIGURE 2
Leda, Stabiae, A.D. 10–20.
Wall fragment from room 26,
Villa Arianna. Naples, Museo
archeologico nazionale,
Inv. 9546.

Photo: Scala/Art Resource, NY.

FIGURE 3
Medea, Stabiae, A.D. 10–20.
Wall fragment from room 26,
Villa Arianna. Naples, Museo
archeologico nazionale,
Inv. 8978.

Photo: From *In Stabiano: Exploring
Ancient Seaside Villas of the
Roman Elite*. Nicola Longobardi
Editore (2004), p. 116.

FIGURE 4
Diana, Stabiae, A.D. 10–20.
Wall fragment from room 26,
Villa Arianna. Naples, Museo
archeologico nazionale,
Inv. 9243.

Photo: Scala/Art Resource, NY.

the eighteenth century but also how much these images appealed to the taste of the Bourbon court.[2] The decontextualization resulting from the Enlightenment practice of selecting, extracting, and reframing Roman frescoes does not, however, explain the scholarly disregard toward such floating figures.[3] After all, their fate in the hands of the Bourbon excavators paralleled that of the larger mythological tableaux, which for the past forty years have been at the center of discussions regarding the symbolism, meaning, and function of Roman painting.[4]

The relegation of such vignettes to a separate, implicitly less significant category derives from *settecento* antiquarian practice. In this regard, the Four Women from Stabiae present a compelling case study. Discovered in 1759 at Gragnano (Castellammare di Stabia) and published for the first time in volume 3 of *Delle antichità di Ercolano* (1762), these paintings stood, from the start, between two different methods of analysis.[5] The texts recording the paintings' discovery and the earliest responses elicited by them reflect a significant methodological split at the heart of antiquarian studies during the Enlightenment: on the one hand, we have the contextual reports submitted by Karl Weber, the Swiss military engineer in charge of the excavations at Gragnano; on the other, we have the erudite commentary written by the members of the Real accademia ercolanese and commissioned by Charles VII of Naples. While Weber's systematic approach to excavating and recording finds has been recognized as a precursor of contemporary archaeological methods, the Ercolanesi favored an earlier model of collecting and interpreting historical evidence. At the same time that Weber argued for the preservation of archaeological context, the Ercolanesi insisted on classifying objects according to medium, presenting them as individual works of art and interpreting them through extensive citation of classical texts.[6]

A study of the first official publication of the Four Women from Stabiae thus offers a synthetic example of how eighteenth-century interpretive models have influenced the writing of Roman art history. To this day the Ercolanesi's omission of context continues to shape our understanding of these images. Rarely considered as a series from a single space, where they appeared amid other paintings, the panels from Villa Arianna still inspire learned exegeses on the identification of each woman. My goal is, then, twofold: to trace how the Ercolanesi's philological approach has defined more recent analyses of these four fragments and to propose new questions that broaden the discussion of them. To do so, I reconstruct, as far as possible, the context in which the paintings were found. Weber's excavation reports, Allroggen-Bedel's careful matching of his descriptions with fragments now in Naples, and comparison with the better-preserved, closely contemporary wall paintings from the Villa della Farnesina in Rome offer a basis for theorizing how *Flora*, *Leda*, *Medea*, and *Diana* engaged ancient viewers through visual and semantic associations that transcend current heuristic boundaries.[7]

The Ercolanesi's work is not simply an outdated model to be discarded. First, it contains the seeds of modern iconographic studies, whereby textual sources and visual comparanda jointly create a range of interpretive possibilities for a given image. Second, the eighteenth-century drive to identify each of the four women securely—a drive perpetuated by subsequent generations of scholars—may be seen as a response to the inherent ambiguity of the paintings. With the exception of the woman holding a swan, traditionally identified as Leda [FIG. 2], the figures in this series have attributes that do not clearly reveal their identity. Rather than seeing such vagueness as a sign of the Roman artist's inability to copy earlier masterpieces, we should consider it as an intended feature of the composition. Designed to hook the viewer's interest and intensify his or her pleasure through the creation of a riddle, the figures' unusual iconography also reflects a stylistic eclecticism typical of early imperial art.[8] Thus, by tracing the history of their interpretation and situating them within the larger context of second- and third-style Roman painting, we may begin to think beyond the panels' 250-year-old frames and look at them again with inquiring eyes.

The Four Women from Stabiae in Delle antichità di Ercolano

From the announcement of the first discoveries at Herculaneum, academics and amateurs hoped that these wondrous finds would soon be published and made accessible to a wider public. But years went by and no such work emerged. Just as the archaeological finds were seen as royal property, so the decision to publish these treasures was perceived as a royal privilege.[9] Charles VII entrusted the task to the fifteen members of the Real accademia ercolanese, established in 1755 to study the king's antiquities. In that same year came the first catalogue of discovered objects, and in 1757—almost twenty years after the excavations had begun—the first volume of the *Antichità* finally appeared. The release of this long-awaited work did little, however, to placate the widespread hunger for information. A hybrid between a learned compendium and a panegyric, the volumes of the *Antichità* were produced as a limited luxury edition not intended for sale, only to be distributed among select noblemen and institutions.[10] As such, they fell short of the scientific community's expectations, for not only was the material presented in the form of earlier catalogues of aristocratic collections of antiquities, but the text also failed to address questions regarding ancient daily life at the fore of contemporary academic debates.[11]

In the first four volumes of the *Antichità*, published between 1757 and 1765, dedicated exclusively to painting, the Ercolanesi opted for a traditional categorization of the objects according to medium. Their choice reflects the great value attached to these objects, which were considered unique and the most prized possession of the Museo ercolanese.[12] No other collection of antiquities could boast a comparable corpus of ancient paintings, known until then only from a few finds in Rome and through studies limited largely to fantastical reconstructions.[13] The order of publication depended on aesthetic worth, with the most beautiful images published as quickly as possible, and others only much later—if ever. Luigi Vanvitelli's comment that the paintings should be divided into three categories—*ottime*, *buone*, *inferiori*—reflects the attitude informing the editors' choices.[14] Within each volume, however, a more subtle and unstated hierarchy further subdivided the paintings.

The first volume exemplifies the Ercolanesi's method. The goal in selecting the images was to offer a representative sample of the various genres of painting described by ancient authors.[15] For this reason, the "most rare and invaluable" marble monochromes from Herculaneum were considered fitting material for the first four plates.[16] In plates 5 to 16 a series of mythological panels follows, with subjects ranging from grave images of heroes to the mirthful misadventures of satyrs and nymphs. Amid these larger tableaux, which are the focus of the Ercolanesi's text, several small vignettes appear with little or no accompanying commentary. On plate 5, for instance, an image of Theseus appears above two still lifes with no original connection to it

[FIG. 5]. Found in different locations, the two depictions of fish simply demonstrate the ancients' taste for this type of painting. Deemed unworthy of in-depth explanation, these small images served as fillers for the occasional blank space.[17] An altogether different category of vignettes occupies the next twenty-two plates. Plates 17 to 28 represent the famous dancers, centaurs, and bacchantes from the Villa di Cicerone in Pompeii, while plates 29 to 38 show a series of *puttini* engaged in everyday activities, all from Herculaneum. The full-page format of the reproductions and the scholars' lavish explications indicate the high value placed on these images. Finally, the book closes with a small selection of architectural details and landscapes (pls. 39–49), reserving the last plate (pl. 50) for "cose egizie."

The hierarchy of genres could not be clearer. Large, figurative narratives corresponding to the established notion of tableaux took pride of place.[18] Small, unframed pieces, on the other hand, appeared in subordinate positions, unless their "perfection and beauty," as in the case of the Pompeian *ballatrici* and Herculanean *puttini*, warranted attention.[19] Architectural fantasies, landscapes, and other genres were treated as addenda, included not only because of their aesthetic refinement but also for their value as curiosities. It is, then, according to this system of classification that we must assess the impression made by the Four Women from Stabiae on the Ercolanesi. Volume 3 of the *Antichità* appeared in 1762, only three years after the discovery of the paintings. Considering that some of the paintings in the first volume had been found as early as 1739 and that the editors had to work with an immense backlog, the speed with which these images were published indicates that they ranked high in the scholars' judgment. Yet their position within the volume itself best illustrates the great regard in which these paintings were held once they entered the collection at the royal palace in Portici.

As in the first volume, volume 3 opens with mythological representations: paintings of Apollo; Bacchus; Selene and Endymion; and Helle and Phryxus occupy plates 1 to 4. Flora appears as plate 5 [FIG. 6]. Although a footnote indicates the location and date of her discovery, the fact that she is part of a larger series of heroines goes unmentioned. Unlike the dancers from Cicero's villa, which the editors carefully described as a sequence found in a single room, the Four Women from Stabiae are isolated from one another: two other paintings from Villa Arianna—*Paris and Helen* and the well-known *Seller of Cupids*—follow *Flora*, while *Leda* [FIG. 2] appears only on plate 8.[20] But because the Ercolanesi think Leda might represent Nemesis, she is paired with another painting of Leda from Portici, also interpreted as Nemesis.[21] Continuing on this theme, *Medea* [FIG. 3] (again thought to be Nemesis) appears next (pl. 10).[22] The *Three Graces* from Pompeii and a painting of Perseus and Andromeda at a spring serve as an interlude. Finally, appearing only in plate 13, *Diana* [FIG. 4] inaugurates a new thematic sequence on the motif of hunting: an anonymous youth with hounds and a *Hippolytus* are the next two plates.[23]

Besides the fragmentation of the ensemble for the sake of a new thematic arrangement, the appearance of the paintings on the pages of the *Antichità* reveals a conscious manipulation of the images that simultaneously enhances their status as precious objects and obscures their original context. According to the orders of the king, the Campanian frescoes had to be presented "just as they were."[24] For this reason, draftsmen and engravers recorded some gaps in the original compositions, such as we see in the painting of Theseus from Herculaneum.[25] But if we compare *Flora* [FIG. 1] to how she appears in the print [FIG. 6], it is evident that the image was subtly touched up. Not only have Flora's small flaws, still visible today, been effaced, but her robes have

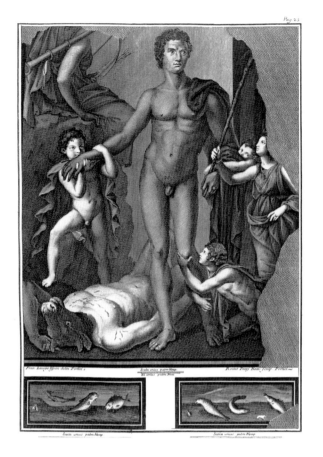

FIGURE 5
Francesco La Vega
(Spanish, 1737–1804)
and Rocco Pozzi
(Italian, d. ca. 1780),
Theseus. Engraving. Plate 5
from *Delle antichità
di Ercolano* (1757), vol. 1.
Los Angeles, Research
Library, Getty Research
Institute, 84-B21058.

FIGURE 6
Giovanni Elia Morghen
(Italian, 1721–after 1789)
and P. Campana (Italian,
life dates unknown), *Flora.*
Engraving. Plate 5
from *Delle antichità
di Ercolano* (1762), vol. 3.
Los Angeles, Research
Library, Getty Research
Institute, N5775.A621 1757.

been rendered more formfitting so that the figure acquires a crisp, relieflike quality.[26] Although the Ercolanesi describe the colors of her garments in detail, the dramatic chiaroscuro of the engraving accentuates the sculpted texture of the image, while the continuous dark ground into which she recedes intensifies the suspended, dreamlike quality of the representation. Presented to the reader as a treasured jewel, Flora is an ambiguous apparition whose form offers no indication of her actual scale or context.

As with every plate in the *Antichità*, *Flora* has a lengthy introduction. Following the Ercolanesi's proclaimed method of offering just a few words to spur the reader on to reflection, the main text limits itself to a brief discussion of subject matter and a detailed formal analysis. Only in the footnotes does a more in-depth discussion take place.[27] In the entry for *Flora* a note of mystery is present from the start: "The nymph that appears before us in this painting, on a green ground . . . could reasonably be thought to be the wife of Zephyrus, whether she is Chloris, or Flora, or one of the seasons. If the green cornucopia she holds with her left arm . . . did not evoke different ideas in the minds of others."[28] Nine footnotes expand this short statement, drawing on a vast array of ancient literary sources. Moving from a discussion of the nymph's yellow dress to a disquisition on her name, the Ercolanesi cite authors such as Aristotle, Pliny, and Ovid, all of whom imply that she must be the goddess of flowers. Horace, on the other hand, is invoked as support for seeing her as one of the Seasons, whom he calls *fugientem horam* (*Od.* 3.2.48). The words of Martianus Capella on Fortuna — "always flowing in contrary plenty, nimble in her inconstant lightness" (1.26) — suggest yet another identification to the authors, who leave the question open-ended.[29]

Thus, the Ercolanesi's words molded the readers' expectations even before they viewed the engravings. In the case of *Flora*, text and image worked together to magnify the painting's worth and mystery. Still, the multiple interpretations do not indicate a broad-minded approach. Despite the ambiguity of these various identifications, the underlying assumption that the figure must represent a specific mythological character and, therefore, have a single, correct identity curtails the semantic fluidity that the scholars' prolific name-dropping might otherwise suggest. The numerous identifications illustrate instead the Ercolanesi's vast knowledge, further corroborated by the little-known literary sources cited. Moreover, their reliance on often-obscure texts rather than visual sources often led them to move from the *lectio facilior* toward more elaborate associations. For example, their grouping of *Leda* and *Medea* under the heading "Nemesis" results directly from their dependence on texts.

Although *Leda* [FIG. 2] does not present a straightforward narrative, the Ercolanesi's effort to identify the woman with a swan as Nemesis, the goddess of justice, is, in comparison, belabored.[30] In fact, in the text preceding plate 8, they admit that she is most likely Leda. Not only has the painter included no sign that she might be a deity, but a passage from Euripides, where he names Leda as Helen's mother (*Helen* 16–22), also strongly supports this identification.[31] Nonetheless, in one footnote they raise the possibility that she might be Nemesis—an identification that is closely linked with their analysis of the next image (pl. 9). The halo around the woman's head in the painting from Portici leads the Ercolanesi to search for a new explanation. Interpreting the halo as a sign of divinity, they recount an obscure version of the myth in which Nemesis was seduced by Zeus in the form of a swan, while Leda served as the mortal guardian of their child.[32] This mythological variant might have justified the Ercolanesi's logic, were it not for the fact that in ancient art Nemesis never appears as Zeus's paramour.[33] Their discussion of *Medea* [FIG. 3] makes clear that they are aware of this other iconographic tradition for Nemesis. But here again problems emerge since none of the goddess's usual attributes—a wheel, a measuring rod, and a set of reins—appear in this image.[34] Furthermore, Medea's attribute, which they interpret as a sword, bewilders the scholars since the only parallel they know is in a painting discussed in volume 1, where the heroine is identified as Dido.[35]

There is, then, a tension between the Ercolanesi's search for a stable identification and the figures' iconographic ambiguity. Despite their intentions, the scholars' efforts to attach an indisputable label to each of these women yielded only polysemy. This multivalence likewise appears in their analysis of *Diana* [FIG. 4], where the proposed identifications gradually unravel the certainty of their initial attribution. Beginning with the obvious idea that the bow and arrow symbolize the goddess of the hunt, the Ercolanesi then point out all the details that problematize this explanation: the absence of a quiver, the unstrung bow, and the figure's long robes and jewels. As a result, they offer alternative interpretations that compete with the initial label but cannot entirely replace it. Could the image show instead the goddess at rest, as described in a passage from Claudianus (*R.P.* 2.31ff.); or Atalanta, the first mortal maiden to have hunted with these weapons; or even Venus, said once to have borrowed the attributes of Diana to appear before her mortal lover, Anchises?[36]

The placement of the Stabiae women within volume 3 of the *Antichità* and the accompanying literary commentaries reflect both the Ercolanesi's preference for iconographic and mythological studies and their understanding of these paintings as separate compositions. Despite the growing concern with archaeological context in the nineteenth and twentieth centuries, their approach has proved long lasting. Perceived by their first commentators as mythological tableaux, the women's nonnarrative form and ambiguous identities failed to spark significant new debates among subsequent scholars. In fact, current interest in the programmatic arrangement of mythological paintings in Roman houses has led to smaller ensembles, such as the Stabiae quartet, slipping out of scholarly sight. Furthermore, their crystallization into precious, isolated objects in the *Antichità* has also rendered their recontextualization more difficult. The few analyses of these paintings since 1762 have limited themselves to iconographical questions in tune with the interests and ambitions of the Bourbon scholars.

After the Ercolanesi: Later Approaches to the Four Women from Stabiae

The identifications put forward by several authors—from Wolfgang Helbig in 1868 to Marisa Mastroroberto in 2001 [TABLE 1]—indicate how much the names of the Four Women from Stabiae have fluctuated. In most texts little or no discussion accompanies the identifications, which are often presented as straightforward and uncontroversial. Clear patterns emerge from this catalogue of interpretations: while Leda and Medea have become standard attributions, no consensus exists for the two other women, especially Flora, whom several scholars refuse to name, opting instead for more anonymous and descriptive titles. The publication of Karl Schefold's *Pompejanische Malerei: Sinn und Ideengeschichte* (1952), however, marked a key change,

TABLE 1 *Scholarly Identification of the Four Women from Stabiae*

Author	Date of Publication	Proposed Identifications
Helbig	1868	Female figure, Leda, Medea, Artemis; Helbig also cites O. Jahn, who proposes Penelope for Diana, and Visconti, who proposes Melpomene for Medea
Cosenza	1907	Maiden with *kalathos*, Leda, Medea, Diana
Ruesch	1908	Maiden with flowers, Leda, Medea, Diana
Reinach	1922	Leda, priestess with key (a.k.a., Medea, Melpomene, Nemesis), Artemis
Rizzo	1929	Flora
Elia	1932	Maiden with flowers, Leda, Medea, Diana
Schefold	1952 (1972)	Persephone or Europa, Leda, Medea, Penelope
Maiuri	1953	Primavera, Leda, Medea, Diana
Elia	1957	Flora, Leda, Medea, Diana
Schefold	1957	A Season, Leda, Medea, Penelope?
Robertson	1975	Persephone, Leda, Iphigenia, Penelope
Allroggen-Bedel	1977	Spring, Leda, Medea, Penelope
Allroggen-Bedel	2001	Persephone, Leda, Medea, Penelope
Mastroroberto	2001	Flora, Leda, Medea, Diana

for his emphasis on the programmatic intention and semantic unity of Roman paint-ing led him to seek a conceptual link that might tie these four panels together into a coherent statement.[37]

According to Schefold, Roman pictorial ensembles use the same structural prin-ciples as first-century Latin poetry; through an orderly game of similarities and oppositions, the pendants on the walls of Roman houses conveyed a larger meaning. Schefold applies this method to the Four Women from Stabiae. Seeing the works as demonstrating the late-third-style preference for themes of love and deification, he interprets the paintings as two maidens seduced by gods and two mortal women, who, having suffered for love, ultimately find happiness. *Flora* represents either Persephone or Europa, both abducted while picking flowers. Given the presence of Leda in this set, Schefold prefers the identification with Europa, which would neatly cast the green-ground pair as two loves of Jupiter.[38] For Schefold, the painter's reduction of narra-tive to static, pregnant moments emphasizes the sublime transport experienced by the god's beloved. Likewise, the solemn, sculptural style of *Medea* and *Penelope* indicates the sober optimism of these two figures. Schefold admits that seeing Medea as a sym-bol of how great good may come from great suffering can seem strange to a modern audience. Such a view, however, derives from a first-century notion of Medea, most powerfully expressed in second-century sarcophagi, where she appears as someone who frees herself from the bonds of death to live the true life. Transformed into a ben-eficial goddess associated with the Bona Dea, this new Medea is appropriately depicted by the Villa Arianna artist as vaporous and ethereal.[39]

Similar notions about content and style shape subsequent interpretations of the paintings. Although he does not offer an overarching theme for the series, Martin Robertson constructs two semantic poles for conceptually pairing the images. He sees in the "slow-moving and heavily clad" form of Diana sufficient indication that she must be Penelope, bringing Odysseus's bow to the suitors. Robertson interprets the sword held by Medea as a large key—an attribute fitting for a priestess, possibly Iphigenia, whose unwavering attachment to the memory of her father would resonate with the pendant's elegantly severe depiction of the most faithful of wives. Moreover, his acceptance of Leda and Persephone as the subjects of the other two panels suggests that they might represent two loves of the gods.[40]

Agnes Allroggen-Bedel presents an almost identical set of names, with the excep-tion of Iphigenia, whom she refers to as Medea. Following Schefold's reasoning, she focuses on the figures' grave, self-absorbed appearance as the key to their decipher-ment. Starting with Leda, she argues that all four paintings reduce the heroines' drama to the moment before the actual event: thus Leda gently receives the swan in her arms; Medea contemplates the murder of her children; Penelope fixes her eyes on the weap-ons that will define her fate; and Persephone innocently picks flowers moments before her rape.[41]

Finally, Marisa Mastroroberto returns to the identifications proposed by Olga Elia in 1957, now adopted as the paintings' official titles by the museum.[42] Mastroro-berto, however, couches her attributions within a unifying program around the ideas of femininity and fertility. Flora, Leda, Medea, and Diana share the common thread of motherhood and the related emotions, *dolcezze e dolori*, that have been elaborated and sublimated in these timeless myths. But tying Flora and Diana to this concept requires a more elaborate explanation, and the author—in the style of the Ercolanesi—finds support in ancient literary sources. Flora, she explains, is the force that presides over all that blooms. Citing Ovid (*Fasti* 5.20ff.), Mastroroberto recounts the nymph's role in creating Mars, said to be the son of Juno, who conceived him by touching a flower offered by Flora. Diana, who is most often thought of as the virgin goddess of the hunt, was also the protector of birthing mothers.[43]

At this point, we have come full circle to the literary, erudite explications of *settecento* antiquarians. In fact, as far as the Four Women from Stabiae are concerned, twentieth-century scholars never moved far beyond the *Antichità*. Despite Schefold's attempt to integrate poetry and painting in his study of Roman art, his approach simply recasts the Ercolanesi's thematic model of analysis as it ignores the images' physical setting and how it might have affected the viewers' perceptions. The innovations proposed by later scholars amount simply to a change of names and organizational leitmotifs for the series. This sustained decontextualization of the images is especially striking in the work of Allroggen-Bedel, who published a catalogue raisonné of the Villa Arianna paintings, organizing the images by the findspots recorded by Karl Weber. The persistence of this traditional methodology, in which ancient frescoes are studied as individual panel paintings, remains an enduring legacy of the Ercolanesi. The aura of preciousness attached to the Four Women from Stabiae has also meant that, in order to write about these small, vaguely narrative compositions, scholars have had to read them as mythological paintings. But must they be mythological? And must they represent only one character or concept? Although we can no longer view them through Roman eyes, looking back at the paintings' original context evokes other readings so far obscured by Enlightenment practices.

The Four Women at Villa Arianna

Although excavations of the architectural complex now known as Villa Arianna began in October 1757, it was not until June 1759 that Karl Weber and his team uncovered the section west of the peristyle where the four women were found.[44] The four cubicula, rooms 23 to 26 in Weber's 1760 plan of the villa [FIG. 7], contained some of the most exquisite and famous examples of Roman fresco painting: *The Seller of Cupids*, *Paris and Helen*, and *A Comedy Scene*.[45] From the archaeologist's description, an image emerges of elegantly appointed spaces with a superb selection of paintings. Room 26, the original location of the four women, had an especially rich decor. In addition to a fine mosaic floor, Weber mentions more than eighteen paintings deemed worthy of extraction.[46] Among these fragments were the so-called Chinese pavilion [FIG. 8], a panel with two lions [FIG. 9], and a series of landscapes [FIG. 10].[47]

Even though Weber describes the process of clearing the rooms as being carried out from top to bottom ("de arriba abajo"), he never specifies which paintings came from which wall or their position in relation to one another.[48] Still, patterns emerge from the fragments in Naples that allow us to sketch a general reconstruction of the decoration in room 26. Both the Chinese pavilion with winged figures [FIG. 8] and the fragment with two lions [FIG. 9] must have appeared close to the ceiling, as was customary for architectural motifs. The landscapes and the four women would have been in the middle zone. In a different context their relatively small dimensions might suggest that these were side panels flanking a larger mythological scene. But, in a mature third-style ensemble, such panels often were the principal focus of the painted walls.[49] As with the finds from rooms 24 and 25, the fragments from room 26 suggest that

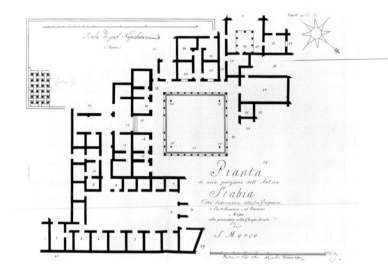

FIGURE 7
Karl Weber (Swiss, 1712–
1764), *Plan of Villa Arianna*,
1760. Engraving. Plate 4
from Michele Ruggiero,
*Degli scavi di Stabia dal
MDCCXLIX al MDCCLXXXII*
(1881). Los Angeles, Research
Library, Getty Research
Institute, DG70.S77 R84
1881.

FIGURE 8
So-Called Chinese Pavilion,
Stabiae, A.D. 10–20.
Wall fragment from room 26,
Villa Arianna. Naples,
Museo archeologico
nazionale, Inv. 9336.

Photo: DAIR neg. 75.1485.

FIGURE 9
Lions, Stabiae, A.D. 10–20.
Wall fragment from room 26,
Villa Arianna. Naples,
Museo archeologico
nazionale, Inv. 9187.

Photo: DAIR neg. 75.1504.

FIGURE 10
Landscape, Stabiae,
A.D. 10–20. Wall fragment
from room 26, Villa Arianna.
Naples, Museo archeologico
nazionale, Inv. 9401.

Photo: DAIR neg. 66.1852.

the four women and the landscapes, like *The Seller of Cupids* and *A Comedy Scene*, appeared amid predominantly white surfaces, attracting the viewer with their brilliant colors.[50] If so, the general composition of the walls in these cubicula in Villa Arianna (A.D. 10–20) may be compared to earlier examples, such as those in the Villa della Farnesina in Rome (ca. 20 B.C.).

The wall paintings from cryptoporticus A in the Villa della Farnesina [FIG. 11] offer a concrete model for reconstructing the arrangement of the panels in room 26. Here, the frescoed walls break into neat sections, reserving the middle zone for the more colorful, framed compositions. Although Weber consistently assigns the red-ground landscapes to room 26, Allroggen-Bedel has argued that they belonged instead to the small hallway connecting the four cubicula.[51] As the Villa della Farnesina example makes clear, however, the landscapes could easily have been integrated into the middle zone alongside the four women. Another example, from the House of the Moralist in Pompeii (3.4.2–3), where landscape paintings appear as framed panels interspersed amid floating women, suggests that this pattern was not uncommon. Like cryptoporticus A, room 26 in Villa Arianna was an enclosed space with limited natural light. In both cases painting the walls white rendered the rooms more luminous and magnified the evanescence of the polychrome figures, especially the unframed images.[52]

Cryptoporticus A exemplifies the transformation of early-empire Roman domestic spaces into *pinacothecae*, private collections of paintings that either reproduced or were inspired by classical Greek and Hellenistic *pinakes* (panel paintings). As Bettina Bergmann has argued, the wall paintings in this space suggest an affinity with outdoor galleries, the essential difference being that, in the Villa della Farnesina, both the masterpieces on the wall and the surrounding architecture are finely executed trompe-l'oeil frescoes. While these panels and their architectural frame were all fictional, the language of display was that of an actual exhibition space;[53] hence the paratactic arrangement of tableaux that invited the viewer to consider one image at a time while moving along this corridor. Rooms 23 to 26 in the Villa Arianna could have formed intercon-

FIGURE 11
Cryptoporticus A. Drawing.
Rome, Villa della Farnesina.

Photo: DAIR neg. 56.1909.

nected exhibition spaces where the dominus and his guests might enjoy the pleasures of cultivated leisure in close proximity to the garden. This collection is an intriguing combination of well-known pieces, such as *A Comedy Scene* and *The Seller of Cupids*, and far less obvious compositions, like the four women in room 26.[54] Having recognized a number of the paintings in the other rooms, viewers conversant with the work of ancient masters would have felt challenged by the puzzling iconography of the Stabiae quartet—their delicacy and ambiguous appearance offering an added thrill to their *otium*.[55]

Stylistic eclecticism also characterizes these domestic, painted collections of art. In cryptoporticus A, for example, an assortment of religious, mythological, and genre scenes, evoking classical and Hellenistic works of art, appears between columns of Egyptian design. Bergmann has interpreted this stylistic mix in Roman frescoed *pinacothecae* as reflecting the collective aspect of the empire.[56] With the artistic treasures of the Greek world available to a wide range of patrons, individuals could now own, copy, and combine them at will. In the case of the Stabiae quartet the figures, both individually and as an ensemble, embody this additive, combinatory aspect of Roman art. As other scholars have discussed, the series breaks down into two sets of pendants: the blue-ground paintings that recall works from the classical period and the green-ground pair that exemplifies a fluid Hellenistic style.[57] Moreover, the women's striking and unique iconography comes from their original recombination of familiar elements.

Although Weber offers few hints as to how these paintings were displayed, it is hard to imagine that the two pairs did not face one another in a physical invitation to compare and contrast them. Besides their stylistic affinity and matching background, *Leda* [FIG. 2] and *Flora* [FIG. 1] were reportedly found together, a fact that further supports the idea that they are a set.[58] Visually, however, there are other clues. The elegant stance of Flora, with her back turned to the viewer and her robes seductively sliding around her body, is the mirror image of Leda, who steps toward the viewer: while one figure attracted viewers with the promise of a bare back; the other rewarded them with a fully exposed torso. Finally, Flora's attributes transformed this visual titillation into an intellectual tease: compared to a seemingly unambiguous swan, the other woman's attribute—whether a cornucopia or a simple basket (*kalathos*)—hardly indicated who she might be.

The other pair played a similar game of semantic hide-and-seek. To the dynamic motion of the first group, *Medea* [FIG. 3] and *Diana* [FIG. 4] present a sober, archaic stillness. Moreover, one woman's profile contrasts with the other's three-quarter view. But, again, the presence of attributes invites further interpretation. The Stabiae *Medea* resembles other Campanian representations of this heroine, where she appears standing and holding a sword.[59] This image would thus have surely elicited comparisons with other examples known in Italy since the late first century B.C. As Allroggen-Bedel shows, however, the Ercolanesi have not been the only ones to be confused by the object held by Medea. Whether the object was a sword, a scepter, or some other instrument, its strange form may well have presented difficulties even to the most skilled Roman interpreter. Nor would the conundrum described in the *Antichità* regarding Diana have been more easily solved by ancient viewers. Although iconographic types representing the goddess in long robes existed, the image of Diana wearing a short chiton was far more familiar. And when the goddess appeared in a long dress, supplementary attributes helped clarify her identity: a quiver, bow and arrow, a torch, a deer, or a small altar.[60]

The desire, however, to see the women's attributes as signs of guaranteed mythological identities may be more of a postantique rather than a Roman preoccupation. *Flora* presents an unusual composition—women with their backs turned to the viewer are not common in ancient art.[61] Therefore, this painting would certainly have drawn attention for its rarity, while its placement within a series might have stimulated the interpretive processes described by Schefold. The idea that these women might represent the loves of Jupiter would have placed the viewer in an empowered, voyeuristic position. But would the women's attributes necessarily have triggered a search for mythological identifications? Perhaps they were seen as more general personifications: flora and fauna; the art of hunting and the art of combat; the bounty of nature and the weapons of civilization. Given the cubiculum's view onto the peristyle, the paintings, especially *Flora*, would have inspired connections between indoor and outdoor pleasures, reiterating pictorially the activities and delights of the villa. None of these readings, however, need be mutually exclusive. Unlike later fourth-style ensembles, where the central mythological tableaux lend a more defined thematic structure to the decoration, the paintings in room 26 left interpretive possibilities open. The viewer could choose how to make sense of these images, which were designed to intrigue.

Within the larger ensemble of room 26, the Four Women from Stabiae were part of a multimedia creation that expressed the house-owner's wealth and sophistication. This complex assemblage of architecture, painting, and mosaic transported viewers to a realm of refined fantasy, where the artistic glories of Greece had been collected for their enjoyment. Transport might, in fact, be the key metaphor of this space. From the remaining fragments we see that the winged women hovering near the ceiling [see FIG. 8] echoed the quartet's ethereal look. Lower down, the idyllic landscapes gave transcendence a more earthbound meaning: echoing the room's constructed view of the garden and other planned panoramas in the villa, the paintings offered bucolic images of places that existed only as triggers for leisurely daydreaming. Looking at paintings in a Roman private gallery was often an interactive endeavor. In the amicably agonistic setting of a learned discussion, a fitting pastime for the villa's splendid grounds, the Four Women from Stabiae offered rich fare for Roman minds. The interpretations they once inspired before being buried by Vesuvius's fatal eruption would probably have left even the Ercolanesi and their descendants speechless.

Notes

I would like to thank Victoria Coates and Jon Seydl for their guidance as editors. For their helpful comments, I am grateful to Bettina Bergmann, Richard Brilliant, Nina Dubin, Ann Giletti, Natalie Kampen, Barbara Kellum, Jessica Maier, Rebecca Molholt, Shilpa Prasad, and Terri Weissman. I must also thank the Department of Classics at Columbia University for generously funding the acquisition of photographs for this essay and the Center for Advanced Study in the Visual Arts at the National Gallery of Art for their support throughout this project. All mistakes and misinterpretations are, of course, my own.

[1]   Johann Joachim Winckelmann, *Sendschreiben von den herculanischen Entdeckungen*, Studien zur deutschen Kunstgeschichte 338 (Baden Baden, 1964), 30. In his letter Winckelmann refers to the well-known vignettes of dancers and centaurs from the so-called Villa di Cicerone in Pompeii. But as Agnes Allroggen-Bedel has observed, his words could also be applied to the paintings from Stabiae. See Agnes Allroggen-Bedel, "Gli affreschi delle ville di Stabiae," in *Stabiae — dai Borbone alle ultime scoperte*, ed. Domenico Camardo and Antonio Ferrara (Naples, 2001), 53.

[2]   Agnes Allroggen-Bedel, "Gli scavi borbonici nelle Ville Stabiane: Pitture antiche e gusto settecentesco," in *Stabiae: Storia e architettura — 250 anniversario degli scavi di Stabiae, 1749–1999. Convegno internazionale, Castellammare di Stabia, 25–27 Marzo 2000* (Rome, 2002), 102–7. See also Paola D'Alconzo, *Picturae excisae: Conservazione e restauro dei dipinti ercolanesi e pompeiani tra XVIII e XIX secolo* (Rome, 2002), 15–45; Peter Werner, *Pompeji und die Wanddekoration der Goethezeit* (Munich, 1970). The dates for the second, third, and fourth styles of Roman wall painting are as follows: second style, ca. 80 B.C.–10 B.C.; third style, ca. 10 B.C.–50 A.D.; fourth style, 50 A.D.–79 A.D.

[3]   Ellen Schwinzer has written the only book dedicated to the study of floating figures. But because she concentrates solely on this genre, focusing on issues of iconography and typology, her work has not bridged the methodological gap between the study of vignettes and that of central narrative panels. See Ellen Schwinzer, *Schwebende Gruppen in der pompejanischen Wandmalerei* (Würzburg, 1979).

[4]   Mary Lee Thompson, "The Monumental and Literary Evidence for Programmatic Painting in Antiquity," *Marsyas* 9 (1961): 36–77; Karl Schefold, *La peinture pompéienne: Essai sur l'évolution de sa signification*, trans. Jean-Michel Croisille (Brussels, 1972); Richard Brilliant, *Visual Narratives: Storytelling in Etruscan and Roman Art* (Ithaca, 1984), 53–89; Bettina Bergmann, "Rhythms of Recognition: Mythological Encounters in Roman Landscape Painting," in *Im Spiegel des Mythos: Bilderwelt und Lebenswelt* (Wiesbaden, 1999), 81–108; idem, "The Pregnant Moment: Tragic Wives in the Roman Interior," *Sexuality in Ancient Art*, ed. Natalie B. Kampen (Cambridge, 1996), 199–21; idem, "The Roman House as Memory Theater: The House of the Tragic Poet in Pompeii," *Art Bulletin* 76, no. 2 (1994): 223–56. For a detailed description of the eighteenth-century process of extraction and preparation for display of ancient Roman frescoes, see D'Alconzo 2002 (note 2).

[5]   On the discovery of Villa Arianna and of the Four Women from Stabiae, see Karl Weber's excavation reports published in Michele Ruggiero, *Degli scavi di Stabia dal MDCCXLIX al MDCCLXXXII: Notizie raccolte e pubblicate da Michele Ruggiero* (Naples, 1881), 3, 63, 96–101.

6   On Karl Weber, see Christopher Charles Parslow, *Rediscovering Antiquity: Karl Weber and the Excavation of Herculaneum, Pompeii, and Stabiae* (Cambridge, 1995). For the development of historical methods in the eighteenth and nineteenth centuries, see Arnaldo Momigliano, "Ancient History and the Antiquarian," *Journal of the Warburg and Courtauld Institutes* 13 (1950): 285–315; and Parslow 1995, 159–97.

7   The frescoes from the section of Villa Arianna where the four women were found are dated to the late Augustan–early Tiberian period (A.D. 10–20). See Allroggen-Bedel 2001 (note 1), 55; Schefold 1972 (note 4), 165. See also Agnes Allroggen-Bedel, "Die Wandmalereien aus der Villa in Campo Varano (Castellammare di Stabia)," *Mitteilungen des deutschen archäologischen Instituts, römische Abteilung* 84 (1977): 27–89. The Villa della Farnesina is dated circa 20 B.C.

8   For the view that the Four Women from Stabiae are copies of Hellenistic works of art, see Allroggen-Bedel 1977 (note 7), 44; Martin Robertson, *A History of Greek Art* (Cambridge, 1975), 575. For a discussion of stylistic eclecticism in early imperial art and the culture of *aemulatio* among Roman artists, see Bettina Bergmann, "Greek Masterpieces and Roman Recreative Fictions," *Harvard Studies in Classical Philology* 97 (1995): 79–120.

9   Fausto Zevi, "Gli scavi di Ercolano," in *Civiltà del '700 a Napoli, 1734–1799* (Florence, 1980), 2:64.

10 See Agnes Allroggen-Bedel and Helke Kammerer-Grothaus, "Il Museo ercolanese di Portici," *Cronache ercolanesi* 13, suppl. 2, *La Villa dei Papiri* (1983): 98; Zevi 1980 (note 9), 60, 64–67. The contemporary reaction to the publication of the *Antichità* is well captured in a November 3, 1760, letter by Ferdinando Galiani to Bernardo Tanucci: "Mi creda, il piú gran castigo di Dio che possa avere chi sta servendo i Re in paesi esteri è questo santo libro che non si vende. La molestia è continua." See *Opera di Ferdinando Galiani*, ed. Furio Diaz and Luciano Guerci (Milan, 1958), 855. On the designers and engravers hired to illustrate the *Antichità* and the high rates charged by these artists, see Ulrico Pannuti, "Incisori e disegnatori della stamperia reale di Napoli nel secolo XVIII: La pubblicazione *Delle antichità di Ercolano*," *Xenia antiqua* 9 (2000): 151–78.

11 Zevi 1980 (note 9), 63ff; Fausto Zevi, "Gli scavi di Ercolano e *Le antichità*," in *Le antichità di Ercolano* (Naples, 1988), 29ff. See also Ferdinando Bologna, "Le scoperte di Ercolano e Pompei nella cultura europea del XVIII secolo," *La parola del passato* 34 (1979): 377–404; idem, "La riscoperta di Ercolano e la cultura artistica del settecento europeo," in *Antichità di Ercolano* (Naples, 1988), 81–105.

12 On their choice of beginning the publication of the *Antichità* with a volume on ancient paintings, see the Ercolanesi's preface to volume 1: "Questo tesoro di cui è stato avvisato il Pubblico col *Catalogo*, si apre ora, e si comunica a tutti co' Rami. Si è cominciato dalle Pitture: queste, che con l'invidia de' più illustri Musei, erano con maggior impazienza dalla curiosità degli Eruditi aspettate." After four volumes on painting, in 1767, the Ercolanesi published the first volume of the *Antichità* dedicated to bronze busts. Another volume on bronze statues came out in 1771. After the frescoes, the bronzes ranked second in importance since other collections either had only a few works in this material or lacked them entirely. In 1779, another volume of paintings was published. Finally, in 1792, came a volume on lamps and candelabra. See Allroggen-Bedel and Kammerer-Grothaus 1983 (note 10), 98.

13 The Ercolanesi themselves were aware of the importance of the Campanian finds for the study of ancient painting: "La negligenza altrui nel conservare quelle poche [pitture], che si erano di tempo in tempo trovate prima, rende più interessante questa parte dell'Opera, che si dà fuora. Si apprenderà da essa molto più di quanto per altri lumi si è saputo finora della Pittura degli Antichi." The painted ceilings of Nero's Domus Aurea, discovered circa 1480, though greatly admired and frequently copied, were allowed to deteriorate in the fifteenth century without scientific study having been carried out. Pirro Ligorio also reports finding ancient *grotteschi* at other sites in and around Rome, but few drawings of these paintings survive. The well-known Aldobrandini Wedding, found in Rome in 1604 or 1605, was heavily restored on its relocation to

the Villa Aldobrandini and did not spur the kind of scholarly inquiry ignited by the discovery of the ancient cities on the Bay of Naples. See Nicole Dacos, *La découverte de la Domus Aurea et la formation des grotesques à la Renaissance* (London, 1969); D'Alconzo 2002 (note 2), 18, 37; Hetty Joyce, "Grasping at Shadows: Ancient Paintings in Renaissance and Baroque Rome," *Art Bulletin* 74, no. 2 (1992): 219–46.

14   *Le lettere di Luigi Vanvitelli della Biblioteca palatina di Caserta*, ed. Franco Strazzullo (Galatina, 1976), 1:577 (cited in Allroggen-Bedel and Kammerer-Grothaus 1983 [note 10], 99). According to D'Alconzo, drawings were made of all the paintings taken to Portici—even if only a selected few were later included in the *Antichità*. In 1765 the practice of drawing the paintings within the fabric of the walls in which they originally appeared became standard. See D'Alconzo 2002 (note 2), 45; Allroggen-Bedel and Kammerer-Grothaus 1983 (note 10), 98; and Giuseppe Fiorelli, *Pompeianarum antiquatum historia* (Naples, 1860), 1:168.

15   "Tutti i diversi gusti del dipingere, di cui si resta memoria ne' libri, si potranno qui riconoscere. Ogni Volume conterrà parte di tutti i diversi generi delle pitture, che finora si son raccolte, e si continuerà così nelle altre, che di mano in mano si anderanno a scavare" (*Delle antichità di Ercolano* [Naples, 1757], 1: preface). See also "Alcune osservazione," ibid., 1:277–78.

16   "Tra i quattro *Monocromi* sopra marmo, perfetissimi nel genere loro, e per la singolarità inestimabili, i quali, nel pubblicarsi le Pitture del Museo Reale, si è creduto esser proprio che a tutte predecessero" (ibid., 1:1).

17   Ibid., 1:24n. 20. See also plate 8, where the painting of Chiron and Achilles is set above two "unrelated" tondi, labeled "Baccanti." On page 65, the Ercolanesi state that the charming landscape on plate 12, alongside an image of Iphigenia and Orestes, is worthy of admiration but not of explanation. On their use of landscapes and still life as *testate* and *finali*, see "Alcune osservazione" 1757 (note 15), 1:278–79. For the practice of including vignettes with the mythological panels, see D'Alconzo 2002 (note 2), 36.

18   On definitions of the tableau in the seventeenth and eighteenth centuries, see Thomas Puttfarken, *The Discovery of Pictorial Composition: Theories of Visual Order in Painting* (New Haven, 2000), 229–43, 263–99; Victor I. Stoichita, *The Self-Aware Image: An Insight into Early Modern Meta-painting*, trans. Anne-Marie Glasheen (Cambridge, 1997), xii–xv.

19   *Antichità* 1757 (note 15), 1:93.

20   On the dancers from Cicero's villa, see ibid. On Paris and Helen (identified as Penelope and Odysseus by the Ercolanesi) and *The Seller of Cupids*, see *Delle antichità di Ercolano* (Naples, 1762), 3: pls. 6–7, 33ff.; Ruggiero 1881 (note 5), 92, 95, 148; Allroggen-Bedel 1977 (note 7), 36, 39. On the afterlife of *The Seller of Cupids* in eighteenth- and nineteenth-century art, see Gina Carla Ascione, "*Wer kauft Liebesgötter?* La fortuna in Europa di un tema stabiano fra rococò e neoclassicismo," in *In Stabiano: Cultura e archeologia da Stabiae, la città e il territorio tra l'età arcaica e l'età romana* (Castellammare di Stabia, 2001), 41–44.

21   *Antichità* 1762 (note 20), 3:43–47.

22   Ibid., 3:51–52.

23   At this point the section on "minor" paintings begins in volume 3. Starting with plate 16, one finds two Nereids from Villa Arianna, a Europa from Herculaneum, another sample of dancers and satyrs from Cicero's villa, and a closing selection of architectural motifs.

24   "Te agradezco lo que me dizes que avias ejecutado de hir el domingo despues de la audiencia a Portici y todo lo que distintamente me dizes que avias visto y ejecutado, y todas las ordenes que avias dado, . . . *pero de lo que deseo que los dibujos que aya de las pinturas sean tales quales ellas son, y enmiendas*" (italics added), letter dated August 5, 1760. Reprinted in *Carlos III: Cartas a Tanucci (1759–1763)*, ed. Maximiliano Barrio (Madrid, 1988), 149–52 (cited in D'Alconzo 2002 [note 2], 36). The Ercolanesi themselves insist that the images reproduced in *Antichità* are "faithfully drawn and incised" (*Antichità* 1757 [note 15], 1:273).

²⁵ The same philological zeal was not, however, applied to the reproductions of sculptures in later volumes of the *Antichità*—a practice much criticized by academics outside Italy, among them Jean-Jacques Barthélémy. See his *Voyage en Italie imprimé sur les lettres originales écrites au comte de Caylus* (Paris, 1801), 356. See also D'Alconzo 2002 (note 2), 35ff.; Zevi 1988 (note 11), 24ff.

²⁶ That the small flaws in the painting were already visible in the eighteenth century is clear from Weber's excavation report. See Ruggiero 1881 (note 5), 97. The eighteenth-century illustrators have also omitted the gold-bead earring on Flora's right earlobe. This practice of gently touching up the paintings was carried out consistently in representations of the Stabiae quartet. For a description of the details missing from the images in the *Antichità*, see Wolfgang Helbig, *Wandgemälde der vom Vesuv verschütteten Städte Campaniens* (Leipzig, 1868), 67–68, 271–72.

²⁷ According to the Ercolanesi, the brief explanations accompanying each illustration were intended to spur the reader to reflection, while notes were meant to "relieve the effort of those content to follow [the scholars'] thoughts": "Le brevissime spiegazioni, che accompagnano i Rami, han per oggetto il risvegliare alla riflessione i Lettori, che vogliano da loro stessi esaminar le cose: le Note alleviaranno la fatica di chi si contenti de' nostri pensieri" (*Antichità* 1757 [note 15], 1: preface). See also 273: "Non fu da prima nostro pensiero il dar giudizio sul merito delle pitture del Museo Reale: credendo che bastasse presentarle al Pubblico disegnate ed incise fedelmente, con dire al più qualche parola sulla conservazione e sul colorito, per porre ognuno nello stato di esaminarle da se."

²⁸ *Antichità* 1762 (note 20), 3:25 (my translation).

²⁹ Ibid., 3:25–27nn. 3–9. In addition to Aristotle, Ovid, and Pliny, the notes also refer to Apuleius, Athenaeus, Callimachus, Catullus, Diodorus Siculus, Hyginus, Lactantius, Pausanias, and Servius.

³⁰ On Leda, see Lilly Kahil, "Leda," in *Lexicon iconographicum mythologiae classicae* (Zurich, 1992), 6:231; Pierre Grimal, *Dictionary of Classical Mythology*, trans. A. R. Maxwell-Hyslop (Oxford, 1985), 254–55.

³¹ *Antichità* 1762 (note 20), 3:43–44.

³² Ibid., 3:47–48. For Nemesis as the mother of Helen, see Davies *Epicorum graecorum fragmenta* F 7; Sappho fr. 166 Voigt; Apollodorus *Bibliotheca* 3 [127].10.7; Hyginus *Astronomica* 2, 8; Athenaeus 2.3.673a; Pausanias 1.33.7; and Pliny the Elder *Natural History* 36.17. Of these authors, Pausanias and Hyginus are mentioned by the Ercolanesi.

³³ By the late fourth century B.C., Leda was already associated with the swan, as the images on an Apulian vase, now in the J. Paul Getty Museum (86.AE.680), and in the *Lexicon iconographicum mythologiae classicae* 1992 (note 30), 6:233, no. 17, make clear. The heroine with her feathery lover is unmistakably identified by an inscription as Leda. It is possible that Euripides, who refers to Leda as Helen's mother (*Hel.* 16–22; *Iph. A.* 794–800), contributed to popularizing this version of the myth. Later, in the first century A.D., Ovid includes Leda and the swan as one of the loves of Jupiter depicted in Arachne's tapestry (*Met.* 6.109). Given the influence of these authors on the shaping of popular perceptions of ancient myths, it is difficult to imagine that a Pompeian audience, for whom the paintings discussed by the Ercolanesi were originally made, would have identified a woman with swans as anyone other than Leda. For ancient iconographic types representing Nemesis, see Pascale Linant De Bellefonds, "Nemesis," in *Lexicon iconographicum mythologiae classicae* 1992 (note 30), 6:733–73.

³⁴ *Antichità* 1762 (note 20), 3:51–52.

³⁵ Ibid., 3:52n. 7. See also *Antichità* 1757 (note 15), 1: pl. 13. This painting, from the Herculaneum basilica, is now identified as Medea (Naples, Museo archeologico nazionale, Inv. 8976). See Margot Schmidt, "Medeia," in *Lexicon iconographicum mythologiae classicae* 1992 (note 30), 6:388, no. 11.

³⁶ *Antichità* 1762 (note 20), 3:69–70. For identification of this figure as Diana, see ibid., 69n. 3, where Callimachus's *Hymn to Diana* and Pindar's *Pythian* 2.16 are presented as the primary

textual supports for this theory. In reference to Atalanta, the Ercolanesi cite Oppian *De Venat* 2.26, and Pliny the Elder *Natural History* 35.3 (*Antichità* 1762 [note 20], 3:69–70nn. 4, 7–8). For Venus, see ibid., 3:70n. 10, where, in addition to the *Homeric Hymn to Aphrodite*, the Ercolanesi cite *Anthology* 4.12.Ep.21.

37   Karl Schefold, *Pompejanische Malerei: Sinn und Ideengeschichte* (Basel, 1952); Schefold 1972 (note 4).

38   Schefold 1972 (note 4), 44–53, 128–32. Martin Robertson includes the Stabiae painting in his catalogue of representations of Europa for *Lexicon iconographicum mythologiae classicae* (Zurich, 1988), 4:89, no. 224. He does, however, call the attribution "doubtful."

39   Schefold 1972 (note 4), 163–67.

40   Robertson 1975 (note 8), 575. His interpretation of Medea's sword derives from Salomon Reinach, *Répertoire de peintures grecques et romaines* (Paris, 1922), 231, fig. 6.

41   Allroggen-Bedel 2001 (note 1), 55. This set of interpretations reflects a slight modification from Allroggen-Bedel's previous attributions, where instead of "Persephone" one finds "Spring." See Allroggen-Bedel 1977 (note 7), 44; see also herein table 1.

42   Marisa Mastroroberto, "Villa Arianna: Affreschi," in *In Stabiano* 2001 (note 20), 129; Olga Elia, *Pitture di Stabia* (Naples, 1957), 68; see also herein table 1.

43   As Mastroroberto points out, it was in this aspect as goddess of fecundity and guardian of the young that Diana was worshiped at the sanctuary in Ariccia, near Lake Nemi (Tacitus *Hist.* 3, 36). Mastroroberto 2001 (note 42), 129.

44   Parslow 1995 (note 6), 45–56, 177ff.

45   *The Seller of Cupids* (Naples, Museo archeologico nazionale, Inv. 9180) was found in room 25; *Paris and Helen* (Naples, Museo archeologico nazionale, Inv. 8982) and *A Comedy Scene*, in room 24. The four women were found in room 26. See Ruggiero 1881 (note 5), 93ff.; Allroggen-Bedel 1977 (note 7), 36–46; Allroggen-Bedel 2001 (note 1), 55.

46   Ruggiero 1881 (note 5), 96–102.

47   Ibid., "Masseria Iraci," pl. 4.

48   Ibid., 99–100.

49   The present dimensions, height by width, of the paintings (Naples, Museo archeologico nazionale): *Flora*, 38 × 32 cm (Inv. 8834); *Leda*, 44 × 32 cm (Inv. 9456); *Medea*, 38 × 26 cm (Inv. 8978); *Diana*, 37 × 27 cm. (Inv. 9243); *Landscape*, 19 × 33 cm (Inv. 9403); *Landscape*, 19 × 33 cm (Inv. 9459); *Landscape*, 22 × 33 cm (Inv. 9397); *Landscape*, 24 × 31 cm (Inv. 9396); *Landscape*, 20 × 33 cm (Inv. 9401); *Landscape*, 19 × 30 cm (Inv. 9402); *Landscape*, 24 × 36 cm (Inv. 9407); *Landscape*, 26 × 40 cm (Inv. 9405); *Landscape*, 20 × 38 cm (Inv. 9398); *The Seller of Cupids*, 23 × 29 cm (Inv. 9180); *A Comedy Scene*, 29 × 38 cm. For the location of the *A Comedy Scene*, see Allroggen-Bedel 2001 (note 1), 55; Allroggen-Bedel 1977 (note 7), 45.

50   Allroggen-Bedel 1977 (note 7), 31–47.

51   Ibid., 45.

52   *La Villa della Farnesina in Palazzo Massimo alle Terme*, ed. Maria Rita Sanzi Di Mino (Rome, 1998), 33.

53   Bergmann 1995 (note 8), 98–102, 105.

54   The popularity of *A Comedy Scene* is attested by the existence of a mosaic from the Villa di Cicerone in Pompeii (Naples, Museo archeologico nazionale, Inv. 9985) that represents the identical composition as the painting from Villa Arianna (Naples, Museo archeologico nazionale, Inv. 9034). *The Seller of Cupids* lacks as exact a copy. A painting from the House of the Colored Capitals in Pompeii and a third-century mosaic from Antioch, however, are related composi-

tions that, in the words of Doro Levi, are "strongly imprinted by the idyllic and epigrammatic spirit of Hellenistic poetry and art." According to him, *The Peddler of Erotes* has its origins in a poem by Moschus, later reworked by Meleager of Gadara. See Doro Levi, *Antioch Mosaic Pavements* (Princeton, 1947), 1:191–95.

55   On the pleasure of Roman viewers in iconographic variations and multiples, see Elizabeth Bartman, "Sculptural Collecting and Display in the Private Realm," in *Roman Art in the Private Sphere*, ed. Elaine Gazda (Ann Arbor, 1991), 71–88; Bergmann 1995 (note 8), 81, 97–98.

56   Bergmann 1995 (note 8), 106.

57   Elia 1957 (note 42), 68; Robertson 1975 (note 8), 575; Mastroroberto 2001 (note 42), 129.

58   Ruggiero 1881 (note 5), 97.

59   Compare *Medea* from the House of the Dioscuri, Pompeii (Naples, Museo archeologico nazionale, Inv. 8977), and *Medea* from Herculaneum (Naples, Museo archeologico nazionale, Inv. 8976). See also herein note 33.

60   For a full discussion of the iconography of Diana, see Erika Simon and Gerhard Bauchhenss, "Artemis/Diana," in *Lexicon iconographicum mythologiae classicae* (Zurich, 1984), 2:792–855. For Diana in a long robe, see ibid., nos. 5, 9–15, 45, 48, 191–208, 216–34. The painting from Stabiae does not appear in their list of representations of the goddess nor is a comparison with extant images of Penelope especially enlightening. No images of Odysseus's wife carrying his bow are known from antiquity (see Christoph Hausmann, "Penelope," in *Lexicon iconographicum mythologiae classicae* [Zurich, 1994], 7:291–95).

61   One thinks of the Three Graces and of a few heroines, such as Daphne. A close parallel to *Flora* can be found in a figure from House 7.2.6 in Pompeii, which is usually identified as a "Season." See Ludwig Curtius, *Die Wandmalerei Pompejis: Eine Einführung in ihr Verständnis* (Hildersheim, 1960), fig. 220.

Hearing Voices:
The Herculaneum Papyri
and Classical Scholarship

James I. Porter

From the ruins of Herculaneum we turn our anxious eyes to far-distant scenes.

William Drummond and Robert Walpole, *Herculanensia* (1810)

UCH OF THIS VOLUME addresses itself to the direct glimpse of a recovered antiquity that the excavations at Pompeii and Herculaneum promised to give the world in the mid-eighteenth century. This response to the past is a natural one and is summed up in a recent account of the discoveries, which proved to be as powerful as they were owing to the opportunities for identification they entailed: "What caught the imagination more than any individual object was the sense that here whole cities lay buried; that here for the first time you could experience how it might feel to look around the ancient world."[1] What I want to focus on in the present chapter, less by way of contrast than by way of complement, is what happens at the site of contact, when the eye meets its object: Why is it that the object can never be taken in directly in an unmediated form? And why is it that the eye so often recoils before its objects? How does it negotiate its field of vision, framing and filtering what it sees? One of the great virtues of dealing with papyri is that they help us view documents of classical antiquity as objects and not only as texts. As we shall see, the papyri found at Herculaneum are no exception, and if anything they are an object lesson in the identificatory processes of classicism.

It is a remarkable but easily forgotten fact that classical objects do not surface from the ground with little labels attached to them that read, "I am classical," like the famous eighth-century B.C. cup from Pithecusae inscribed with the seductively misleading tag "I am the cup of Nestor." The reason they do not is simple: no object is intrinsically or even formally classical. Classicism—the classical ideology that took shape during Winckelmann's generation (although there are clear precedents in Greek and Roman antiquity)—is a product of the struggle over what counts as classical, and consensus is rather rarer than our handbooks let on. By *classicism* we may understand the reverence for the value and heritage of the cultures and civilizations of classical Greece and Rome and their prolongation in various forms, whether through imitation, revival, adaptation, enshrinement (most often, in museums), and so on.[2] Because classicism is bound up with a presumption about what it is to be classical, the coherence of classicism hinges on the coherence of what is claimed as classical—and those claims prove rather fragile. As we shall see, not all antiquity was always considered "classical," even when it was recognized to be antique. If this is right, then what ought to be of interest to us are the ways in which objects get classified as classical— what permits their classicism to take hold of them, and then of us. Now, it ought to be understood, but it rarely is, that classical antiquity is full of surprises and uncertainties: it never ceases to astonish, to seem strange, and to fall disobediently out of its expected frames of reference and understanding. Is classicism a way of perceiving these surprises or is it a way of preventing them from happening, a way of containing these and other uncertainties? If classicism is the latter, then this raises a troubling prospect. Is an unmediated view of antiquity not only never possible but also something never really desired?

These questions could take us well beyond the confines of the present volume, but they are of special importance for the library of Herculaneum, the discovery and subsequent appropriation of which provide a case study in lofty expectations and their being dashed and reversed.[3] The Herculanean library has had this polarizing effect on modern observers for a few different reasons. These have to do with the incoherencies that are native to the classical ideal and with the intractability—the native resistance, if you like—of classical materials, which comes in the first instance simply from their never ceasing to be physical objects (as is true, surprisingly, of the parallel case of the Parthenon marbles and as was also true of the paintings discovered at Herculaneum and at Pompeii) but also, in the case at hand, from the particulars of the library's unusual contents.[4] One outstanding peculiarity of the library of Herculaneum is that most of its holdings are stamped by the ancient philosophical school of Epicurus, a tightly controlled sect that was first established in Athens early in the third century B.C. and then later spread its gospel to Rome, where it attracted followers among the educated elite. Epicureanism offered a compelling alternative to the chaos of political turmoil and the stress of urban existence: psychological hedonism and the promise of simple pleasures. It did so on the foundations of an alienating atomistic physical hypothesis: the belief that the universe was in essence composed of atoms and void. Here, eighteenth-century classicism found itself doubly challenged, facing not only strange bits of matter (charred papyrus rolls) but also—what was in ways worse for a world reared on classical idealism—exponents of philosophical materialism.[5] The question that naturally arises is what happens when the empiricism, but also the materialism, of the archaeological gaze—the classical or classicizing gaze—falls not just on the material remains of antiquity but also on ancient materialism. That, in a nutshell, is what the present paper is about.

"The wreck of Herculanean lore"

Let us begin by quoting a contemporary reaction in verse to the discovery of books at Herculaneum:

> O ye, who patiently explore
> The wreck of Herculanean lore,
> What rapture! could ye seize
> Some Theban fragment, or unroll
> One precious, tender-hearted, scroll
> Of pure Simonides.
>
> That were, indeed, a genuine birth
> Of poesy; a bursting forth
> Of genius from the dust:
> What Horace gloried to behold,
> What Maro loved, shall we enfold?
> Can haughty Time be just![6]

The expectations voiced by William Wordsworth in 1819 were shared by an entire generation that had been exposed to the discovery and gradual unrolling of the papyri found at Herculaneum between 1752 and 1754. At first tossed aside because of their sorry condition—they were carbonized and resembled lumps of black coal or burnt wood [FIG. 1]—and only later discovered to contain traces of writing [FIG. 2], the papyri were unearthed by Bourbon excavators tunneling at different locations through the buried remains of what became known as the Villa dei Papiri, later (with less justification) dubbed the library of Philodemus. Approximately two thousand papyrus rolls were discovered on the site, in different locations and in whatever spot they happened to occupy when the lava of Vesuvius submerged the town in A.D. 79.

Wordsworth's hopes for recovering pure poets from the Greek and Roman past were thoroughly in line with classical paradigms. But Herculaneum does not appear to obey the rules of classicism, and the poem expresses this fact in the form of an unfulfilled wish that is ambiguously tinged with conditional despair: "What rapture!

could ye seize . . . That were, indeed, a genuine birth of poesy." The poet's excitement, his expectations, and his frustration remain as valid today as they were in 1819. No new Theban fragments of Pindar have been found and no Simonides either. In their place something far less satisfying was found: a library of mostly Greek philosophical writings evidently formed by the tastes of an Epicurean but also of a rather unglamorous sort—no lost dialogues of Aristotle, let alone any pre-Socratic treatises, but instead several hundred titles, the bulk of them the writings of an obscure professional philosopher, Philodemus of Gadara, who was active in Italy in the first half of the last century B.C. and whose works tend (like those of many professional academics) to be tedious, polemical, and unstylish in the extreme. As the papyri were gradually and painstakingly unrolled and deciphered over the next centuries, scholars and other enthusiasts of antiquity learned to adjust to a postclassical, if not unclassical, archive. Tremors of excitement were felt whenever a snatch of Ennius or Virgil or, failing that, Lucretius or even Caecilius Statius was detected. The mere mention of some classical great personage, at times forced on the texts by overexcited editors, worked in much the same way to validate the findings that in other respects were anything but glamorous. Today, the fervent hopes of finding another library with a complete run of Latin classics are a symptom of this same desire.[7]

In what follows, I will trace three different aspects of this problem. Let us call these three aspects "objects," because that is how they come to be reified by the gaze of classical scholarship. First, there are the connections between the villa and Philodemus, which are hardly straightforward. Second, a shift takes place if one turns away from Philodemus as a source of interest in his own right and instead looks at him as an object of philological scrutiny or of philosophical reconstruction and as a source of information about other developments in antiquity (which we can best glean from looking at his opponents). Third, an irony of recuperation happens when Epicureanism oddly becomes embedded again in the classical ideal. These three aspects will all require a certain amount of unfolding in what follows. And because Herculaneum will prove to be an object lesson in how classical scholarship in its very methods negotiates with the unwieldy idea and ideal of the "classical," my approach will necessarily raise questions with larger implications, such as: what are the aesthetic biases of classical scholarship? and, can scholarship itself be classicizing? The story of the Herculaneum papyri contains many surprises and ironies in this regard. But first a few more details about the process by which the original discoveries were made known and integrated into a hypothetical picture of Herculaneum's antiquity will be needed.

The first attempt at recuperation sought (and still seeks) to anchor the villa in late Roman republican politics and culture, which is to say the bulk of the last century B.C. down to the reign of Augustus (27 B.C.). The standard view of the villa was already in place in the eighteenth century: L. Calpurnius Piso Caesoninus, who was connected to the family of Julius Caesar and was consul in A.D. 58, owned the villa; and Piso was the patron of Philodemus of Gadara, an Epicurean schooled in Athens but living in Italy and consorting with Roman elites and intellectuals who gathered at the Bay of Naples to indulge their sympathies for Epicureanism (this group would have included Virgil and Horace, who are imagined to have visited with Philodemus in Herculaneum).[8] Accordingly the library in Herculaneum must represent Philodemus's private workshop, where he prepared his writings for private circulation and teaching. All aspects of the villa's finds (architectural, sculptural, and inscriptional) have since been marshaled to flesh out this picture, often ingeniously and sometimes fantastically. And although alternative reconstructions of the evidence have been put forward, most scholars have accepted this picture in its outlines as a highly probable interpretation of the villa.[9]

That said, the consensus view is more than simply fragile: it has little to stand on at all. Most of this picture is wishful, and the key evidence is almost entirely circumstantial. Piso's ownership of the villa and his links to Virgil and Horace are a mere speculation. (Some half-dozen candidates have been plausibly put forward as the villa's owner.)[10] A dedication to a certain Piso in one work by Philodemus, *On the Good King according to Homer*, in itself establishes nothing, any more than does Cicero's mention, in his *Against Piso*, of Piso's association with Philodemus.[11] When the library was formed, and where, is anybody's guess—and the options for chronology run down to as late as A.D. 79 when Vesuvius erupted. In a word, the library could easily postdate Philodemus's *floruit* by as much as a century. These last points need to be developed.

Philodemus's last preserved work dates from around 40 B.C. While a handful of the papyri date to Epicurus's lifetime, including his opus maximum, *On Nature*, the last hand in the papyri from Herculaneum dates from the end of the first century B.C. or the early part of the next century, which, in one view, attests to later accessions.[12] But no titles postdate Philodemus, and Vesuvius would not erupt for another sixty to a hundred years. Accordingly, the accessions represent either copies of earlier Epicurean writers, including Epicurus, or copies of Philodemus's own writings on the history of his school and the earlier history of philosophy.[13] In other words, no fewer than eight decades can have passed between the formation of the collection and the eruption of Vesuvius. When was the collection actually formed? It may have existed only at a later date, say at some point after Philodemus's death in around 35 B.C. and until A.D. 79. Or it can have existed during or after Philodemus's lifetime, but in another location, before finding its way to the villa in Herculaneum, a prized possession gleaned from the book market rather than a private heirloom passed down in a family estate, such as that of the gens Calpurnia, from one generation to the next, until passing (possibly) out of its hands.[14] We simply do not know.

Speculations abound. But their status as speculation must be emphasized. Was the library a working library, a collector's gallery, or a storage room? In fact, the papyri were not found in a library at all. They were found in five different locations, some shelved in cabinets and boxes and others massed in heaps. Most were found in a small chamber off to the side of a peristyle. One speculation is that the scene they presented was a snapshot of disaster and thwarted recovery; the papyri must have been caught in a state of rescue. Another is that the villa was undergoing reconstruction at the time of the eruption, which is supported archaeologically, possibly indicating a change of hands in the villa's proprietorship. Consequently, the library's contents had merely been stored in provisional locations.[15] As with most aspects of the villa's history, there is no way of deciding the question. The more romantic option has its attractions, not least of all because it matches the instincts of classicists, for whom the salvaging of the precious library is naturally their foremost concern, and so it surely must have been for the library's owners or keepers as well. Much better to imagine this salvage operation than to picture the equally likely image of a chaos of boxes threatened not by the hazards of nature but by those of remodeling.

As for Philodemus, his sole connection to Herculaneum is the findspot of his writings. He need not have ever set foot there, and there is no evidence that he ever did. Piso's Epicurean leanings and Philodemus's confirmed Epicureanism aside, the notion that the villa was a haven of Epicurean teaching, a college or retreat where acolytes

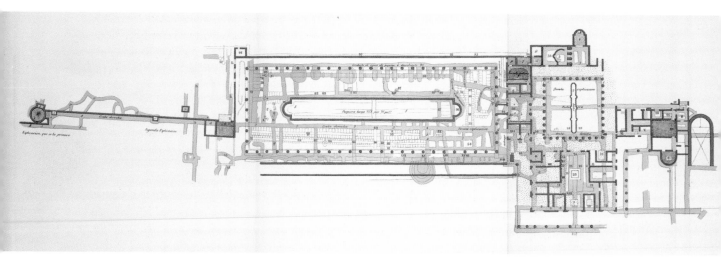

could meet and discuss Epicurean philosophy and even live out Epicureanism in an idyllic setting, gathered, for example, around the so-called belvedere at the end of the property [FIG. 3] to gaze thoughtfully on the setting sun and glistening sea, free from cares and indulging in the simplest of pleasures (wine, not in overabundance, goat cheese, olives, and loaves of bread), while not strictly impossible or even improbable, nevertheless is based on nothing more than a desire to see things in this way. True, we do have a delightful epigram by Philodemus that points to some such setting:

> Tomorrow, friend [φίλτατε] Piso, your musical
>   [μουσοφιλής] comrade drags you to his
>   modest digs at three in the afternoon,
> feeding you at your annual visit to the Twentieth [in
>   honor of Epicurus]. If you will miss udders
>   and Bromian wine *mis en bouteilles* in
>   Chios,
> yet you will see faithful comrades, yet you will hear
>   things far sweeter than the land of the
>   Phaeacians.
> And if you ever turn an eye to us too, Piso, instead
>   of a modest feast we shall lead a richer one.

Philodemus *Epigram* 27 Sider [= AP 11.44]

But nothing guarantees that the villa in Herculaneum provided the physical setting for this versified banquet, and indeed the poem itself suggests the contrary.[16] Future excavations might help solve many of these puzzles by bringing to light fresh details about the ground plan and layout of the library and the villa or by revealing further chambers containing new papyrus rolls (for instance, a separate collection of Latin books or a collection of non-Epicurean Greek texts)—if these exist to be found at all. Or we may never discover the answers to these puzzles. Time is haughty indeed!

In sum, the villa is for us the Villa dei Papiri, which was devoted to preserving the heritage of a Greek philosophical sect that was transmitted (and in cases physically

FIGURE 3
Karl Weber (Swiss, 1712–1764), Plan of the Villa dei Papiri, Herculaneum. Plate 24 from Domenico Comparetti and Giulio de Petra, *La Villa ercolanese dei Pisoni: I suoi monumenti e la sua biblioteca* (1883). Los Angeles, Research Library, Getty Research Institute, 85-B13214.

transported) from Athens. But seeing things in this way is a modern fantasy, and the picture it represents remains to be proved. In fact, the villa need not have been any more than a place of retreat for a wealthy Hellenizing Roman with a collector's yen for Epicurean writings or simply for pretty and impressive-looking books. Our picture of the villa is a romanticized one.

Hearing Voices

The library of Herculaneum presents a unique opportunity to recover voices from the past. But whose voices do we hear? The question has plagued the study of the papyri from the start. Wordsworth's hopes will have been raised by the publication of transcriptions of the papyri, a tedious process that began immediately upon their unrolling in nearby Naples.[17] Nor were conditions exactly propitious to the texts that were found. The papyri have existed in a fragile and disintegrative condition since their discovery, and they suffered a bumpy early history. I have already mentioned how some unspecified number of rolls were thrown away, being mistaken for lumps of charcoal. Later, the papyri were removed to Palermo when the court fled the Parthenopean revolution in 1798, taking its treasures with it. The papyri returned to Portici in 1802, although a large number (around eighty) appear to have been broken in transit.[18] But even earlier, the papyri suffered the damages of impatience once it was determined that they contained writing and were not mere rubbish to be tossed aside: countless precious books were destroyed when the briquettes were initially sliced open, their outer husks peeled away to reveal the more legible "tender-hearted" or better-preserved middles (*midolli*, literally, "marrows"). Even then, once unrolled, the papyri had to be deciphered. Transcription had its own perils. Graphic artists (*disegnatori*) were hired for the job. For the most part illiterate in ancient Greek and therefore more faithful witnesses than their supervisors, who occasionally sought to improve upon and correct the diplomatic transcripts made for them, the *disegnatori* would trace in pencil whatever they could see on sturdy paper sheets, allotting one sheet per column of text [FIG. 4]. These drawings were then published as engravings, which were copied freely onto copper plates (but with a certain fidelity to the original *disegni*, or apographs, which mimicked, as best they could, the peculiarities of scripts and hands) in two editions (*Herculanesium voluminum quae supersunt collectio*), the first from 1793 to 1855, the second from 1862 to 1876, each in eleven volumes.

The original *disegni*, now housed in the Biblioteca nazionale in Naples and the Bodleian Library in Oxford, are a priceless witness to papyri that were either destroyed during the unrolling process or lost during the various dislocations of the treasures or that have since deteriorated, owing to their exceedingly fragile condition. The papyri themselves (see FIG. 2), once peeled away from their briquettes, were mounted on cardboard backings and stored in wooden and later metal trays. These originals are with few exceptions archived in Naples, and, although in some cases visible to the naked eye, they typically have to be read with prosthetic devices, whether magnifying glasses, binocular microscopes, or (most recently) digital multispectral imaging scanners. The result is that today one can read both more and less than those who first laid eyes on the papyri. The current techniques of reading reveal much that went unnoticed previously, but nothing can restore what is no longer there to be seen.

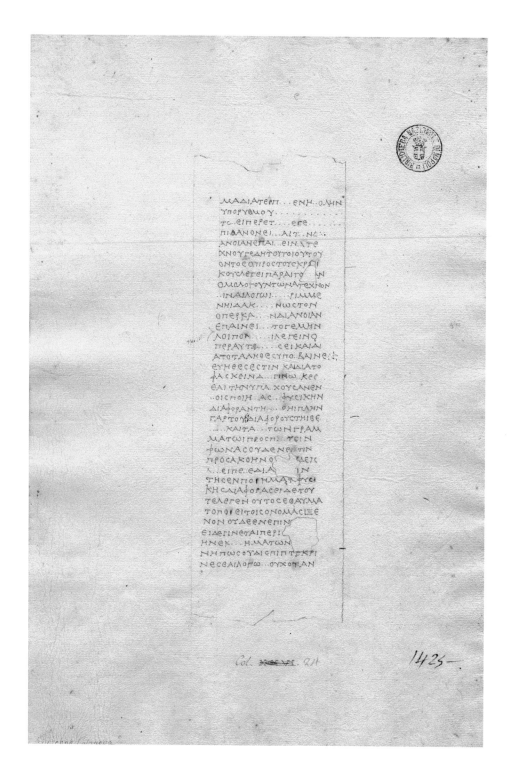

FIGURE 4

Disegno of Herculaneum
papyrus 1425 (*De poem.*
5 col. 24N) drawn
by Giuseppe Casanova
(1733–1844), ca. 1807.
Biblioteca Nazionale
"Vittorio Emanuele III"
di Napoli.

Wordsworth's wistfulness in 1819 was already strangely anachronistic and possibly ill-informed (the harsh truth about the contents of the papyri had been more or less known for several decades already). It is conceivable that he took his inspiration from *Herculanensia* (1810), a published report to Prince George by William Drummond and Robert Walpole as part of a bid to secure financing and political support for a renewed investigation of the papyri, which the Prince of Wales had been underwriting and which eventually resulted in a set of *disegni* made under the supervision of John Hayter (the series that is now kept at Oxford).[19] In their preface Drummond and Walpole share an entire generation's expectations of discovery:

> The lost books of Livy, and the Comedies of Menander, presented themselves to the imagination of almost every scholar. Each indeed anticipated, according to his taste, the mental pleasures, and the literary labours, which awaited him. Some connected the broken series of historical details; some restored to the light those specimens of eloquence, which, perhaps, their authors believed incapable of being ever concealed from it; and others opened new springs, which should augment the fountains of Parnassus. Varius again took his seat by the side of Virgil; Simonides stood again with Sophocles and Pindar by the throne of Homer; and the lyre of the Theban was struck to themes and to measures, that are remembered no more. (ix–x)

The authors here are plainly anticipating Wordsworth's rapturous exclamations over "some Theban fragment" and "scroll of pure Simonides" surfacing from the wreckage and "tender-hearted" scrolls of Herculaneum.[20] But they also bear witness to his disillusionment: "These enthusiastic hopes were perhaps too suddenly repressed, as they had been too easily excited." They go on to explain:

> When we walk among the remains of temples and palaces, we must not expect to meet only with fragments of sculpture, with the polished column, or the decorated capital. Where the ruin has been great, the rubbish is likely to be abundant. The first *papyrus* which was opened, contained a treatise upon music by Philodemus the Epicurean. It was in vain that Mazzochi and Rosini wrote their learned comments on this dull performance: the sedative was too strong; and the curiosity which had been so hastily awakened was as quickly lulled to repose. A few men of letters, indeed, lamented that no further search was made for some happier subject, on which learned industry might be employed; but the time, the difficulty, and the expense, which such an enterprize required, and the uncertainty of producing any thing valuable, had apparently discouraged and disgusted the Academicians of Portici. (x)

At first, scholars were dazed by what they found. Unused to papyrus formats and reduced to utter desperation, they turned to the oddest of hypotheses. One of these was advanced by Giacomo Martorelli, a Neapolitan scholar who claims to have been the first "to see and touch" the papyri (an empiricist archaeological impulse if there ever was one) when they were originally unearthed. Despite his admiration for what he saw, Martorelli found himself puzzled beyond belief. He denied they were books at all (because they were not in codex form): they must be documents of a mundane kind (contracts, testaments, and the like), and the villa must be the official public archive of Herculaneum. For support, he turned, now like a literal-minded philologist, to the silence of the lexica: precisely because the Greeks lacked a word for papyrus roll (*volumen* in Latin) they cannot have known what a papyrus roll was. And anyway, the ancients were far too clever to have submitted to a system as awkward as the book roll; a codex was so much simpler to use.[21] Puzzled, a second time, by the strange appearance of the writing (most likely due to the distortions in the papyri and to the clinging of overlapping layers when these were imperfectly separated), Martorelli advanced the thesis that beyond texts in Greek and Latin one could find a form of writing that was hitherto unknown: Sabine.[22] He was soon joined by Alessio Simmaco Mazzocchi, a local erudite from Ercolano, who professed to be able to detect in the least legible of the papyrus finds the Ur-language of Campania, Oscan.[23] The desperations of these earliest responses to the papyri are symptomatic of a larger anxiety, one that anticipated Wordsworth by more than half a century.

In this context a new player entered the stage, Johann Joachim Winckelmann, who visited the royal museum in Portici in February and March 1758 and again four years later in February 1762 and then a final time in March 1764, where he saw the collection after the first unrolling of the papyri had taken place and as the unrolling process progressed. Winckelmann's descriptions, in two open letters, published after his second and third visits (1762 and 1764), helped bring knowledge of the discoveries at Herculaneum to a wider European public.[24] In the first report he gives a picture of the current state of play. Four books had been unrolled and transcribed:

> Until now, and first off, four rolls of writing have been completely unrolled, and the remarkable fact was that all four are by one and the same author. His name is Philodemus, and he was from Gadara in Syria and a member of the sect of Epicurus: both Cicero, in whose time he lived, and Horace mention him. The first writing is known to be a treatise against music, in which the author wants to show how music is harmful to moral conduct and to the State. The second writing to be unrolled was the second book of his *Rhetorica*. . . . I've been assured by somebody who was able to study this text bit by bit as it was unrolled [bit by bit (*nach und nach*) is an understatement, seeing how slowly the unrolling process proceeded, at about a millimeter or so an hour, on the ingenious *macchina* devised by Padre Antonio Piaggio delle Scuole Pie (FIG. 5)], that in this book . . . Philodemus quotes the *Politica* of Epicurus and Hermarchus. The third writing . . . is the first book of a work on the considered art of rhetoric [in fact, this is another book from the same work, the *Rhetorica*], and the fourth writing is about virtues and vices.[25]

Already at the time it was suspected that one of these works was an autograph in draft by Philodemus,[26] "and this [assumption]," Winckelmann writes, "leads to the suspicion that the villa in which the writings were found possibly belonged to this same philosopher"—to which he adds in the next breath, "but this [in turn] would give rise to the *fear that nothing but Philodemean writings are to be found*, given that the first four pieces of writing to have turned up, in a purely random selection, are from his pen" or his workshop (italics added).[27] Winckelmann lays out the grounds for this fear a few pages later with a remarkable confession (especially for those who tend to see him as an ahistorically minded idealizer of antiquity): "One would have wished to find historians, such as the lost books of Diodorus, the history of Theopompus and that of Ephorus." But a moment later, the more familiar side of Winckelmann emerges clearly: "and [one would also have wished to find] other writings, such as Aristotle's criticisms of the dramatic poets [doubtless, the lost dialogue *On Poets*], the

FIGURE 5
Mechanism used to unroll
papyrus scrolls, designed
by Padre Antonio Piaggio
delle Scuole Pie. Plate 4
from Giacomo Castrucci,
Tesoro letterario di Ercolano
(1852). Los Angeles,
Research Library,
Getty Research Institute,
88-B5582.

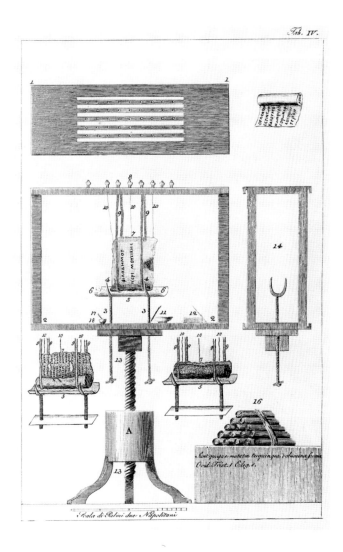

lost tragedies of Sophocles and Euripides, the comedies of Menander and of Alexis,
the *Symmetry* of Pamphilus [a handbook for painters], and a few works on architecture: for who cares about a hypochondriacal and twisted complaint about music?"[28]
In retrospect, we can see now that the litany of complaints about ancient authors and
works that were never found at Herculaneum, and which runs like a broken record from
Drummond and Walpole to Wordsworth, originates here in Winckelmann. And in the
second of his reports Winckelmann laments the Epicureans' characteristically defiant
neglect of style in their writing:

> If we can make an inference about the value of the Philodemean writings in view of
> their style, based on the style of Epicurus and Metrodorus [a contemporary follower
> of Epicurus], we would have to conclude that there is not much in the way of orna-
> ment to be sought for in them. For we know that Epicurus paid no attention at all to
> the selection, ordering, or composition of words and expressions, and that he taught
> that nature is the only arbiter of speech, while art contributes nothing. That is why
> he forbad his students to resort to the ornaments of [artful] style, just as he is said to
> have disparaged the arts and sciences [*Wissenschaften*] generally.[29]

All in all, the disappointment was great: "there is not much to hope for here."[30] And the feeling was shared. One plan contemplated by those in charge was to unroll and examine only the initial columns of a great number of papyri "until they could find a few with useful contents" and to continue the work on these and to lay the others aside until this work was completed.[31] Luckily for the papyri, no such plan was ever undertaken. Even so, Winckelmann's worst fears and suspicions would be borne out only over the next century of unrolling, deciphering, and transcription: the library was a philosophical one and almost exclusively Epicurean.

Here, the empiricism driving classicism and classical scholarship arrived at an impasse: classicism was forced to confront its own sources in the form of an impediment, in the sheer inert materiality of its objects. (Winckelmann's despairing description begins on this same note: "so much for the formal side [*dem Förmlichen*] of the writing; the material side of the writing [*das Materialische derselben*] is ....")[32] But worse still, classicism had no choice but to face the realities of an ancient school of materialism, an uneasy prospect. Ancient atomism has never been a staple of classicism, for obvious reasons. Presenting the rebarbative spectacle of atoms jostling in a cosmic void, undirected by divinity, reason, or teleology, atomism is anathema to worshipers of form, beauty, or ideals of any kind. It goes against the Platonic grain of classical idealism, and its official study by classicists was retarded for a century or more for identical reasons.[33] Likewise, the aestheticizing tendency of classical scholarship was stymied in the face of the Herculanean writings. In search of new music from the classical past, nobody could comprehend how antiquity could have produced such a complete rejection of music. It turns out that in addition to his works on music and rhetoric, Philodemus also wrote a work in five books on poetry called *On Poems*, but this text was not identified until later in the nineteenth century. Once identified, the work drew intense interest and rekindled the waning hopes of scholars, who had all but given up on discovering some salvageable bit of classical antiquity in the papyri, which had languished in neglect for more than half a century. Whence the heady fervor of Theodor Gomperz in 1865, who felt that here, in the poetic writings of Philodemus, one could finally point to "*the — until now — fully unknown aesthetics of the Epicurean school*" (italics in original).[34] Does the hope express a desire to bring Epicurus back into the fold of classical culture (*paideia*), which Epicurus was known to have repudiated?

"*That were, indeed, a genuine birth of poesy*"

However alluring Gomperz's hope may be — and it is still shared by most scholars in the field today — Philodemus brings us no closer to an Epicurean poetics than did Epicurus himself (Epicurus was notoriously hostile not just to music but to poetry and its study). Instead, the writings of Philodemus contain a wealth of information about developments in aesthetic theory outside the Epicurean school and especially after Aristotle, many of which are attested nowhere else. Philodemus reports the teachings of mainly anonymous sources, apparently filtered through either his teacher from Athens, Zeno, or the Pergamene grammarian Crates of Mallos, who flourished in the early to mid-second century B.C. and who is known to us elsewhere principally for his bold and often bizarre allegories of Homer. The theories assembled and passed under critical review by Philodemus seem to be largely Hellenistic in origin but with roots that can be traced to the fifth century and possibly earlier—indeed, they are rooted in the very character of early Greek poetry as oral literature. As it happens, mystifyingly and somewhat uncannily, these developments are for the most part taken up with the question of the voice ($\varphi\omega\nu\acute{\eta}$)—of the sound and aural surface of music, poetry, and rhetoric. In the writings on poetics in particular, the emphasis of these non-Epicurean sources, while apparently aimed at a theory of euphony (an analysis of how poems sound), is in fact focused on how texts from the remote postclassical era, when read out loud, resurrect the voices of classical authors in a powerfully immediate, sensuous, and pleasurable way.

On both intellectual and moral grounds, scholars today remain baffled by these teachings, for the critics opposed by Philodemus appear to offer a theory according to which what counts in a poem is not what it means but only how it sounds. Poetic excellence is determined solely by the sound, which is appreciated by the irrational sense of hearing and not by the mind (although the mind can appreciate the artfulness by which poetic sounds are arranged and so produced). This reductive euphonism is an affront to most things precious to ancient literary criticism and to conventional sensibilities today. Genre boundaries, the appropriateness of thought to expression, content, moral utility, and even the specific relevance of meaning are sacrificed; euphony and pleasure are made into the irrational criteria of rational meaning; and nature begins to look like the convention it, in fact, was in classical antiquity.

The introduction to Richard Janko's magnificent edition of the remains of Philodemus's *On Poems*, book 1, closes with the forbidding thought (which would surely have been shared by a more prescient Philodemus): "The theories of the euphonists…did much to reverse the progress of human rationality for many centuries, until at last enlightened thinkers like Giambattista Vico came to reject [such a view], first as applied to Homer and then to more 'sacred' texts. In their own times Lucretius, Philodemus, Horace, Seneca, and Plutarch did well to resist it. Theories of language and interpretation have a profound importance for civilization as a whole; we get them wrong at our peril."[35] But this concern is merely the latest revulsion of modernity in the face of an antiquity it cannot ever completely assimilate. In the brief space that remains, I want to indicate two final ironies of the Herculaneum papyri and their reception among classical scholars.

The rejection of the euphonists over the centuries completely misgauges the thrust of their undertaking, which is, in fact, multifaceted. The purpose of these critics is both critical (destructive of literary critical commonplaces) and uncritical (conservative and classicizing). On the one hand, euphonist criticism is bound up with the culturally critical and ideological aspects of aesthetic criticism in antiquity, an aspect of ancient aesthetics that tends to be neglected—wrongly.[36] Presumed theoretical analyses often turn out to have wider conceptual and critical implications, as here. An aesthetics such as that of the euphonists contrasts with the formalism and the moralism of mainstream criticism familiar from Plato and Aristotle. Materialism in aesthetics highlights problems of conventional value in striking ways. If literary criticism implies a discussion of cultural biases, norms, and values (from morals to meaning), criticism in a materialistic vein—criticism centered on the phenomenal experience of art as registered through the pleasures of the body (as disseminated through the ear or eye)—can be intensely critical of conventional values and especially of the conventions of nature that underpin them. Appearances notwithstanding, a sensuous aesthetics such as the euphonists' need not be grounded in naturalism or even in the senses. On the contrary, it can make strategic use of the postulates of naturalism in order to loosen the grip of deeply seated (and naturalized) conventions of aesthetic perception and criticism. And indeed, their provocative counteraesthetics sharply call into question these latter conventions (for instance, the difficult problem of how to reconcile aesthetic pleasure with poetic and cultural value). Here the euphonists are good candidates for representing a form of anticlassicism.

But a more immediate motivation for their theory is to be found in the very situation of ancient literary criticism. The focus on the voice as a substance that is simultaneously an abstract and fleeting entity (a *spiritus* or $\pi\nu\varepsilon\hat{\upsilon}\mu\alpha$) recalls the perpetual problem of postclassical Greek literary culture: how to breathe life into the lifeless matter of a canonical text. Readers, Longinus writes, are "possessed by a spirit [$\pi\nu\varepsilon\hat{\upsilon}\mu\alpha$: breath or voice] not their own" (13.2). Sublimity makes "a kind of lustre bloom upon our words as upon beautiful statues; it gives things life [$\psi\upsilon\chi\acute{\eta}\nu$] and makes them speak [$\varphi\omega\nu\eta\tau\iota\kappa\acute{\eta}\nu$]" (30.1; trans. Russell). "Books," Cicero writes, recalling a theme dating to the fourth century, "lack that breath of life [*spiritu illo*] which usually makes . . . passages seem more impressive [*maiora*] when spoken [*aguntur*] than when read [*leguntur*]" (*Orator* 130; trans. Hubbell). And it is probably Pausimachus, one of Philodemus's euphonist sources and otherwise an unknown entity, who says, "When Homer's verses are read out [$\dot{\alpha}\nu\alpha\gamma\iota\nu\acute{\omega}\sigma|[\kappa\eta\tau]\alpha\iota$], they all appear greater and more beautiful [$\pi\acute{\alpha}\nu\tau\alpha \mu[\varepsilon]\acute{\iota}\zeta\omega|[\kappa\alpha\grave{\iota} \kappa\alpha]\lambda\lambda\acute{\iota}\omega \varphi[\alpha\acute{\iota}\nu\varepsilon]\tau\alpha\iota$]."[37] Seen in this light, the euphonists offer us, among other things, a theory of reading, a way of reading the voice buried in the voiceless script of Greek texts from the distant past.

If this way of reading their program is right, then these exponents of poetic sensualism and materialism are not questioning classical values but are only reinforcing them.[38] The sheer seductiveness of what is classical about classical literature, never previously named as such, is here being, in fact, named—as sweet sound, transport, and sublimity. Classical seductions, always irrational (a matter of feeling rather than of reason), are not being dismissed. On the contrary, they are being shown to be sublime. What remains, on this critical reduction of sense to sound, is thus not only sound but also the feeling that the sound both evokes and represents. What remains, in other words, is a pure ideological effect, absent any meaning or content, namely, the ideological effect of classicism itself. That the euphonist critics are also highlighting the contingency of this value, by directing attention in the first instance to its material coordinates (in sound, in its existence in and for "the ear") and then to its convention-bound nature and to its sheer imaginary value (it is no more than a *phainomenon* or sensuous experience), is a possibility that cannot be foreclosed.[39] But if that is the case, then their apparent conservatism has a hidden critical edge: they are laying bare the phenomenology of ancient classical values and exposing to view the sheer fragility and the material foundation of those values. For how, exactly, does a *written* text *sound*? What remains, on this critical reduction of sense to sound, is thus not only sound but also, or rather above all, the *feeling* that the sound evokes and represents. The euphonists isolate without naming this quality of classical literature. "Euphony," "pleasure," and occasionally "ecstasy" compete with one another without providing a focused concept that would correspond to all these terms. Perhaps the modern term *classical* captures it best of all. But then, it captures just a movement of breath.

And so, although the writers in aesthetics described by Philodemus are not classical authors in the narrow sense (they date from the age of the Alexandrian library, from the third to first centuries B.C., although their intellectual roots can be traced back to such fifth-century B.C. thinkers as Democritus and Prodicus and to the earliest musical and philological traditions), they do represent, or else lay bare, a strongly classicizing tendency of postclassical antiquity and not only of ancient literary, musical, and rhetorical theory. What they give us is an aesthetics of classicism in the guise of a theory of sensuous perception (of sound, hearing, euphony, and so on). And while they might therefore be said to justify classicism and reinforce its structures of feeling through their advocacy of an extreme and irrational aesthetic hedonism, what they are in fact doing is pointing out the foundational beliefs of literary classicism, which is, after all, rooted in the pleasure of the text and which reinforces its values through a regime of pleasure. This last insight is what drew the ire of the Epicureans, and it accounts for the preservation of these theorists by Philodemus—unlike their earlier atomist forebears, Epicureans, being the moral hedonists that they are, are rationalists at bottom as well as non-reductive materialists—but it does not yet account for their complete lack of attestation elsewhere in our ancient sources.[40] Classicism, after all, is itself a pleasurable practice. Thus, the Herculaneum papyri ironically do bring us back to classicism again, albeit via a most unexpected route.

Now for the second irony, which this time has to do with classicism in its modern form. We have seen how the Herculaneum papyri repulsed Winckelmann, who found them to be narrowly sectarian and unaesthetic in the extreme. Yet by the strangest of reversals, even Winckelmann found a way of fully recuperating the recovered antiquity of Herculaneum in all its Epicurean splendor, for as surprising as it may seem to us, Winckelmann's foundational concept of the classical ideal—noble simplicity and tranquil grandeur—is, in fact, a calque on Epicurus's idealization of divinity. Winckelmann's ideal of flesh rendered transparent and finally unseen (a prerequisite of idealization) is explicitly supported by a reference to Epicurus's account of the gods, as we have it from Cicero:

> But if the human figure is superior to all other shapes of animate beings, and god is animate, he certainly possesses that figure which is most beautiful of all. And since the gods are agreed to be supremely blessed, and since no one can be blessed without virtue, and virtue is impossible without reason, and reason can exist only in the human form, it must be admitted that the gods are of human appearance. However, that appearance is not body [*nec tamen ea species corpus est*] but quasi-body [*sed quasi corpus*], and it does not have blood [*nec habet sanguinem*] but quasi-blood [*sed quasi sanguinem*]. (Although these discoveries of Epicurus's are too acute, and his words too subtle, to be appreciated by just anyone, I am relying on your powers of understanding....) Epicurus, who not only sees hidden and profoundly obscure things with his mind but even handles them as if they were at his fingertips, teaches that the force and nature of the gods is of such a kind that it is, primarily, viewed not by sensation but by the mind, possessing neither the kind of solidity nor the numerical distinctness of those things which...Epicurus calls *steremnia* [solid bodies]; but that we apprehend images by their similarity and by a process of transition [through *simulacra* and by mental focusing].[41]

What stands out is not only the gods' human form ("for nature supplies us all, whatever our race, with no other view of the gods than as human in form") but also the evanescence of that form when it is invested with divinity: God "possesses that figure which is most beautiful of all," even more beautiful than humanity, because it is the quintessence of humanity—but also, by the same token, no longer quite human: in Epicurus's words, their "appearance is not body but quasi-body, and it does not have blood but quasi-blood." The same thoughts are repeated verbatim in Winckelmann's *History of Art*, published in 1764, the same year as the second of his accounts of Herculaneum:

> The beauty of the gods in their virile age consists in the quintessence of strength that comes with mature years and the joyfulness of youth—and this consists *in the lack of nerves and sinews*, which are little in evidence in the full flowering of life. Herein lies at the same time an expression of divine self-sufficiency, which has no need of certain parts of the body such as we need for the nurture of our own. And that explains Epicurus's view of the form of the gods, upon whom he bestows a body, *albeit a quasi-body*, and blood, *albeit quasi-blood*, a view that Cicero finds obscure and incomprehensible.[42] (italics added)

Winckelmann's classical ideal of beauty is generally felt to be Neoplatonic. But it is, in fact, suffused with Epicurean features. The gods of Epicurus preeminently display grandeur in their tranquility (*ataraxia*) and in their blissfulness (*voluptas*): they are ideals of human happiness—despite, or just because of, their essential inhumanity.[43] How Winckelmann could ever reconcile his two attitudes regarding Epicureanism—his distaste for Epicurean aesthetics and its implied aesthetics of divinity or, more concretely, his distaste for Epicurean philosophy when encountered in the flesh, as it were, and his attachment to its (classicized) idealizations—is another story, which would lead us into the thickets of the classical ideal, which, I believe, thrives on just this kind of incoherence. But it is no understatement to suggest that Winckelmann owed at least some of his theory of Greek beauty to his contact with Herculaneum and that he manifestly sublimated that contact into his theory of classical beauty.

◻ ◻ ◻

The history of Herculanean philology makes vivid a widespread tension within classical scholarship: the desire of scholarship to recover voices from the past and the unexpected and sometimes unwanted voices that the past can at times return. One of the great ironies of the library of Herculaneum, at least concerning the writings on poetry, is that what it contains are not so much products of the high classical era that stretches from Homer to Plato as perspectives as wistful as our own on that vanished past. The voices we can recover from Herculaneum at times mirror our own aestheticizing and classicizing desire to recover the voices of the classical past. This is a disconcerting prospect—for what we hear, and then refuse, is a distant echo of ourselves.

Notes

My sense of the issues surrounding the library at Herculaneum has been greatly sharpened thanks to informal discussions over the years with David Blank, Richard Janko, and Dirk Obbink, whom I wish to thank here but who in no way should be assumed to bear responsibility for any of my conclusions. Thanks, too, go to Robert Connor and David Sider for helping me improve a version of this chapter and to Victoria Coates and Jon Seydl for their encouragement and keen editorial insights. The publication version of this essay was written while I was a fellow of the Council of the Humanities at Princeton University in the fall of 2004.

1   Mary Beard and John Henderson, *Classical Art: From Greece to Rome* (Oxford, 2001), 11.

2   For a survey of eighteenth-century classicism, often called "neoclassicism," see Hugh Honour, *Neo-classicism* (Harmondsworth, 1968), an introduction that remains unsurpassed.

3   For new approaches to the categories of the classical and classicism in relation to the conduct of classical studies, ancient and modern, see the essays collected in *Classical Pasts: The Classical Traditions of Greece and Rome*, ed. James I. Porter (Princeton, 2006); and Salvatore Settis, *Futuro del classico* (Turin, 2004).

4   On the checkered history of the Elgin marbles and especially the initial resistance to their acceptance as classical works of art, see Mary Beard, *The Parthenon* (London, 2002); and Timothy Webb, "Appropriating the Stones: The 'Elgin Marbles' and English National Taste," in *Claiming the Stones/Naming the Bones: Cultural Property and the Negotiation of National and Ethnic Identity*, ed. Elazar Barkan and Ronald Bush (Los Angeles, 2002), 51–96. On the equally mixed reaction to the paintings discovered at the Bay of Naples in the eighteenth century, see Agnès Rouveret, *Histoire et imaginaire de la peinture ancienne: Ve siècle av. J.-C.–Ier siècle ap. J.-C.* (Rome, 1989), 5–6.

5   On the resistance in classical studies to the materiality of its own objects, see James I. Porter, "The Materiality of Classical Studies," *Parallax* 29, no. 4 (2003): 64–74.

6   William Wordsworth, "Upon the Same Occasion" (September 1819), in *Shorter Poems, 1807–1820, by William Wordsworth*, ed. Carl H. Ketcham (Ithaca, 1989), 286 (vv. 50–60).

7   See Robert Fowler, "Herculean Task for Modern Scholars," *London Times*, April 5, 2002, 42. A veritable war has been waged over the past half decade between philologists, keen to inaugurate a new excavation of the villa in the hope of uncovering a second Latin library and further Greek volumes, and archaeologists, equally keen to maintain and preserve the site as it currently stands, given the limited funds available (and pessimistic about the prospects for recovering new books). See further the open letter signed by eight leading classicists in the *London Times*, March 13, 2002, 23, pleading the case for reopening the excavations.

8   For a social history of this milieu, see John D'Arms, *Romans on the Bay of Naples and Other Essays on Roman Campania* (Bari, 2003).

9   See Marcello Gigante, *Philodemus in Italy: The Books from Herculaneum*, trans. Dirk Obbink (Ann Arbor, 1995), 1–13.

10 Mario Capasso, "Congedo," in *Manuale di papirologia ercolanese* (Lecce, 1991), 53.

11 Cicero does not mention Philodemus by name here, but the identification is given by an intermediary source, Asconius, in a commentary on Cicero's *In Pisonem* 68.

12 Guglielmo Cavallo, *Libri scritture scribi a Ercolano: Introduzione allo studio dei materiali greci* (Naples, 1983), 60–61, 65 (refuting an earlier view, such as that of Walter Scott, *Fragmenta herculanensia: A Descriptive Catalogue of the Oxford Copies of the Herculanean Rolls Together with the Texts of Several Papyri, Accompanied by Facsimiles* [Oxford, 1885], 11–12: "not a single Greek roll has been found which can be shown to be of later date than Philodemus").

13 Cavallo 1983 (note 12), 65.

14 For a similar thought, see *The Epigrams of Philodemos*, ed. David Sider (New York, 1997), 15, who, however, insists on the connection between Philodemus, Piso, and the villa (passim, with the exceptions mentioned in note 16). See now, too, idem, *The Library of the Villa dei Papiri at Herculaneum* (Los Angeles, 2005), 5–8. For a different set of arguments, likewise severing the connection, see Phillip De Lacy, "Review of Mario Capasso, *Manuale di papirologia ercolanese* (1991)," *American Journal of Philology* 114 (1993): 178–80.

15 Maria Rita Wojcik, *La Villa dei Papiri ad Ercolano: Contributo alla ricostruzione dell'ideologia della nobilitas tardo repubblicana* (Rome, 1986), 36–37, 151–56; Capasso 1991 (note 10), 53–54, 81–82.

16 See De Lacy 1993 (note 14), 179, who points out that it is Philodemus who invites Piso to Philodemus's "modest digs," not the other way around; and that there are several possible "Pisones" who could serve as the addressee. See further, Cicero, *In L. Calpurnium Pisonem oratio*, ed. R. G. M. Nisbet (Oxford, 1961), 187–88; Sider 1997 (note 14), 14n. 7, 154 (ad 1).

17 On this process, see especially David L. Blank, "Reflections on Re-reading Piaggio and the Early History of the Herculaneum Papyri," *Cronache ercolanesi* 29 (1999): 55–82 (for the techniques); Capasso 1991 (note 10), chap. 4; and Franco Strazzullo, *P. Antonio Piaggio e lo svolgimento dei papiri ercolanesi* (Naples, 2002).

18 The record is confusing and often misrepresented. I owe this information to David Blank. See further Mario Capasso and Francesca Longo Auricchio, "John Hayter nella Officina dei papiri ercolanesi," in *Contributi alla storia della Officina dei papiri ercolanesi*, 2 vols. (Naples, 1980), 1:164n. 16; Capasso 1991 (note 10), 100–101.

19 William Drummond and Robert Walpole, *Herculanensia, or Archeological and Philological Dissertations, Containing a Manuscript Found among the Ruins of Herculaneum* (London, 1810).

20 Ibid., ix–x. They lay all their cards on the table early in the dedication: "We certainly know of no period since the revival of letters, when, if classical acquirements be of any value, it has been so necessary to ascertain what that value is, as at present. Among the many extraordinary features of the revolutionary system, which is rapidly changing the state of Europe, the neglect of ancient literature is not the least remarkable" (v). L. Varius Rufus was a friend of Virgil's (he published the *Aeneid* upon Virgil's death) and dwelt in the same circle of influence as did Horace. Quintilian compared his Theban plays to Sophocles' (10.1.98); he also wrote a didactic poem, *De morte*, in the Epicurean vein (Quintilian 6.3.78). The "lyre of the Theban" may be an allusion to Thomas Gray's ode "The Progress of Poesy: A Pindaric Ode" (1757), vv. 111–17:

> But ah! 'tis heard no more—
> Oh! lyre divine, what daring spirit
> Wakes thee now? Though he inherit
> Nor the pride, nor ample pinion,
> That the Theban Eagle bear
> Sailing with supreme dominion
> Through the azure deep of air.

21 Johann Joachim Winckelmann, *Herkulanische Schriften Winckelmanns*, vol. 1, *Sendschreiben von den herculanischen Entdeckungen* (Mainz, 1997), 1:114–15; Capasso 1991 (note 10), 70.

22 Winckelmann 1997 (note 21), 1:119.

23 Ibid. Winckelmann calls this hypothesis *lächerlich* (risible).

24 Johann Joachim Winckelmann, *Lettre de M. l'Abbé Winckelmann, antiquaire de Sa Sainteté, à Monsieur le Comte de Brühl, chambellan du roi de Pologne, electeur de Saxe, sur les découvertes d'Herculanum* (Dresden, 1764); idem, *Critical Account of the Situation and Destruction by the First Eruptions of Mount Vesuvius of Herculaneum, Pompeii, and Stabia: The Late Discovery of Their Remains, the Subterraneous Works Carried On in Them…in a Letter (Originally in German) to Count Bruhl, of Saxony, from the Celebrated Abbé Winckelmann…; Illustrated with Notes Taken from the French Translation* (London, 1771). There were translations in French and English; the English version from 1771 was based on the French translation from 1764.

25 Winckelmann 1997 (note 21), 1:125–27; cf. Strazzullo 2002 (note 17), 5–13.

26 The notion is refuted by Gigante 1995 (note 9), 17.

27 Winckelmann 1997 (note 21), 1:123.

[28] Ibid., 1:127.

[29] Johann Joachim Winckelmann, *Herkulanische Schriften Winckelmanns*, vol. 2, *Nachrichten von den neuesten herculanischen Entdeckungen* (Mainz, 1997), 2:38.

[30] Winckelmann 1997 (note 21), 1:127.

[31] Ibid.

[32] Ibid., 1:123.

[33] On the resuscitation of ancient atomism and its history by F. A. Lange and Friedrich Nietzsche in the mid-nineteenth century, in conscious opposition to the legacy of Plato and the idealism of contemporary philosophy, see James I. Porter, *Nietzsche and the Philology of the Future* (Stanford, 2000), esp. chaps. 1–2.

[34] Theodor Gomperz, "Die herculanischen Rollen I," *Zeitschrift für die österreichischen Gymnasien* 16 (1865): 724.

[35] *On Poems: Philodemus*, ed. Richard Janko (Oxford, 2000), 189.

[36] See James I. Porter, "Content and Form in Philodemus: The History of an Evasion," in *Philodemus and Poetry: Poetic Theory and Practice in Lucretius, Philodemus, and Horace*, ed. Dirk Obbink (New York, 1995), 136; idem, "Feeling Classical: Classicism and Ancient Literary Criticism," in Porter 2006 (note 3).

[37] Herculaneum papyrus 466 fr. 5.9–12 = col. 43.9–12 Janko.

[38] For an argument to this effect, see Porter 2006 (note 36).

[39] James I. Porter, "Des sons qu'on ne peut entendre: Cicéron, les 'kritikoi' et la tradition du sublime dans la critique littéraire," in *Cicéron et Philodème: La polémique en philosophie*, ed. Clara Auvray-Assayas and Daniel Delattre (Paris, 2001), 315–41.

[40] Although the euphonists named by Philodemus appear nowhere else in surviving sources, the literary writings of Dionysius of Halicarnassus constitute a major exception, being closely affined (but betraying no lineages or dependencies). And although brief smatterings of euphonist criticism appear in various ancient writings, they never materialize in such concentrated doses, nor, again, do they lead us directly back to the Philodemean evidence.

[41] Cicero *De natura deorum* 1.47–49; trans. Long and Sedley.

[42] "Die Schönheit der Gottheiten im männlichen Alter besteht in einem Inbegriffe der Stärke gestezter Jahre, und der Fröhlichkeit der Jugend, und diese besteht hier *in dem Mangel der Nerven und Sehnen*, welche sich in der Blüthe der Jahre wenig äußern. Hierinn aber liegt zugleich ein Ausdruck der göttlichen Genugsamkeit, welche die zur Nahrung unseres Körpers bestimmten Theile nicht von nöten hat; und dieses erläutert *des Epicurus Meynung* von der Gestalt der Götter, denen er einen Körper, *aber gleichsam einen Korper*; und Blut, *aber gleichsam Blut*, giebt, welches Cicero dunkel und unbegreiflich gesagt findet" (Johann Joachim Winckelmann, *Herkulanische Schriften Winckelmanns*, vol. 4, *Geschichte der Kunst des Alterthums* [Mainz, 2002], 4:274–76; italics added).

[43] Compare also ibid., 4:250–53. For the argument, see Hans Zeller, *Winckelmanns Beschreibung des Apollo im Belvedere* (Zurich, 1955), 227–35, who insists, more so than Walther Rehm (*Götterstille und Göttertrauer: Aufsätze zur deutsch-antiken Begegnung* [Bern, 1951]), on the specifically Epicurean hue of the Winckelmannian ideal.

Picnic at Pompeii: Hyperbole and Digression in the Warm South

Chloe Chard

Eating and Drinking

ANNA JAMESON, in her *Diary of an Ennuyée* (1826), observes: "Our excursion to Pompeii yesterday, was 'a Pic-nic party of pleasure,' *à l'Anglaise*." After an account of viewing wall paintings in a newly excavated building, she describes the gastronomic components of this "party of pleasure":

> Hurried on by a hungry, noisy, merry party, we at length reached the Caserna.... The central court of this building has been converted into a garden; and here, under a weeping willow, our dinner table was spread. Where Englishmen are, there will be good cheer if possible; and our banquet was in truth most luxurious. Besides more substantial cates, we had oysters from Lake Lucrine, (or Acheron), and classically excellent they were; London bottled porter, and half a dozen different kinds of wine. Our dinner went off most gaily, but no order was kept afterwards: the purpose of our expedition seemed to be forgotten in general mirth: many witty things were said and done, and many merry ones, and not a few silly ones.[1]

Too luxurious a banquet, in other words, prompts a "general mirth" that detracts from the experience that the traveler expects and desires: the experience of wonder and enthrallment. After describing one of the party mounting the rostrum of "the School of Eloquence" and giving "an oration extempore; equally pithy, classical and comical," Jameson reaffirms that she is capable of responding to the sights of the warm south with an enthralled intensity, undiminished by her participation in such scenes of frivolity: "of all the lovely scenes I have beheld in Italy, what I saw to-day has most enchanted my senses and imagination." She then, however, explains that gastronomy, better managed, might have been recruited in the service of yet greater enthrallment:

> Thus ended a day which was not without its pleasures:—yet had I planned a party of pleasure to Pompeii, methinks I could have managed better. *Par exemple*, I would have deferred it a fortnight later, or till the vines were in leaf; I would have chosen for my companions two or at most three persons whom I could name, whose cultivated minds and happy tempers would have heightened their own enjoyment and mine. After spending a few hours in taking a general view of the whole city, we would have sat down on the platform of the old Greek Temple which commands a view of the mountains and the bay; or, if the heat were too powerful, under the shade of the hill near it. There we would make our cheerful and elegant repast, on bread and fruits, and perhaps a bottle of Malvoisie or Champagne: the rest of the day should be devoted to a minute examination of the principal objects of interest and curiosity: we would wait till the shadows of evening had begun to steal over the scene, purpling the mountains and the sea; we would linger there to enjoy all the splendours of an Italian sunset; and then, with minds softened and elevated by the loveliness and solemnity of the scenes around, we would get into our carriage, and drive back to Naples beneath the bright full moon; and, by the way, we would "talk the flowing heart," and make our recollections of the olden time, our deep impressions of the past, heighten our enjoyment of the present; and this would be indeed a day of *pleasure*, of such pleasure as I am capable of feeling—of imparting—of remembering with unmixed delight. Such was *not* yesterday.[2]

Joseph Forsyth, in his *Remarks on Antiquities, Arts, and Letters during an Excursion in Italy in the Years 1802 and 1803* (1813), also touches on the relation between the imaginative pleasures of enthrallment and the pleasures of consuming wine. In describing Virgil's Tomb, he considers two categories of sightseers: those who have visited the tomb reverentially and carved their names and a drunken party of foreigners whom the traveler himself witnesses "reeling down" to see it:

> The tomb itself resembles a ruined pigeon-house where the numerous *columbaria* would indicate a family sepulchre; but who should repose in the tomb of Virgil, but Virgil alone? Visitors of every nation, kings and princes have scratched their names on the stucco of this apocryphal ruin, but the poet's awful name seems to have deterred them from versifying here. I met a party of foreigners who had filled themselves with the God in the vineyard above, and were then reeling down between two precipices to kiss the dust and make further libations to the shade of Virgil.[3]

Hyperbole and Digression

The eruption of drinking into Forsyth's commentary initially prompts an expectation of a plunge into bathos: the author distances himself from the "reeling" foreigners by ironically assigning them an absurdly elevated motive for their drunkenness—a devotion to the memory of the poet. It is the party "who had filled themselves with the God," however, rather than the name-scratchers, too timorous for "versifying," who most strongly affirm the status of the tomb as one of the major sights of Naples. While the "libations" of the foreigners express a digressive, disorderly approach to sightseeing, they nonetheless veer toward an approach that, in travel writing, is frequently set in sharp opposition to digression and divagation: a hyperbolic responsiveness. Irony, in other words, coexists with hyperbole and even protects the traveler-narrator's vision of a dramatically destabilized response to a wonder. In allotting this response to others, Forsyth avoids the need to defend its intensity or sincerity. The foreigners' "reeling," physical gesture of acknowledgment of the tomb, taking the place of any coherent form of words, supplies a variant on one of the hyperboles most frequently employed in travel writing of this period: a hyperbole of inexpressibility, in which the traveler, transported by the emotions induced by a particular sight, is at a loss for words. Anna Jameson, for example, ascending Vesuvius, declares: "I can hardly write, my mind is so overflowing with astonishment, admiration, and sublime pleasure."[4] In Byron's five stanzas of hyperboles acclaiming the Venus de' Medici in canto 4 of *Childe Harold's Pilgrimage* (1818), the traveler refuses to "describe the indescribable" and declares that "there need no words, nor terms precise" to confirm the statue's transcendent beauty; he then introduces a metaphorical response of reeling intoxication of the kind that Forsyth ironically literalizes:

> We gaze and turn away, and know not where,
> Dazzled and drunk with beauty, till the heart
> Reels with its fullness.[5]

Jameson, like Forsyth, is concerned with the relation between hyperbole and digression—or wonder and disorderly distraction—and with the role of drinking (and, in her case, eating) within each of these tropes. The picnic at Pompeii degenerates into disorder ("no order was kept afterwards: the purpose of our expedition seemed to be forgotten in general mirth"), and this dissipation of the exalted attention that the site demands is implicitly attributed to the excessive variety of drinks offered: the "London bottled porter, and half a dozen different kinds of wine" and attests to an absence of the simplicity required to promote a sense of wonder. A less complicated meal, of "bread and fruits, and perhaps a bottle of Malvoisie or Champagne," on the other hand, would allow the sightseers to speak the hyperbolic language of wonder: to "'talk the flowing heart,' and make our recollections of the olden time, our deep impressions of the past, heighten our enjoyment of the present."

The Metaphor of Taste

When traveler-narrators marshal eating and drinking as forms of gratification that can intensify visual and imaginative pleasure, the continuity that they establish between the gastronomic and the aesthetic is implicitly authenticated by an unspoken awareness that these two domains are already linked by the double range of reference of the term *taste*: writings of the mid- to late eighteenth century often assume that there must be some continuity between taste in gastronomy and taste in the arts, however swiftly they then point out the differences between the two, or the limitations of taste as a metaphor. Martin Sherlock, for example, in his *Nouvelles lettres sur l'Italie* (1780), reflects:

Le terme goût est une métaphore prise du palais. Une bonne perdrix est servie à trois hommes; un la trouve bonne; un autre la trouve mauvaise; le troisième est un homme sans goût; le premier a le goût bon. Menez un Grenadier Allemand voir l'Apollon de Belvedere, il ne le trouvera ni beau, ni laid; celui-ci est un homme sans goût: montrez cette statue à un Bourgmestre Hollandois, il la trouvera trop svelte, il la voudroit un peu plus lourde; c'est un homme d'un goût perfide; montrez-la alors à dix Italiens, dix François et dix Anglois, ils la trouveront tous belle; et cependant chacun d'eux peut avoir un goût différent.[6]

Around the end of the eighteenth century, however, accounts of the pleasures of the imagination begin to deploy a new option: the strategy of forcibly opposing the elision of taste in food and wine with taste in art and literature. Wordsworth, in the preface to the second edition of *Lyrical Ballads* (1800), refers scornfully to "men who speak of what they do not understand; who talk of Poetry as of a matter of amusement and idle pleasure; who will converse with us as gravely about a *taste* for Poetry, as they express it, as if it were a thing as indifferent as a taste for rope-dancing, or Frontiniac or Sherry."[7] Coleridge endorses the same opposition when he reflects upon his own definition of poetry as "the excitement of emotion for the purpose of *immediate* pleasure, through the medium of beauty." He explains: "To take a trivial but unexceptionable instance, the venison is agreeable because it gives pleasure; while the Apollo Belvedere is not beautiful because it pleases, but it pleases us because it is beautiful."[8] Stendhal, in a fragment of 1818 on Naples, meets some English travelers at Paestum, reflects digressively on "le sombre des Anglais," and exclaims:

Y a-t-il rien de plus plaisant...que la gravité ridicule avec laquelle les Anglais traitent les plus petites choses? N'est-il pas bien bon de trouver l'art de la cuisine discuté en ces termes dans les in-4° de M. Dugald Stewart, un de leurs prétendus philosophes *écossais*?

Agreeably to this view of the subject, *sweet*, may be said to be intrinsically pleasing, and *bitter* to be relatively pleasing; which both are, in many cases, equally essential to those effects which in the art of cookery correspond to that composite beauty which it is the object of the painter and of the poet to create.[9]

Once it becomes possible to separate taste in food so definitively from taste in the arts, and to exclude taste in its primary sense from the domain of the aesthetic, an elision between the two areas of experience, or a sudden movement from one to the other, can readily generate an effect of comic incongruity, as they do for Stendhal in this account of his visit to Paestum. The expectation of bathos in Forsyth's account of Virgil's Tomb is another such comic effect, produced by the assumption that the pleasures of viewing sites with antique literary associations are different in kind from those of drinking. It might, therefore, seem surprising that gastronomic pleasure also assumes another role in Forsyth's commentary: the same role that Jameson ends up assigning to it in Pompeii, when she uses the delights of a "cheerful and elegant repast" to intensify the traveler's hyperbolic affirmation of the pleasure to be derived from sites of antiquity. One way of charting the preconditions for this use of food and wine in support of a language of intensity is to explore some of the ways in which hyperbole and digression interact with each other in travel writings of the late eighteenth and early nineteenth centuries.[10]

The conflict between these two tropes that is delicately mapped out in Jameson's analysis of a picnic and Forsyth's narrative of visiting Virgil's Tomb is discernible in many other texts that consider encounters with foreign places. In exploring the role of each of the rhetorical figures in travel writing, however, it becomes evident that the relations and boundaries between the two are not fixed and that odd areas of collusion between them make it easier for traveler-narrators to suggest that gustatory gratification might, in fact, reinforce the aesthetic delights of Italy.

Hyperbole and Its Dangers

Hyperbole is repeatedly defined as crucial to travel writing; in its movement beyond mundane utterance, travel writings assume, it necessarily reaches out beyond the tame and the familiar and allows the subject of commentary to proclaim as strongly as possible his or her ability to invest the objects of commentary with drama and alterity. Travelers regularly criticize other travelers who have failed to utter hyperboles as unequal to the task of discerning the foreign as a domain of dramatic difference. Byron, in a famous passage of his Alpine Journal, mentions with amused disdain a woman who, "in the very eyes of Mont Blanc," exclaims: "'Did you ever see any thing more *rural*?'—as if it was Highgate or Hampstead—or Brompton—or Hayes."[11] Robert Gray, in his *Letters during the Course of a Tour through Germany, Switzerland, and Italy* (1794), lambastes the younger Pliny for a note of detachment that diminishes the hyperbolic force of his account of Vesuvius erupting in A.D. 79: "Pliny describes the eruption, from which his uncle suffered, with great spirit; but it was surely pedantry or affectation unworthy a philosopher, to pretend to read during such an event. With such a scene to contemplate he had no occasion for tablets but to record his sensations. . . . When he was hunting he might have taken his pen with his spear to catch the ideas of the imagination, enlivened by exercise; but it was insensibility to talk of writing when Vesuvius was casting out its tremendous destruction."[12]

Travel writing from the late eighteenth and early nineteenth centuries is full of hyperbolic language of a specific kind: a language of emotional responsiveness, in which the traveler-narrator claims to have reacted intensely, spontaneously, and sincerely to the objects of commentary. Hyperboles, however, are, at the same time, defined as rhetorically risky. They leave the traveler who utters them open to the suspicion of being far too easily impressed—as registered in Hester Piozzi's observation at Mantua, in her *Observations and Reflections Made in the Course of a Journey through France, Italy, and Germany* (1789): "The gentleman who shewed us the Ducal palace, seemed himself much struck with its convenience and splendour; but I had seen Versailles, Turin, and Genoa."[13] Hyperboles also leave the traveler vulnerable to the accusation of merely repeating conventionalized formulations. Travelers often mock the propensity of their precursors to fall into this rhetorical trap. Sir James Edward Smith, at Baia, brusquely dismisses a line quoted—as he observes—by many other travel writers:

All the ground hereabouts is covered with ruins of the ancient Baiæ, so celebrated by writers of the Augustan age; yet surely one passage of Horace, "*Nullus in orbe locus Baiis prælucet amœnis*," is very improperly quoted by those who now describe this place. The poet only imagines those words as if spoken by a rich man about to

choose a country retreat; and they can no more be quoted as a direct commendation
of Baiæ, than

"————drinking tea, on Sunday afternoons,
At Bagnigge-wells, with china and gilt spoons."[14]

Yet more alarmingly, hyperboles invite the suspicion of pretentiousness and affectation. Piozzi summarizes this risk, while at the same time emphasizing that avoiding
hyperbole is an equally dangerous strategy, at least for travelers aware of the critical
scrutiny of other foreigners; she notes that the Italians themselves are not inclined
to feign emotions that they do not feel and observes: "So removed are they from all
affectation of sensibility or of refinement, that when a conceited Englishman starts
back in pretended rapture from a Raphael he has perhaps little taste for, it is difficult to
persuade these sincerer people that his transports are possibly put on, only to deceive
some of his countrymen who stand by, and who, if he took no notice of so fine a picture, would laugh, and say he had been throwing his time away, without making even
the common and necessary improvements expected from every gentleman who travels
through Italy."[15]

Disordering the Language of Wonder

One way in which travelers keep at bay the damning suspicion of affectation is
to recognize and exploit yet another of the risks of hyperbole: its tendency to
surge out of control and reach such heights that it cannot help but tip over into bathos
[FIG. 1]. Travel writings of this period often employ a self-protective effect of irony
or comedy, which acknowledges the potential for a plunge from the sublime to the
ridiculous, and turns it to the traveler-narrator's advantage, reminding the reader that
even when travelers allow themselves to be tempted by the rhetorical force of hyperbole, they may nonetheless retain some powers of critical detachment. Piozzi, ascending Vesuvius, and anticipating dramatic contrasts of "snow and flame!" allows the
trivial and the mundane to displace the sublime. She expresses her delight at becoming
embroiled in a conversation with the resident hermit: "'Did I never see you before,
Madam?' said he; 'yes, sure I have, and dressed you too, when I was a hair-dresser in
London, and lived with Mons. Martinant, and I dressed pretty Miss Wynne too in the
same street. *Vit-elle encore? Vit-elle encore?* Ah I am old now,' continued he; 'I remember when black pins first came up.'"[16]

Peter Conrad, summarizing the aesthetics of Jean Paul Richter, has defined the
disarming quality of irony in a way that precisely pinpoints the rhetorical effect that
Piozzi produces here: "In the sublime the senses and imagination despair of responding adequately to the grand phenomenon with which they are confronted; in irony
they abandon the attempt and instead lovingly contemplate their own weakness."[17]
Sydney Morgan, describing her own ascent of Vesuvius in *Italy* (1821), makes similar
use of a disarming relinquishment of the sublime. She relates how her party reaches
a spot "which a few days before had been liquid fire, and from which smoke and a
sulphureous vapour were emitted at frequent air-holes" and is startled when, "by the
sudden turn of an angle, we came unexpectedly upon a group of English dandies, of
both sexes, of our acquaintance—the ladies with their light garments something the
worse for the adventure, and all laughing, flirting, and chattering over a chasm, which

exhibited the lava boiling and bubbling up within a few feet below where they stood." Lady Morgan ironically maintains the language of aesthetic theory in her observation that "this was a terrible sacrifice of the sublime to the agreeable!"[18]

In such moments of ironic or comic reversal, the traveler usually shifts from hyperbole to digression. The structure of hyperbole is transgressive: the figure of speech entails a "throwing beyond," in which the speaker moves beyond the boundaries of everyday speech and, in some cases, beyond the bounds of verisimilitude. The trope of digression, then, readily throws hyperboles into confusion, by diverting their transgressive thrust; it proclaims an ironic detachment that precludes any affected pretentiousness. The strategy of wandering off the point ineluctably establishes some degree of critical distance from the utterances from which the speaker has diverged: as Ross Chambers observes, in *Loiterature* (1999): "once one has digressed, the position from which one departed becomes available to a more dispassionate or ironic analysis: it must have been in some sense inadequate or one would not have moved away from it."[19]

Throughout the history of travel writing, digression has played a role as crucial as hyperbole in translating the topography of the foreign into forms of language. Within the genre of the first-person travel narrative, the traveler-narrator moves freely between different domains of interest and different discourses—shifting at will from art to botany to demography, for example. During the late eighteenth and early nineteenth centuries, the rhetorical function allotted to hyperbolic responsiveness, as a major source of authority for the subject of commentary, produced a corresponding proliferation of self-conscious digressiveness, as travelers distanced themselves from the language of wonder. Responsiveness, in other words—in commentaries such as Piozzi's account of ascending Vesuvius—is defined as too readily channeled into reverential acclamations of sights in a formalized itinerary: in digressing, the traveler-narrator claims for his or her responses a more disorderly spontaneity.

In Laurence Sterne's *Sentimental Journey through France and Italy* (1768), the founding text of this divagatory tradition, the traveler-narrator, Yorick, is yet more uncompromising than Piozzi in his determination to avoid uncritically devoting his attention to the great sights of Europe. Defining to a French count the precise role played by exchanges with women in his travels, he declares: "I could wish . . . to spy the *nakedness* of their hearts, and through the different disguises of customs, climates, and religion, find out what is good in them, to fashion my own by." The nakedness of the female heart, he reveals, is actually displacing more orthodox objects of observation and reflection in his itinerary of sights and wonders: "It is for this reason, Monsieur le Compte, continued I, that I have not seen the Palais royal—nor the Luxembourg—nor the Façade of the Louvre—nor have attempted to swell the catalogues we have of pictures, statues and churches—I conceive every fair being as a temple, and would rather enter in, and see the original drawings and loose sketches hung up in it, than the transfiguration of Raphael itself."[20]

Yorick is at pains to emphasize the impulsive spontaneity of such an approach: "The thirst of this, continued I, as impatient as that which inflames the breast of the connoisseur, had led me from my own home into France—and from France will lead me through Italy."[21] The rhetorical uses of such impulsiveness, in suggesting a more sincere capacity for emotional response than that which the traveler can express through the language of wonder, are enthusiastically exploited by Martin Sherlock, in his *Nouvelles lettres d'un voyageur anglois* (1779). Sherlock addresses his correspondent, in a letter describing the Borromean Islands: "Me blâmez-vous, mon cher ami, de ce que je quitte trop souvent mon sujet? J'écris sans art et je vous présente un mélange de mouvements et d'idées dans le même désordre qu'ils se sont offerts à moi."[22]

Chambers suggests some of the sequences of association that such disorderliness may follow when he argues that "what makes digression a pleasurable experience is the relaxation of the vigilance, the abandonment of discipline that becomes associated . . . with the way the body impinges on (or distracts from) the activities of the mind, the unconscious on those of consciousness, and with the way desire interferes in matters that are supposed to have nothing to do with libido."[23] Shifts from aesthetic to gastronomic pleasure offer the reader a promise of such a distraction from "the activities of the mind" by concerns more closely associated with the body. Digressions of this kind are frequently deployed in early-nineteenth-century travel writings to register a spontaneous responsiveness that resists the constraints of conventional, reverential sightseeing. Henry Matthews, at the Uffizi, in his *Diary of an Invalid* (1820), signals an irreverence in the face of the room that houses one of the greatest wonders of Italy—the Venus de' Medici—by a plunge not merely into divagatory impulsiveness but into downright infantile greed: "Upon the same principle that a child picks out the plums, before he eats the rest of his pudding,—I hurried at once to the Sanctum Sanctorum of this Temple of Taste;—the Tribune."[24] Sydney Morgan cites the "culinary criticism" of a director of this same museum, the Cavaliere Puccini, in order to suggest the possibility of responding to the Venus in a spirit not of awe and wonder but of gently ironic gastrolatry; the sculpted figure, in the Cavaliere's reference to her as a "cosa da mangiare," is drawn not only into a domain of everyday, unaffected pleasure

("the kitchen" as opposed to "the cabinet") but also into a space in which epicureanism merges with affectionate intimacy: "Of this arduous director of the museum, and
zealous guardian of the Venus de Medicis, the Hesperian dragon 'was but a type': one
object only had ever divided his passion for the fine arts, and that was his taste for
the gastronomic ones. Torn by contending inclinations towards the cabinet and the
kitchen, he is said to have habitually confounded the phraseology of both—to have
talked of the Venus as a 'cosa da mangiare,' and of 'mouton à la braise,' as being of the
true French school."[25]

Hazlitt, in his *Notes of a Journey through France and Italy* (1826), turns, like Matthews, to uncompromisingly bathetic instances of gastronomic pleasure: at Terni, he
reflects on Byron's description of the famous cascade there in *Childe Harold's Pilgrimage* and comments on this scene of wild nature:

> It has nothing of the texture of Lord Byron's terzains, twisted, zig-zag, pent up and
> struggling for a vent, broken off at the end of a line, or point of a rock, diving under
> ground, or out of the reader's comprehension, and pieced on to another stanza or
> shelving rock.—Nature has
>> "Poured it out as plain
>> As downright Shippen, or as old Montaigne."
> To say the truth, if Lord Byron had put it into *Don Juan* instead of *Childe Harold*, he
> might have compared the part which her ladyship has chosen to perform on this occa-
> sion to an experienced waiter pouring a bottle of ale into a tumbler at a tavern. It has
> somewhat of the same continued, plump, right-lined descent.[26]

In the description of Raphael's *Fornarina* in this same travel book, Hazlitt once again
uses gastronomic metaphors to protect his hyperboles from any suspicion that he
might be too easily impressed:

> Assuredly no charge can be brought against it of mimini-piminee affectation or shrink-
> ing delicacy. It is robust, full to bursting, coarse, luxurious, hardened, but wrought
> up to an infinite degree of exactness and beauty in the details. It is the perfection of
> vulgarity and refinement together. The Fornarina is a bouncing, buxom, sullen, saucy
> baker's daughter—but painted, idolized, immortalized by Raphael! Nothing can be
> more homely and repulsive than the original; you see her bosom swelling like the
> dough rising in the oven; the tightness of her skin puts you in mind of Trim's story of
> the sausage-maker's wife—nothing can be more enchanting than the picture.[27]

Another category of digression from the cerebral to the physical is that in which
a work of antique sculpture, which, it is assumed, must be viewed primarily with
reference to the ideal, is shifted into a domain of robust sexuality. Henry Matthews
concludes his account of the sculptures in the Belvedere courtyard by expressing his
surprise "at the squeamishness which has induced the ruling powers at Florence and
Rome, to deface the works of antiquity by the addition of a tin fig-leaf, which is fas-
tened by a wire to all the male statues." He remarks, high-mindedly: "Nothing can
be more ridiculously prudish. That imagination must be depraved past all hope, that
can find any prurient gratification in the cold chaste nakedness of an ancient marble.
It is the fig-leaf alone that suggests any idea of indecency, and the effect of it is to
spoil the statue." A female spectator, however, supplies just the slightest hint that some

element of "prurient gratification" might, in fact, play a part in the pleasures of the antique: "I was complaining loudly of this barbarous addition, when an Italian lady of the party assented to my criticism, and whispered in my ear,—that I must come again in the *Autumn*."[28]

Living women who invoke the antique ideal, such as Emma Hamilton, in her famous attitudes, and Paolina Borghese, posing to Antonio Canova as Venus, are readily adopted as the starting points for digressions from abstracted aesthetic experience to untrammelled sexuality: Emma is often described as a woman who exhibits an extraordinary vulgarity and immoderation in everyday life, and the Princess Borghese prompts a variety of comic anecdotes of unrestraint, not to mention remarks such as Anna Jameson's: "Of the stories told of her, I suppose one half may be true—and that half is quite enough."[29]

Hyperbolic Digression

Digressions, however, are more unpredictable than the analysis so far has suggested. Even the commentaries just cited, with their effects of comic bathos, offer telling evidence of the ability of hyperbole and wonder to resurge, as a shift of attention to the mundane paradoxically invests the objects of commentary with renewed intensity and fascination. Both Emma Hamilton and Paolina Borghese are imbued with a power to reanimate the antique—and enthrall the viewer—that is defined as the product of the same immoderation that prompts travelers to gossip about them. As women who appear to be decidedly of flesh and blood, they infuse the classical ideal with a dramatic immediacy.[30] Matthews's Italian woman, too, rescues the antique sculptures in the Vatican from their abstracted aloofness and reveals within them an erotic charge that highlights their pleasures in a more unexpected—and therefore more dramatic—manner than the conventional comparison between the Apollo and the Venus de' Medici that has preceded her appearance on the scene.

Many digressions reach out beyond established boundaries, both of language and of credulity, but do so in distractingly unpredictable ways. As Mark Twain points out in *Following the Equator* (1897), the information offered to travelers is often outrageously hyperbolic, while nonetheless displaying a combination of irresponsibility and capricious randomness that marks it out as comically digressive. Spring in Sydney, Twain himself suggests, might pass for summer in Canada. The locals, however, insist that the city will get a great deal hotter and then proceed to visions of even greater heat in other parts of the country: "They said that away up there toward the equator the hens laid fried eggs." The traveler comments urbanely:

> Sydney is the place to go to get information about other people's climates. It seems to me that the occupation of Unbiased Traveler Seeking Information is the pleasantest and most irresponsible trade there is. The traveler can always find out anything he wants to, merely by asking. He can get at all the facts, and more. Everybody helps him, nobody hinders him. Anybody who has an old fact in stock that is no longer negotiable in the domestic market will let him have it at his own price. An accumulation of such goods is easily and quickly made. They cost almost nothing and they bring par in the foreign market.[31]

One form of digression invests relatively familiar places with an especially dramatic degree of alterity: a sudden deflection from the topography of the Grand Tour to some more remote part of the world. In many topographical digressions, the hyperbolic force of the movement beyond the familiar largely displaces the awareness of digressiveness. Hester Piozzi registers some satisfaction at discovering, in Genoa, "chesnuts, which would not disgrace the forests of America."[32] James Johnson, in *Change of Air; or, The Pursuit of Health* (1831), describes a disturbance of the waters of Lake Lugano: "a tremendous gust of wind, which ploughed the water into white furrows." He then allows this sudden turbulence to acquire an unexpected excitement, simply by proclaiming: "I had witnessed a Chinese *tiffoon*, an eastern tornado, and a western hurricane; but the scene which for seven hours passed under our eyes, might claim kindred with the wildest of these."[33]

Accounts of foreign manners, in particular, make ebullient use of hyperbolic allusions to the exotic. The Neapolitans are regularly classified as inviting comparison with more remote peoples: Piozzi and Louis Simond liken their sexual mores to the uninhibited behaviour of the Tahitians, while Sherlock, in his *Lettres d'un voyageur anglois* (1779) observes that Naples is "aussi sauvage que la Russie."[34]

Such deflections to the exotic readily increase the hyperbolic charge of the traveler's language by investing a sight with the localized singularity that allows it to be classified as a wonder: the exotic reference serves to remove the sight from the topography around it and marks it out as demanding a more intense responsiveness. Lady Morgan, in her account of Naples, uses deflection to a range of rather more remote spots to define the city as a site of topographical paradox—and so of extreme singularity:

> Its great, its distinguishing feature is the singular and sublime character stamped on its region by Nature! In this point of view Naples stands alone; taking her perilous position on the brink of destruction, reposing her luxurious villas on the edge of a crater, and raising her proud towers on the shifting surface of an eternally active volcano. Such fatal but inevitable engines rarely allure the proximity of man: they are found lording the desolation where human interests end, amidst the ice deserts of Kamtschatka, the altitudes of the Andes, the outskirts of the world; but the gay, brilliant, fantastic city, which pours its restless, busy, bustling population at the foot of Vesuvius, with an electric fluid for its atmosphere, and rivers of flame, and showers of ashes, for its ordinary phenomena—such a city is well worth visiting, though it had not one attraction besides that of its awful and uncertain site.[35]

Wonder, here, reaches out impatiently beyond a mere attentiveness to the visual character of the sight in question. Gastronomic digression, too, can map out this same impatience of limits. Both Jameson and Forsyth, when they suggest that eating and drinking can be deployed in the service of hyperbole, also register a determination that pleasure should not be limited to the sphere of the imagination and of visual experience. Their forays into gastronomy implicitly claim that gastronomic digression can, in effect, intensify hyperbole as dynamically as does topographical digression.

Drinking and eating, it might be argued, are rather different in their ability to invest expressions of hyperbolic responsiveness with yet greater drama and intensity; drinking and drunkenness, through their long association with poetic inspiration and heightened emotion, readily lend themselves to a rhetorical traversal of limits, whereas eating has repeatedly been defined as a more bathetic activity. As Leigh Hunt puts it in his essay "Eating-Songs" (in which he inquires into the lack of a "class of compositions" of this kind): "With wine you are 'elevated'; with turtle you sink down—feel, perhaps, even a difficulty of getting up—are more willing to sleep than to sing."[36]

Writings of the late eighteenth and early nineteenth centuries, however, confidently draw eating as well as drinking into accounts of the visual and imaginative delights of sightseeing. Benjamin Hobhouse, in *Remarks on Several Parts of France, Italy, &c.* (1796), recounts a visit to the hermit on Vesuvius and observes:

> An English gentleman and lady, and myself, made him a visit. We carried cold meat, which we washed down with some of his *lacryma christi*, a most delicious kind of wine. The terrace before his little cottage commands the most lovely prospect in nature. You have the ocean studded with the islands Proscida, Nicida, Ischia, and the still larger Caprea, made famous by having been the retreat of TIBERIUS: you have two spacious bays bordered by hills in the form of a crescent. On the declivity of the most central you have the city of Naples, which appears to greater advantage than from the Certosa, a monastery directly above it upon the summit of the same hill, or than from a boat in the centre of the bay.[37]

Robert Gray, at Vesuvius, is more contained when he indicates the pleasures of merely drinking there and selecting the crater as a spot that bears a sufficient charge of imaginative and emotional intensity to prompt a toast: "When, after much fatigue, though without being obliged, as Sir W. H. sometimes has been, to run over the incrustation of the lava, we reached the verge of the crater, we drank our friends' health in some English porter."[38]

In commentaries that touch upon antiquity, moreover, digression to both food and drink has a particular rhetorical usefulness: like the digressions to robust sexuality prompted by Emma Hamilton and Paolina Borghese, reference to food and wine hauls the remote past into the here and now. Charles Dupaty, at Tivoli, describes the delights of the Temple of the Sibyl as immeasurably increased by dining in the building with a waitress whose beauty supplies a point of comparison for the untainted simplicity of the fare that she serves to them: he notes "l'arrivée imprévue d'une charmante Tivolienne, qui nous apportait du lait blanc et pur, comme ses belles dents, et des fraises, aussi vermeilles que ses jeunes lèvres, qui rougissoit de nos souris et de nos regards."[39] Henry Swinburne, at Sorrento, in his *Travels in the Two Sicilies* (1783–85), moves happily back and forth between classical fabulation and gastronomic immediacy:

> Of all the places in the kingdom, this is blest with the most delightful climate. It was renowned for it in ancient times: Silius Italicus extols its soft and wholesome zephyrs. At present, it enjoys shady groves, excellent water, fruit, fish, milk, butter, the finest veal in the world, good wine, and almost every necessity of life at an easy rate. Mountains screen it from the hot autumnal blasts. The temper of the inhabitants is said to resemble the climate in mildness. A few inscriptions and reservoirs of water are all the remnants of antiquity it can shew. It derives its name from the residence or worship of the Syrens.[40]

The concept of free-floating imaginative pleasure that is formed within such commentaries—a pleasure that moves easily beyond the limits of the visual—supplies a crucial precondition for Jameson's vision of a perfect picnic at Pompeii. On the one hand, description of food and wine, or even mere listing of foodstuffs, digresses from the domain of visual and imaginative experience that constitutes the traveler's central preoccupation. On the other hand, the ease with which digression can be deployed to reach out for subsidiary, intensificatory pleasures allows the traveler to reinforce hyperbolic accounts of visual and imaginative delight by suggesting that food and wine might be consumed in visually alluring places or might serve as metaphors or metonyms for the attraction of such places.

Gastronomy, Geniality, and the Antique

There is, moreover, a particular reason why gastronomic digression should prove rhetorically useful in accounts of visits to ancient places. Such places are consistently presented by travelers as spots that are ineluctably mediated by classical literature. Swinburne, for example, at once follows up an acclamation of the "delightful climate" of Sorrento by affirming that this climate was "renowned in ancient times" and, more specifically, extolled by Silius Italicus.[41] Such mediation, by definition, deprives the traveler-narrator of the authority to be derived from effects of impulsive immediacy, which proclaim an on-the-spot, personal responsiveness.[42] Leigh Hunt, in his essay "An Effusion upon Cream," which endorses the "animal spirits" of a poem entitled "A Can of Cream from Devon," laments the lack of such "spirits" in English poetry and equates them with an absence of spontaneity. He places "geniality . . . that is to say, the impulse to enjoy, to create, and to sing" in opposition to the "artificial" effect produced by literary mediation: "Milton himself was in some respects an artificial poet; for he spoke Greek and Latin, and saw Nature, to a certain extent (as Dryden beautifully expresses it), 'through the spectacles of books.'"[43]

In his subsequent essay "On Poems of Joyous Impulse," Hunt cites a number of verses concerned with drinking—and also Robert Herrick's metaphorically gastronomic "Cherry-Ripe"—as instances of such "animal spirits."[44] His claim that such literary invocations of gustatory pleasure produce the effect of impulsiveness and animation suggests one way of reading accounts of the food and drink on offer in spots with antique associations: by invoking pleasures that are readily identified with immediate gratification, traveler-narrators find a means of shifting historical time into personal time and so claiming that their response to such spots has been sincere, unmediated, and personal. Jameson, Forsyth, and many of their contemporaries are, in their travel books, concerned with accomplishing a shift of this kind.

In a witty twist on this device of using food and drink as a gesture of imaginative appropriation when visiting sites associated with ancient history and literature, Samuel Rogers, at the beginning of a culminatory prose section to *Italy: A Poem* (1822–28), describes gastronomic offerings so meager that they defeat any expectation that gustatory and imaginative pleasure might fuse: "It was in a splenetic humour that I sat me down to my scanty fare at TERRACINA; and how long I should have contemplated the lean thrushes in array before me, I cannot say, if a cloud of smoke, that drew the tears into my eyes, had not burst from the green and leafy boughs on the hearth-stone. 'Why,' I exclaimed, starting up from the table, 'why did I leave my own chimney-corner?'"[45]

After the traveler meditates on the antique associations of the road on which he is traveling, however, his view of the gustatory offerings before him undergoes a dramatic reversal; exclaiming, "But am I not on the road to BRUNDISIUM?" he reflects: "And are not these the very calamities that befel HORACE and VIRGIL, and MÆCENAS, and PLOTIUS, and VARIUS? HORACE laughed at them—Then why should not I? HORACE resolved to turn them to account; and VIRGIL—cannot we hear him observing, that to remember them will, by and by, be a pleasure?"

Cultural memory, from this point onward, is made to rescue even the "scanty fare" of Terracina and allow food and wine to reassume their more usual role in shifting ancient history into a domain of the personal, in which gustatory and imaginative pleasures reinforce each other—and, in this case, galvanize the traveler into a renewed state of literary fervour:

> My soliloquy reconciled me at once to my fate; and when for the twentieth time I had looked through the window on a sea sparkling with innumerable brilliants, a sea on which the heroes of the Odyssey and the Iliad had sailed, I sat down as to a splendid banquet. My thrushes had the flavour of ortolans; and I ate with an appetite I had not known before. "Who," I cried, as I poured out my last glass of Falernian (for Falernian it was said to be, and in my eyes it ran bright and clear as a topaz-stone). "Who would remain at home, could he do otherwise? Who would submit to tread that dull, but daily round; his hours forgotten as soon as spent?" and, opening my journal-book and dipping my pen in my ink-horn, I determined, as far as I could, to justify myself and my countrymen in wandering over the face of the earth. "It may serve me," said I, "as a remedy in some future fit of the spleen."[46]

For Rogers, then, as for Jameson, food and drink require careful management if they are to serve as gratifying bearers of memory. These two travelers, explaining how to manage gastronomic experience in such a way as to produce the greatest effect of pleasure and exaltation, suggest very different strategies. Both, however, conclude that gastronomy is, in the end, not so difficult to recruit in the service of hyperbole and wonder.

This essay is dedicated to the memory of my adored husband, Vincent Woropay, with whom I spent many happy times in ancient places.

Notes

The author is grateful to the Getty Research Institute, the Leverhulme Foundation, McMaster University Library, and the Yale Center for British Art for a scholarship, research grant, and fellowship that allowed her to carry out research on a number of the themes discussed here. She would also like to express her gratitude to Karen Gunterman, her research assistant during her year as a scholar at the Getty Research Institute, for tracking down some crucial references.

[1] Anna Jameson, *Diary of an Ennuyée* (London, 1826), 241–42, 245–46. For a more prosaic account of a picnic at Pompeii, in which the traveler-narrator nonetheless defines food and wine as an integral part of her enjoyment of the town, see Mariana Starke, *Travels in Italy, between the Years 1792 and 1798, Containing a View of the Late Revolutions in That Country*, 2 vols. (1800; London, 1802), 2:97.

[2] Jameson 1826 (note 1), 246–48.

3   Joseph Forsyth, *Remarks on Antiquities, Arts, and Letters during an Excursion in Italy in the Years 1802 and 1803* (London, 1813), 302. Melissa Calaresu, in her essay "Looking for Virgil's Tomb: The End of the Grand Tour and the Cosmopolitan Ideal in Europe," in *Voyages and Visions: Towards a Cultural History of Travel*, ed. Jás Elsner and Joan-Pau Rubiés (London, 1999), 138–61, uses the tomb as a starting point for an exploration of the reactions of Neapolitan writers to travelers on the Grand Tour. Neapolitans, she argues, were often sharply critical of foreign visitors, whom they saw as singling out ancient monuments such as tombs as objects of reflection while failing to explore the complexities of Neapolitan society and manners.

4   Jameson 1826 (note 1), 226.

5   [George Gordon Noel] Byron, *The Complete Poetical Works*, ed. Jerome J. McGann, 7 vols. (Oxford, 1980–), 2:142 (stanza 53, line 5), 141 (stanza 50, line 6), 140 (stanza 50, lines 1–3).

6   Martin Sherlock, *Nouvelles lettres sur l'Italie*, 2d ed. (London, 1780), 156–57. In *New Letters from an English Traveller . . . Now Translated into English by the Author* (London, 1781), 156–57, Sherlock translates this passage as follows:

> The term *taste* is a metaphor taken from the *palate*. A good partridge is served up to three men: one finds it good; another finds it bad; the third finds it neither good nor bad. The third is a man without taste; the second man's taste is bad; the first man has a good taste. Bring a German grenadier to see the Belvedere Apollo, he will neither find it beautiful nor ugly; this is a man without taste: shew this statue to a Dutch Burgo-master, he will find it too light, he would wish it a little heavier; this is a man of a perfidious taste: shew it afterwards to ten Italians, ten Frenchmen, and ten Englishmen, they will all find it beautiful, and yet each of them may have a different taste.

Sherlock then goes on to distinguish between the literal and metaphorical senses of *taste* (Sherlock 1780, 152–53; Sherlock 1781, 157–59). See also, for example, Edmund Burke, *A Philosophical Enquiry into the Origin of Our Ideas of the Sublime and Beautiful*, ed. James T. Boulton (Oxford, 1987), 13–16; and David Hume, "Of the Standard of Taste," in David Hume, *Essays: Literary, Moral, and Political* (London, [1875]), 134–49.

7   [William] Wordsworth, *Poetical Works*, ed. Thomas Hutchinson (Oxford, 1981), 737.

8   At another point in this essay, Coleridge cites both the great works of literature and those of art—including the Venus de' Medici and the Apollo Belvedere—and speculates on the absurdity of a situation in which we regarded these as works that merely "please us because they please us," in which case "we could be no more justified in assigning a corruption or absence of just taste to a man, who should prefer Blackmore to Homer or Milton, or the Castle Spectre to Othello, than to the same man for preferring a black-pudding to a sirloin of beef." S[amuel] T[aylor] Coleridge, "On the Principles of Genial Criticism Concerning the Fine Arts, More Especially Those of Statuary and Painting, Deduced from the Laws and Motions which Guide the True Artist in the Production of His Works," in *Biographia literaria, with His Aesthetical Essays*, ed. J. Shawcross, 2 vols. (Oxford, 1907), 2:224, 227.

9   Stendhal [Henri Beyle], *Voyages en Italie*, ed. V. del Litto ([Paris], [1973]), 253: "Is there anything more amusing than the ridiculous gravity with which the English treat the most trivial matters? Isn't it good to find the art of cookery discussed in these terms in the quarto volumes of Mr Dugald Stewart, one of their so-called Scottish philosophers?" Stendhal quotes from Dugald Stewart, *Philosophical Essays* (Edinburgh, 1816), 310; Stewart is commenting on Burke in the passage cited.

10 The present analysis concerns the range of relations constructed between visual and gustatory pleasure within a specific context: that of writing about the encounter with the foreign. These questions are explored in a slightly different way in Chloe Chard, *Pleasure and Guilt on the Grand Tour: Travel Writing and Imaginative Geography, 1600–1830* (Manchester, 1999), 238–48. Jocelyne Kolb, in *The Ambiguity of Taste: Freedom and Food in European Romanticism* (Ann Arbor, 1995), offers a much more wide-ranging analysis of changes in the way in which

the metaphor of taste is employed in literature over this period. During the eighteenth century, Kolb argues, "to speak of food or eating in an elevated context already constitutes a breach of neoclassical decorum" (16); the very indecorousness of such a punning metaphor, however, marks it out as a device of particular use in romantic writing: "The pun on taste unites the elevated and the ordinary, because it combines contradictory meanings and conflicting diction. Its fusion of form and significance exemplifies the dualities of Romantic poetry, and indeed of modern literature as a whole" (16).

[11]   *Byron's Letters and Journals*, ed. Leslie A. Marchand, 13 vols. (London, 1973–94), 5:97; this part of the poet's Alpine Journal, written for his sister Augusta Leigh, is dated September 18, 1816, and recounts the events of September 17.

[12]   Robert Gray, *Letters during the Course of a Tour through Germany, Switzerland, and Italy, in the Years MDCCXCI and MDCCXCXII. With Reflections on the Manners, Literature, and Religion of These Countries* (London, 1794), 419; after the observation that "he might have taken his pen with his spear," Gray appends the reference "See Letter VI" in a footnote.

[13]   Hester Piozzi, *Observations and Reflections Made in the Course of a Journey through France, Italy, and Germany*, 2 vols. (London, 1789), 1:119.

[14]   Sir James Edward Smith, *A Sketch of a Tour on the Continent, in the Years 1786 and 1787*, 3 vols. (London, 1793), 2:99–100; the quotation is adapted from the prologue, by George Colman the Elder, to David Garrick's *Bon-Ton; or, High Life above Stairs: A Comedy in Two Acts* (1775), lines 21–22. See [John Bell], *Supplement to Bell's British Theatre, Consisting of the Most Esteemed Farces and Entertainments Now Performing in the British Stage*, 4 vols. (London, 1784), 4:187. Bagnigge Wells, in eighteenth-century London, was a place of amusement, between Clerkenwell and King's Cross.
    Among the many travel writings that quote this same line of Horace are Fynes Moryson, *An Itinerary, Containing His Ten Yeeres Travell through the Twelve Dominions of Germany, Bohmerland, Sweitzerland, Netherland, Denmarke, Poland, Italy, Turky, France, England, Scotland, and Ireland*, 3 pts. (London, 1617), 1:118–19; George Sandys, *A Relation of a Journey Begun An: Dom: 1610. Foure Bookes Containing a Description of the Turkish Empire, of Ægypt, of the Holy Land, of the Remote Parts of Italy, and Ilands Adjoyning* (London, 1615), 290; John Evelyn, *Diary*, ed. E. S. de Beer, 6 vols. (London, 1955), 2:348–49 (February 8, 1645); and Sherlock 1780 (note 6), 54 (translated in Sherlock 1781 [note 6], 65).

[15]   Piozzi 1789 (note 13), 2:214.

[16]   Ibid., 2:61, 63; Piozzi translates the hermit's words in a footnote as "Is she yet alive? Is she yet alive?"

[17]   Peter Conrad, *Shandyism: The Character of Romantic Irony* (Oxford, 1978), 23.

[18]   Sydney, Lady Morgan, *Italy*, 2 vols. (London, 1821), 2:343–44.

[19]   Ross Chambers, *Loiterature* (Lincoln, Neb., 1999), 15.

[20]   Laurence Sterne, *A Sentimental Journey through France and Italy by Mr Yorick, with the Journal to Eliza; and, A Political Romance*, ed. Ian Jack (Oxford, 1984), 84.

[21]   Ibid.

[22]   Martin Sherlock, *Nouvelles lettres d'un voyageur anglois* (London, 1779), 103–4. In Sherlock 1781 (note 6), 100, Sherlock translates this sentence as: "Do you blame me, my dear friend, for too often quitting my subject? I write without art, and present you a mixture of emotions and ideas in the same disorder in which they offered themselves to me." See also, for example, [Lewis Engelbach] *Naples and the Campagna Felice. In a Series of Letters Addressed to a Friend in England, in 1802* (London, 1815), 66–67. Launching into his account of Pompeii and Herculaneum, Engelbach disingenuously claims to his correspondent that he will make a great effort to force himself to be systematic, despite his usual "antipathy to systems" and concludes, "a few side-way flights, however, I fear you will have to put up with."

23   Chambers 1999 (note 19), 12.

24   Henry Matthews, *The Diary of an Invalid. Being the Journal of a Tour in Pursuit of Health in Portugal, Italy, Switzerland, and France in the Years 1817, 1818, and 1819*, 2d ed. (1820; London, 1828), 40.

25   Morgan 1821 (note 18), 2:71. Morgan adds in a footnote: "Pointing out the best pictures of the gallery one day to a Roman gentleman, in his usual strain of culinary criticism, he observed of *one*, 'Come questo quadro è buttiroso' (how buttery this picture is!); of another, 'Come è *midolloso!*' (how full of marrow is this!) 'If you say another word,' interrupted the Virtuoso, licking his lips, 'I shall eat them';—'*State ʒitto; se no, lo mangio!*'"

26   W[illiam] Hazlitt, *Notes of a Journey through France and Italy* (London, 1826), 239. See *Childe Harold's Pilgrimage*, canto 4, stanzas 69–72, in Byron 1980 (note 5), 2:147–48. The quotation is adapted from Alexander Pope, "Satire 1: To Mr. Fortescue," in "Satires and Epistles of Horace Imitated," lines 51–529 (Alexander Pope, *Collected Poems* [London, 1951], 267).

27   Hazlitt 1826 (note 26), 262–63.

28   Matthews 1820 (note 24), 133.

29   Jameson 1826 (note 1), 273. For other comments on Paolina Borghese, see, for example, Charlotte Eaton, *Rome in the Nineteenth Century; Containing a Complete Account of the Ruins of the Ancient City, the Remains of the Middle Ages, and the Monuments of Modern Times. With Remarks on the Fine Arts, on the State of Society, and on the Religious Ceremonies, Manners, and Customs, of the Modern Romans. In a Series of Letters Written during a Residence at Rome, in the Years 1817 and 1818*, 3 vols. (Edinburgh, 1820), 3:47; and James [Jacques Augustin] Galiffe, *Italy and Its Inhabitants: An Account of a Tour in That Country in 1816 and 1817*, 2 vols. (London, 1820), 1:254–55; the latter account of the princess's behavior is adapted by Thomas Love Peacock in *Crotchet Castle (Nightmare Abbey, Crotchet Castle)*, ed. Raymond Wright (Harmondsworth, 1969), 189; *Crotchet Castle* was first published in 1831.
       For accounts of Emma Hamilton's ebullient unrestraint, see, for example, [Charlotte-Louise-Éléonore-Adélaïde] de Boigne, *Mémoires de la Comtesse de Boigne*, ed. Charles Nicollaud, 4 vols. (Paris, 1907), 1:113–15; *Life and Letters of Sir Gilbert Elliot, First Earl of Minto, from 1751 to 1806*, ed. the countess of Minto, 3 vols. (London, 1874), 2:364–66; *Souvenirs de Madame Louise-Élisabeth Vigée-Lebrun* (1835–37; Paris, 1891), 1:193–200.
       The role assigned to the two women, as figures who revive and reanimate the antique past, is explored in Chard 1999 (note 10), 147–53.

30   See, for example, Vigée-Lebrun's account of Emma Hamilton's animated appearance when posing as a bacchante (*Souvenirs* 1891 [note 29], 1:193).

31   Mark Twain, *Following the Equator: A Journey around the World* (1897; New York, 1989), 114.

32   Piozzi 1789 (note 13), 1:63.

33   James Johnson, *Change of Air; or, The Pursuit of Health; An Autumnal Excursion through France, Switzerland, and Italy, in the Year 1829, with Observations and Reflections on the Moral, Physical, and Medical Influence of Travelling-Exercise, Change of Scene, Foreign Skies, and Voluntary Expatriation*, 4th ed. (London, 1831), 60.

34   Sherlock 1779 (note 22), 96; "as savage as Russia," idem, *Letters from an English Traveller, Translated from the French Original Printed at Geneva, with Notes* (London, 1780), 45.
       Piozzi says of a Milanese informant: "His account of female conduct, and that even in the very high ranks, was such as reminded me of Queen Oberea's sincerity, when Sir Joseph Banks joked her about Oteroo" (Piozzi 1789 [note 13], 2:28).
       Louis Simond, *Voyage en Italie et en Sicile* (Paris, 1828), 2:142: "L'on pourrait comparer les mœurs des Napolitains à celles d'Otahiti, telles qu'elles étaient au temps de Cook; et ces mœurs sont celles de la nature! Quand leur intérêt immédiat paraît s'y trouver, ils font le mal sans honte et sans remords, faute de principes et en quelque sort innocemment. La même irréflexion fait

qu'ils jouissent de la vie au jour la journée, sans penser au lendemain." In Louis Simond, *A Tour in Italy and Sicily* (London, 1828), 431, this passage is translated as follows: "The manners of the Neapolitans are those of Otaheite, or of Nature. They do wrong without shame or remorse whenever it suits their immediate purpose, enjoying animal life day by day without the smallest care about the next."

35   Morgan 1821 (note 18), 2:335–36.

36   "Eating-Songs," dated May 1, 1854, in Leigh Hunt, *Leigh Hunt's Literary Criticism*, ed. Lawrence Huston Houtchens and Carolyn Washburn Houtchens (New York, 1956), 2:553, 554. For a useful survey of the range of roles assigned to alcoholic drink in writing (and in everyday life) over this period, see Anya Taylor, *Bacchus in Romantic England: Writers and Drink, 1780–1830* (New York, 1999).

37   [Sir] Benjamin Hobhouse, *Remarks on Several Parts of France, Italy, &c. in the Years 1783, 1784, and 1785* (Bath, 1796), 250–51.

38   Gray 1794 (note 12), 417.

39   Charles Dupaty, *Lettres sur l'Italie en 1785*, 2 vols. (Rome, 1788), 1:256. "A charming girl of Tivoli brought us milk, pure and white as her own fine teeth, together with strawberries, that vied in colour with the natural vermilion of her lips; she blushed at our smiles, and our attentive looks" (Charles Dupaty, *Sentimental Letters on Italy*, trans. J. [Giovanni] Povoleri, 2 vols. [London, 1789], 1:199).

   For an account of the strategy of using food as a metonym for Italy's natural luxuriance, in writings of the late eighteenth and early nineteenth centuries, see Chard 1999 (note 10), 238–40.

40   Henry Swinburne, *Travels in the Two Sicilies, in the Years 1777, 1778, 1779, and 1780*, 2 vols. (London, 1783–85), 2:87.

41   Ibid.

42   For a more detailed discussion of the role of personal, on-the-spot responsiveness in travel writing, see Chard 1999 (note 10), 95–108.

43   Leigh Hunt, "An Effusion upon Cream and a Desideratum in English Poetry," in *Leigh Hunt's Literary Criticism* (New York, 1956), 2:528–39 (dated February 1, 1854). The quotation in this last sentence is from John Dryden, *Of Dramatick Poesie: An Essay* (London, 1668), 69 (Dryden observes that Shakespeare "needed not the spectacles of Books to read Nature").

44   Leigh Hunt, "On Poems of Joyous Impulse: A Sequel to the 'Effusion on Cream,' Intended as Much for Musical, as for Literary Consideration," in Hunt 1956 (note 43), 2:540–51. In "Eating-Songs" (1956 [note 36], 557), before eventually reaching the conclusion that "eating can never be properly sung of, except in jest," Hunt enthusiastically endorses the "gusto on the subject of eating" displayed by Milton—evidence, it would seem, of the poet's less "artificial" side (556)—and notes that "in Paradise Lost, Eve is not only described as being skilful in paradisaical cookery ('tempering dulcet creams'), but the angel Raphael is invited to dinner, and helped by his entertainers to a series of tid-bits and contrasted relishes" (556; Hunt quotes from Milton's *Paradise Lost*, book 5, line 347, and, in describing Eve's assiduity in entertaining the angel Raphael, line 336).

45   Samuel Rogers, *Italy: A Poem* (1822–28; London, 1830), 169.

46   Ibid., 169–70. After the word *Falernian*, Rogers adds the note: "We were now within a few hours of the Campania Felix. On the colour and flavour of Falernian consult Galen and Dioscorides."

The Visible and the Visual: Pompeii and Herculaneum in the Getty Research Institute Collections

Claire L. Lyons and Marcia Reed

Pompeii and herculaneum have generated a wealth of secondary texts and images almost as vast as the trove of artifacts and buildings unearthed within their walls. The literature furnishes an essential source of information about antiquities that were haphazardly excavated and then lost or dispersed during the early years of exploration. In addition to publications and archival records, the visual tradition constitutes a series of parallel representations that express historical responses to antiquity and the demands made on its legacy. In illustrating antiquities, artists recast what was objectively visible into ideal visions of the classical world. Book design and technologies of reproduction, in their turn, exerted an insistent authority over the material remains. The achievements of the graphic arts coincide with the progress of archaeological investigations made in this same period, when the study of ancient history shifted from awed admiration for monuments from the remote past and aimed instead to extract something of the context, conduct, and vigor of lives lived within them.

This essay considers the impact of ancient Pompeii on several generations of artists and architects, from the early topographical depictions of the territories surrounding the volcano to the advent of modern forms of documentation in the mid-nineteenth century. Drawing on selected materials from the Research Library at the Getty Research Institute, our intention is to describe some ways that illustrations shaped the reception of Roman antiquity and to show how the sensational finds of cities buried virtually intact spurred the genre of archaeological publication. From its beginning in 1983, the Research Library has taken the history of archaeology and ancient art as a focal point. Building on this strong foundation, the recent donation of the Vander Poel Campanian Collection added a notable group of original sources both for reconstructing the excavations of Pompeii and for gauging their resonance in the modern era.[1]

Recovering antiquity depends in part on mining the archives. The theme of this volume provides an opportune moment to introduce several recently acquired and as-yet-unpublished documents in which the Vesuvian cities—the quintessential archaeological sites—were reconstituted in the visual imagination. Beginning with sixteenth-century regional studies, this essay first surveys landmark publications that disseminated a generally conservative, neoclassical vision of Pompeian antiquity. By and large the most influential printed editions circulated with the approval of the Neapolitan court and orthodox academic authorities. These works offer a context in which to consider Pompeii through the eyes of several less well-known observers, who studied its remains once the site was more regularly opened to outsiders. As archaeological illustration became more scientifically rigorous, it also began to address the diverse needs of audiences newly engaged with the past. The nineteenth-century iconography of Pompeii and Herculaneum reflects the growing awareness of architectural theorists, artists, and the public, who saw the ruins of Roman seaside resorts and the fate of their inhabitants as signposts for contemporary society.

Volcanic Vistas and Early Excavations

The earliest printed maps and views of the Bay of Naples emphasize the looming profile of Mount Vesuvius, the region's natural wonder and ominous threat to human habitation. The settlements of Herculaneum, Stabiae, and Pompeii appear as tiny architectural symbols in an etched bird's-eye view in Ambrogio Leone's *De Nola* (1514), where they cluster between the bay and the centrally positioned volcano [FIG. 1]. Topographical texts and illustrations of the sixteenth and seventeenth centuries portray the Bay of Naples as an ancient region whose mythic ancestry was heralded by its given name of Herculaneum. An etching on an early-seventeenth-century German broadside describing the eruption on December 16, 1631, with Naples in the foreground, shows figures fleeing the conflagration. At the base of the volcano the letter *h* marks "the village Somma completely buried by the mountain" [FIG. 2]. Publications proliferated whenever the volcano stirred. As the title of William Curk's 1808 book, *The Fiery Museum, or the burning Mountains: Containing authentic accounts of those dreadful eruptions*, indicates, the production of texts accompanied by dramatic colored prints of nature's fireworks continued well into the nineteenth century.[2] Volcanic wonders and antiquities, relics that could be used to reconstruct the natural and human history of ages past, were frequently linked in printed works issuing from Naples.

The eighteenth-century excavations commenced at a formative moment for the discipline of art history. Significant advances in art and archaeological publishing included Johann Joachim Winckelmann's first history of ancient art in 1764, catalogues of sites such as *Delle antichità di Ercolano*, and catalogues of specific genres, such as ancient vases. News about the discoveries at Herculaneum first came out in the form of reports and printed versions of letters from eminent visitors, who provided their own veneer of celebrity and benediction concerning the importance of the finds. Publications by the antiquarians Gori, Venuti, Moussinot, Brosses, and Requier launched a flood of literature on the discoveries, but these publications were not well illustrated.[3] A popular book in erudite circles, Venuti's text was quickly translated into English and published in an edition dedicated to Hans Sloane, founder of the

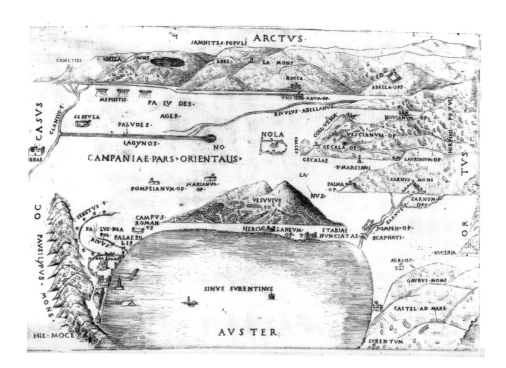

British Museum.[4] A slightly different approach, still following the handbook format, appeared in the French publication by the artist Charles-Nicolas Cochin and the architect Jérôme-Charles Bellicard. Introduced by maps and plans, charming etched illustrations depict a selection of paintings, vases, candelabra, and tables [FIG. 3].[5] These prints were based on drawings made surreptitiously by Bellicard during his visits to the region in 1750 and 1751 with Cochin, accompanying Abel-François Poisson de

Vandières, future marquis de Marigny [see p. 47, FIG. 3].[6] William Hamilton wrote his 1777 description, illustrated with views of the sites, specifically for colleagues at the Society of Antiquaries in London. Winckelmann issued several much-anticipated reports first published in German, and—owing to the significance of the subject and the reputation of the author—later in translations.[7] These texts were all published in smaller formats and could have served as onsite travelers' guides, but they were intended in large measure to bring the discoveries to distant, learned audiences. It is important to stress the lack of originality in the succession of publications on Pompeii. Rather than firsthand observation, the new titles, editions, and translations that followed Cochin's and Winckelmann's books drew heavily on a limited number of previously published sources.

Following these reports of the initial discoveries, an innovative type of publication developed that responded to the excitement generated by the Vesuvian cities and a growing appetite for collecting ancient art. Heavily illustrated catalogues of objects from specific regions, such as Rome, Etruria, and Naples, were produced following the format of earlier collection catalogues. An archaeological style of illustration emerged that promoted the artistry and value of individual objects, depicting them in detail and setting the objects off in separate plates with attractive frames. More sophisticated than the amateur schematic depictions, these aestheticized images drew on well-established graphic traditions of vedute and reproductive prints. Some decorative illustrations were intended to be displayed as well as collected for eminent libraries.[8] Prints were occasionally issued with subscription announcements for books or sold separately to collectors.

FIGURE 3
Jérôme-Charles Bellicard (French, 1726–1786). *Theseus and the Minotaur from Herculaneum*. Etching. Plate 15 from Charles-Nicolas Cochin and Jérôme-Charles Bellicard, *Observations sur les antiquités de la ville d'Herculanum* (1754). Los Angeles, Research Library, Getty Research Institute, 92-B22942.

FIGURE 4
Pietro Fabris (Italian, act. 1768–78), *Discovery of the Temple of Isis at Pompeii*. Hand-colored engraving. Plate 41 from William Hamilton, *Campi Phlegræi* (1776), vol. 2. Los Angeles, Research Library, Getty Research Institute, 84-B29643.

Three nearly contemporary mid-eighteenth-century publishing enterprises on antiquities stand as landmarks in the history of art: Giovanni Battista Piranesi's extended body of work on the magnificence of Rome past and present initiated in 1748; Pierre d'Hancarville's *Antiquités étrusques, grecques, et romaines tirées du cabinet de M. Hamilton* (1766–76); and *Delle antichità di Ercolano*, published between 1757 and 1792 by the Real accademia ercolanese. Contributing equally to scholarly polemics and the tradition of fine illustrated books, these works featured imagery whose value rivaled or exceeded that of the written word. These major publication projects thus inaugurated the creation and communication of an image of antiquity that inspired classicizing styles in art, architecture, and design for the coming century.

Beginning with his 1748 *Prima parte*, Piranesi's works monumentalize Rome in order to argue for the preeminence of the city and its legacy of imperial architecture for classical studies. His illustrated books and prints cleverly promote their subjects through book design and decorative pages incorporating architecture and antique motifs. In collages of fragments and artifacts, Piranesi's layouts and print compositions parallel contemporary reconstructions of monuments and sculpture restoration. These works are not necessarily accurate but reveal an eighteenth-century ideal notion of antiquity. The stunning presentations of views and objects are beautifully printed in black ink on large sheets of heavy, creamy white paper. Piranesi's dense texts, replete with historical references, archaeological data, and polemics, were virtuoso publications that became both models and benchmarks in the production of luxury illustrated editions.

Shortly thereafter, in 1766, William Hamilton and Pierre d'Hancarville began the publication of *Antiquités étrusques, grecques, et romaines tirées du cabinet de M. Hamilton*, a compendium of ceramics found in the region of Campania and elegantly reproduced in the colors of Athenian red-and-black figure vases and south Italian polychrome pottery. In these volumes Hamilton established an important class of antiquities as desirable historic and decorative collectibles. Published in tandem with *Campi Phlegræi* (1776; 1779) on the eruptions of Vesuvius with views of Pompeian ruins [FIG. 4], this book is the first illustrated edition on art with colorplates.[9] While not noted for accuracy, the lavish plates are striking in their dramatic use of color and the inventive recasting of subsidiary decoration from vases into elaborate ornamental borders that surround each illustration.[10] The *Antiquités* includes other well-known works of ancient art and architecture as well as objects and monuments from the region, which are used as decorative motifs in the initial letters and chapter heads.[11]

Delle antichità di Ercolano (hereafter *Antichità*) was the fruit of an association of scholars purposely founded for this project, the Real accademia ercolanese, and was aimed at royal patrons and aristocratic collectors. Both government funded and authorized, it was one of the earliest systematic attempts to record finds from an archaeological excavation.[12] Compared to earlier guidebooks and reports on the excavations, the *Antichità* was distinctive as a luxury edition of newly recovered Pompeian art treasures and a surrogate paper museum of objects. Such impressive multivolume editions as *Museum florentinum* (1731–66) and Bernard de Montfaucon's *Antiquité expliquée* (1719) had established models for this publication.[13] A five-part, 2,678-page *Prodromo* (1752) by Ottavio Antonio Baiardi introduces the eight volumes, focusing on the ancient history and mythology of the region and including a catalogue with brief listings of the finds.[14] Forgoing the bravura of Piranesi's prints, the *Antichità* presents decoratively ornamented text pages that complement the beautifully rendered prints of various genres of objects. The Neapolitan academy integrated fine printing and elegant page design in its presentation of the antiquities, using heavy paper stock in creamy white and classicizing fonts. The specially designed initial letters allude appropriately to regal and regional themes (*C* with a crown, *T* with a temple). As frames for the texts, the chapter heads and tailpieces present volcanic and architectural scenes as well as vignettes from the frescoes. In the Getty copy from the Vander Poel Campanian collection, illustrations have been annotated to cross-reference objects and their illustrations in earlier and later works, making this copy a comparative chronicle of publications through the twentieth century. This commentary offers useful identifications, provides context not included in the volumes, and points to developing relations among visual representations over time. The illustrations were not colored but follow the practice of reproductive prints in which color is designated by varying weights and textures of black lines to create a grisaille image of the original.[15]

The *Antichità* focuses on individual objects and does not include architectural plans. Baiardi's *Prodromo* attempted to illuminate the historical background of the region, and a map at the beginning of the *Antichità* locates the sites. Although locations are usually identified in the text, the images isolate objects by virtually ignoring the archaeological and urban context of the settlement. With no visual attention paid to the excavated context or relative sizes of objects (although measurements are included), the full-page etchings monumentalize their subjects. Indeed, the placement of objects in the *Antichità* echoes the Bourbon court's practice of excising artifacts from their findspots and reinstalling them in different arrangements in the royal museum.

Instead of placing images in context or surrounding them with text (as Piranesi had done), the printmakers of the *Antichità* focus on the aesthetic qualities of objects, which are smartly framed and often set against dark backgrounds. Striking plates balance pages of descriptions with elucidatory notes. The graceful presentations and sheer splendor of the books made them highly desirable among European connoisseurs of art and antiquities. Two types of collectibles—antiquities and works on paper—were thus closely allied. In folios suitable to a grand library setting, the visual presentation of the volumes plays to the sensibility of a personal cabinet in ways not anticipated by encyclopedic assemblages like those of Montfaucon. Adding to the aura of private collecting, plates from the *Antichità* were sold separately, underscoring their appeal as beautiful possessions independent of the scholarly contents of the book. Their success stems from the ingenious translation of original works into stunning black-and-white images of objects that were jealously guarded from the eyes of the public.

At the end of the eighteenth century the general fascination with the subject of Pompeii placed the *Antichità* among the most sought-after books in Europe and America. The volumes could not be purchased but were distributed solely as gifts from the king—a scarcity that in turn fueled the interest of collectors. For example, as Britain's ambassador plenipotentiary to Naples, Hamilton received letters from friends back in England inquiring about his vase books and asking him to obtain copies of the *Antichità*.[16] The popularity of the deluxe edition sparked copycat versions that took liberties with the texts but always reproduced the art and artifacts from the sites. The quality of the work produced by the Portici school for the *Antichità* is, however, immediately evident when compared with the illustrations in the impressive number of foreign editions and translations that continued to appear through the beginning of the nineteenth century.

THE VISIBLE AND THE VISUAL

In England, *The Antiquities of Herculaneum* was published in a one-volume translation by Martyn and Lettice in 1773. The title page notes that this volume "contain[s] the PICTURES," continuing the emphasis on illustration in the original volumes.[17] Although the book itself is in quarto format, the illustrations are almost the same size as the originals. The preface notes the Neapolitan government's lack of enthusiasm for the appearance of editions over which it had little control.[18] The list of subscribers, which includes academics, clergy, and libraries, demonstrates that the intended audience was scholarly rather than the elite class of aristocrats to whom the court presented the original volumes.

Subsequent editions oscillated between the artistic poles of documentation and design. One of the first Continental versions was Georg Christoph Kilian's German edition with texts in Italian and new outline plates [FIG. 5] that crudely reproduce the original prints [FIG. 6] but provide basic images and information on the discoveries.[19] In Paris, François-Anne David's stylish collector's edition *Les antiquités d'Herculanum* was published in the same format as his abridged edition of Hamilton's vases.[20] While the vases were shown in terracotta and black colorplates, the Pompeian antiquities appear in decorative black-and-white plates that are close to the Neapolitan originals. David's books promoted Pompeian style and reflect the luxurious standard for which eighteenth-century French illustrated books are known.

In Paris, Tommaso Piroli and Piranesi's sons, Francesco and Pietro, issued a new edition of the *Antichità* in 1804.[21] Their stated purpose was to make the collection accessible to more amateurs and artists and also to supplement the large folios published in Naples, now rare and *très dispendieuse*. In fact, Piranesi's sons provide lifeless reproductions of the elegant prints from the *Antichità*. Francesco Piranesi published

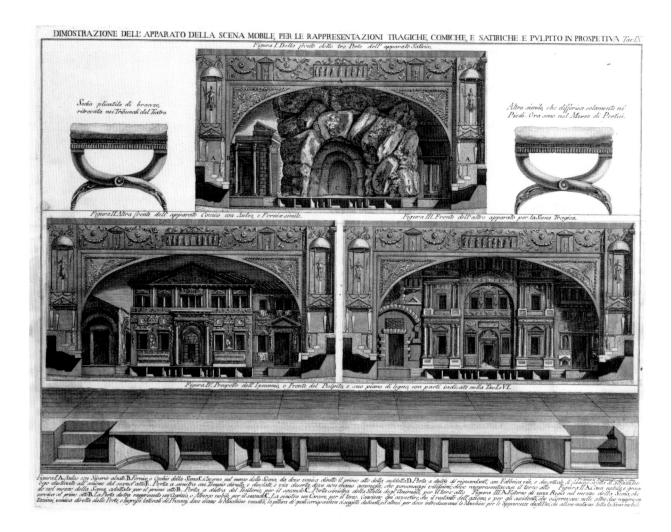

another early work on one of the signal structures at Herculaneum. His 1783 *Teatro d'Ercolano* is one of the few works from the Piranesi printshop on a non-Roman subject and one of the earliest publications to address the architecture of an individual structure at Herculaneum.[22] The final plate, *Dimostrazione dell'apparato della scena mobile, per le rappresentazioni tragiche, comiche, e satiriche, e pulpito in prospettiva*, shows the theater with elaborate Pompeian-style interior architecture and furnishings, including ancient chairs found in situ [FIG. 7]. Francesco continues his father's penchant for minute architectural details, elaborate decorative motifs, and furniture designs that could be used for classical reproductions.

In the early decades of the nineteenth century, *Les ruines de Pompéi* (1824–38) by the French architect François Mazois set a new standard in its systematic and scientific approach based on a completely new study of the remains. The impressive scale and quality of these works—even more grandiose than that of the Real accademia ercolanese—continued to promote the international reputation of Pompeii. A comparison of title pages from the *Antichità* and *Les ruines de Pompéi* illustrates a change in style, moving toward grand, yet severe, decorative patterns and away from the evocative presentation of discoveries created and preserved by the disastrous eruptions [FIGS. 8–9]. Writing that the public has known the finds from the *Antichità* as

FIGURE 7
Francesco Piranesi
(Italian, ca. 1756–1810),
*Dimostrazione dell'apparato
della scena mobile, per le
rappresentazioni tragiche,
comiche, e satiriche,
e pulpito in prospettiva.*
Etching. Plate 9 from
Francesco Piranesi, *Il Teatro
d'Ercolano* (1783). Los
Angeles, Research Library,
Getty Research Institute,
90-B21846.

well as from sketches made surreptitiously at the site, Mazois notes that everyone has been awaiting an exact and complete work on the antiquities, and that his publication will fulfill this need with its painstaking analysis of the finds.[23] The illustrated deluxe edition marks the French appropriation and manipulation of cultural heritage in a way that parallels Napoleon's *Description de l'Égypte* (1809–28), a similar government-sponsored inventory in luxury format. Firmin Didot, a Parisian printer specializing in scholarly editions and elegant typography, produced *Les ruines de Pompéi*. Just a few splendid colorplates convey the hues that were so important in the transmission of Pompeian style [FIG. 10] and illustrate Mazois's text. Most importantly, in addition to updating information on all buildings discovered since 1755, Mazois provides context, presenting general plans, sections, and elevations set within the landscape of the site.

Popularizing Pompeii

In the wake of the grand and ambitiously inclusive projects initiated by the Real accademia ercolanese, the subsequent literature reflects the changing character of the latest finds and their ever-widening audiences. The eighteenth-century reception of Pompeii and Herculaneum can be broadly inferred from the media through which the excavations were transmitted. Strongly inflected by the predominant neoclassical style, illustrations of objects, paintings, and buildings took their place in the canon of classical art that served as a paradigm to be emulated by those with the requisite training and cultivation. Artists' prints—desirable objets d'art in their own right—and luxury editions were the province of a select audience. The visual iconography was closely controlled as much by academic convention and artistic training as by the politics and self-interest of the Neapolitan court.

In the nineteenth century, in contrast, the focus shifted from the site as a coffer of art masterpieces to an inhabited urban space that manifests the lives of its human residents. In response to the clamor for information, increased access by scholars and visitors, and improved scientific practices, a spate of richly illustrated publications appeared with the goal of disseminating a more accurate and holistic picture of the finds and their contexts. Modern technologies of reproduction, color printing, and eventually photography played a significant part in the dissemination—and commodification—of Pompeii's legacy. Still fired by the spectacular and lurid nature of their destruction, popular perceptions of the Vesuvian cities nevertheless reveal contemporary ideas about how the past could serve the purposes of the present. Contradictions between the visible remains and their visual representations, which characterized the earlier iconography, are still evident. As the following examples taken from several recent Getty acquisitions suggest, ephemeral and personal records in the form of sketches, training exercises, and memorabilia disclose some of the shifting understandings and cultural agendas that redefined Pompeii.

Just as architects like Mazois were enticed by a nearly intact ancient city, French artists in Italy were drawn to Pompeii because it furnished a fresh and unparalleled source of antique paintings, sculptures, and bronzes. Immersion in the study of ancient art honed drawing skills and instilled a classicizing sensibility championed by the academic art establishment. The painter Élie-Honoré Montagny was one of several students of Jacques-Louis David who spent years in Italy in this pursuit, copying works of art from Rome to Sicily. Although not formally affiliated with the French Academy in Rome, Montagny impressed the academy directory, Joseph-Benoit Suvée, with his exceptional drafting abilities. Suvée's patronage led Montagny on a two-year mission to southern Italy between 1804 and 1805, which eventually resulted in the artist's appointment as court painter to Queen Caroline Murat from 1808 to 1815. In Naples the young painter also pursued a commission to execute drawings for a grand publi-

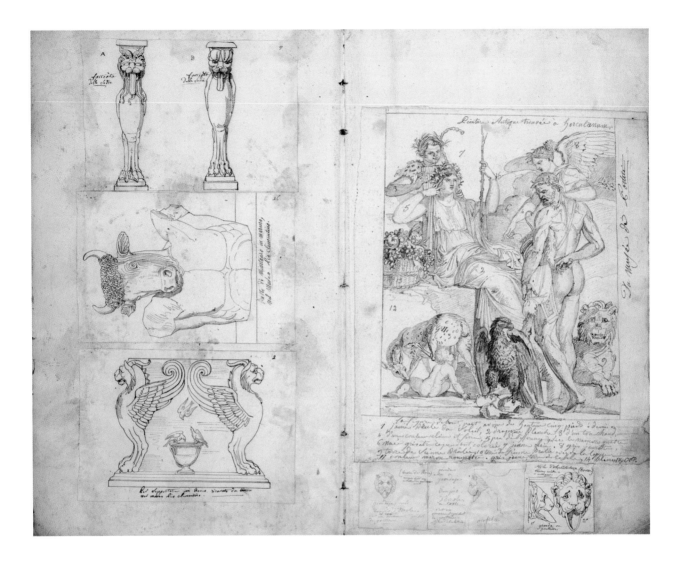

cation project, *Iconographie ancienne*, directed by Ennio Quirino Visconti, the famous antiquarian and head of the Musée Napoléon in Paris.

One of Montagny's unpublished albums of drawings and sketches from this trip demonstrates the lure of Roman wall paintings, which were believed to derive directly from Greek masterworks of the classical age [FIG. 11]. The album, entitled *Recueil d'antiquités dessinées d'après des peintures trouvées à Herculanum, Stabia et Pompéia qui sont maintenant au Musée de Portici à quatre milles de Naples*, contains eighty-nine leaves of drawings. They include not only sculptures and portraits, which were the focus of the *Iconographie*, but also frescoes that had been removed from buildings and relocated to the royal museum in Portici. The artist's copy of the Hercules and Telephus panel from Herculaneum is annotated and keyed to indicate the original colors. Whether the drawings were intended for publication or simply served as personal records of ancient iconography and technique is unclear. In any case, the hold that this rich repertoire of mythological scenes exerted on artists is evident in Montagny's attentive and highly finished copies. Pompeian wall painting, transmitted in numerous colorplate publications over the next decades, became one of the chief vectors of neoclassical style in the nineteenth century.

Sir William Gell and John Peter Gandy's *Pompeiana*, published in 1817–19, brought the first comprehensive account of the excavations to English-speaking readers. Unlike the *Antichità* and its audience of court favorites and connoisseurs, *Pompeiana* was a guidebook in a small format suitable for use by educated amateurs and the growing ranks of travelers. Numerous editions issued over the next six decades influenced popular culture through a skillful illumination of fact with lively pictorial images. The first edition is a topographical tour covering major public and domestic structures, illustrated by Gell and written by Gandy, while the revised sequel of 1832 (by Gell alone) presents the results of recent exploration, in the course of which a number of spectacular residences and baths were uncovered.[24] Bringing to light noteworthy examples of mythological paintings, excavations carried out during the 1820s opened a window into the living quarters of Romans whose libraries and walls were replete with the texts and images of classical mythology.

The revelation of interior spaces and private lives literally embodied in the ruins resonated immediately in contemporary literature and the performing arts. Artists and illustrators found irresistible the opportunity to populate antiquity with actors, costumes, and words. First staged at the Teatro di San Carlo in Naples in 1825, Pacini's opera *L'ultimo giorno di Pompei* opens in the House of Sallust, reconstituted for the Milan production in striking stage designs by Alessandro Sanquirico [FIG. 12]. Edward

FIGURE 12
Alessandro Sanquirico
(Italian, 1777–1849),
Atrio della Casa di Salustio,
ca. 1832. Aquatint. From
Alessandro Sanquirico,
*Raccolta di varie decorazioni
sceniche: Inventate ed
eseguite per il R. Teatro alla
Scala di Milano* (ca. 1832).
Los Angeles, Research Library,
Getty Research Institute,
93-B15110.

Bulwer-Lytton dedicated his best-selling morality tale of the same title, *The Last Days of Pompeii* (1834), to William Gell, whose elaborate reconstruction drawings of sumptuous interiors inspired the backdrop of the novel. Gell's facility for making ancient history vivid to the modern viewer, whether traveler abroad or reader at home, was particularly enhanced by theatrical re-creations of Roman dwellings, staged to evoke a lifestyle of aesthetic refinement. In scholarly publications no less than in popular culture, personal spheres hitherto unavailable to archaeology were re-created and animated with figures whose lifelike attitudes belie the pathos of their impending doom.

Gell's illustration techniques were not, however, limited to the genre of fantasy revival. As he notes in the prefaces to both editions, the drawings were made by means of "Dr. Wollaston's prism," a camera lucida that helped a draftsman visualize the scene as if it were projected onto the surface of the paper. An adept artist could produce highly accurate drawings using this optical device, and Gell was among a group of pioneering historical topographers—including his friend Edward Dodwell in Greece—who used this precursor of photography to good effect. Ironically, the goal of precision was undermined when he later corrected the drawings by referencing the engraved images from the Real accademia ercolanese.[25] Other illustrations for *Pompeiana* include measured ground plans, aerial perspectives, and reproductions of paintings based on tissue tracings taken directly from frescoed walls. Thus better contextualized, the illustrations and lucid text are informative and appealing. Gell was a popular cicerone among British tourists, and not unexpectedly his publication describes Pompeii with well-informed familiarity. The publication's accessibility reflects the increasing openness of the site to visitors and scholars and represents a departure from works like the *Antichità*, in which antiquity—translated into black and white by the conventional reproductive technologies of engraving and etching—is confined to the rarified world of aristocrats and antiquarians.

Gell recorded his observations on the progress of the excavations in a notebook dated to circa 1830, which he compiled during near-daily visits to the site. The notebook is one of several held in various repositories and represents research gathered for his 1832 revision of *Pompeiana*.[26] Its fifty-eight leaves are crowded recto and verso with drawings and watercolor views of the baths, the Fullonica, the House of the Dioscuri, the House of the Tragic Poet, and nearby structures around region 6, uncovered during the 1826–29 excavations [FIG. 13]. Inscriptions, measurements, and notes on color and location annotate the drawings and were used in the composition of the sequel. As several series of sextant angles taken from prominent vantage points show, his mission also entailed mapping the surrounding territory. Well connected with the British monarchy and the Real accademia ercolanese and respected by virtue of his position as resident minister of the Society of Dilettanti in Naples, Gell enjoyed more liberty than most to document the discoveries. Although applauding the 1828 lifting of the ban on drawing, he was nevertheless discontented with the continued restrictions placed on scholars and the slowness with which Italian publications emerged. Responding to the criticism of Andrea de Jorio, a prominent local author of a guide to Pompeii, that a foreign publication contained inaccuracies, Gell commented pointedly that "probably the stranger was prevented from drawing it, as they have yet to learn at Naples that the only use or glory in the possession of these antiquities and curiosities would consist in the promulgation of them to the world."[27]

Gell's great achievement was in combining correct topographical information with a creative sensibility. His work integrates art and architecture into an overall con-

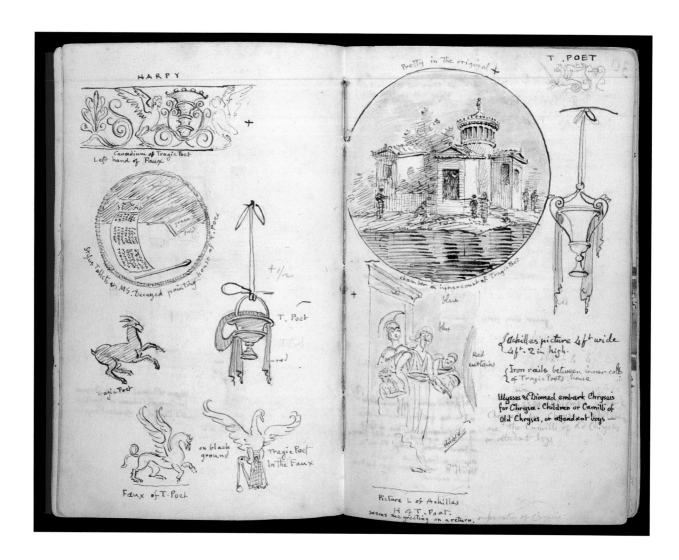

sideration of the site as a treasury of Roman daily life. Reconstructions such as that of
the atrium in the House of the Tragic Poet represent an assemblage of fragments found
in situ or excerpted from other locations. The cycle of large paintings with scenes from
Homer's *Iliad* are the focus of the text, along with the delightful *Cave canem* mosaic of
a chained dog guarding the entrance and a second mosaic of actors dressing for a satyr
play. His confident outline drawing of the Alcestis and Admetus scene restores fragmentary sections that may have been more visible at the time. Several vignettes that
have since disappeared, such as one showing a papyrus scroll and stylus that decorated
a wall in cubiculum 17 (pointing to the early identification of this room as a library),
help fill gaps in our knowledge of the decoration. The papyrus scroll was assimilated
into a collage of writing apparatus in a vignette that, as Gell notes, "though not existing
in any one place as a painting at Pompeii, may nevertheless be considered antique"
[FIG. 13].[28] *Pompeiana* engages in the cosmetic practices of luxury publications like
those of Piranesi and the *Antichità*, relying on truthful fiction to re-create an inclusive vision of a virtual Pompeian world. Yet the author's combination of technical and
restored illustrations brought the buried city to life and shaped perceptions of the site
across a broader constituency of professional and amateur readers.

At the same time that Gell was recording structures in insula 6, the French architect
Jules-Frédéric Bouchet had embarked on a thorough study of the House of the Tragic
Poet. A residency at the French Academy in Rome in 1824 allowed his immersion in
antiquity and assured his career as a neoclassical draftsman and prominent teacher.
Commissioned to produce the plates for Désiré Raoul-Rochette's 1828 *Choix de monuments inédits*, his deluxe publication was one of the first to examine the architecture and
painted decoration of an individual villa [FIG. 14].[29] Accompanying the text, twenty-
seven hand-colored engravings depict elevations of villa interiors and vibrantly hued
copies of its mythological frescoes. A student of Charles Percier, Bouchet demonstrates the virtuoso drafting skills inculcated by the classical curriculum of the École
des Beaux-Arts. Up to this point few students at the French Academy in Rome turned
their attention to Pompeii, where the horizontal aspect of the ruins did not inspire
meticulous restorations of imposing structures or engineering wonders that student
architects were required to produce for their *envois*. Domestic architecture, on the
other hand, appealed to Bouchet's antiquarian instincts. This interest laid the ground-
work for his reconstruction on paper of the Laurentine villa of Pliny the Younger. Private residences were taken as models for this famous, still undiscovered villa otherwise
known only from Pliny's letters. Bouchet's contribution to the traditional exercise of
reconstructing the building from a textual description was to re-create Pliny's resi-
dential complex in archaeologically convincing terms by means of impressive axono-
metric aerial perspectives, sections, and elevations.[30] Inclining toward an imaginative
response to antiquity, however, his frontispiece and the final view of a family scene in
the restored atrium reveal the architect's true calling as a designer.

An album containing more than four hundred drawings attributed to Bouchet
traces his forty-year career through a variety of decorative, salon, and publishing
projects and signals his aptitude as a perspectivist. The album represents an eclectic
compendium of iconography extracted not only from the Pompeian context but also
from the available literature on classical sculpture, Greek vase painting, and Roman
frescoes. Among the illustrations probably made during his 1825–28 period of study in
Naples are a watercolor restoration of the atrium of the House of Sallust [FIG. 15] and a
sketch elevation of the House of the Baker. Many drawings offer repeated elaborations

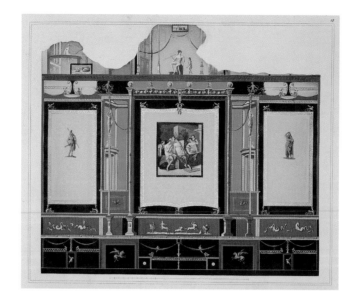

FIGURE 14
Jules-Frédéric Bouchet
(French, 1799–1860), Wall
Painting of Venus and Cupids
in the Triclinium of the House
of the Tragic Poet, ca. 1825.
Hand-colored engraving.
Plate 11 from Désiré Raoul-
Rochette, *Choix de
monuments inédits. 1ère
partie: Maison du Poète
Tragique à Pompéi* (1828).
Los Angeles, Research Library,
Getty Research Institute,
2643-730.

FIGURE 15
Jules-Frédéric Bouchet
(French, 1799–1860),
Reconstructed Atrium of
the House of Sallust,
ca. 1825–28. Watercolor.
Los Angeles, Research Library,
Getty Research Institute,
2003.M.6.

of antique scenes and book frontispieces, where motifs and figures recur interchangeably. These designs were destined for a subsequent publication of neoclassical "compositions" that merge Pompeian visual sources into utopian tableaux, a logical step in the
architect's progress from documentation to reconstruction and, finally, to invention.[31]

Bouchet exhibited *restitutions* at the salons of 1849 and 1850 and also produced
similar neoclassical fantasies for a popular Parisian monthly, *Le magasin pittoresque*.
Such enterprises circulated a visual homage to Pompeian style in which archaeological
reality—fragmentary, impressionistic, and ambiguous—was reconfigured in the crisp
regularity of contour drawing. Human figures were copied from Greek vases, probably taken directly from the Hamilton volumes, lending the illustrations the sort of rigid
perfection that Beaux-Arts architectural drawings imposed on Pompeian facades.

Bouchet's editorial collaboration with Raoul-Rochette bridged the period from
the 1820s to the 1840s, which saw the transition from hand-colored prints to chromo-
lithography. Mounting evidence that sculptures and temple entablatures were once

richly painted spurred a preoccupation with the use and meaning of color in antiquity. That the profusion of frescoes and painted plaster at the Vesuvian cities applied
not only to villa interiors but also to civic and sacred structures demonstrated beyond
doubt how central polychromatic decoration was to the idiom of classical architecture.
The issue of color—and how to preserve, record, and transmit it faithfully—informs
many publications of this era. It generated keen discussions among scholars who were
more accustomed to reflecting on antiquity as expressed in white marble or mono-
chrome engravings. For the generation of architects that followed Bouchet's path
south of Rome, polychromy was not merely a matter of superficial ornamentation but
a point of departure for intense aesthetic and philosophical debate.[32]

Three albums of drawings in the Getty collections made by traveling architects
Simon Claude Constant-Dufeux (1825–33), Charles-Edouard Isabelle (1826–27), and
Matthieu Prosper Morey (1836–37) reveal the impact of ancient polychrome buildings
on modern architectural theory.[33] Constant-Dufeux's drawings record unconventional
orders and building types such as Etruscan and Roman tombs [FIG. 16], the archaic
temples of Paestum and Sicily, and megalithic walls. He was attracted by the multicul-
tural built heritage of central and southern Italy, from its richly colored church mosaics
to a painted terracotta revetment from the ancient Greek site of Metaponto. Isabelle's
extensive portfolio of architectural studies made on-site represents his intense engagement with the materials, design, and techniques of Roman construction. Morey mixes
measured elevations with copies of colorplates from Raoul-Rochette's publication, a
procedure that student architects consciously adopted to stress objective documentation
over subjective, intuitive interpretation. The concept that buildings were not defined
by a set of unchanging external forms but responded to the spirit and vitality of the
surrounding culture was promoted by this generation of young architects, who resur-
rected ancient architecture as a philosophical and stylistic paradigm for design in the
present.[34] Stylistically their record drawings resemble those by Bouchet and the earlier
generation in their meticulous precision, but an archaeological preoccupation with
rendering historical forms, functions, and decoration infuses their work.

Marvelous sculptures and artifacts in precious metals were preserved in the ashes
of Vesuvius and were a highlight of the royal museum in Naples. These works inspired
a unique publication by Beauvalet de Saint-Victor, a Paris-based painter who traveled
in Italy from 1833 to 1836 and witnessed the 1835 eruption of Vesuvius. During visits
to museums and private collections, the artist made drawings of ancient art objects,
which he then reelaborated in a series of inventive decorative illustrations. Created by
means of superimposed stencils finished with applied pigments to imitate the sheen
of metal and glazed terracotta, the handmade plates were available for purchase by
subscription (one of the scarce complete sets was ordered by Louis Philippe, king of
France).[35] Saint-Victor also directed his commercial efforts toward instructing amateurs in the stencil technique. Several objects depicted are likely to have come from the
excavations of Pompeii, such as a bronze bull [FIG. 17] and various bronze vessels and
utensils. These idiosyncratic illustrations recast classical objects in a fanciful mélange
of shapes and imagery depicted in lustrous colors unknown to the ancient palette.
Exceeding the traditional bounds of neoclassical taste as transmitted by artists and
designers of architectural interiors, porcelains, and furniture, the renditions of Saint-
Victor represent a personalized vision of antiquity as a source of creative inspiration.

The demise of an idealizing approach to archaeological illustration came about
gradually but inevitably through the agency of the camera. Archaeology had emerged

as a science, and recording original contexts — as opposed to merely collecting art treasures — was now the central goal of exploration. The Bay of Naples was a primary destination for practitioners of the new technology. Photographs complemented the documentary function of drawings in their accuracy and truthfulness, but they were likewise subject to the aesthetic impulses and political objectives of their creators. Skillfully composed, some early photographs display close links with the picturesque traditions of Piranesi's prints and gouache *vedute* by Neapolitan artists. For example, daguerreotype views of Pompeii made by Alexander John Ellis between 1840 and 1841 depict established stops along the tourist itinerary, views that had previously been sketched from similar vantage points.[36] Painting and photography shared reciprocal influences, as we see in Giacinto Gigante's startlingly precise watercolor view of the Street of the Tombs in sepia tones that emulate photographs.[37]

The multiplication of photographic images, a key benefit of William Henry Fox Talbot's paper-negative process, further facilitated the inscription of Pompeian iconography onto the popular imagination. Although the potential of this reproductive technology for archaeological investigation was great, recognition of its advantages was slow to take hold in academic circles.[38] Accomplished amateur photographers like Calvert Richard Jones, George Wilson Bridges, and Stefano Lecchi were among the first to pioneer documentation of the site. As Bridges reported in letters to Talbot in May 1847, Ferdinand II, king of Naples, was impressed with photographs — "especially those of the frescoes Paty discovered" — and granted permission to "copy, move, or measure throughout the Kingdom."[39]

Jones's application of color doubtless enhanced the appeal of his work, as his photograph of the House of Sallust demonstrates: "I have lately been coloring some of the copies of views which I have taken," he wrote to Talbot, "and the effect is so wonderfully beautiful that it exceeds my hopes and expectations: a very intimate knowledge of the local colour by the Artist himself is necessary for this operation, which I much desire to shew you, and think you will be much charmed with this extension of the Art."[40] The king's positive reaction suggests that there was official interest in the application of photography to reproduce fugitive wall paintings that faded soon after exposure, a problem continuously lamented by Bridges's predecessors, including Gell. Lecchi, who was successful with his own innovative process for making salted-paper prints, apparently had a royal commission for a photographic campaign at the site

FIGURE 16
Simon Claude Constant-Dufeux (French, 1801–1871), *Pompeia voie des tombeaux*, ca. 1825–33. Watercolor. From Simon Claude Constant-Dufeux, *Record Drawings of Ancient Monuments* (ca. 1825–33), 1. Los Angeles, Research Library, Getty Research Institute, 890252.

FIGURE 17
Beauvalet de Saint-Victor (French, act. 19th century), *Taureau*, ca. 1836–45. Watercolor stencil. Plate 44 from Beauvalet de Saint-Victor, *Vases grecs et étrusques* (1836–45). Los Angeles, Research Library, Getty Research Institute, 2004.M.14.

as early as 1846.[41] Just as Bourbon court-sponsored publications enhanced the prestige of an enlightened monarch in the preceding century, photography began to be seen as a valuable tool of state self-representation in potentially even more powerful visual terms.

Most significant for the public appreciation of the ancient patrimony of Naples was the photographic oeuvre of Giorgio Sommer, whose studio catered to the mounting tide of tourism. By 1863 his work for the eminent archaeologist Giuseppe Fiorelli had established Sommer as a premier architectural photographer. Their collaboration eventually resulted in a comprehensive illustration of all the major areas of the excavation and museum collections. Taken from the perspectives of archaeological science, Sommer's views compress picturesque architectural space into a flattened plane, aggregating sculptures and columns into matrices of brick and masonry.[42] Fiorelli turned to him for photographs of his most compelling finds, the imprints of human cadavers encapsulated in the ash. Fiorelli sent photographs of these and other key finds to senior cultural administrators in Florence and collected for himself several hand-colored examples.[43] Sommer's studio was particularly famous for its lifelike hand-colored views, which enhanced the realism of the visual experience [FIG. 18]. Before the advent of color photography, applied pigments overcame the deficits of albumen prints, particularly for wall paintings, which could be reproduced in rich tones used by Beaux-Arts architects. Sommer distributed an album of photographs of drawings of frescoes, which were then tinted, blurring the lines between art and photography [FIG. 19].

⊡ ⊡ ⊡

During the centuries between Ambrogio Leone and Giorgio Sommer, the imagery of the unfolding excavations constructed a visual rhetoric for an emblematic place, bringing it from the speculative realm of myth ever closer to present reality. Aiming to circulate instructive illustrations of the discoveries, various technologies and styles of reproduction persuasively re-created the site to suit contemporary ambitions. The qualities of line, design, paper, and especially color further advanced this mission. The visible and the visual remained nearly inseparable in the graphic tradition until the advent of photography. Bringing its own subjectiveness, the camera nevertheless transformed the archaeological enterprise. A world frozen in time, Pompeii was its ideal subject.

Notes

[1]   Much of the Getty's collections on the historiography of archaeology around the Bay of Naples came as a generous donation of Halsted B. Vander Poel. All materials cited in this article are in the Research Library at the Getty Research Institute.

[2]   William Curk, *The Fiery Museum, or the burning Mountains: Containing authentic accounts of those dreadful eruptions which have so frequently broke out at mounts Vesuvius and Aetna: with a circumstantial narrative of their eruptions in one of which, (at Vesuvius) the town of Ottaiano was nearly reduced to ashes: with every particular relative to those great volcanoes which have so astonished the surrounding nations, and the world . . . To which is added, a very remarkable trial concerning a man who was driven into the flames of Stromboli* (Lewes, 1808).

[3]   Anton Francesco Gori, *Notizie del memorabile scoprimento dell'antica città Ercolano* (Florence, 1748). The small book includes accounts of visits from such notables as the Venuti brothers (Marcello and Ridolfino), P. M. Paciaudi, and Matteo Egizio, among others, as esteemed testimonials on the significance of the discoveries. Niccolò Marcello Venuti, *Descrizione delle prime scoperte dell'antica città d'Ercolano* (Rome, 1748). Venuti's brother, Ridolfino, was the papal antiquary (Venuti 1748, ix). Abbé Moussinot's *Mémoire historique et critique sur la ville souterraine, découverte au pied du Mont-Vésuve* (Paris, 1748) appeared originally in French and was translated quickly into Italian (Venice[?], 1748[?]) and English (London, 1750). Promoting his publication with a barbed critique of Venuti's account, the author writes, "its being so mixed with Fable, and Criticisms on Inscriptions, &c. would prevent its pleasing the Generality of Readers, and the more so, as he had not been upon the Spot for the last ten Years" (sig. A2). Charles de Brosses's *Lettres sur l'état actuel de la ville souterraine d'Herculée et sur les causes de son ensevelissement sous les ruines du Vésuve* (Dijon, 1750) was sometimes bound together with Jean-Baptiste Requier's *Recueil general, historique et critique de tout ce qui a été publié de plus rare sur la ville d'Herculane* (Paris, 1754).

[4]   Niccolò Marcello Venuti, *A Description of the First Discoveries of the Ancient City of Heraclea . . . by Wickes Skurray* (London, 1750).

[5]   The first report on the paintings by Charles-Nicolas Cochin, *Lettre sur les peintures d'Herculanum, aujourd'hui Portici* (Paris, 1751), was written in the form of a fictitious letter from Brussels and published anonymously. Later, Cochin and Jérôme-Charles Bellicard collaborated on *Observations sur les antiquités de la ville d'Herculanum*, published by the print publisher Antoine Jombert in Paris in succeeding editions and translations from 1754 onward. See Christian Michel, *Charles-Nicolas Cochin et le livre illustré au XVIIIe siècle* (Geneva, 1987), 262–63, 382.

6   Alden R. Gordon, "Jérôme-Charles Bellicard's Italian Notebook of 1750–51: The Discoveries at Herculaneum and Observations on Ancient and Modern Architecture," *Metropolitan Museum Journal* 25 (1990): 49–142.

7   Johann Joachim Winckelmann, *Sendschreiben von den herculanischen Entdeckungen an den hochgebohrnen Herrn. Heinrich von Brühl* (Dresden, 1762); his *Nachrichten von den neuesten herculanischen Entdeckungen* (Dresden, 1764) was addressed to Heinrich Füssli. The first 1762 edition was republished in Germany in 1792, indicating continuing interest in the site. Translations include *Critical Account of the Situation and Destructions by the First Eruptions of Mount Vesuvius of Herculaneum, Pompeii, and Stabia* (London, 1771); and *Recueil de lettres de M. Winckelmann, sur les découvertes faites à Pompeii, à Stabia, à Caserte & à Rome* (Paris, 1784).

8   "Les planches qui composent ce recueil, sont aussi propres à meubler un Appartement, qu'à enrichir un Porte-feuille d'estampes, ou à tenir leur place dans une Biblioteque." [The plates that comprise this collection are just as appropriate to decorate an apartment as to augment a print portfolio or to take their place in a library.] Pierre d'Hancarville, *Antiquités étrusques, grecques, et romaines tirées du cabinet de M. Hamilton* (Naples, 1766–76), 1:[i].

9   William Hamilton, *Campi Phlegræi: Observations on the volcanoes of the two Sicilies . . . with 54 plates illuminated from drawings taken and colour'd after nature* (Naples, 1776); and idem, *Supplement to the Campi Phlegræi* (Naples, 1779).

10   François Lissarrague and Marcia Reed, "The Collector's Books," *Journal of the History of Collections* 9, no. 2 (Fall 1997): 275–94; Nancy Ramage, "The Initial Letters in Sir William Hamilton's 'Collection of Antiquities,'" *Burlington Magazine* 129 (1987): 46–56; and idem, "Piranesi's Decorative Friezes: A Source for Neoclassical Border Patterns," *Ars ceramica* 8 (1991): 14–19.

11   Many of the black-and-white plates include measurements but lack identifications of the vases.

12   An excellent summary of the publication, with full collation and list of participants, appears in the Royal Architectural Library, Royal Institute of British Architects, *Early Printed Books, 1478–1840* (London, 1994), 1:59–62.

13   *Museum florentinum exhibens insigniora vetustatis monumenta quae Florentinae sunt* (Florence, 1731–66) is made up of twelve volumes covering gems, statues, coins and medals, and portraits of famous painters, with texts by the antiquary Anton Francesco Gori and the publisher Francesco Moucke. Bernard de Montfaucon, *L'antiquité expliquée et représentée en figures* (Paris, 1719), comprises five volumes in ten parts, organized according to religious significance and quotidian uses of the objects.

14   Ottavio Antonio Baiardi, *Prodromo delle antichità d'Ercolano*, 5 vols. (Naples, 1752); and idem, *Catalogo degli antichi monumenti dissotterrati dalla discoperta città di Ercolano* (Naples, 1755).

15   Colors were occasionally applied later as the prints circulated among collectors and dealers.

16   Requests for the *Antichità* to Sir William Hamilton on behalf of James, first Earl of Charlemont, and from Joshua Reynolds, as well as an acknowledgment for them from William, second Earl of Bessborough, appear in *The Hamilton and Nelson Papers*, The Collection of Autograph Letters and Historical Documents Formed by Alfred Morrison, 2d ser. (London, 1893), 1:10–12. "So great indeed was English interest in the subject that the King ordered 500 sets to be reserved for English dilettanti alone" (*Early Printed Books* 1994 [note 12], 1:61).

17   *The Antiquities of Herculaneum, Translated from the Italian*, by Thomas Martyn and John Lettice (London, 1773).

18   The authors note that the Neapolitan court did not favor the English edition and attempted to stifle the work (ibid., v).

19   Georg Christoph Kilian, *Li contorni delle pitture antiche d'Ercolano*, 8 vols. (Augsburg, 1777–1802); later translated as *Abbildungen der Gemälde und Alterthümer*, 8 vols. (Augsburg, 1793–99).

20 François-Anne David, *Les antiquités d'Herculanum avec leurs explications en françois*, 8 vols. (Paris, 1780–89); and Pierre d'Hancarville, *Antiquités étrusques, grecques et romaines, ou les beau vases étrusques, grecs et romains, et les peintures rendues avec les couleurs qui leur sont propres*, 5 vols. (Paris, 1787). The title of the second set emphasizes the colored illustrations.

21 Tommaso Piroli, *Antiquités d'Herculanum, gravées par Th. Piroli, et publiées par F. et P. Piranesi frères*, 6 vols. (Paris, 1804–5).

22 Francesco Piranesi also illustrated Pompeii in *Les antiquités de la grand Grèce* (Paris, 1804). His prints were based on fourteen drawings made at the site by his father in 1770–76. See Oreste Ferrari, "Pompei e i pittori di vedute," in *Pompei: Pitture e mosaici*, vol. 10, *La documentazione nell'opera di disegnatori e pittori dei secoli XVIII e XIX*, ed. Giovanni Pugliese Carratelli (Rome, 1995), 1.

23 "Les monuments de Pompei ne sont encore connus que par l'ouvrage de l'Académie de Naples sur les mosaïques et les peintures de la Maison de Campagne, ou par des gravures faites d'après des dessins levés furtivement, et dès lors peu fidèles: aussi les savants, les artistes, les amateurs, attendent'ils avec impatience, depuis près de cinquante ans, un ouvrage exact et complet sur les antiquités de cette ville" (François Mazois, *Les ruines de Pompéi* [Paris, 1824], 1:5–6).

24 William Gell and John P. Gandy, *Pompeiana: The Topography, Edifices, and Ornaments of Pompeii* (London, 1817–19); William Gell, *Pompeiana: The Topography, Edifices, and Ornaments of Pompeii: The Result of Excavations since 1819* (London, 1832).

25 J. H. Hammond and Jill Austin, *The Camera Lucida in Art and Science* (Bristol, 1987), 92.

26 For other sketchbooks and manuscripts located in Paris, Naples, and London, see Andrew Wallace-Hadrill, "Roman Topography and the Prism of William Gell," in *Imaging Ancient Rome: Documentation, Visualization, Imagination*, ed. Lothar Haselberger and John Humphrey (Portsmouth, R.I., 2006), 285–96.

27 See Gell 1832 (note 24), 2:198. On the secrecy surrounding the Bourbon excavations, see Alison Shell, "Publishing Pompeii: A Study in Cultural Censorships," *Bulletin of the New York Public Library* 4, no. 2 (1996): 17–34.

28 See Gell 1832 (note 24), 2:189.

29 Désiré Raoul-Rochette, *Maison du poète tragique à Pompéi, publiée avec ses peintures et ses mosaïques fidèlement reproduites et avec un texte explicatif* (Paris, 1828). On Bouchet, see *Pompéi: Travaux et envois des architectes français au XIXᵉ siècle* (Paris, 1981), 285; and on Raoul-Rochette, see Jean Leclant, "Raoul-Rochette," in Michel Sapin, *Peintures à Pompéi: Peintures en Gaule* (Le Blanc, 1999), 21–25.

30 Jules-Frédéric Bouchet, *Le Laurentin: Maison de campagne de Pline-le-consul, restitué d'après sa lettre à Gallus* (Paris, 1852). On this influential restoration, see Pierre de la Ruffinière du Prey, *The Villas of Pliny from Antiquity to Posterity* (Chicago, 1994), 99–103.

31 Jules-Frédéric Bouchet, *Compositions antiques* (Paris, 1851).

32 David van Zanten, *The Architectural Polychromy of the 1830s* (New York, 1977); Barry Bergdoll, *Léon Vaudoyer: Historicism in the Age of Industry* (New York, 1994), 75–79.

33 Charles-Edouard Isabelle, *Drawings of Ancient Sites in Italy*, 1826–27, Los Angeles, Research Library, Getty Research Institute (acc. 900096*); Matthieu Prosper Morey, *Architectural Drawings*, ca. 1836–37, Los Angeles, Research Library, Getty Research Institute (acc. 870626*).

34 David van Zanten, "Architectural Polychromy: Life in Architecture," in *The Beaux-Arts and Nineteenth-Century French Architecture*, ed. Robin Middleton (Cambridge, 1982), 215.

35 Beauvalet de Saint-Victor, *Vases grecs et étrusques*, 1845. The copy in the Getty Research Institute (2004.M.14), a presentation folio containing ninety-six plates, bears a label stating that the collection was commissioned by King Louis Philippe.

36   Seven daguerreotype views of Pompeii by Alexander John Ellis are in the National Museum of Photography, Film, and Television, Bradford, United Kingdom. On Ellis, see *L'Italia d'argento, 1839/1859: Storia del dagherrotipo in Italia* (Florence, 2003), 34–40.

37   Pugliese Carratelli 1995 (note 22), 1005, no. 28.

38   Photographs were regularly used on-site beginning in the early 1860s, in the excavations of Pietro Rosa in the Roman Forum and Giuseppe Fiorelli in Pompeii: Maria Antonietta Tomei, *Scavi francesi sul Palatino: Le indagini di Pietro Rosa per Napoleone III (1861–1870)* (Rome, 1999), 41. Rosa sent photos of the excavations to Napoleon III in 1861. On Fiorelli, see Roberto Cassanelli, "Pompei reprodotta: Dall'incisione alla fotografia," in *Le case e i monumenti di Pompei nell'opera di Fausto e Felice Niccolini*, ed. Roberto Cassanelli (Novara, 1997), 48–51. On the impact of photography on the study of ancient art and archaeology, see Claire L. Lyons, "The Art and Science of Antiquity in Nineteenth-Century Photography," in *Antiquity & Photography: Early Views of Ancient Mediterranean Sites*, ed. Claire L. Lyons, John K. Papadopoulos, Lindsey S. Stewart, and Andrew Szegedy-Maszak (Los Angeles, 2005), 22–65.

39   Robert E. Lassam, *The Romantic Era: Reverendo Calvert Richard Jones, 1804–1877: Reverendo George Wilson Bridges, 1788–1863: William Robert Baker di Bayfordbury, 1810–1896: Il lavoro di tre fotografi inglesi svolto in Italia nel 1846–1860, usando il procedimento per Calotipia (Talbotipia)* (Florence, 1988), 21.

40   Calvert Richard Jones, letter to Talbot, dated November 11, 1846, transcribed in www.foxtalbot.arts.gla.ac.uk. The colored view of the House of Sallust is reproduced in Wendy Watson, *Images of Italy: Photography in the Nineteenth Century* (South Hadley, Mass., 1980), 32, no. 45.

41   See Lassam 1988 (note 39), 21. One example of Lecchi's work at Pompeii is included in an album entitled *Fotografi di Roma*, 1849, Los Angeles, Research Library, Getty Research Institute (2002.R.45*). See also Maria Pia Critelli, *Stefano Lecchi: Un fotografo e la Repubblica romana del 1849* (Rome, 2001).

42   Brigitte Desrochers, "Giorgio Sommer's Photographs of Pompeii," *History of Photography* 27, no. 2 (2003): 111–29.

43   I am grateful to Eugene Dwyer for drawing my attention to relevant letters, which were sent by Fiorelli to the Ministry of Public Instruction in Florence (May 1868) describing the finds of a bronze bed and a cadaver and enclosing photographs: see Paola Poli Capri, *Pompeii: Letters and Documents*, vol. 1, *Oct. 31, 1863–May 26, 1869* (Rome, 1996), 80–81. For two hand-colored photographs from Fiorelli's collection, see Raleigh Trevelyan, *The Shadow of Vesuvius: Pompeii AD 79* (London, 1976), 18, 86.

The Sentinel of Pompeii: An Exemplum for the Nineteenth Century

Lee Behlman

DR. JOSEPH C. STILES, an influential Presbyterian minister and chaplain to the Army of Northern Virginia, stood up to address his Richmond congregation during a moment of crisis on February 17, 1865. Union troops were poised to invade the city, and a sense of doom pervaded. As he rallied his audience to defend the city, he invoked a historical parallel from eighteen hundred years in the past: the Sentinel of Pompeii, the Roman soldier who kept his post even as the pumice and ash of Vesuvius destroyed his city.

> The earth beneath him heaved and rocked, but he kept his post! The air was whirling madly around him, but he kept his post! Before him the mountain was belching forth its bowels of fire—but he kept his post! Behind him the terrified people were fleeing in dismay, and he kept his post!
>
> My countrymen!... That old sentinel is the model man for you![1]

During the eighteenth-century excavations of Pompeii, the skeleton of a soldier in full armor was supposedly found in the ruins of a sentry post. The story of the Sentinel of Pompeii originated with this early archaeological legend, but it came to fruition in the nineteenth century. This iconic example of noble masculine suffering, this *exemplum virtutis* for the age, appeared in nineteenth-century novels, letters, popular travel accounts, children's inspirational literature, and, most strikingly, Edward John Poynter's popular 1865 painting *Faithful unto Death* [FIG. 1] and Harriet Hosmer's 1878 sculpture *The Pompeian Sentinel* [FIG. 2].[2] This essay traces the history of this pervasive story in British and American writing and its transmission into the fine arts at midcentury. I will establish the context for the sentinel story among earlier artistic representations of the destruction of Pompeii and its exemplary men and women and then turn to the various articulations of the sentinel story itself. In a final section I will

address how Poynter's painting and Hosmer's statue served to thematize the construction of an ancient male moral precedent. Notably, both works deploy a visual language of Stoicism, which in its Victorian manifestation was a markedly sentimental mode.

The Sentinel of Pompeii was the last *exemplum virtutis* of neoclassicism, a final set piece of ancient moral instruction in the face of rapidly modernizing art practice and theory. Even late in the century, when any claim to the sentinel's historical accuracy had become unlikely at best, the narrative maintained its tenacious appeal, operating as a common reference point and a resource for new storytelling. The various articulations of the sentinel and the critical response to them combine to form a late bloom in the heroic art tradition, the art of the "model man."

Painting Pompeii: Storytelling and Archaeological Pretexts

For more than half a century after excavations began at Pompeii's Civitas Hill in 1748, Continental and British landscape artists showed a greater interest in Mount Vesuvius itself than in the topography of the ancient cities that were being unearthed around it.[3] Painters such as Pietro Antoniani, Jacob Philipp Hackert, Joseph Wright of Derby, and Pierre-Jacques Volaire presented broad topographic views of the mountain in mideruption, often featuring contemporary onlookers in the foreground who point at the conflagration in amazement.[4] New information about ancient Pompeii and Herculaneum gradually became available with the open-air excavations of Karl Weber and Francesco La Vega, but the major advance in general European knowledge occurred in 1812, when François Mazois published the first two volumes of *Les ruines de Pompéi* [see p. 141, FIG. 9]. After the publication of *Les ruines*, artists became increasingly interested in representing an erupting Vesuvius with ancient Pompeii in the foreground or middle ground, showing the features of buildings that had recently been uncovered by contemporary archaeologists. When individuals first appeared in these panoramic landscapes of Pompeii, they were often historical figures drawn from Pliny the Younger's two letters to Tacitus.[5] In these letters he offered an eyewitness account of his own experiences and the death of his uncle, Pliny the Elder.[6] Even before the publication of Mazois's *Ruines*, late-eighteenth-century writers and artists were already turning from established ancient accounts of Vesuvius's victims to the recent archaeological evidence, in particular the new discoveries of human remains that began in the 1760s. Anonymous maidens, misers, looters, prostitutes, and waifs replaced the familiar exemplary Roman figure of Pliny, and the archaeological foundation for their stories could be based on the narrowest of pretexts.[7] An especially vigorous extrapolation from the evidence is Joseph Franque's *Scene during the Eruption of Vesuvius* [FIG. 3]. Franque's catalogue text for the painting's exhibition claimed a valid historical source for his image. His painting represented the deaths of a mother and her three daughters, whose remains were found near the western gate of Pompeii in 1812.[8] The Roman matron and her daughters occupy the entire frame, and local artifacts include their cart and some household objects (a mirror, a lyre) that they have taken with them in flight. The mother clasps a small child and an adolescent daughter to her bosom in the middle of the image, while the voluptuous, prostrate naked form of the third daughter stretches across the bottom. Whereas artists such as John Martin and Pierre-Henri de Valenciennes presented gigantic tableaux that show the full force of the effects of Pompeii's destruction, Franque presents a more intimate scene featuring revivified skeletons. Franque's figures, like the figure of the sentinel, dominate the landscape in part because they are anonymous; their stories can take on the force and dimensions of abstraction and nearly unrestrained fantasy.

Birth of a Story: The Sentinel of Pompeii

With the sentinel, we witness a process of modern cultural mutation as many hands transformed the story, from a reference in an archaeological report through tour guide patter to a subject for diaries, novels, and didactic art. The first report of the sentinel can be traced to the discovery of a street. In December 1762 Camillo Paderni, an artist and excavator as well as the curator of the Real museo ercolanese, shifted his group of laborers to Pompeii from what had been a fruitless search for artifacts at Stabiae. Using techniques established by Weber, Paderni located and followed the path of an ancient street. Beginning from outside the city walls, Paderni soon uncovered a set of tombs along this Street of the Tombs, leading up to the Herculaneum Gate at the northwestern entrance to the city.[9]

On August 13, 1763, eight months after excavation along the Street of the Tombs had begun, Weber recorded in his notebook the discovery of a minor structure, a small vaulted niche just outside and to the left of the gate. Inside was an empty statue base made of travertine and a recessed seating area. An inscription inside listed the name "M. Cerrinius Restitutus." More than a century later this site would be correctly identified as Restitutus's tomb, but for many years it was known chiefly as the final resting place of the sentinel.[10]

FIGURE 3
Joseph Franque (French, 1774–1833), *Scene during the Eruption of Vesuvius*, ca. 1827. Oil on canvas. Philadelphia Museum of Art: Purchased with the George W. Elkins Fund, E1972-3-1.

Sir William Gell's popular *Pompeiana* (1817–19) was the first publication to mention the sentinel: "[In an] arched recess, around and without which seats are formed … was found a human skeleton, of which the hand still grasped a lance. Conjecture has imagined this the remains of a sentinel, who preferred dying on his post to quitting it for the more ignominious death, which, in conformity with the severe discipline of his country, would have awaited him."[11] Although he acknowledges that the identification of the skeleton as the sentinel requires some guesswork—"conjecture has imagined" it—Gell nevertheless takes for granted the skeleton's existence. But, in fact, Weber and other excavators at this site never mention finding a skeleton or any lance, helmet, or armor. How had these details coalesced and become associated with this site by 1819?

It is impossible to reconstruct the origins of this story fully, but in a recent article Eric Moormann has plausibly suggested that the cicerones, who were well known for providing romantic accounts of Pompeian ancient life for the delight of tourists, produced the legend of the sentinel by embellishing on details from other recent discoveries.[12] Such details abounded: for example, on June 20, 1767, a male skeleton—a rare find for the time—was found in the Barracks of the Gladiators, where parade armor had already been unearthed. Similar finds occurred near the amphitheater beginning in 1766.[13] It is possible that these discoveries, as well as the proximity of the tomb to the Herculaneum Gate, helped inspire the sentinel story.

As Gell tells it, the sentinel is both brave for having chosen this noble death and helpless because in a sense he had to choose it. His alternative would have been to die a coward's death at the hands of the state. Gell's perspective is not explicitly critical of the stern Roman military ethos, but neither is it fully sympathetic to it: his voice instead evinces an anthropological coolness. Later representations of the sentinel story would draw from Gell's account, often showing variations in such details as the setting, props, costume, and posture of the figure, but they would also offer new explanations of the context and meaning of the sentinel's sacrifice.

The most influential literary treatment of the sentinel story was Edward Bulwer-Lytton's *Last Days of Pompeii* (1834).[14] Drawing the story from Gell, Bulwer-Lytton provides the sentinel with a cameo appearance, standing upright by the Herculaneum Gate as the novel's heroes run past him to escape from the dying city. Two features of Bulwer-Lytton's account of the sentinel story would be crucial for later versions. First, the author implicitly compares the sentinel to other Pompeian citizens. Just before the sentinel appears, we see the callow priests of Isis prepare to gather their "gold and precious mummeries" from the temple. One of them "greedily" wolfs down food. "Nothing," the narrator concludes, "could, perhaps, be more unnaturally horrid than the selfish baseness of these villains, for there is nothing more loathsome than the valor of avarice."[15] The sentinel's nobility contrasts with the priests' despicable and pointless grasping for material goods in their final moments, just before columns of boiling seawater inundate them.

Although Bulwer-Lytton juxtaposes the sentinel with other, lesser Pompeians, the figure's heroism is problematic: "The fugitives hurried on—they gained the gate—they passed by the Roman sentry; the lightning flashed over his livid face and polished helmet, but his stern features were composed even in their awe! He remained erect and motionless at his post. That hour itself had not animated the machine of the ruthless majesty of Rome into the reasoning and self-acting man. There he stood, amidst the crashing elements: he had not received the permission to desert his station and escape."[16] The sentinel is magnificent, statuelike, frozen in a moment of noble fortitude, but for Bulwer-Lytton his immobility is also a minor tragedy. Imperial Rome has constructed a machine instead of the "reasoning and self-acting" man who might have been produced by a republic. Bulwer-Lytton goes further than Gell in his depiction of the sentinel as a victim of circumstance, for in this version the imperial ethos of his society has reduced and betrayed him. The soldier's status as a victim of the imperial machine is made more poignant by the sense that he is experiencing the emotions he denies.

Details of the sentinel story began to be questioned in 1853, and in 1867 Thomas Dyer was the first to argue that the entire story was pure fable.[17] Such critiques did not penetrate the public consciousness, however. Numerous retellings of the sentinel story would be produced well into the late nineteenth and early twentieth centuries, and usually they were enthusiastic about the sentinel's value as a role model for both adults and children.[18] Even Mark Twain, who is hilariously skeptical about the claims of tour guides in *The Innocents Abroad* (1869),[19] accepts the sentinel story as "perhaps the most poetical thing Pompeii has yielded to modern research."[20] Twain famously used the sentinel story as the setup for a joke about modern-day policemen, who, he says, would have stayed on the scene not out of a sense of duty but for the sake of a good nap. Still, this joke did nothing to tarnish the reputation of the original Roman model.

Poynter's Sentinel: Faithful unto Death and *Victorian Stoicism*

In nineteenth-century archaeological and travel writing, in fiction, and in didactic literature for children, the sentinel appears along the way as a colorful anecdote, a minor character, or an instructive example. But with *Faithful unto Death*, Poynter places this figure at the center of his canvas and invites his audience's sustained attention. Even as balls of fire besiege the citizens hunched over in the background, the soldier stands at the ready in the foreground, his forearms and right calf tensed in preparation. He stands monumental, in the contrapposto of classical statuary.[21]

Poynter makes a straightforward argument for the sentinel's value as an example through the same kind of moral juxtapositions evident in Bulwer-Lytton's *Last Days of Pompeii*. Coins, a statuette, and other signifiers of Roman luxury are strewn across the painting's foreground, but they do not attract the sentinel's attention. A man lies prostrate, still clutching a precious object, while another man stands upright, holding a large metal vessel. Their suffering is an ironic reversal of fate for those who had before seemed so blessed by its gifts. The soldier seems oblivious to this drama of moral retribution even as he participates in it as the exemplum of virtue.

Like his fellow "Olympian" painters, Frederic Leighton and Lawrence Alma-Tadema, Poynter employed various classical elements in his paintings, but his emphasis on ancient episodes of male martyrdom and self-sacrifice distinguish his early work.[22] Poynter's soldier evinces a masculine self-control in his rigid posture, rebuking not only Roman decadence and avarice but also sentimental excess, the overflow of grief or fear that can expose the male body as a site of disorder or weakness. In his *constantia* (firmness), the soldier promises to eliminate the creeping modern effeminacy that Thomas Hughes, Charles Kingsley, Charlotte Yonge, and other Victorian writers meant to suppress.[23] The two women of Poynter's work, who struggle to protect themselves against falling objects by stooping and shielding their faces, represent this weak response. In his 1867 travel memoir William Dean Howells establishes a similar connection between Roman moral weakness and the weakness of women's bodies in describing a set of plaster casts of the Pompeian dead:

> The man in the last struggle has thrown himself upon his back, and taken his doom sturdily—there is a sublime claim in his rigid figure. The women lie upon their faces, their limbs tossed and distorted, their drapery tangled and heaped about them, and in every fibre you see how hard they died. One presses her face into her handkerchief to draw one last breath unmixed with scalding steam; another's arms are wildly thrown abroad to clutch at help; another's hand is appealingly raised, and on her slight fingers you see the silver hoops with which her poor dead vanity adorned them.[24]

While the rigidity of the man's body suggests "sublime" composure to Howells, the contortion of the women's bodies indicates pain and fear, and the jewelry one of them wears marks a characteristically female vanity.

By resisting threats to his masculine self-control, Poynter's sentinel stands as a common mid-Victorian type, the Roman Stoic. Stoic exemplars were nothing new— beginning in the early modern period Stoic heroes such as Cato and Seneca were celebrated in Britain for their opposition to imperial hegemony—but in the Victorian era imperial Roman Stoicism captured many writers and artists' imaginations.[25] To them, the early Greek Stoic virtues of *apatheia* (freedom from violent passion) and *sophrosyne* (self-control or moderation) appeared to be most fully manifested in the Roman military ethos, specifically, the earnest morality and pervasive Roman appetite for duty and self-sacrifice.[26] In *Faithful unto Death* the temporal and moral distance between the soldier's enactment of this Roman tradition of martial bravery and the male viewer's own, presumably fallen, time convicts modern men of having strayed from the Stoic path of honor. Still, the viewer is offered the possibility of following the sentinel's example. As Joseph Kestner has observed, the sentinel figure is suggestively reproduced in miniature in the painting itself, for scrawled on the left side of the gate is a tiny Pompeian graffito of a soldier standing at attention, spear at the ready.[27] The potential influence of the sentinel's example is further suggested by his long shadow, which takes up the middle foreground.

In *Faithful unto Death* Poynter encourages imitation not only through such self-reflexive gestures but also by depicting the sentinel's heroic stance as requiring sustained effort. The struggle to maintain a soldierly rigidity is obvious in the tension of the forearm and calf muscles. This sentinel's eyes gaze upward, nervously, toward the ashy sky. They are dewy with apprehension about his impending destruction. Because the sentinel's body reveals an emotional susceptibility, Roman Stoicism fails to emerge intact. *Faithful unto Death* becomes either an active rebuttal to the Victorian desire to constitute an earlier, hard imperial masculinity or an unwitting record of its failure. But for Poynter, the Pompeian soldier's nervous eyes do not eliminate the possibility of transmitting Roman Stoicism to the modern male viewer; rather, it is enabled through the possibility of its failure. This viewer recognizes sympathetically the soldier's emotional and bodily control even as he senses the possibility that he could surrender to a fearful wince at the last moment. This intended manipulation of viewer response is detailed in Charlotte Yonge's guide for children, the *Book of Golden Deeds* (1864). For Yonge, the "very appreciation of suffering only . . . [quickens] the sense of the heroism that risked the utmost, till . . . [young readers] learn absolutely to look upon danger as an occasion for evincing the highest qualities."[28]

Harriet Hosmer's Pompeian Sentinel

An important element of the appeal of Poynter's soldier is that he is young and beautiful: his smooth, healthy skin is shown to advantage by the red glow of the volcanic eruption. The fact that his eyes are turned away from the viewer only draws the viewer in further, for like a contemporary female nude, they invite lingering considerations of his charms. The fearful yet resigned expression of his eyes recalls a more vulnerable, voluptuous image of male sacrifice, Saint Sebastian. This painting's direct appeal to the audience to imitate the sentinel's bodily self-sacrifice is supplemented by the surface appeal of that body itself. Its beauty is enhanced, too, by its proximity to death.

The youthful beauty of Poynter's figure stands in high relief when compared with the other major visual representation of the sentinel, Harriet Hosmer's sculpture *The Pompeian Sentinel* [see FIG. 2]. In the summer of 1878 this leading American-born sculptor exhibited the 2.5-meter plaster-and-wax statue at Colnaghi's Gallery in London.[29] Hosmer had likely seen one of the many magazine reproductions of Poynter's *Faithful unto Death* before creating her *Sentinel*, but her treatment is strikingly different. Our basis for comparison is limited by the fact that only a photograph of the upper torso and head of Hosmer's statue has survived, yet it is clear that her figure is at least twenty years older than Poynter's, and his face and neck appear weathered by hardship. Imperfections riddle his skin, and his lips are pressed firmly together. These features combine to form a more somber and monumental figure than Poynter's sentinel.

In the lack of classical balance and proportion of his facial features, the contrast between the high level of anatomical detail and comparative simplicity of the armor design, and an older, more rugged manliness, Hosmer's sentinel draws from a particular ancient tradition: Roman verism. The main features of this mode of portraiture, prevalent during the first two centuries A.D., have been ably described by Sheldon Nodelman:

> [Veristic portraits consist] exclusively of portraits of men in later life, often balding and toothless, upon whose faces the creases, wrinkles, and blemishes inflicted by life upon aging flesh are prominently and harshly displayed with a kind of clinical exactitude which has aptly been called "cartographic." The insistent presentation of unflattering physiognomic irregularities, apparently, from their diversity, highly individualized, extends also to the representation of emotional states; the expressions of these faces are without exception grim, haggard, and ungenerous, twisted by fixed muscular contractions.[30]

These portraits often represented Roman republican heroes of the past such as Brutus and Cicero, whose "grim restraint," as Nodelman further notes, stood in contrast to the "emotional pathos, the exaltation of spontaneity which had illuminated Hellenistic royal portraiture."[31] As scholars have noted, in its ancient context Roman verism was not a mode of realism devoted to a perfect mimesis of the human face but was instead a programmatic resistance to foreign Greek values, which ostensibly overlapped with the tyrannical rule favored by the new emperors. These old Roman faces, with their sagging flesh and dignified, crumbling aspects, resembled each other more than they differed.[32]

Hosmer's *Sentinel* is equally no work of straightforward realism, and in drawing on a distinctively Roman veristic art practice Hosmer associates her sentinel with the earlier resistance to contemporary "decadence." Her canny use of this early Roman mode results in a more historically resonant approach to representing the sentinel than Poynter's. But there is a key difference between Hosmer's *Sentinel* and Roman veristic portraits: The eyes of Hosmer's sentinel are closed, probably a reference to the appearance of wax death masks used at Roman funerals (a legendary form of Roman art that scholars recently have suggested influenced Roman veristic portraiture).[33] Whatever the reason, the closed eyes challenge the kind of immediate identification offered by Poynter's painting.

Two contemporary reviewers admired this feature, arguing that the shut eyes suggest, in one case, "concentration," and in the other, "calm."[34] The reviewers diverged, though, in their appraisal of the statue's posture (which we cannot now fully appraise) and facial expression. The reviewer for the *Art Journal* observed:

> [He is] leaning with both hands upon his spear. There is a slight inclination of the head, which, at first glance, does not altogether accord with the manly proportions and muscular development of the figure, but which, on closer inspection, will be found in perfect harmony with the expression on his face. The moment chosen, indeed, is that immediately before the poor sentinel is choked by the sulphurous air and ashes of the terrible eruption. His eyes are calmly closed, and his whole face has about it the grand, unflinching "consent to death."

This description presents the sentinel's body as already having achieved a successful resignation and an exemplary physical stasis. His placidity in the face of death is so complete that we cannot see the struggle that must have preceded it—it is an "everlasting stillness." The *London Times* critic, on the other hand, saw a body caught in struggle: "Looking at the figure in profile, we see that he already staggers and can scarce sustain himself by aid of his lance, hard clutched and pressed as a point of support against his knee.... The muscles of his limbs are in strong tension, the bones firmly set, giving emphasis to the impression that the man's energies are bent up to their very utmost." Here, the slight downward tilt of the sentinel's torso indicates not a preparation for suffering but suffering itself.

Despite the differences between these two readings of Hosmer's sentinel, neither suggests that he is contending with fear, which is consistent with the photographic evidence that has survived of the statue. Hosmer's veteran soldier shows no sign of losing dignity or self-confidence. In fact, the closest approximation to the appearance and the ethos of this figure is not Poynter's *Sentinel* but Hosmer's own earlier work *Zenobia* (1859).[35] Joy S. Kasson and Deborah Cherry have demonstrated how Hosmer's rendering of the captive and chained yet resolute Palmyrean queen represented dramatic resistance to male authority.[36] In the context of her career Hosmer's *Sentinel* appears as a late male variant of an established female Stoic type. Both statues feature dramatically tall human figures with proud, resigned, relatively impassive faces, who command respect but not necessarily easy sympathy. With regard to technique, however, this little-noticed statue stands apart from the rest of Hosmer's oeuvre and resembles what we know of the *Sentinel*. Nearly all of Hosmer's other statues emphasize pure Hellenic or Hellenistic classical form over the kind of ugly beauty evident in Roman veristic portraits. But for *Zenobia* and the *Sentinel*, the sculptor clearly believed this more morally rigorous tradition was the appropriate classical model.

▣ ▣ ▣

Edward Poynter and Harriet Hosmer represent two important facets of Victorian depictions of the Sentinel of Pompeii. Hosmer's *Pompeian Sentinel* projects a certain authenticity in its depiction of this Stoic hero but also suggests a sense of distance between the modern viewer and the ancient exemplum by depicting him with eyes that are firmly shut against fear and other damaging emotions. We are presented with a heroic Stoic product but not, as with Poynter, a clear process of establishing a contemporary connection to the image. In his book *Duty* (1880) Samuel Smiles defines the ne plus ultra of such impassivity, positing a sentinel who lacks any fear at all: "It was his Duty. He had been set to guard the place, and he never flinched.... Duty, in its purest form, is so constraining that one never thinks, in performing it, of one's self at all. It has to be done without any thought of self-sacrifice."[37] This exemplum is defined by an exterior call to service, whereby circumstances demand action. He lacks any countervailing feelings or deliberation, including an inner sense that he is behaving like an exemplum. Hosmer's sentinel does not, like Smiles's, necessarily lack self-consciousness, but his appeal lies in his seductive inaccessibility.

A sense of distance from the Roman past is evident in many representations of the sentinel, and, indeed, the inescapable pathos of loss in modern reconstructions of antiquity may exacerbate such a distance. But alongside it is a stronger force of sympathetic, imaginative connection represented in Poynter's sentinel, with his upturned eyes and exaggerated stiffness. Like Gell's sentinel, Poynter's version made evident to a nineteenth-century male audience the pressures impinging on him from both within and without, a figure who showed weakness but ultimately "preferred dying on his post."[38]

Notes

Many thanks to Eric Moormann, Christopher Parslow, Ann Kuttner, Meilee Bridges, Rev. Joseph L. Curran, and the staff of the Watertown Free Public Library for their advice and assistance.

1   Cited in Ernest B. Furgurson, *Ashes of Glory: Richmond at War* (New York, 1996), 301.

2   On the *exemplum virtutis* in eighteenth-century art, see Robert Rosenblum, *Transformations in Late Eighteenth-Century Art* (Princeton, 1967), 50–106; on Poynter's use of the *exemplum virtutis* tradition, see Elizabeth Prettejohn, "Recreating Rome in Victorian Painting: From History to Genre," in *Imagining Rome*, ed. Michael J. H. Liversidge and Catharine Edwards (London, 1996), 54–69.

3   As Alexandra R. Murphy has noted (*Visions of Vesuvius* [Boston, 1978], 4), depictions of the topography of an erupting Vesuvius increased in the 1750s as the mountain again became geologically active. Murphy also notes that later images of Vesuvius were likely encouraged by popular treatises on the mountain by Francesco Serao (*Istoria dell'incendio del Vesuvio accaduto nel mese di maggio dell'anno 1737* [Naples, 1738]); and William Hamilton (*Campi Phlegræi: Observations on the volcanoes of the two Sicilies ... with 54 plates illuminated from drawings taken and colour'd after nature* [Naples, 1776]; and idem, *Supplement to the Campi Phlegræi* [Naples, 1779]).

4   See, for examples, Pietro Antoniani, *Eruption of Vesuvius*, 1767 (Naples, private collection); Jacob Philipp Hackert, *Vesuvius in Eruption*, 1774 (Kassel, Museen), and 1779 (Cologne, Wolfgang Kronig); Joseph Wright of Derby, *Vesuvius*, ca. 1774 (Derby Museum and Art Gallery); and Pierre-Jacques Volaire, *The Eruption of Mount Vesuvius*, 1777 (Durham, North Carolina Museum of Art).

5   Gaius Plinius Caecilius Secundus *Epistulae* 4.16, 20 (see *The Letters of the Younger Pliny*, ed. and trans. Betty Radice [Baltimore, 1963], 166–68, 170–73).

6   See, for example, Pierre-Henri de Valenciennes's *Eruption of Vesuvius and the Death of Pliny*, 1813 (Toulouse, Musée des Augustins), which depicts the younger Pliny's account of his uncle's death at Stabiae. Valenciennes's painting emphasizes the old man's isolation at his death as two slaves hold him up on a nearly empty patch of shoreline. See also Angelica Kauffmann's *Pliny the Younger and His Mother at Misenum, A.D. 79*, 1785 (Princeton University Art Museum);

and John Martin, *The Destruction of Pompeii and Herculaneum*, after 1821 (University of Manchester, Tabley House).

7   In 1843 an American visitor, J. T. Headley, was struck by the pervasiveness of such stories. After starting to discuss the last moments of a fallen woman found in the Villa of Diomedes, he interrupted himself to write, "But I cannot go into details. They have been written over a hundred times" (J. T. Headley, *Letters from Italy* [New York, 1854], 71).

8   See Murphy 1978 (note 3), 15.

9   As Michael Grant has noted, the ancient name for the gate was Porta Saliensis because it led to a "village of salt-pan workers" (*Cities of Vesuvius: Pompeii and Herculaneum* [New York, 1976], 53). On the early excavations along the Street of the Tombs, see Valentin Kockel, *Die Grabbauten vor dem Herkulaner Tor in Pompeji* (Mainz, 1983). For a fine history of early Pompeian excavation, see Christopher Charles Parslow, *Rediscovering Antiquity: Karl Weber and the Excavation of Herculaneum, Pompeii, and Stabiae* (Cambridge, 1995).

10 For Weber's August 13 account in his excavation diary, see Giuseppe Fiorelli, *Pompeianarum antiquitatum historia* (Naples, 1860), 1:152–53.

11 William Gell and John P. Gandy, *Pompeiana: The Topography, Edifices, and Ornaments of Pompeii* (London, 1817–19), 94.

12 Eric Moormann, "Literary Evocations of Ancient Pompeii," in *Tales from an Eruption: Pompeii, Herculaneum, Oplontis: Guide to the Exhibition*, ed. Pietro Giovanni Guzzo, trans. Jo Wallace-Hadrill (Milan, 2003), 14–33. On cicerones, see Eric Moormann, "Guides in the Vesuvius Area Eternalised in Travelogues and Fiction," *Rivista di studi pompeiani* 14 (2003): 31–48. I will cite Moormann, "Literary Evocations," 2003, when quoting from his cited sources.

13 On October 31, 1766, a helmet and what appears to be leg armor were discovered during the early excavation of the Barracks of the Gladiators. In Giuseppe Abbati's 1854 catalogue of artifacts from the museum in Portici, *Raccolta de' più belli ed interessanti dipinti, musaici ed altri monumenti rinvenuti negli scavi reali di Ercolano, di Pompei e di Stabia, che ammiransi nel Museo reale borbonico* (Naples), he includes sketches of a gladiatorial helmet, four gladiatorial shields, and four spears (17–19). At least the first helmet and the fourth shield derive from excavations made at the Quadriporticus of the Theaters, which began in 1766 and were completed in 1796 (see photographs from Tiziana Rocco, "The Quadriporticus of the Theatres," in Moormann, "Literary Evocations," 2003 [note 12]), 100–101). Thirty-four male skeletons were eventually found at this site.

14 Edward Bulwer-Lytton, *The Last Days of Pompeii* (1834; New York, 1940). Bulwer-Lytton, like some other writers and artists, does not use the term "sentinel," instead using the term "sentry." For the sake of consistency, I will use the term "sentinel" throughout this essay. On Bulwer-Lytton and Pompeii, see Wolfgang Leppmann, *Pompeii in Fact and Fiction* (London, 1968).

15 Bulwer-Lytton 1940 (note 14), 293.

16 Ibid., 294–95.

17 In his *Handbook for Travellers in Southern Italy* (London, 1853), Octavian Blewitt casts doubt on the identification of the sentinel's supposed resting place as a sentry box near the Herculaneum Gate, but he does not question the validity of the on-site discovery of the skeleton (332). See Thomas Dyer, *Pompeii: Its History, Buildings, and Antiquities* (1867). For later critiques of the sentinel story, see the seventh edition of the *Handbook for Travellers in Southern Italy* (London, 1873), 230; Johannes Overbeck, *Pompeji in seinen Gebäuden, Alterthümern und Kunstwerken für Kunst und Alterthumsfreunde dargestellt*, ed. August Mau, 7th ed. (Leipzig, 1873), 230. The latter two are cited in Moormann, "Literary Evocations," 2003 (note 12), 23–24.

18 See, for example, Charlotte M. Yonge, *A Book of Golden Deeds* (1864; London, 1893), 3–4; Samuel Smiles, *Duty, with Illustrations of Courage, Patience, and Endurance* (1880; London,

1883), 2; Anthony Baden-Powell, *Scouting for Boys* (London, 1908), 234. The latter is cited in Joseph A. Kestner, *Masculinities in Victorian Painting* (Brookfield, Vt., 1995), 99.

19 At one point, Twain writes of a tree with a bullet hole in it, "The guides will point it out to visitors for the next eight hundred years, and when it decays and falls down they will put up another there and go on with the same old story just the same" (*The Innocents Abroad* [1869; New York, 2002], 97).

20 Ibid., 272.

21 On Poynter, see Christopher Wood, *Olympian Dreamers* (London, 1983); George P. Landow, "Victorianized Romans: Images of Rome in Victorian Painting," *Browning Institute Studies* 12 (1984): 29–51; Joseph A. Kestner, *Mythology and Misogyny* (Madison, 1989); Kestner 1995 (note 18); Prettejohn 1996 (note 2); and Joanna Madeleine Kear, "Victorian Classicism in Context: Sir E. J. Poynter (1836–1919) and the Classical Heritage" (PhD diss., University of Bristol, 1999).

22 Three other works on this theme appear in Poynter's oeuvre besides *Faithful unto Death*, 1865 (Liverpool, Walker Art Gallery), including an 1864 painting, *On Guard, in the Time of the Pharaohs* (private collection); an 1872–73 fresco on the martyrdom of Saint Stephen (Dulwich, Saint Stephen's Church); and an 1884 painting, *The Ides of March* (Manchester Art Gallery), which includes a Roman sentinel figure in the background. *On Guard, in the Time of the Pharaohs* was exhibited at the Royal Academy in 1864. An 1870 reviewer tantalizingly referred to the painting as the "Egyptian sentinel" (Philip Gilbert Hamerton, "English Painters of the Present Day," *Portfolio* [London, 1870], 2). Two of the Saint Stephen fresco panels feature angels bearing scrolls, including the respective phrases "Be thou faithful unto death" and "And I will give thee the crown of life," from Revelation 2:10. These are the words of comfort and reward sent by God to the Christians at Smyrna, who would suffer trials at the hands of the "synagogue of Satan." The fresco is briefly discussed by Herbert Sharp in "A Short Account of the Work of Edward John Poynter RA," *Studio* [London] 7 (1896): 3–15.

23 On Hughes, Kingsley, and the rejection of effeminacy in favor of Christian manhood, see Norman Vance, *The Sinews of the Spirit: The Ideal of Christian Manliness in Victorian Literature and Religious Thought* (Cambridge, 1985), 78–165; and essays by David Rosen, Donald E. Hall, Laura Fasick, Dennis W. Allen, and Patricia Srebrnik in *Muscular Christianity: Embodying the Victorian Age*, ed. Donald E. Hall (Cambridge, 1994). On masculinity in the novels of Charlotte Yonge, see Catherine Wells-Cole, "Angry Yonge Men: Anger and Masculinity in the Novels of Charlotte M. Yonge," in *Masculinity and Spirituality in Victorian Culture*, ed. Andrew Bradstock, Sean Gill, Anne Hogan, and Sue Morgan (New York, 2000), 71–84.

24 William Dean Howells, *Italian Journeys* (1867; New York, 1901), 92–93.

25 Much of the early writing on Stoicism in England addressed the issue of suicide, for which the Stoics, especially Seneca, were often cited as advocates. On suicide and British Stoicism, see S. E. Sprott, *The English Debate on Suicide from Donne to Hume* (La Salle, Ill., 1961); and Michael MacDonald and Terence R. Murphy, *Sleepless Souls: Suicide in Early Modern England* (Oxford, 1990). In *Death, Desire, and Loss in Western Culture* (New York, 1998), Jonathan Dollimore includes readings of Seneca and Marcus Aurelius that focus on their varying positions on "the perception and the acceptance of, even the yearning for, oblivion" (32). Reaching beyond the issue of suicide, Gordon Braden's *Renaissance Tragedy and the Senecan Tradition* (New Haven, 1985) contains a helpful overview of the literary influence of Senecan writers on medieval and early modern England (see esp. 63–98). Julie Ellison's *Cato's Tears and the Making of Anglo-American Emotion* (Chicago, 1999) examines Addison's *Cato* (London, 1713) in the context of eighteenth-century Whig politics.

26 The Victorian revival of interest in Roman Stoicism began with three key texts: John Stuart Mill's encomium to Marcus Aurelius in *On Liberty* (London, 1859); A. A. Long's influential translation of *Thoughts of Emperor M. Aurelius Antoninus* (London, 1861); and Matthew Arnold's response to both in his 1863 "Marcus Aurelius" essay (*Complete Prose Works of Matthew Arnold*, ed. R. H. Super [Ann Arbor, 1962], 3:133–57).

27   Kestner 1989 (note 21), 214–15.

28   Yonge 1893 (note 18), 2. Yonge specifically invokes the sentinel in her description of Dr. Hay, a British hero of the 1857 Indian Mutiny: "this was the Roman sentry's firmness, more voluntary and more glorious" (ibid., 7).

29   While it received favorable reviews in the *Times of London* and the *Art Journal* ("Miss Hosmer's 'Sentinel of Pompeii,'" *London Times*, August 10, 1878, 12, col. 2; and "The 'Pompeian Sentinel' by Miss Hosmer," *Art Journal* [New York] 4 [1878]: 355), this press amounted to relatively little attention compared to the reception of earlier works such as *Beatrice Cenci* and *Zenobia*. On the *Pompeian Sentinel*, see Dolly Sherwood, *Harriet Hosmer: American Sculptor, 1830–1908* (Columbia, Mo., 1991), 311.

30   Sheldon Nodelman, "How to Read a Roman Portrait," in *Roman Art in Context*, ed. Eve D'Ambra (1975; Englewood Cliffs, N.J., 1993), 11.

31   Ibid., 13.

32   See ibid., 13–15; J. J. Pollitt, *Art in the Hellenistic Age* (Cambridge, 1986), 141–47; Sheldon Nodelman, "The Portrait of Brutus the Tyrannicide," in *Ancient Portraits in the J. Paul Getty Museum* (Malibu, 1987), 41–86; *Roman Portraiture: Images of Character and Virtue: Selections from the J. Paul Getty Museum*, ed. John Pollini (Los Angeles, 1990), 8–13; and Mary Beard and John Henderson, *Classical Art: From Greece to Rome* (Oxford, 2001), 227–30.

33   Pollini 1990 (note 32), 9.

34   See "Miss Hosmer's 'Sentinel of Pompeii,'" 1878 (note 29) and "The 'Pompeian Sentinel' by Miss Hosmer," 1878 (note 29). In both reviews the critics assert that the sentinel's skeleton was discovered on April 20, 1794, and that his "helmet, lance, and breastplate" were still on display at the Real museo borbonico in Naples. There is no evidence in Fiorelli 1860 (note 10) or elsewhere for this claim; it is possible (Moormann, "Literary Evocations," 2003 [note 12]), that tour guides may have pointed to such items at the museum and attributed them to the sentinel.

35   The original 1859 *Zenobia* has not survived.

36   See Joy S. Kasson, *Marble Queens and Captives: Women in Nineteenth-Century American Sculpture* (New Haven, 1990), 141–65; and Deborah Cherry, *Beyond the Frame: Feminism and Visual Culture, Britain, 1850–1900* (London, 2000), 101–41. See also Gail Marshall, "Harriet Hosmer and the Classical Inheritance," *Forum for Modern Language Studies* 39, no. 2 (2003): 202–13.

37   Smiles 1883 (note 18), 2.

38   Gell and Gandy 1817–19 (note 11), 94.

Science or Morbid Curiosity?
The Casts of Giuseppe
Fiorelli and the Last Days
of Romantic Pompeii

Eugene Dwyer

W
ITH THE WANING of the romantic movement in the second half of the nineteenth century, the feverish international interest that had focused on the Bay of Naples archaeological sites also appeared to dissipate. For a brief period in the 1860s imported cotton covered the fields lying above the unexcavated parts of Pompeii.[1] Fortuitously coincidental political and scientific developments, however, quickly returned the eyes of the world to Pompeii as a shocking new epoch of response to the discoveries began. In 1860, the newly created kingdom of Italy assumed the patrimony of the king of Naples and transformed a land that had languished for more than half a century. The agent of this larger change at Pompeii was Giuseppe Fiorelli, an energetic young man who had been imprisoned under the Bourbons but who in the new regime was appointed professor of archaeology at the University of Naples and director of museums and archaeological excavations in the new provinces of a united Italy.[2] Although Fiorelli already was a respected epigrapher and numismatist, his sensational 1863 invention of a method of casting the bodies of Pompeian victims carried his fame throughout Europe and America. But the fame of the casts and their creator came with a price, as they created their own moral dilemma for both excavators and visitors to the site.

Although previous attempts had been made to cast bodies from impressions left in the volcanic mud (fango), these new casts confronted the public with the agony of death, a sight that had been reserved only for the excavators themselves. All were taken aback by the grisly spectacle, but the response of both public and learned communities varied. In the mind of the scientifically inclined director, total disclosure was the best course even if some delicate sensibilities might be injured. Survivors of the recently ousted Bourbon regime, who might have been expected to entertain an opposing view, were silent in hopes of keeping their jobs. Foreigners, such as the recently arrived American consul in Naples, William Dean Howells, viewed the new discoveries in the broader context of contemporary events, which for Howells meant the modern horrors of the American Civil War. He saw four bodies in a city house restored as a temporary museum when he visited Pompeii in November 1864:

> You have read, no doubt, of their discovering, a year or two since, in making an excavation in a Pompeian street, the moulds of four human bodies, three women and a man, who fell down, blind and writhing, in the storm of fire eighteen hundred years ago; whose shape the settling and hardening ashes took; whose flesh wasted away, and whose bones lay there in the hollow of the matrix till the cunning of this time found them, and, pouring liquid plaster round the skeletons, clothed them with human form again, and drew them forth into the world once more. There are many things in Pompeii which bring back the gay life of the city, but nothing which so vividly reports the terrible manner of her death as these effigies of the creatures that actually shared it. The man in the last struggle has thrown himself upon his back, and taken his doom sturdily — there is a sublime calm in his rigid figure. The women lie upon their faces, their limbs tossed and distorted, their drapery tangled and heaped about them, and in every fibre you see how hard they died. One presses her face into her handkerchief to draw one last breath unmixed with scalding steam; another's arms are wildly thrown abroad to clutch at help; another's hand is appealingly raised, and on her slight fingers you see the silver hoops with which her poor dead vanity adorned them.
>
> The guide takes you aside from the street into the house where they lie and a dreadful shadow drops upon your heart as you enter their presence. Without, the hell-storms seem to fall again, and the whole sunny plain to be darkened with its ruin, the city to send up the tumult of her despair.
>
> What is there left in Pompeii to speak of after this? The long street of tombs outside the walls? Those that died before the city's burial seem to have scarcely a claim to the solemnity of death.[3]

Where the dead are concerned at Pompeii, compassion had at first been mixed with indifference, perhaps to be expected where the discovery of cadavers became routine. Responses to human remains at Pompeii begin with the first official, dispassionate notice of the discovery of a corpse: "A cadaver was discovered this morning, between the lapilli [the layer of pumice] and the soil, found together with eighteen bronze and one silver coin, which I am sending enclosed to the hands of Your Excellency."[4] As the official record of the excavation was a journal of expenses and receipts meant to justify the continuation of the efforts, the unprofitable human remains often assumed second place to more valuable finds. It did not take the excavators long, however, to observe that the discovery of a body often meant the discovery of coins, jewelry, or other treasure. Furthermore, philosophical contemplation of the dead amid the ruins of Pompeii had become a time-honored practice when the casting technique was perfected. There had even been a certain amount of stagecraft employed in the arrangement and display of skeletons to enhance this experience.[5] The discovery of the body of a person who had died a violent death held a certain thrill, all the more so if it belonged to a godless pagan. The casts made by Fiorelli instantly transformed public perception of the suffering of the Pompeians. Consequently, we must reflect on how the earlier presenters and consumers of the Pompeian experience conceived of the death and suffering of the victims. It can hardly be accidental that the period from the discovery of Pompeii to the perfection of Fiorelli's casting technique (about 120 years) coincided with the birth and death of romanticism and its replacement (or displacement) within the sphere of archaeology by a new scientific attitude.

Even before Fiorelli, the encounter with death was a memorable part of every tourist's experience of Pompeii, though it was usually mediated by art in the course of a promenade along the Street of the Tombs, with its ironic inscriptions and emblems of death or a visit to a subterranean cellar where a group of skeletons had once been found huddled together. The human imagination is ever active, and the public wanted to know what had happened in morbid detail. For those with a knowledge of classical languages, several passages in ancient literature conveyed some idea of the terrible experience of the victims of Vesuvius. Indeed, the population of Naples knew too much about sudden, catastrophic mortality brought about by disease or volcanic eruption. The city had been visited regularly by the plague and in the nineteenth century by cholera. An eruption of Vesuvius in 1631 killed at least four thousand in a few hours. During the worst of these periods of devastation the corpses literally piled up in the cemeteries. Terror interfered with the survivors' respect for the dead. The same saint, San Gennaro, who protected the Neapolitans from the plague and the volcano, on occasion withheld his protection. Such death was popularly viewed as divine retribution: "Naples sins, and Torre [del Greco] pays," was—and still is—commonly heard.[6] In the popular imagination, the Pompeians, known for their sybaritic lifestyle, deserved their fate. Pompeii and Herculaneum were a kind of Sodom and Gomorrah.[7] Even the man of science Stefano Delle Chiaje, who was the first to study the human remains of the Pompeians, believed their physiognomy showed evidence of a "relaxed and libidinous lifestyle."[8] If they had been Christian, things might have been different, but the treatment of human remains from Pompeii has had little or nothing in common with the treatment of remains from the Roman or Neapolitan catacombs.[9] Quite to the contrary, it might almost be said that Christians felt it their duty to display contempt for the victims' remains at Pompeii.[10]

Forensic interest in the bodies is noticeably lacking from the first official accounts, but some visitors had more curiosity about the circumstances of the victims' fate. As in many other aspects of Pompeian archaeology, Johann Joachim Winckelmann anticipated both the scientific method and the humane response of future generations of visitors. He did not know of any bodies found at either Pompeii or Herculaneum but only at Stabiae: "Three female bodies, one of which appeared to be the maid of the other two, and was carrying a wooden casket: this lay beside her, and had decomposed in the ash. The two other ladies both had golden bracelets and earrings, which were sent to the museum."[11] In Pompeii, though he did not find evidence of the bodies, he deduced from the locations of heavy items that these artifacts had been discarded as the flight of the inhabitants grew increasingly desperate.[12] Unfortunately, he gave no examples in support of this attractive theory, but it does suggest a human as well as an archaeological interest in the victims' plight.

Winckelmann's sympathy heralded a new era of interest in the human remains. The Stabian women observed by Winckelmann interested neither the authorities nor the learned Neapolitans charged with publishing the discovered treasures. As open-air excavation proceeded, however, the study of the archaeological context began to attract more attention, even while treasure hunting (*collezionismo*) continued to fund operations. In late 1766 the discovery of what was believed to be a military barracks at Pompeii produced a remarkable collection of arms, which eventually proved to be those of gladiators. The same building yielded thirty-four fugitives (*fuggiaschi*),

including some women laden with jewelry. One room housed an apparatus designed to hold ten prisoners by their legs; also found were four skeletons. Some at the time speculated that they were prisoners who had met their death in the stock, including Giovanni Battista Piranesi, who drew a sketch of the wretches held by their legs with a row of skulls looking down on them from a shelf at the back of the room [FIG. 1].[13] Significantly, in the twelve or so years between the discovery of the room and Piranesi's drawing, several dramatic discoveries compelled people to focus on the archaeological context of the fate of the victims as a novel, and perhaps defining, feature of the Pompeian excavations.[14]

The Austrian emperor Joseph II, brother of Queen Maria Carolina of Naples, was a notable beneficiary of Winckelmann's teachings. On a visit to Pompeii in 1768 Joseph was taken to a subterranean room in the structure that became known as the House of the Emperor Joseph II. There he and the rest of the party saw an intact skeleton, presumably of a victim who had perished in that place. Egon Cesar Conte Corti, referring to Joseph's correspondence with the empress Maria Theresa, noted that "for a long time the Emperor stood reflectively before these tokens of an intense human drama."[15]

This imperial tableau vivant attained symbolic status and it was re-created on numerous occasions with different participants. Several years later Pierre Jacques Onésme Bergeret de Grancourt together with his party, including the painter Jean-Honoré Fragonard, visited the same place. In his journal Bergeret noted that "in one house, among others, in the room downstairs where they must have done the washing, we could see all the implements, the stove, the washtub, etc....and a heap of volcanic ash upon which rested the skeleton of a woman, as if, having tried to escape from the choking ashes coming in from all sides, she had finally fallen backwards and died. Everything about the placement and position of her bones indicated that this was clearly what had happened, and one remains stunned at the contemplation of the events of 1,700 years ago."[16] A drawing by Fragonard recorded a virtual replay of the same scene as witnessed by a French party, including Abbé de Saint-Non, as published in the latter's *Voyage pittoresque* in 1781 [FIG. 2], a choice that demonstrates how the remains had gained a status equal to the antiquities.[17]

Between 1771 and 1774, the center of attention at Pompeii was the villa suburbana, thought to belong to Arrius Diomedes, whose name was known from an adjacent

FIGURE 1
Giovanni Battista Piranesi (Italian, 1720–1778), *Prisoners in the Barracks of the Gladiators at Pompeii*, ca. 1778. Pen and brush and blackish-brown ink on paper, squared in black chalk. Kupferstichkabinett. Staatliche Museen zu Berlin, Berlin, Germany.

Photo: Bildarchiv Preussischer Kulturbesitz/Art Resource, NY.

FIGURE 2
Jean-Honoré Fragonard (French, 1732–1806), *Travelers Viewing a Skeleton at Pompeii*, 1775. From Jean Claude Richard de Saint-Non, *Voyage pittoresque, ou description des royaumes de Naples et de Sicile* (1781). Los Angeles, Research Library, Getty Research Institute, DG821.S14 1781.

monument on the Street of the Tombs. Excavations in the cellar had revealed a grisly sight: twenty or so women and children "of whose flesh there remained nothing but an impression in the earth, with the bones fallen into disorder, the hair partly preserved around some of the heads, and [even] some of the plaited tresses. Of their clothing there was nothing but ashes to be found, but these preserved the texture of the material which had surrounded their forms, permitting one to distinguish very clearly the fineness of the weave and the weight of the fabric."[18] The director of the excavations, Francesco La Vega, sent sixteen pieces cut from the volcanic impressions to the museum "in order to give evidence."[19]

When F. P. Latapie toured the villa in 1776 the bones had been laid out on tables and were gradually disappearing as successive visitors came through. He admitted to having taken for his personal museum "a bone more than seventeen centuries old."[20] Charles Dupaty, who saw the impressions in the museum at Portici, wrote: "One [impression] represents half of her bosom, which is of exquisite beauty; another a shoulder, a third a portion of her shape, and all concur in revealing to us that this woman was young, and that she was tall and well made, and even that she had escaped in her shift; for some pieces of linen are still adhering to the ashes."[21] This last observation of Dupaty's was to prove helpful to the woman's—and, indeed, all the Pompeians'—reputations and comforting to a subsequent, more prudish generation.

Seventy years later Charles Dickens responded viscerally to the Bay of Naples, in particular to the residual sense of death that still hung about Pompeii: "In the cellar of Diomede's house, where certain skeletons were found huddled together, close to the door, the impressions of their bodies on the ashes, hardened with the ashes, and became stamped and fixed there, after they had shrunk, inside, to scanty bones."[22] His success in reconstructing the progress of the destruction surpassed that of most visitors: "Nothing is more impressive and terrible than the many evidences of the searching nature of the ashes, as bespeaking their irresistible power, and the impossibility of escaping them. In the wine cellars, they forced their way into the earthen vessels: displacing the wine, and choking them, to the brim, with dust. In the tombs, they forced the ashes of the dead from the funeral urns, and rained new ruin even into them. The mouths, and eyes, and skulls of all the skeletons, were stuffed with this terrible hail."[23]

Dickens must be placed among the romantic visitors to Pompeii for his imaginative reconstruction of the terrible fate suffered by the ancient Pompeians. For one, the impressions of the bodies, or what could be conserved of them, had been removed first to Portici and then to the Real museo borbonico in Naples long before Dickens saw them. He might, in fact, have seen them in the latter place and restored them to their original context as an act of artistic license, or he might have borrowed the observation from contemporary tour guides. One detail that stands out is the tendency of the fine volcanic ash to penetrate virtually every cavity in the ruins. This phenomenon had long been noted, especially in the cellar of the Villa of Diomedes, where the skeletons mentioned by Dickens had been found. So completely had the ashes penetrated this space that the excavator, La Vega, believed they had arrived in liquid form. Others had even gone so far as to argue that a flood, and not a volcanic eruption, had destroyed Pompeii. A contemporary scientific report, however, contradicts Dickens's morbid but compelling assertion that the victims had been invasively violated by the insidious ash. In an 1854 study the pathologist Stefano Delle Chiaje found only one skeleton among the seventy-odd examples that he collected with ash from the eruption within the cranial cavity. There can be little doubt that Dickens invented or exaggerated this memorable detail to re-create the disaster according to his romantic fantasy.[24]

Pity for the victims emerges as a recurring theme among visitors' accounts from the 1780s onward. For example, Dupaty described a scene that is all too familiar to students of Pompeii: "But what do I perceive in that chamber. They are ten deaths heads. The unfortunate wretches saved themselves here, where they could not be saved. This is the head of a little child: its father and mother then are there! Let us go up stairs again; the heart feels not at ease here."[25]

On May 12, 1812, an excavation in the Street of the Tombs produced a piteous spectacle: a woman and three children were uncovered in the vicinity of the Mammia hemicycle. The architect Carlo Bonucci supplied the following analysis of the scene in his popular guide of the 1820s:

> Vesuvius had for an instant suspended his fury, when an unfortunate mother bearing an infant in her arms, and with two young daughters, endeavoured to profit by the opportunity, and to fly from their country-house to Nola, the city least threatened by this unspeakable catastrophe! Arrived at the foot of [the Mammia hemicycle], the volcano recommenced its ravages with redoubled fury. Stones, cinders, fire, melted and boiling substances, rained from all sides, and surrounded the miserable fugitives. The unfortunates sought refuge at the foot of a tomb, where reposed perhaps the ashes of their fathers; and invoking in the most frightful despair the gods, deaf to their prayers, they closely embraced their mother as they breathed out their last sigh, and in this situation they remained.[26]

Bonucci explained the victims' arrival at the Mammia tomb as an interruption in their futile attempt to flee from a country house to the city due north of Pompeii, which was known to have escaped the fury of the eruption. Unfortunately, as Bonucci and his audience knew, such a flight would have taken the mother and her children even closer to Vesuvius and was therefore doomed to end in failure, which only added to the poignancy of this scene.

Joseph Franque selected the subject of the mother and her children for his large history painting *Scene during the Eruption of Vesuvius* [see p. 161, FIG. 3]. Standing in the remains of their chariot, the figures embrace at the moment they are overcome by the irresistible volcanic surge. Dressed in loosely flowing and revealing garments, the mother and her children recall the Vatican sculpture of Laocoon and his sons as they succumb to their fate. The pathos and beauty of their delicate and shapely limbs and the sensitive, terrified expressions on their faces elicit both admiration and pity from the viewer.

Thanks to the popularity of Bonucci's guide and Franque's painting, the mother and her children became an established icon in Pompeian lore prefiguring Fiorelli's sensational casts. Thomas Gray wrote the same victim into his 1830 novel, *The Vestal*, as the character Favilla:

> "I can go no farther," said she. "Kiss me and leave me, my children." With one voice they declared that her fate should be theirs. . . . She was just able to reach the hemicycle on the left hand, near the gate, when she sank exhausted. Her daughters knelt beside her, and she threw her arms around them and blessed them. Faithfully did these girls redeem their promise to save her or to die with her. From that embrace

they rose not. The thick falling ashes closed over them, as the waves of the sea close over their victims.[27]

Gray, like Edward Bulwer-Lytton after him, introduced Christian morality into the lives of his heroes, thus separating them from the rest of the decadent Pompeians, who, the reader must suppose, deserved their fate. In the course of his novel he made use of the notorious sexual emblems found in Pompeii to indicate widespread moral depravity. He was heartened, however, by Dupaty's observation that the women in the cellar of the villa suburbana were clothed, thus refuting the opinion of some that the fugitives had fled "almost naked."[28]

Gray's pioneering use of the new archaeological context to reconstruct the last moments of the victims' lives anticipated the technique of Bulwer-Lytton's *Last Days of Pompeii* (1834). Through this popular novel, which fused archaeology and fiction, a worldwide audience became familiar with the Temple of Isis, the House of the Tragic Poet, the House of Pansa, the villa suburbana of Arrius Diomedes, and other stops on the Pompeian itinerary of the day, and they also read plausible explanations of the deaths of certain victims.

Appreciation of Pompeii usually required the visitor to look beyond the horror of the destruction to see beauty amid death. Bulwer-Lytton was able to achieve this necessary quality of good fiction by coloring in features not present in the archaeological record and sometimes going well beyond the outlines of the historical evidence. By Bulwer-Lytton's time, it was well known that many fleeing victims carried lamps or lanterns, presumably to help them find their way in the ash-darkened streets.[29] Bulwer-Lytton's invention of the blind girl, Nydia, who alone was able to guide her companions through the confusion, was a brilliant way to extricate his heroes from the dying city—but, unlike Franque's pictorial and Gray's fictional depiction of the mother who perished with her children at the Mammia sepulcher, Bulwer-Lytton's invention had no supporting archaeological evidence.

In the wake of Bulwer-Lytton, Ferdinand Gregorovius composed *Euphorion* (1858), a long narrative poem in German hexameters about the escape from disaster and at the same time from slavery by a fictional Pompeian Greek artist.[30] Although for the most part he was faithful to the archaeological record in his tale, Gregorovius concentrated more on the art of Pompeii than on the death of its inhabitants. But he soon became a convert to the new science. In August 1864, between the publication of the first and second editions of *Euphorion*, Gregorovius viewed the casts of the victims in the presence of Fiorelli. He was moved in particular by the fate of "the young girl, who, in despair, has lain down to sleep the sleep of death; the figure as graceful as that of a slumbering Hermaphrodite."[31] In response, he added a note to the 1884 edition concerning the new casts, calling them examples of "life incarnate in its most awful tragedy" and "most noteworthy of all statues." He added, "what once only the fantasy of the poet might have conjured up, he [now] has in full-blown reality in front of him, and as evidence of the moment itself."[32]

The confusion of pity, vulnerability, and erotic attraction is a familiar topos in nineteenth-century art and literature.[33] A prominent Pompeian example of this phenomenon was Théophile Gautier's resurrection of the famously admired young woman from the cellars of the villa suburbana as femme fatale in his Pompeian novel *Arria Marcella*, published in 1852.[34] Enchanted by the sight of the impressions in the Real museo borbonico, Gautier's hero Octavian embarks on an adventure that eventually leads to a tryst with the spirit of the dead woman. As Octavian and the dead woman are on the verge of fulfilling their desires, the sudden arrival of Arria's father, who has just embraced Christianity and now condemns his daughter's pagan sensuality, interrupts the scene. To Gautier, the Pompeians represented an exotic, eroticized antiquity not far removed from its contemporary equivalent, the Orient, which would become more immediately accessible through Fiorelli's casts.

Gautier's fantasy derived from an object exhibited in the Naples museum, which had been admired by many before him, and an erotic element had always been implicit in the making and exhibiting of the plaster casts of victims. This element of sexual fantasy had been present, if in more conventional form, since the discovery of the first female body impressions. The impressions from the Villa of Diomedes can be considered the beginning of a romantic quest to recover lost beauty. After their removal to the museum and the discovery of the mother and her children at the Mammia tomb, an attempt was made to cast the body of a woman found in the atrium of the House of the Faun in March 1831. This unfortunate person had dropped and scattered the collection of gold jewelry she had been carrying and sought refuge in one of the rooms surrounding the atrium. The position of her body showed her frantic effort to protect herself from the collapsing ceiling. The traces of her fine clothing were clearly visible in the ash that had solidified around her. But what caught the attention of the excavators was the impression of her beautiful foot and elegant sandal. Unfortunately efforts to make a cast of her body were unsuccessful.[35] Gautier's imaginative fantasy was, nevertheless, the fictional analogue to an actual archaeological effort.

This survey brings us to 1863, when Fiorelli made his epoch-making casts. Although plaster of paris had been used previously to cast wooden objects such as cabinets and doors, and even parts of cadavers, a casting of a complete body had never been attempted. By ordering his workers to stop digging and to inform him at the first appearance of a cavity in the fango, Fiorelli set the stage for a dramatic new discovery.[36] He lost no time in displaying his casts to the visitors who flocked to Pompeii in the 1860s in response to the news of his discovery. With the exhibition of plaster casts of victims in their death throes, a new element of shock was added to the experience of the visit. For the most part, the public responded positively to Fiorelli's casts [FIG. 3], and the exhibition played a critical part in Fiorelli's plan to finance the excavations by charging an admission fee.[37]

Most visitors and scholars regarded the innovation as positive and did not object much to the exhibition of the casts.[38] A typical reaction was that of the archaeologist Heinrich Brunn, who praised Fiorelli's ingenious discovery and published a careful description of the excavation in the *Bullettino della corrispondenza archeologica* for May–June 1863. Brunn admired the casts for the clarity of the bodily forms and the "artistic beauty of the figures themselves." The aesthetic, sculptural qualities of the casts were widely appreciated, and the sculptor Tito Angelini petitioned to have the admission fee waived while he transformed two bodies, a mother and her daughter [FIG. 4], into a work of art.[39]

Brunn further noted that the nudity to which students of ancient civilization had become accustomed in art was not found in real life, "vita stessa degli antichi." The inhabitants of ancient Pompeii were, in fact, clothed no more scantily than the modern Neapolitans, though the clothing worn by the Pompeian victims had lost its normal contours in the fango. But the evidence suggested that both men and women wore trousers. One of the women wore a scarf "all'uso degli orientali."[40]

FIGURE 3
Giacomo Brogi (Italian 1822–1881). *Interior of the Pompeii Museum,* Photograph. Private collection.

Photo: Courtesy Eugene Dwyer.

FIGURE 4
Giorgio Sommer (German, 1834–1914), *Cast of a Mother and Daughter.* Photograph. Private collection.

Photo: Courtesy Eugene Dwyer.

FIGURE 5
Cast of a Man. Photograph. Private collection.

Photo: Courtesy Eugene Dwyer.

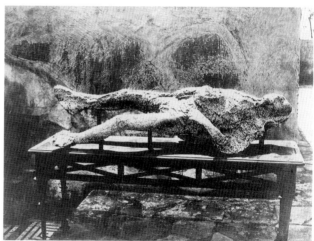

This moral rehabilitation of the ancient Pompeians suited the program of the new archaeologists. The fact that the ancients wore pants [FIG. 5] was a detail of exaggerated importance. Before Fiorelli's discovery, the wearing of trousers had been thought to distinguish the moderns from the ancients—not simply in the trousers' practicality but also in the greater degree of modesty they afforded. Transported back into ancient times, Gautier's Octavian was a ridiculous sight in his frock coat and trousers. The new archaeological evidence contrasted with the picture of ancient dress gleaned from Pompeian paintings. Even while the heavily clothed Pompeian victims were being uncovered, Hippolyte Taine was writing of the Naples frescoes: "The painters of these pictures enjoyed a unique advantage, one which no others have possessed, even those of the Renaissance, of living amid congenial social customs, of constantly seeing figures naked and draped in the amphitheater and in the baths, and besides this, of cultivating the corporeal endowments of strength and fleetness of foot. They alluded to fine breasts, well-set necks, and muscular arms as we of the present day do to expressive countenances and well-cut pantaloons."[41]

Ironically, Taine based his vision of ancient dress on a vision of ancient life that was relatively new to Europeans, having been revealed and promulgated through the publication of the Pompeian and Herculanean frescoes only a century before.[42] This view of antiquity represented contemporary European social currents and a desire for freedom and erotic license more than the ancient reality. Brunn and his colleagues, representing the new spirit of scientific archaeology, gave the lie to the claimed archaeological correctness of neoclassicism and asserted that the evidence now proved this vision wrong. The dream of antiquity was now shown to be just that—a dream. Yet dreams, especially dreams based on aspirations of freedom, die hard. The rejection of an erotically charged vision of the antique in favor of a banal realism required the sacrifice of many cherished ideas about the ancients. The ghosts of the morally debased, pagan Pompeians had always enjoyed a certain celebrity.

Fiorelli, the pioneer in exhibiting physical human remains to the public, was also the pioneer in demonstrating this new morality. Not surprisingly he deliberately reversed the Bourbon policy in each area. While the rejection of neoclassical fashion was part of a general change in European taste following the fall of Napoleon, the Neapolitan reaction was specifically linked to the political events in Naples under the Bourbon restoration.[43] The reign of the scholarly but pious Francis I (1825–30) brought mixed fortune for antiquities. Francis actively supported the museum and the excavations at Pompeii, and he encouraged the resumption of excavations at Herculaneum. But his religious zeal and the need to reassert his control over his possessions led him to order strictures concerning the museum's collection of erotic artifacts. Even before his accession, he had suggested in 1819 that all obscene items in the museum's collections be kept in a closed room, to be known as the Cabinet of Obscene Objects (Gabinetto degli oggetti osceni), with admission limited to "persons of mature age and established morals."[44] In 1823 the name was changed to the less provocative Cabinet of Reserved Objects (Gabinetto degli oggetti riservati), with admission only by permission of the king. Many visitors of the time agreed with the morally conservative monarch in expressing their distaste for erotic Pompeii, no doubt in reaction to excesses of the Napoleonic period. Others were interested in Pompeian culture but preferred to veil this interest in conventional morality by condemning the manners of the Pompeians when the opportunity presented itself.

Many Neapolitans and visitors, however, harbored republican ideals, and these ideals were closely associated with the unique archaeological patrimony of the region. In 1848 political events gave Neapolitan liberals the opportunity to establish a constitution limiting royal power. Some liberal party members immediately challenged the status of the museum—then known as the Real museo borbonico—as the repository of the inherited wealth of King Ferdinand II. They argued that material from the archaeological sites belonged to the kingdom, not to the king. The constitutional program, containing a lengthy proposal for the reorganization of the Naples museum, was largely the work of Fiorelli.[45] Under Fiorelli's plan the pornographic objects were to remain closed to girls and boys, but women might view them with permission of the superintendent.[46] The proposal also called for the establishment of a museum at Pompeii intended to hold, in addition to artifacts of various common types, "human and animal skeletons."[47] This plan, however, came to nothing because the constitutional government failed and the king regained power. In addition to rejecting the planned reorganization of the museum, the king rebuffed a further proposal of Fiorelli's to send the human remains from Pompeii to the Istituto di anatomia of the University of

Naples.[48] Even more publicly, Ferdinand demonstrated his regained power by tightening his hold on the Cabinet of Reserved Objects. In 1849, in response to the failed attempt to establish a constitution and in anticipation of Pope Pius IX's visit to Naples, "the religious hypocrisy of government agents provoked strict orders that the door of this collection be closed and riveted, and all the Venuses and other painted and sculpted nudes, regardless of artist, be withdrawn from public view."[49]

The pope's arrival in Neapolitan territory and his reception by the devout King Ferdinand was celebrated as a triumph of Catholicism, and the political barometer of the Cabinet of Reserved Objects sank to its lowest register as once again the depravity of the Pompeians offered a suitable foil for the demons of contemporary politics. On the occasion of an elaborately staged visit to Pompeii on October 22, 1849, the pope blessed the people assembled in the amphitheater, and according to Stanislas d'Aloe, "his blessing served as well to sanctify that place so brutally profaned by the bloody spectacles of the ancients." Not only the amphitheater but also the forum and the temples of the gods were considered by d'Aloe as "place[s] profaned by the idolatry and by the depravity of the ancient inhabitants."[50] In a florid commemorative inscription written for this occasion, the learned Abate Gaetano Leofreddi likewise referred to the city's ruined monuments as "evidence of divine vengeance" ("ultionis divinae vestigia") and made an explicit comparison between ancient depravity and modern revolution.[51] Further suppression of the pornographic collection followed in 1852 and 1856, the last possibly in pious reaction to the cholera epidemic of 1855.

The scholarly, positivist attitude of Fiorelli toward human behavior and human remains firmly opposed the religious and moralizing perspective of many of his contemporaries.[52] Nevertheless, despite attempts to prevent it, a republican spirit and a scientific attitude toward the ancients eventually won out over "religious hypocrisy" (to use Fiorelli's term). With the victory of Giuseppe Garibaldi and the abdication of the Bourbon dynasty, the fortunes of the pornographic collection rose immediately. By a proclamation of Garibaldi, the collection was reopened on September 18, 1860, and under Fiorelli's supervision, a scholarly catalogue was prepared for publication in 1866. Women and boys, "uomini di fresca età," were still not permitted to view the objects, according to Raffaele Gargiulo's 1864 guidebook, though access was otherwise much freer than under the previous regime.[53]

As I have noted, the period from the discovery of Pompeii to the perfection of Fiorelli's casting technique coincided with romanticism and its replacement within the sphere of archaeology by a new scientific attitude. By a fortunate coincidence the latter part of this change in historical mentality fell directly within the life experience of a prominent archaeologist of the age, Charles Ernest Beulé. In his *Drame du Vesuve* of 1872 Beulé summed up a lifetime of experiencing Pompeii:

> The burial of five towns by Vesuvius is a proper drama to strike the imagination. Some poetic details have been added; the subject is fit for a novel. Bulwer draped it in his color. Today the prejudices have taken root, the errors have become popular.
>
> As a youth I experienced in their simplicity the delights of a sudden intimacy with antiquity. Later, after a period of four years in Greece, I found Pompeii small and its art seemed to me that which it is—an art of decadence. Finally, having arrived at mature age, I sought the explanation of extraordinary occurrences for which I, like so many others, had accepted banal explanations. I realized that the truth has more charm than convention and that the strongest poetry is the poetry of facts.

That which the ignorant call a wonder is nothing but a natural phenomenon for science. I wanted to account for the circumstances of this phenomenon. Vesuvius is the author of disasters that one believes are without precedent. I have conducted my inquiry with the patience of a magistrate who prepares a case and follows the clues of a crime: these are the results of the investigation which I lay before the judgement of the public.[54]

True to his promise, Beulé gave a meticulous description of the four bodies cast by Fiorelli in 1863. He began with the woman who had fallen on her back [FIG. 6]. Although her features were indistinct, she had obviously died of suffocation. She strained her head upward to breathe the air, supporting herself with her right hand, while she drove off an invisible foe with her left.[55] Her hair was wrapped about her head in a crown. Her chest was flattened and her breasts compressed under the weight of the soil. The sleeves of her tunic were harmoniously curved, but the glass-paste buttons that held them had deteriorated. In her flight she had gathered up her skirts about her hips, so that she appeared pregnant. Her thighs were covered by a fine garment like a slip, similar to those that had been noted in the impressions of the villa suburbana. Such a garment was intended to protect the dignity of the wearer from accidental gusts of wind. Ancient sculptors usually ignored such garments, though soldiers on the Column of Trajan wore them. In Pompeii even slaves and women of the people wore them. In conclusion, Beulé wrote, the woman was "grand, elegant, with a leg '*bien prise et charmante*,' and a foot '*admirablement cambré*.'" This last was well covered to protect her from the hot cinders over which she had to flee. She wore a silver ring and gold earrings. She carried a silver mirror and a miniature amber statuette of Amor. From these curious treasures, and from the proximity to the place where the body was found, Beulé suggested that this woman—whose fine clothing and treasures were inconsistent with the humble quarter—might have been a prostitute. "The evidence is slight; let us leave in peace not their bodies, which we must examine forever, but their memory." Austen Henry Layard, who examined her no less carefully, identified her as a housewife on the strength of the iron key she had with her. Yet here too the writer's eye for beauty prevails. "Her garments are gathered up on one side, leaving exposed a limb of beautiful shape. So perfect a mould of it has been formed by the soft and yielding mud, that the cast would seem to be taken from an exquisite work of Greek art."

FIGURE 6
Giorgio Sommer (German, 1834–1914). *Cast of a Pregnant Woman*. Photograph. Private collection.

Photo: Courtesy Eugene Dwyer.

FIGURE 7
Cast of a Young Woman. From an album of photographs of Pompeii by various artists, 1870–82. Los Angeles, Research Library, Getty Research Institute, 89.R.14 (8).

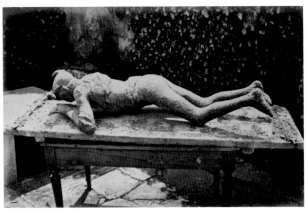

The woman, most often identified in the guidebooks and on photographs as "the pregnant woman," remained at the center of attention at Pompeii until 1875, when a still more beautiful woman was successfully cast [FIG. 7].⁵⁶ From that day until the present, the woman of 1875 has continued to be celebrated—most recently by Yusef Komunyakaa.⁵⁷ Fiorelli's "pregnant woman," however, has disappeared without trace —proving, perhaps, that novelty and physical beauty were the keys to the casts' popularity.⁵⁸

The advent of the casts marked a new era in the history of interpretation of Pompeii. The innovation coincided with the Risorgimento, which brought freedom from certain kinds of religious oppression to Naples and Pompeii. A new spirit in archaeology suited the change in government, in which, as Beulé wrote, the poesy of facts eclipsed that of the imagination. Even during the earlier, romantic period the novelists were beholden to archaeologists such as Andrea de Jorio and Carlo Bonucci for their information. After Fiorelli, however, materialist history came to monopolize the Pompeian discourse. Gregorovius bore witness to this change in his testimony to the evocative power of the casts. Popular literature saw Bulwer-Lytton and Gautier give way to Overbeck and Mau.⁵⁹ In the graphic arts, photography, which replaced engraving, suited the historians more than the novelists. But even as the characteristic image of the Pompeian victims shifted from half-nude to trousered men and women, pity and Eros remained constant sentiments in the hearts of the viewers. And the viewers in both periods were assumed for the most part to be male, although the American Thomas Gray and the Englishman Bulwer-Lytton wrote for a more gender-balanced audience. Both the old and new periods witnessed horrified shock among some viewers. Dupaty and Piranesi conveyed their dismayed response at an early date, but in 1847 Luigi Settembrini gave this discomfort its most compelling expression: "But now you, my friend Fiorelli, have discovered human pain, and whoever is human can feel it."⁶⁰ In the end, the question—still unresolved—lies in the decision to study or to bury the victims.⁶¹

Notes

¹   William Dean Howells, *Italian Journeys* (1867; Marlboro, Vt., 1988), 57–68, esp. 61.

²   On the life and career of Giuseppe Fiorelli, see G. Kannès, "Fiorelli, Giuseppe," in *Dizionario biografico degli Italiani* (Rome, 1997), 48:137–42.

³   Howells 1988 (note 1), 67. When William Dean Howells saw them, they were exhibited in the House of the Skeletons (VI, Ins. Occ., 27: Casa degli scheletri or Casa dei cadaveri di gesso). Hence, his reference to the Street of the Tombs, which began nearby, is topographical as well as topical.

⁴   Giuseppe Fiorelli, *Pompeianarum antiquitatum historia* (Naples, 1860), 1:2 (April 19, 1748). The body was probably that of a fugitive (*fuggiasco*), who had begun his flight after the rain of pumice (lapilli) had stopped and before the surges that followed the pumice. The word "soil" (*tierra*) here probably indicates not the ancient ground level but the modern cultivated surface.

⁵   I have in mind the skeleton displayed in a lower room of the House of the Emperor Joseph II. I am not aware of any outright falsification of evidence of human remains.

⁶   Haraldur Sigurdsson (*Melting the Earth: The History of Ideas on Volcanic Eruptions* [New York, 1999], 13) reminds us of the novelty of the Scottish physician James Hutton's declaration made

in 1788: "A volcano is not made on purpose to frighten superstitious people into fits of piety nor to overwhelm cities with destruction."

7   In 1789 Father Pietro d'Onofri wrote that when the gate of Pompeii was uncovered in 1755 the sculpted image of a phallus was to be seen on it, indicating that the city had dedicated itself to "the most sordid impudence," for which crimes it deserved divine destruction by fire. See Pietro d'Onofri, *Elogio estemporaneo per la gloriosa memoria di Carlo III, monarca delle Spagne e delle Indie* [Naples, 1789], xcv. The remark is cited by Michele Arditi, in *Il fascino e l'amuleto contra il fascino presso gli antichi* (Naples, 1825), 1–2, where d'Onofri's facts as well as his conclusions are contested.

8   Stefano Delle Chiaje, "Cenno notomico patologico sulle ossa umane scavate in Pompei," is cited and summarized in Giulio Minervini, "Ossa e scheletri diseppeliti in Pompei," *Bullettino archeologico napolitano*, n.s. 3, no. 51 (July 1854): 1–3.

9   In the Roman catacombs Christian remains have usually been reburied under the authority of the Vatican. In Naples certain ossuaries filled up in time of the plague may strike visitors as "presenting a very disgusting appearance," in the words of Thomas Gray, *The Vestal, or a Tale of Pompeii* (1830; Louisville, 1977), 213n. 38, though the effect is more bizarre than disrespectful. The search for Christians in Pompeii has been disappointing. Novelists from Gray onward and even Gaetano Leofreddi, in his commemorative inscription of 1849 (*Diario della venuta e del soggiorno in Napoli di sua beatitudine Pio IX. P. M.* 18 [October 1849], reprinted in Soprintendenza archeologica di Pompei, Biblioteca apostolica vaticana, *Pio IX a Pompei: Memorie e testimonianze di un viaggio* [Naples, 1987], appendix), allowed the possibility that Saint Peter had preceded Pius. Raffaele Garucci, however, leaves the matter unresolved in his article "Si è rinvenuto finora alcuna cosa di cristiana credenza in Pompei?" *Bullettino archeologico napolitano* n.s. 2, no. 1 (July 1853): 8. Excavations in the 1860s revealed a house that was quickly named the "hostel of the Christians" (VII, 9, 11–12) on the basis of a graffito (*Corpus inscriptionum latinarum* IV.679). The graffito disappeared and Fiorelli was openly skeptical (see *Descrizione di Pompei* [Naples, 1875], 278–80). Matteo Della Corte later championed the site as evidence for Christians in Pompeii (*Case ed abitanti di Pompei*, 3d ed. [Naples, 1965], 204–5, nos. 398–401, and literature cited).

10   This attitude is inferred more from the obligatory condemnation of the manners of the ancient Pompeians found in virtually every traveler's account than it is from evidence regarding the actual treatment of human remains—about which surprisingly little has been written. The popular (and official) hostility shown toward Protestant burials in Rome in the eighteenth and nineteenth centuries gives some possible parallels. See Johan Beck-Friis, *The Protestant Cemetery in Rome* (1956; Malmö, 1988).

11   Johann Joachim Winckelmann, *Herkulanische Schriften Winckelmanns*, vol. 1, *Sendschreiben von den herculanischen Entdeckungen* (Mainz, 1997), 1:75.

12   Ibid.

13   Hylton A. Thomas, "Piranesi and Pompeii," *Kunstmuseets årsskrift* 39–42 (1952–55): 13–28, esp. 24, fig. 15.

14   The appearance of archaeological contexts, such as the Barracks of the Gladiators, helped Pompeii emerge from the shadow of Herculaneum as a center of learned and popular attention and to be established as the new paradigm in Vesuvian archaeology.

15   Egon Cesar Conte Corti, *The Destruction and Resurrection of Pompeii and Herculaneum*, trans. K. and R. Gregor Smith (London, 1951), 147–48. As sources Corti uses the *Giornale* and a letter from Emperor Joseph II to Empress Maria Theresa, Florence, April 21, 1769, in the Vienna State Archives (147n. 1). See also Fiorelli 1860 (note 4), 1:1.230 (April 7, 1768): "Dopo i Sovrani passarono ad osservare alcune stanze sottoposte, dove ancora si conserva uno scheletro intatto." Lawrence Richardson (*Pompeii: An Architectural History* [Baltimore, 1988], 234–40) carefully describes the house, including the bakery-bath suite on the lowest level.

16   Pierre Jacques Onésme Bergeret de Grancourt, *Voyage d'Italie, 1773–1774, avec les dessins de Fragonard*, ed. Jacques Wilhelm (Paris, 1948), 110–11, as cited in *The Golden Age of Naples: Art and Civilization under the Bourbons, 1734–1805* (Detroit, 1981), 2:279–80.

17   For the drawing, see *Pompei: Pitture e mosaici*, vol. 10, *La documentazione nell'opera di disegnatori e pittori dei secoli XVIII e XIX*, ed. Giovanni Pugliese Carratelli (Rome, 1995), 1, 5–6, 9 (fig. 9). The engraving after Fragonard's drawing, by Claude Fessard, is reproduced by Raleigh Trevelyan (*The Shadow of Vesuvius: Pompeii AD 79* [London, 1976], 48, fig. 29). Another drawing, by Pietro Fabris, dated 1774, is in the collection of the Society of Antiquaries, London. See Jan Jenkins and Kim Sloan, *Vases and Volcanoes: Sir William Hamilton and His Collection* (London, 1996), 43, fig. 16.

18   "One clearly sees that these... were overcome in the part of the house that was the most secure, but that they were powerless against the rain of ashes, which fell after that of the pumice, and one sees clearly that it was accompanied by water which fed into every part where the first rain of pumice had not" (Fiorelli 1860 [note 4], 1:268; my translation). Victims are for the first time referred to as "unfortunates" (*infelici*).

19   "Per dare una qualche testimonianza di quello che si asserisce avere osservato" (ibid.). La Vega described his excavation with unusual care, thus demonstrating an awareness of the importance of the archaeological context and the historic nature of this discovery. See ibid., 1:268–70 (December 12, 1772).

20   F. P. Latapie, "Description des fouilles de Pompéii (a. 1776)," *Rendiconti dell'Accademia di archeologia di Napoli* 28 (1953): 223–48, esp. 240.

21   Charles-Marguerite-Jean-Baptiste Mercier Dupaty, *Travels through Italy, in a Series of Letters; Written in the Year 1785, by President Dupaty* (London, 1788), 320.

22   Charles Dickens, *Pictures from Italy* (London, 1846), 159.

23   Ibid.

24   Dickens's understanding of the process of the eruption was probably prompted by that of the English antiquary Sir William Gell, who wrote: "Pompeii was not destroyed by an inundation of lava; its elevated position sheltered it from that fate: it was buried under that shower of stones and cinders of which Pliny speaks. Much of this matter appears to have been deposited in a liquid state; which is easily explained, for the vast volumes of steam sent up by the volcano descended in torrents of rain, which united with the ashes suspended in the air, or washed them, after they had fallen, into places where they could not well have penetrated in a dry state. Among other proofs of this, the skeleton of a woman was found in a cellar, enclosed within a mould of volcanic paste, which received and has retained a perfect impression of her form." Gell continued: "In the great eruption of 1779, minutely described by Sir William Hamilton, Ottaiano, a small town situated at the foot of Somma, most narrowly escaped similar destruction. The phenomena then observed may be presumed to correspond closely with that which occurred at Pompeii" (William Gell, *Pompeii: Its Destruction and Re-discovery* [New York, n.d. (after 1832)], 17).

25   Dupaty 1788 (note 21), 383. See also Chantal Grell, *Herculanum et Pompéi dans les récits des voyageurs français du XVIIIᵉ siècle* (Naples, 1982), 119.

26   Carlo Bonucci, *Pompei* (Naples, 1828), translated in Gray 1977 (note 9), 183.

27   Ibid., 181–82. See also T. L. Donaldson, *Pompeii, Illustrated with Picturesque Views* (London, 1827), 2:23.

28   Gray 1977 (note 9), 187.

29   Some fleeing victims may, in fact, have left their places of shelter before dawn—visible or no—on August 25, thus requiring lanterns in any event.

30   Ferdinand Gregorovius, *Euphorion: Eine Dichtung aus Pompeji* (Leipzig, 1858).

31   Idem, *The Roman Journals of Ferdinand Gregorovius, 1852–1874*, ed. Friedrich Althaus and trans. Mrs. Gustavus W. Hamilton (London, 1911), 212 (Naples, August 15, 1864). Gregorovius was presumably referring to the younger of the two women who were cast together, though his interpretation of her fate contrasts noticeably with that of Layard and other observers.

32   See Ferdinand Gregorovius, *Euphorion: Eine Dichtung aus Pompeji*, trans. Theodore Grosse, 2d ed. (Leipzig, 1884), 100.

33   Poe wrote in his "Philosophy of Composition," first published in 1846, that "the death, then, of a beautiful woman is, unquestionably, the most poetical topic in the world." The classic study of this theme is Mario Praz, *The Romantic Agony*, trans. Angus Davidson, 2d ed. (London, 1951), esp. chap. 3, "The Shadow of the 'Divine Marquis,'" 93–186. For the eroticism of misfortune, see also Fritz Laupichler, "Misfortune," in *Encyclopedia of Comparative Iconography*, ed. Helene E. Roberts (Chicago, 1998), 2:609–13.

34   Gautier's novel *Arria Marcella* has been discussed in Wolfgang Leppmann's *Pompeii in Fact and Fiction* (London, 1968), 136–40. Ironically, Gautier's character was seen as an example of modesty by earlier writers on Pompeii, like Donaldson 1827 (note 27) and Gray 1977 (note 9).

35   Fiorelli 1860 (note 4), 2:248 (January–June 1831) and 3:114–15 (March 3–7, 1831); Robert Etienne, "Die letzten Stunden der Stadt Pompeji," in *Pompeji: Leben und Kunst in den Vesuvstädten*, 2d ed. (Recklinghausen, 1973), 53–58, esp. 56. The enthusiasm of certain male connoisseurs for a woman's foot may be found, for example, in pages of George Du Maurier's novel of artistic life, *Trilby* (New York, 1894); and Wilhelm Jensen's novel of Pompeii, *Gradiva: Ein pompejanisches Phantasiestück* (Dresden, 1903).

36   Although Fiorelli was given full credit for the innovative discovery at the time and has ever since been recognized as the inventor of the process, descriptions of the actual casting technique have always been vague, lending support to the argument that credit should have been more widely given. Adolfo Venturi was the most prominent scholar to challenge Fiorelli's sole claim to the discovery. See Adolfo Venturi, *Memorie* (Milan, 1911), 101.

37   Fiorelli proposed a standard admission fee in 1861, and the sum of two lire was instituted toward the end of the following year. The intent of the fee was to abolish tips and to raise money for additional custodians. In January 1863, after a month's receipts, Fiorelli reported that the excavations were running at a handsome profit. It was just as these preliminary results were being tabulated that the first of the casts was made (February 3, 1863). The publicity that followed the discovery helped draw more visitors to the excavations. On the admission fee, see *Pompeii: More Letters and Documents*, ed. Paola Poli Capri, 12 vols. (Rome, 1998), 1:26–32, 89–90, 97–103.

38   Some visitors, like Edward Hutton, objected to the exhibition: "And if you have the courage to creep into that new museum by the gate you may see the images of those who suffered.... There they lie, the young matron beside the slave, the mother by the daughter, close together. ...Ah, why should our curiosity demand so horrible an outrage as this?" (Edward Hutton, *Naples and Campania Revisited* [London, 1958], 192–93). The museum opened in 1875 and was still "new" when Hutton wrote the essay on Pompeii, circa 1910. Compare also Augustus J. C. Hare, *Cities of Southern Italy and Sicily* (Philadelphia, [1882]), 218. Fiorelli's ministerial colleague Luigi Settembrini published an open letter to Fiorelli, in the first public response, that was both laudatory and critical. Settembrini evidently resented the celebrity then being accorded to Fiorelli, but this aspect of the event must be examined in another place. See Felice Barnabei, *Le "Memorie di un archeologo"* (Rome, 1991), 405–6, 415n. 3; and Giuseppe Fiorelli, *Appunti autobiografici*, ed. Stefano De Caro (Sorrento, 1994).

39   Angelini, a prominent Neapolitan sculptor of the day, expressed his request and his intentions for the work in a letter from Naples to the Ministry of Public Instruction dated January 16, 1865. The letter, contained in the archive of the ministry, now in the Archivio centrale dello Stato in Rome, has been transcribed in *Giornale degli scavi di Pompei*, ed. Halsted B. Vander Poel and Paola Poli Capri (Rome, 1994), 7:X–XIV.

40 See Heinrich Brunn, "Scavi di Pompei, Cuma e Pesto," *Bullettino dell'Instituto di corrispondenza archeologica* (May–June 1863): 86–105, esp. 88–90. Fiorelli was the closest student of the casts, as attested by Brunn in the *Bullettino*. After his description of the four victims, Brunn deferred to Fiorelli, "who has not only examined these bodies more closely than anyone, but has also collected the observations made in his presence by archaeologists and antiquaries, artists, anatomists, and others." Brunn clearly expected that Fiorelli would eventually produce a definitive publication of the remains. It remains somewhat of a mystery that he did not produce such a study.

41 Hippolyte Taine, *Travels in Italy* (1865), cited by Robert Etienne, *Pompeii: The Day a City Died*, trans. Caroline Palmer (New York, 1992), 159.

42 See Anne Hollander, *Seeing through Clothes* (Harmondsworth, 1975), esp. 274–87.

43 For the modesty in women's dress favored by the court of the saintly Maria Christina, see Harold Acton, *The Last Bourbons of Naples* (London, 1961), 75–76. In addition to the young queen's influence, Ferdinand II was, for most of his reign (1830–59), under the influence of his confessor, Monsignor Celestino Cocle.

44 For the history of this collection, see *Il gabinetto segreto del Museo archeologico di Napoli*, ed. Stefano De Caro (Naples, 2000), esp. 9–22.

45 Società napoletana di storia patria, manuscript XXIX.C.I. See Mario Pagano, "Una legge ritrovata: Il progetto di legge per il riordinamento del R. museo di Napoli e degli scavi di antichità del 1848 e il ruolo di G. Fiorelli," *Archivio storico per le provincie napoletane* 112 (1994): 351–414.

46 Pagano 1994 (note 45), 393 (art. 72).

47 Ibid., 412 (art. 289, item 13); see also 370.

48 Ibid., 370n. 41 (Archivio di Stato di Napoli, Ministero della pubblica istruzione, FS. 317/9): "ma la proposta fu respinta dal Re il 14 novembre 1848." The plan was eventually implemented.

49 Giuseppe Fiorelli, *Museo nazionale di Napoli: Raccolta pornografica* (Naples, 1866), preface. Concerning Fiorelli's charge of "religious hypocrisy," a contemporary anecdote illustrates the extent to which religion and government worked together in the last days of the Bourbons of Naples. "When Victor Emmanuel first entered Naples to take possession of his new kingdom, he received, amidst many congratulations and submissions, one of strange character. An ecclesiastical dignitary approached towards his Majesty, and inquired in a low voice, but with an air of the utmost candour and simplicity, to whom he was to make his *report of the confessions*." One is meant to conclude that the secrets of the confessional had been regularly transmitted to the Bourbon police under the previous regime. See *Blackwood's Magazine* 101 (April 1867): 420.

50 See *Pio IX a Pompei: Memorie e testimonianze di un viaggio: Catalogo della mostra; Pompei scavi, Casina dell'Aquila, luglio–settembre 1987* (Naples, [1987]), 71–72.

51 Ibid., 72. The papal visit and the respect shown toward the excavations, as well as the gracious acceptance of a selection of artifacts, may well have been intended to answer the challenge to papal infallibility shown several years earlier (in 1845) by the Seventh Congress of Italian Scientists, whose session at Pompeii had been presided over by the youthful Fiorelli himself.

52 The new freedom did not immediately result in universal sympathy with the ancient way of life, as an 1861 observation made by Pedro de Alarcón indicates. The Spanish man of letters found in the pornographic collection "the Providential explanation of the destruction of Pompeii," a sentiment with which Thomas Gray thirty years earlier would have concurred. Alarcón is cited in De Caro 2000 (note 44), 19. Thomas Gray wrote: "the indecent paintings in the bed-rooms of the young girls, the charm *contra sterilitatem* which there seems little reason to doubt were worn by the ladies about the neck, as in modern times a cross or an eye-glass; the symbol over the oven [i.e., the phallus], etc., all serve to show how deep was the moral degradation from which Christianity rescued mankind" (Gray 1977 [note 9]), 203n. 20).

53   Raffaele Gargiulo, *Cenni storici e descrittivi dell'edificio del Museo nazionale* (Naples, 1864), 40.

54   Charles Ernest Beulé, *Drame du Vesuve* (Paris, 1872), 1–2.

55   Modern forensic pathologists would interpret this gesture as a "pugilistic stance," character-istic of victims whose bodies had been burned or exposed to high temperatures at the time of death.

56   See *Giornale degli scavi di Pompei*, n.s. 3 (1875): 173: [23 April 1875] 23 (Reg. VI, Is. 14). The cast has been illustrated in many books on Pompeii. See, for example, Pierre Gusman, *Pompei* (London, 1900), 17. (In his text Gusman confuses this woman with the "pregnant woman" of 1863.) Amedeo Maiuri illustrated the woman of 1875 ("una giovane e bella vittima dell'eruzione") in the many editions of his guide to Pompeii in the popular Ministry of Public Instruction series.

57   "Body of a Woman (Cadavere di donna)," in Yusef Komunyakaa, *Talking Dirty to the Gods: Poems* (New York, 2000), 42. I am indebted to Angela Salas for this reference.

58   Amedeo Cicchitti, who in the 1980s refined the casting process to obtain "the first transparent cast," was at that time unable to locate Fiorelli's first cast of the pregnant woman. See Amedeo Cicchitti, *Pompei: Il primo calco trasparente (Diario di uno scavo)* (L'Aquila, [1993]), 24.

59   For example, Joannes Overbeck, *Pompeji in seinen Gebäuden, Alterthümern und Kunstwerken für Kunst- und Alterthumsfreunde dargestellt* (Leipzig, 1856); August Mau, *Pompeii: Its Life and Art*, trans. Francis W. Kelsey (London, 1899); idem, *Pompeji in Leben und Kunst* (Leipzig, 1900). Both authors enjoyed great popularity in the heyday of historiography that was foreseen by Beulé.

60   Luigi Settembrini was the author of the revolutionary pamphlet *Protesta del popolo delle Due Sicilie*, published anonymously in 1847. He was imprisoned for revolutionary activities but con-tinued to use his pen effectively until the fall of the Bourbons in 1860. Subsequently he became inspector general of public instruction and held the chair of Italian literature in the Univer-sity of Naples. The excerpt from Settembrini's contemporary open letter to Fiorelli is cited in Emilio Magaldi, *Pompei e il suo dolore* (Naples, 1930), 103–4, 105n. 78.

61   It may be inferring too much from the quoted passage to say that Settembrini favored the burial (reburial?) of the victims, yet his youthful habit of reciting from Ugo Foscolo's poem "I sepol-cri" of 1806 reflects a lifelong respect for the honored dead. See Luigi Settembrini, *Ricordanze della mia vita* (Milan, 1964), 1:38. The church has frequently opposed the cult of the dead in Italian nationalism, as the history of the Roman Pantheon illustrates.

"A Picture Painted in Fire": Pain's Reenactments of *The Last Days of Pompeii,* 1879–1914

Nick Yablon

It is in the nature of things that all spectacles represent something....
Those fireworks that only represent a kind of repetition through the play
of different colors, movements, and brilliant effects...no matter how
cleverly designed, will never amount to anything more than the frivolous
charms of paper cutouts. In all the Arts it is necessary to paint.
In the one that we call Spectacle, *it is necessary to paint with actions.*

Jean-Louis de Cahuzac in Denis Diderot, *Encyclopédie* (1751–52)

I N HIS 1897 COMPENDIUM of the latest conjuring tricks, *Magic: Stage Illusions and Scientific Diversions,* Albert A. Hopkins included a chapter on the phenomenon of the pyrodrama. A fusion of two ancient arts—theater and fireworks—the pyrodrama was at the same time a distinctly modern creation. Advances in the chemical formulation and propulsion of combustible materials [FIG. 1] converged with mechanical developments in the manipulation of stage scenery [FIG. 2] to allow pyrodramatists to produce spectacles of unprecedented scale, realism, and intensity. The most ambitious and advanced of these impresarios, according to Hopkins, was James Pain, a British entrepreneur who in 1879 had brought his "spectacular productions" from London's Crystal Palace to Brooklyn's Manhattan Beach at the southeastern tip of Coney Island and had since exhibited in thirty cities across the United States. The subject matter of his shows varied considerably, encompassing past military campaigns such as Napoleon's siege of Moscow and historical disasters such as the Great Fire of London as well as more recent political disturbances such as the Paris Commune uprising—events that culminated in "some stirring catastrophe...[some]

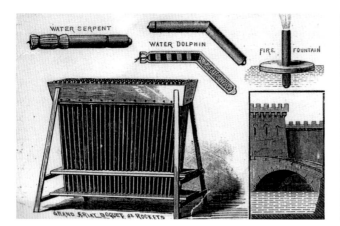 

FIGURE 1
New developments in
pyrotechnics. From *Magic:
Stage Illusions and
Scientific Diversions*, ed.
Albert A. Hopkins (1897),
366.

FIGURE 2
Lowering the flats backstage
during the reenactment
of Napoleon's siege
of Moscow. From *Magic:
Stage Illusions and
Scientific Diversions*, ed.
Albert A. Hopkins (1897),
364.

awful cataclysm" that could be reenacted with the aid of "colored fire." But the most popular of all Pain's Coney Island productions, and the one with which his name had become indelibly associated, was *The Last Days of Pompeii* [FIG. 3]. On the periphery of American cities, and on an almost nightly schedule, thousands of spectators were transported for only fifty cents to Flavian Pompeii to witness its final moments of decadence and destruction.[1]

In recent years, art, cultural, and film historians have become increasingly interested in the commercial spectacles and visual simulations that preceded the advent of cinema in 1895. Previously understudied media such as the stereograph, the panorama, and the diorama are now understood as central to the emergence of the new perceptual habits and spectatorial positions demanded by the medium of film.[2] One could make a similar case for locating Pain's pyrodramas, with their dramatic visual effects and mass audiences, within that emerging visual culture. Indeed, the subsequent success in the United States of the various film versions of *Gli ultimi giorni di Pompei* executed by the Italian producers Arturo Ambrosio (1908, 1911, 1913) and Ernesto Maria Pasquali (1911, 1913) might be attributed to audiences' prior experience of Pain's Pompeian epics.[3] This article, however, will interrogate the post hoc fallacy of characterizing such entertainments as "precinematic." To regard them as precursors or antecedents to the cinema is to misrepresent their historical contingency in a number of respects. First, it suppresses their kinship—in terms of audience, subject matter, and special effects—with the older institution of the theater. Second, it leads to the assumption that the eclipse of these entertainments by the early twentieth century was the natural and inevitable result of the advent of cinema, with whose capacity for verisimilitude they could not compete. But most critically the formal identification of these productions with the visual tricks and attractions of early cinema has the effect of eliding their distinctive content. Their spectacularity is thus emphasized at the expense of the narratives they enacted.[4]

Suspending the teleology that would characterize the pyrodrama as precinematic —as an important but ultimately unsuccessful prototype for the technology of motion pictures—this article will instead situate Pain's spectacles within their own specific contexts. It will examine his borrowings, as well as departures, from the apocalyptic melodramas performed in antebellum theaters, while also showing how he responded to the changing social composition and cultural tastes of late-nineteenth-century audiences. And it will place as much emphasis on his shows' literary content as on their

FIGURE 3

Pain's "Last Days of Pompeii" at Manhattan Beach, 1885. Advertisement from *Harper's Weekly* 29 (July 25, 1885): 476.

spectacular aspects. Indeed, their success arguably lay not only in the presentation of novel technical effects but also in the creative treatment of established themes such as the Last Days of Pompeii. Episodes from ancient history have served as a recurrent source for American plays and films, from the nineteenth-century plays of Robert Montgomery Bird, through the cinematic epics of *Ben-Hur* (1959), *Spartacus* (1960), and *Cleopatra* (1963), to the new wave of sword-and-sandal blockbusters, *Gladiator* (2000), *Troy* (2004), *Alexander* (2004), and most recently the dramatized documentary, *Pompeii: The Last Day* (2005).[5] While it is tempting to see the recurrence of these productions as a cyclical phenomenon, it is important to recognize the particular uses and meanings to which such narratives were assigned in each respective period. In the late nineteenth century, both critics and celebrants of various facets of an urbanizing and industrializing America—especially of its increasingly commercialized and spectacular popular amusements—found a powerful allegory in the destruction of Pompeii.

◱ ◱ ◱

Rather than viewing Pain's show as heralding an entirely new kind of entertainment, late-nineteenth-century audiences would have understood its content (if not its format) as indebted to a tradition of Pompeiana dating to the early nineteenth century. Pain derived both the narrative framework and the title from the famous historical melodrama written in 1834 by the English novelist Edward Bulwer, later Lord Lytton.[6] Bulwer-Lytton's novel, while motivated by English liberal politics, specifically the Whig call for electoral reform and the Christian moralist critique of an aristocratic class more concerned with its own self-gratification than with pressing social problems, could easily be translated into various American contexts. Indeed, the narrative existed in a public domain, open to all manner of appropriation and reappropriation during the remainder of the nineteenth century, with Bulwer-Lytton's blind slave girl serving, for example, as the inspiration for George Henry Boker's *Nydia; A Tragic Play* (1885), and Randolph Rogers's eponymous sculpture of about 1853–54, reproduced perhaps as many as one hundred times to satisfy popular demand.[7]

The earliest and most frequently performed of the American dramatic adaptations of Bulwer-Lytton's text was written in 1835 by the British-born playwright Louisa Medina.[8] The transference from page to stage, and from Britain to the United States, required certain modifications on Medina's part. The attention to archaeological artifacts and historical details that marked Bulwer-Lytton's extensively researched novel could not be carried over into the medium of theater. Many of his secondary characters were similarly omitted, and tangential subplots elided. But the novel's political and social meanings underwent the most comprehensive modification. Bulwer-Lytton had articulated a caustic critique of his own aristocratic class by portraying a Pompeian ruling class morally enfeebled by its appetite for luxury and material display. In Medina's version, the Pompeian ruling class now appears to refer to a more local "aristocracy of labor" that reflects the emergent class of petit bourgeois industrialists in northeastern cities like New York and Philadelphia, who had enriched themselves by mechanizing the manufacturing sector, implementing stricter divisions of labor, and imposing lower wages on their skilled workers.[9] In a melodramatic turn of events typical of American antebellum theater, the concluding eruption inflicted divine, even apocalyptic, retribution on these parasitic, neoaristocratic villains, thereby reaffirming the personal honor and pride of those who worked with their hands.[10]

By rearticulating Bulwer-Lytton's narrative in the language of radical republicanism, Medina was able to address a particular audience: the closely knit subculture of male, native-born artisans and mechanics who frequented the theater operated by her husband, Thomas Hamblin. Officially named the New York Theater when it opened in October 1826 and originally funded by "gentlemen-subscribers" from the city's leading mercantile families, by 1830 the Bowery Theater and its surrounding neighborhood had become the haunt of workingmen.[11] In the same way that Medina would appropriate *The Last Days of Pompeii* from its aristocratic author, the local artisanal classes set about appropriating this theater from its elite owners. With the lowering of its admission prices, the house was soon "packed from ceiling to pit, with its audience mainly of ... full-blooded young and middle-aged men, the best average of American-born mechanics," a single "mass" of "flush'd ... faces and eyes" and "full-sinew'd" arms, as one member of the audience, Walt Whitman, later reminisced. Before long, the Bowery's original patrons abandoned it for the more genteel Park Theater on fashionable Park Row.[12] Recent cultural historians have exaggerated the rowdiness and vulgarity of the Bowery's antebellum audience and characterized its spectatorial practices as the primitive and authentic "other" of bourgeois theater.[13] In fact, as Whitman himself recalled, Bowery performances were serious affairs. Eschewing the lighthearted comedies and operas favored at the Park Theater, the Bowery identified itself "more decidedly" with "the heavy tragedy business," at least until the 1840s. The actors cast by Hamblin and so fondly remembered by Whitman were famous for long-drawn-out death scenes: not only Edwin Forrest and Junius Brutus Booth but also J. Hudson Kirby, John R. Scott, and Hamblin himself.[14] Medina likely had these actors and audiences in mind when she transformed Bulwer-Lytton's gladiator-hero Glaucus into a thinly veiled portrayal of a native-born skilled artisan.

Medina—an English expatriate like James and Henry Pain—thus initiated the process whereby Bulwer-Lytton's novel was simultaneously theatricalized, Americanized, and radicalized. Contemporary theater critics believed that this latitude with respect to her literary sources was precisely that which guaranteed her success as a playwright. "It has been objected to them that their story departs from that of the novels on which some of them are based," wrote the *New-York Mirror* in 1838, "and this objection, as we think, redounds to her praise."[15] An indication of this success can be gleaned from the frequency with which *The Last Days of Pompeii* was performed at the Bowery. Opening there on February 9, 1835, it ran for twenty-seven consecutive nights until March 7, at that time the "longest and most comfortable uninterrupted run" in the history of New York theater according to its annalist, George Odell.[16] Medina and Hamblin thus contributed to a new and enduring feature of New York theatrical culture: the "long-running play." It established a precedent for the repetition of Pain's erupting Vesuvius, the lava of which, again according to Odell, would soon be seen throughout Coney Island's summer season, "flar[ing] into the sky every evening except Mondays."[17]

But the route by which Vesuvius was relocated from the streets of the Bowery to the beaches of Coney Island was not direct. By the time Pain arrived in the United States in the late 1870s, the legend of Pompeii had begun to accrue new class meanings. No longer allegorizing the punishment of the capitalist entrepreneur and the vindication of the surviving artisan, it now appeared to prefigure the wholesale destruction of

American civilization through a more general class apocalypse. With the eclipse of the craft system of production and the collapse of the Working Men's movement, a large industrial working class emerged, performing unskilled labor for long hours and at fixed wages and becoming increasingly militant in its demands for union recognition. The ensuing strikes and riots of the 1870s and 1880s led many to resort to volcano-logical metaphors to express their sense of impending doom. Henry George's 1879 political tract, *Progress and Poverty*, warned of the "volcanic forces" that were being generated among "the festering mass"—"pent-up forces" that would eventually cause "the very foundations of society [to] begin to quiver," unless his panacea of the "Single Tax" was adopted.[18] Utopian and dystopian novelists also capitalized on what one historian has called "a late nineteenth-century volcano vogue."[19] Ignatius Donnelly's cataclysmic vision, *Caesar's Column* (1890), presents an industrialized America of the future as a latter-day Pompeii. While a "molten mass" of misery and horror swirled beneath the surface threatening at any moment to discharge its "volcanic explosions," the rich continue to gratify themselves, "as thoughtless of the impending catastrophe as were the people of Pompeii in those pleasant August days in 79."[20] If, in the pre-industrial worldview of artisanal theater, the volcanic destruction once represented the power of divine retribution to restore an older economic order, the volcano now served as a metaphor for the vast socioeconomic forces unleashed by modern indus-trial capitalism itself.

Pain's show marked a further break from Medina's play in its balance between narrative and spectacle. Critics labeled Medina one of the Bowery's more sensational-ist playwrights ("partial to startling and terrible catastrophes," wrote the *Mirror*) and Whitman remembered her *Pompeii* to be one of its more "spectacular pieces," but her plays largely focused on themes of aristocratic villainy and artisanal revenge.[21] The special effects made possible by the newly invented gaslighting systems—installed in the Bowery before any other New York theater—were still primitive and rudimen-tary. Technical artifice was subordinated to the actors' performance, just as industrial processes of production were resisted in the workshop in favor of the manual labor of skilled artisanship.[22] Thus, limelighting, another apparatus available in theaters by the 1830s, was mobilized not as a means of distraction but rather to concentrate attention on the oratorical skills and personal charisma of the actors.[23]

Pain, on the other hand, deemphasized his actors and promoted the extranarra-tive elements of the show. The printed advertisements for his Pompeii spectacles (and others of the period) gave the pyrotechnics, rather than the dramatics, top billing [FIG. 4]. And during the performance Bulwer-Lytton's narrative was freely interrupted to introduce various sideshow acts and attractions, ranging from orchestral interludes, gladiatorial fights, chariot and foot races, swimming feats, dancing Pompeian girls, acrobatic routines, and, of course, the concluding fireworks display [FIG. 5]. Indeed, while the range of programs remained fairly constant from one season to the next, the fireworks would be improved almost nightly to keep pace with the audience's appetite for ever greater visual effects. In the case of Pompeii, "raft-born fireworks bobbing down in transparent glass water-troughs" were employed to simulate the "cascades of lava descending" the slopes of Vesuvius.[24] The large artificial lake, which served as the Bay of Naples, enhanced the fireworks' spectacular nature by reflecting the colors in the water while distancing the audience from the performance. Through such displays Pain helped redefine the function of fireworks in America. In place of the haphazard, recreational use of fireworks by untrained individuals (a "menace" that a national Safe

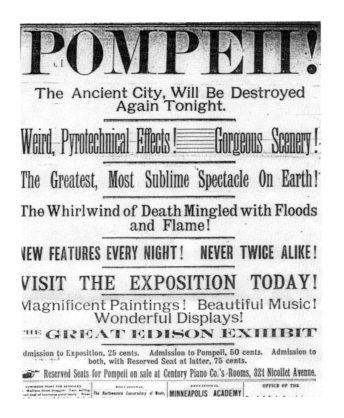

and Sane Fourth of July movement was at that time campaigning against), Pain reconceived fireworks as a mass spectacle to be produced by experts and consumed at a distance by audiences.[25]

Moreover, from the remote perspective of that "pier on Ischia . . . across the Bay of Naples," the audience would barely have been able to distinguish the expressions of Pain's actors, let alone hear their voices.[26] Indeed, as Hopkins himself pointed out, it is "perhaps more proper to speak of" the sideshows and fireworks as the main attraction and the actors as mere "accessories," so "loosely hung together" was the plot, minimal the dialogue, and underdeveloped the characters.[27] This subordination of the actors to the totality of the spectacle was not necessarily a function of any technological advance or innovation. The reduction of their lines from long soliloquies to a handful of shouted words (accompanied by gesticulated movements) and the effacement of their names from the advertising posters—their demotion, in effect, to the status of anonymous mime artists—were attributable in larger part to the altered composition of the audience. The native-born artisanal subcultures that had dominated antebellum theater by now had been supplanted by new immigrant audiences from eastern and southeastern Europe who had different recreational tastes. Pain's pyrodramatic version of Pompeii appealed to those less-cohesive audiences as it did not require or presume any knowledge of the linguistic codes of melodrama or even the English language.

Given the challenges of representing the volcanic eruption, of rendering what one art historian has called the "eruptive sublime," Pompeii acquired an additional significance during the course of the nineteenth century as a proving ground for modern techniques of visual display.[28] For several decades, American and British audiences had almost come to expect that the pioneers of each successive form of exhibition and entertainment would soon turn to the downfall of Pompeii for appropriate subject matter. John Burford, a pioneer of the panorama (an all-encompassing view fixed to the interior of a circular hall), showcased that medium with a *Ruins of the City of Pompeii* exhibition at the Strand in London in 1824—which was subsequently sold to the American artist and architect Frederick Catherwood for his rotunda at Prince and Mercer streets in New York [FIG. 6].[29] Similarly, the transformation of the static panorama into a moving panorama by attaching the painted canvas to a roll and gradually unscrolling it before a seated audience—a more practicable device for remote American audiences due to its greater portability and adaptability—prompted a number of Pompeian features, the most successful of which was *Mirror of Italy, or Italia*. Painted in 1849 by the Philadelphia artist Samuel B. Waugh, with a denouement that revealed the eruption of Vesuvius and scenes of Pompeii, this panorama toured a number of American cities and was particularly popular among New York audiences.[30] When special effects such as front and back gaslighting, colored lantern-slide projections, noise machines, and rotating platforms were incorporated, giving birth to the mechanical diorama, an erupting Vesuvius again demonstrated the enhanced capacity for spectacular realism.[31] Finally, the electrification of the diorama was consummated in that laboratory of illumination, Coney Island's Dreamland amusement park, with the 1904 installation of *The Destruction of Pompeii*, a two-hundred-thousand-dollar exhibition of electrical effects by E. C. Boyce and paintings by Charles S. Shean, all rather incongruously contained within a classical Greek temple.[32]

As these pictorial displays became increasingly sophisticated in their mechanical artifice, so the commitment to archaeological authenticity made by Bulwer-Lytton's novel diminished. The early-nineteenth-century panoramas had been promoted as living documents of ancient history, with "every stone" of Pompeii's ruins "painted with the utmost accuracy in detail" and further particulars about the everyday life of Pompeians on the eve of the eruption provided by printed souvenir booklets and by narrators lecturing within the auditorium.[33] By the late nineteenth century, on the other hand, emphasis had shifted to the moment of the eruption itself, executed with steam, electricity, or fireworks. Utopian novelists imagining the mass media of the future, including the picture-making devices that would ultimately succeed the panoramas, dioramas, and pyrodramas of the present, already detected this drift away from the narrative and the didactic. The inhabitants of Saturn in Cyrus Cole's 1890 novel, *The Auroraphone*, would employ an "Electro-Camera-Lucida-Motophone" to project

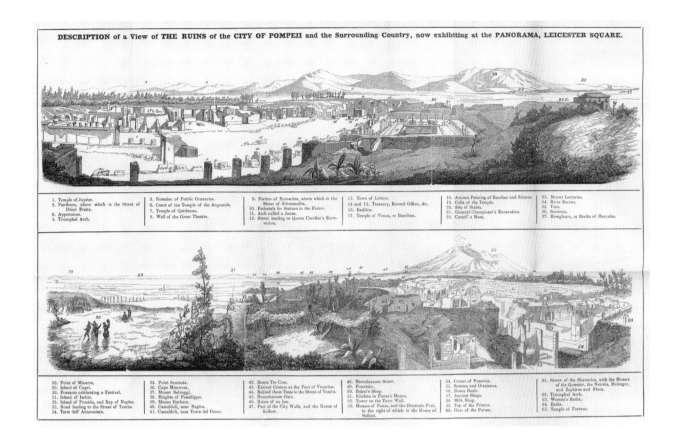

FIGURE 6

John Burford, *Description of a View of the Ruins of the City of Pompeii and the Surrounding Country, Now Exhibiting at the Panorama, Leicester Square*, 1824. From J. [John] Burford, *Description of a Second View of the Ruins of Pompeii and Surrounding Country* (1824), n.p. Bloomington, Indiana University, Lilly Library.

their "spectacular entertainment[s]," including "animated tableaux" of temporally and spatially distant events such as the eruption of Vesuvius. Stripped of all didactic or moralistic content, such projections, wrote Cole, would be "presented purely as exciting combinations of movement, sound, and color."[34]

Even with the greater emphasis on spectacle over narrative, however, the Pompeian theme was more than simply a passive vehicle for demonstrating the technological capabilities of new (and anticipated) media of pictorial exhibition. Precisely through this heightened association with new exhibition practices, the myth of Pompeii had also come to represent the excesses of a culture that demanded and craved commercialized spectacles. By the time Pain arrived at Coney Island the identification of the American amusement industry with the supposedly excessive and decadent entertainments of imperial Rome was firmly established. The pleasure-seeking masses of American industrial cities now resembled, for many critics, the vulgar "plebeian rabble" in their demand for a regular supply of *panem et circenses*. Pain's achievement lay not merely in his striking technical achievements but equally in his ability to allude to and exploit these subtextual meanings. Significantly, his audience would witness Pompeii's destruction not within a modern, post-theatrical space, such as a panorama or a diorama, but within a historicized space, a reconstructed Roman amphitheater. Seated or standing in a ten-thousand-capacity open-air arena that deliberately evoked the amphitheater built in Pompeii in 70 B.C. (purported to have been large enough to accommodate the population of the entire town), the audience could identify with the Roman spectators assembled on the stage or figured in the painted backdrop.[35] As a city that had by now become a byword for the love of large-scale spectacle and extravagant display, to which only Bulwer-Lytton's blind Nydia had been immune, Pompeii offered a pertinent allegory for America's own apparent transition from a popular culture grounded in local, clearly defined artisanal rituals to a mass culture of commercialized entertainment consumed across class, ethnic, and gender boundaries. Just as the volcano consumed Pliny the Elder as he attempted to get a better view, so too did the love of spectacle appear to consume American audiences. Within this context, the spectacular form of Pain's *Last Days of Pompeii* also became its content, as audiences could reflect on the fate of a society in thrall to visual pleasure.

Given this perceived relationship between Pompeian antiquity and American modernity, arguments for or against the new mass culture taking shape in Coney Island were frequently reinforced by allusions—both explicit and implicit—to Pain's pyrodrama. Within the context of an ongoing debate over the political and aesthetic value of modern commercial amusements, the nature of those allusions correspondingly alternated between unqualified adulation and outright excoriation.[36] *Battle of Lights, Coney Island*, painted in 1913 by the Italian immigrant Joseph Stella, appears to be unequivocally celebratory [FIG. 7]. With this first major painting after his return from Europe, Stella sought to employ the aesthetic doctrines of the Italian Futurist movement.[37] The Futurist goal of a synaesthetic embrace of the flux of modern city life, with its chaotic and dynamic merging of the senses, led him straight to the "surging crowd," "revolving machines," and "dazzling lights" of Coney Island.[38] Inspired by what he termed "the new polyphony" of electrical illumination, Stella orchestrated a discordant "ringing" of neon letters, searchlights, roller coasters be-decked in light bulbs, and, in the center, the electric tower of Luna Park. Crowning this "dynamic arabesque" of electrical motifs are several arcs of pointillist dots that appear to trace the outline of a fireworks display.[39] If Stella had visited Manhattan Beach, he would have found Pain's shows to be themselves synaesthetic in their combination of melodramatic theater, symphonic music, intense illumination, and even the "smell of brimstone and powder"—a *Gesamtkunstwerk* for the masses.[40] Indeed, another version of *The Battle of Lights*, painted on a larger canvas, elevates the fireworks display to its central subject [FIG. 8]. In his efforts to render the ephemeral vision of the exploding rocket in a two-dimensional format, Stella evoked an older tradition of firework imagery dating to the etchings, engravings, and paintings of the *feux d'artifice* of the seventeenth and eighteenth centuries.[41] But while those earlier artists depicted the fireworks display as courtly entertainment, celebrating the victory, wedding, or coronation of a royal figure and marking the absolute authority of the sovereign, Stella represents the transformation of the fireworks display into a popular spectacle, celebrated by and for the masses. Significantly, those fireworks erupt from the apex of the composition, as if giving vent to the volcanic energies of mass commercial amusement.

The assessment made by another European visitor, the Russian Marxist Maxim Gorky, was less favorable. Even if Gorky did not cite Pain's show directly, pyrotechnic and volcanic metaphors nonetheless saturated his prose, in particular his 1907 magazine article on Coney Island, succinctly titled "Boredom." Appalled by the stultifying and reifying effects of capitalism's latest mode of recreation, Gorky invoked an array of apocalyptic imagery that may well have been inspired by a visit to Pain's Pompeian amphitheater. Coney Island is a "fantastic city all of fire…a flaming city," "a city made up of millions of fires." Even the water encircling the piers of these amusement parks has come to resemble "whimsical blotch[es] of *molten* gold" (italics added). And

FIGURE 7
Joseph Stella (American, 1877–1946), *Battle of Lights, Coney Island*, 1913. Oil on canvas. New Haven, Conn., Yale University Art Gallery, Gift of Collection Société Anonyme, Object No. 1941.689.

FIGURE 8
Joseph Stella (American, 1877–1946), *Battle of Lights, Coney Island*, ca. 1914–18. Oil on canvas. Sheldon Memorial Art Gallery and Sculpture Garden, University of Nebraska–Lincoln, UNL-F.M. Hall Collection.

Photo: © Sheldon Memorial Art Gallery.

like Pain's own incendiary devices, this fire burns but "does not consume," leaving the structures of the city intact for yet another night of monotonous entertainment.[42]

Approaching the spectacles of Coney Island through the lens of neither Italian Futurism nor Russian Marxism, the middle-brow cultural critic for the *New York Sun*, James Huneker, assumed a more ambivalent stance. On the one hand, Huneker's self-confessed "bourgeois" tastes predisposed him against that "whole horrible aggregation of shanties, low resorts, shacks masquerading as hotels." Describing a visit to Coney Island in 1907, Huneker echoed Gorky's longing for a real, apocalyptic fire—as opposed to the routinized simulacra of fire—in his vision of those booths and shacks "swept off the earth by some beneficent visitation of Providence, [for which] the thanksgivings of the community would be in order." Such an eschatological outcome is already prefigured by those apocalyptic illuminations that transform the island every night into a "glorified city of flame." The trope parallels that of Gorky, except here Huneker goes on to allude to Pain explicitly:

> After seeing the aerial magic of that great pyrotechnic artist Pain, a man who could, if he so desired, create a new species of art, and his nocturnes of jeweled fire, you wonder why the entire beach is not called Fire Island. The view of Luna Park from Sheepshead Bay suggests a cemetery of fire, the tombs, turrets, and towers illuminated, and mortuary shafts of flame.... Everything is fretted with fire. Fire delicately etches some fairy structure; fire outlines an Oriental gateway; fire runs like a musical scale through many octaves, the darkness crowding it, the mist blurring it. Fire is the god of Coney Island after sundown, and fire was its god this night, the hottest night of the summer.[43]

Thus, even as Huneker decries the booths and shacks of the amusement park landscape, he admits the "joys [he] experienced" that night, and concedes a certain admiration for the spectacles exhibited there by "artists" like Pain.[44] Resisting the temptation to dismiss the shows as excessive or indulgent, Huneker offered only one criticism of Pain: he did not take the spectacle far enough. Fireworks, Huneker argued in another article written at the time, had the potential not merely to become an art form—the eighth art, perhaps—but indeed to transcend (in a Hegelian sense) the preceding seven. The medium of fireworks, neither encumbered by historical precedents and aesthetic principles nor physically bound to any material support, could achieve a formal purity that would allow it to surpass even painting and poetry: "Its chief merit lies in its inability to express ideas, above all, didactic ideas. It must not tell a story, insinuate a moral, or imitate any earthly form. It is the ideal art of the arabesque." Huneker urged pyrotechnicians to free this new form from its residual content, thus dedicating it not to narratives (such as the fall of Pompeii) but rather to "form and hue, pattern and emotional meanings." He writes that, "Professor Pain, virtuoso in the art, delights in showing us historic happenings in a coruscating pragmatic blaze; yet we believe if left to follow his own devices this firesmith would give the world a nobler style of art."[45] Huneker thus instructs Pain to "have the courage of his fiery fugues"—to jettison the literary deadweight of Victorian melodramas such as those of Bulwer-Lytton or Medina. Only then will the "art of pyrotechny" redeem itself to become a "universal" art form that will "need no preliminary initiations, one immediately underst[ood by] the people."[46]

In any event, the cancellation of Pain's shows the following year, in 1914, prevented him from further exploring the artistic aspects of the pyrodrama. The near conjunction of those final shows of *The Last Days of Pompeii* with the release of the two eponymous films produced in 1913 by the rival Italian directors Eleuterio Rodolfi and Mario Caserini might lead one to endorse the common assumption—outlined at the outset of this article—that cinematic spectacle rendered the precinematic obsolete. Certainly, the Italian directors developed film techniques that allowed for narrative structures of greater complexity and they constructed sets that were deeper and less stagelike than Pain's. With access to thousands of extras available at low wages and to growing international networks of printing and distribution, they could unquestionably produce larger epics to wider audiences at lower costs than could Pain, who was required to rebuild his sets for each performance, design and manufacture his own chemicals, hire expensive American actors, and enter into partnerships with local businessmen.[47] The presumption, however, that one medium supersedes another according to a logic of escalating spectacle elides several other conditions. Pain's decision to suspend his pyrodramas appears not to have been motivated by any decline in popularity. Instead, other pressures appear to have affected the business. The *New York Times'* 1935 obituary for Pain cited his company's growing concentration on producing military munitions for the Great War and its diminishing sales of fireworks to American consumers because of the legal restrictions brought about by the Safe and Sane Fourth of July movement.[48] Moreover, the art of pyrotechnics survived the birth of cinema, and would, in fact, go on to satisfy Huneker's desire for a pure spectacle, liberated entirely from narrative content, in the form of patriotic "aerial spectaculars" produced in recent decades for the centennial celebrations of the Brooklyn Bridge and the Statue of Liberty, the Bicentennial of Independence, and the inaugurations of presidents. But in the process these later spectacles marked a break with a long-standing tradition in the history of fireworks—the belief that they should aspire to something more than the "frivolous charms of paper cutouts."

Notes

I would like to thank Lauren Rabinovitz, Paula Amad, Jon Seydl, and Victoria Coates for their comments on earlier drafts and presentations of this article; and John Deeker of Pains Fireworks Ltd.; and for assistance with research, the staffs of the Research Library of the Getty Research Institute; the Regenstein Library, University of Chicago; the UCLA Arts Library; and the Lilly Library, Indiana University.

[1]   The title of this essay, "A Picture Painted in Fire," is quoted from "A Saturday by the Sea," *New York Times*, June 18, 1882, 7. The epigram is from Jean-Louis de Cahuzac, "Feux d'artifice," in Denis Diderot, *Encyclopédie, ou, Dictionnaire raisonné des sciences, des arts et des métiers* (1751–72; Elmsford, N.Y., 1969), 1:1418, translated and cited in Kevin Salatino, *Incendiary Art: The Representation of Fireworks in Early Modern Europe* (Los Angeles, 1997), 23.
   On pyrodramas, see *Magic: Stage Illusions and Scientific Diversions*, ed. Albert A. Hopkins (New York, 1897), chap. 8, "Fireworks with Dramatic Accessories," quotations on 362, 365. The Pain family's involvement in explosives dates to 1593 (one of their early customers was allegedly Guy Fawkes, preparing for his gunpowder plot of 1605) and continues to this day. James Pain returned from the United States to England in either 1884 or 1885, leaving his son Henry to continue the shows (see the obituary "Henry J. Pain Dies in England at Eighty," *New York Times*, February 15, 1935, 19, which dates Pain's arrival to 1877 rather than 1879). As it is difficult to determine any divergence in their approaches, this article will hereafter use the surname "Pain" to refer to the company itself rather than to specify father or son.

2   Jonathan Crary, *Techniques of the Observer: On Vision and Modernity in the Nineteenth Century* (Cambridge, Mass., 1990); *Cinema and the Invention of Modern Life*, ed. Leo Charney and Vanessa R. Schwartz (Berkeley, 1995), esp. chaps. 3, 8, 11; Lynne Kirby, *Parallel Tracks: The Railroad and Silent Cinema* (Durham, 1997), esp. 42–48; Vanessa R. Schwartz, *Spectacular Realities: Early Mass Culture in Fin-de-Siècle Paris* (Berkeley, 1998), 149–76; Angela Miller, "The Panorama, the Cinema, and the Emergence of the Spectacular," *Wide Angle* 18, no. 2 (1996): 34–69.

3   Paolo Cherchi Usai, "Italy: Spectacle and Melodrama," in Geoffrey Nowell-Smith, *The Oxford History of World Cinema* (Oxford, 1996), 123–30. Ambrosio's 1913 versions of *Pompeii* was introduced to approving American audiences (apparently including D. W. Griffith) by the distributor George Kleine. See Kleine's program of Italian epics, complete with descriptions of each film, *George Kleine's Cycle of Film Classics* (New York, 1916).

4   Angela Miller's essay on the "emergence of the spectacular," in which she makes the case for viewing the various types of panoramas as "antecedents of the cinema," provides an example of all three tendencies. The "new experiences" offered by this medium, she writes, "had no precedents in the culture of the theater." The decline of the medium at the turn of the century was "assured" by the coming of cinema. And "its ability to reproduce an experience in its maximum visual intensity" was predicated on its liberation "from narrative requirements," its "independen[ce] [from] content" (Miller 1996 [note 2], 38, 41, 36, 49). See also A. Nicholas Vardac's earlier genealogy of the cinema, *Stage to Screen: The Theatrical Origins of Early Film: David Garrick to D. W. Griffith* (1949; New York, 1968).

5   On Hollywood's fascination with Rome, see Maria Wyke, *Projecting the Past: Ancient Rome, Cinema, and History* (London, 1997); and Peter Bondanella, *The Eternal City: Roman Images in the Modern World* (Chapel Hill, N.C., 1987), 207–55. For a discussion of how narratives and images of ruins and antiquity have been used to articulate the upheavals of American urbanization, see Nick Yablon, *American Ruins: An Archaeology of Urban Modernity, 1830–1920* (Chicago, forthcoming).

6   Edward Bulwer-Lytton, *The Last Days of Pompeii* (1834; New York, 1957).

7   On Rogers's *Nydia*, see Wayne Craven, *Sculpture in America* (1968; Newark, 1984), 312–14. According to Craven, Rogers's *Nydia, the Blind Girl of Pompeii* became a "symbol of the [Victorian] age," remaining a "stellar attraction" even as late as 1876, when exhibited at the Philadelphia Centennial Exposition (313–14). Less well received was the *Nydia* made in 1839 by the Cincinnati sculptor Edward Augustus Brackett, a statue that should have been "destroy[ed]," wrote one critic, as soon as it was "finished" (187).

8   Louisa Medina (Hamblin), *The Last Days of Pompeii: A Dramatic Spectacle* (1835; New York, 1856).

9   On this "bastardization" of the artisanal system and efforts by those artisans to voice their resistance through a vision of "radical democracy," see Sean Wilentz, *Chants Democratic: New York City and the Rise of the American Working Class, 1788–1850* (Oxford, 1984), esp. 107–42, 326–59. See also Richard B. Stott, *Workers in the Metropolis: Class, Ethnicity, and Youth in Antebellum New York City* (Ithaca, 1990), 34–67.

10   On this melodramatic quest, which structures a number of other popular plays of the period, see Bruce A. McConachie, "The Earthquake! The Earthquake!" in *Melodramatic Formations: American Theater and Society, 1820–1870* (Iowa City, 1992), 119–55.

11   According to Wilentz (1984 [note 9], 257), the Bowery "in the 1830s was swiftly becoming New York's plebeian boulevard" and its "most renowned attractions were its scores of sideshows and theatricals, esp. those staged at the Bowery Theatre." See also Stott 1990 (note 9), 222–29.

12   Walt Whitman, "The Old Bowery," in *November Boughs* (1888), reprinted in *Prose Works 1892*, ed. Floyd Stovall (New York, 1964), 2:595. When the Bowery first opened, its admission prices were 37½¢ for the pit, 75¢ for the boxes, and 25¢ for the gallery (Charles Haswell, *Reminiscences of New York by an Octogenarian, 1816–1860* [New York, 1896], 191). Whitman described the

Park Theater, which charged fifty cents for the pit and one dollar for the boxes, as "the more stylish and select theatre...a large and well-appointed house on Park Row" (*Prose Works* 1964, 2:592).

13   On the supposed unruliness of early-nineteenth-century artisanal audiences, see Lawrence Levine, *Highbrow/Lowbrow: The Emergence of Cultural Hierarchy in America* (Cambridge, Mass., 1988), 13–81; and John Kasson, *Rudeness and Civility: Manners in Nineteenth-Century Urban America* (New York, 1990), 217–22.

14   *Prose Works* 1964 (note 12), 2:592. Whitman continues: "It was at the Bowery I first saw Edwin Forrest...and it affected me for weeks; or rather I might say permanently filter'd into my whole nature....[C]ertainly the main 'reason for being' of the Bowery Theatre those years was to furnish the public with Forrest's and Booth's performances....For some reason or other, neither Forrest nor Booth would accept engagements at the more fashionable theatre, the Park. And it is a curious reminiscence, but a true one, that both these great actors and their performances were taboo'd by 'polite society' in New York and Boston at the time—probably as being too robustuous. But no such scruples affected the Bowery" (2:593–94).

15   *New-York Mirror*, April 28, 1838, 351, cited in Rosemarie K. Bank, "Theatre and Narrative Fiction in the Work of a Nineteenth-Century American Playwright, Louisa Medina," *Theatre History Studies* 3 (1983): 56; see also *The Ladies Companion and Literary Expositor*, which "ascribe[d] the success of Miss Medina's plays wholly to the liberties she takes with the authors" (April 1837, 30, cited in Bank 1983, 56); Bank cites only one negative review, in which her plays are described as "those fanfaronades of dramatic flummery" (*The Spirit of the Times*, September 10, 1836, 233, cited in Bank 1983, 57).

16   George Clinton Densmore Odell, *Annals of the New York Stage*, 12 vols. (New York, 1927–49), 4:31.

17   Ibid., 12:557. In the winter Pain took his Pompeii pyrodrama to the Southern Hemisphere, exhibiting it at cricket grounds and pleasure gardens in Melbourne between 1886 and 1890 and in 1904. See Mimi Colligan, *Canvas Documentaries: Panoramic Entertainments in Nineteenth-Century Australia and New Zealand* (Melbourne, 2002), 141–56.

18   Henry George, *Progress and Poverty: An Inquiry into the Cause of Industrial Depressions and of Increase of Want with Increase of Wealth...the Remedy* (1879; New York, 1960), 537, 551.

19   Kenneth Roemer claims that "by far the most common image of the turbulent and potentially destructive forces culminating during the transition period was the volcano" (*The Obsolete Necessity: America in Utopian Writings, 1888–1900* [Kent, Ohio, 1976], 22; the reference to a "volcano vogue" is on 23); see also Frederic Cople Jaher, *Doubters and Dissenters: Cataclysmic Thought in America, 1885–1918* (New York, 1964).

20   Edmund Boisgilbert [Ignatius Donnelly], *Caesar's Column: A Story of the Twentieth Century* (1890; Cambridge, Mass., 1960), 62, 70; see also the allusions to volcanic eruption later in the novel, when the violent revolution finally takes place (256).

21   *New-York Mirror*, April 28, 1838, 351 (cited in Bank 1983 [note 15], 56). *Prose Works* 1964 (note 12), 2:594.

22   Haswell 1896 (note 12), 191. In 1816 the first stage gaslighting system was installed in Philadelphia at the Chestnut Street Theater.

23   I would thus question whether we can date the ascendancy of the spectacular from the availability of certain technologies of illumination. See, for example, McConachie's claim that "gas was crucial to the success of apocalyptic melodrama" and that "without this technology [of gas illumination], it is doubtful that apocalyptic melodrama [such as Medina's *Last Days of Pompeii*] would have been written or produced" (McConachie 1992 [note 10], 142–43); and Christopher Kent's assertion that "the audience were further, and literally dazzled by the employment of high intensity lime light" among other special effects ("Spectacular History as an Ocular Discipline," *Wide Angle* 18, no. 3 [1996]: 4). Limelighting, invented by Thomas

Drummond in 1816 and in wide use by the mid-nineteenth century, was, in fact, employed to focus rather than derange the attention of the spectator.

24   David Mayer, *Playing Out the Empire: Ben-Hur and Other Toga Plays and Films, 1883–1908; A Critical Anthology* (Oxford, 1994), 94; idem, "Romans in Britain, 1886–1910: Pain's 'The Last Days of Pompeii,'" *Theatrephile* 2, no. 5 (Winter 1984–85): 46.

25   This turn-of-the-century campaign against the personal use of fireworks was led by the American Medical Association and by prominent reformers such as Mrs. Isaac L. Rice, whose article, "Our Barbarous Fourth," appeared in *Century Magazine* 76 (June 1908): 222. In 1908 Cleveland passed the first citywide ban on consumer fireworks.

26   "A Drama in Pyrotechnics: The Last Days of Pompeii Enacted at Manhattan Beach," *New York Times*, June 12, 1885, 2.

27   Hopkins 1897 (note 1), 362, 364; see also "Fireworks with Dramatic Accessories," *Scientific American* 55, no. 5 (July 31, 1886): 69; and "Fireworks as an Adjunct to Dramatic Entertainment," *Scientific American*, July 11, 1896, 25.

28   Salatino 1997 (note 1), 54–76.

29   See also J. [John] Burford, *Description of a View of the Ruins of the City of Pompeii and the Surrounding Country: Now Exhibiting in the Panorama, Strand; Painted from Drawings Taken on the Spot by Mr. Burford* (London, 1824). Burford produced a third panorama, *Ruins of Pompeii, the City of the Dead*, in 1849; see Curtis Dahl, "Panoramas of Antiquity," *Archaeology* 12 (Winter 1959): 259. On Frederick Catherwood's 1838 rotunda, see Dahl 1959, 260–62; and Stephan Oettermann, *The Panorama: History of a Mass Medium*, trans. Deborah Lucas Schneider (1980; New York, 1997), 317–23.

30   Samuel B. Waugh, *Italia; A Hand-Book Descriptive of the New Series of Italian Views* (1855; Philadelphia, 1867). Other panoramas of Pompeii and Vesuvius include one exhibited by a Mr. Mondelli in Saint Louis in 1830 (see J. F. McDermott, "Newsreel—Old Style; or Four Miles of Canvas," *Antiques* 44 [July 1943]: 10), and those painted in the 1890s in watercolor by the amateur panoramists Lawrence W. Ladd and Ilseph Beck (collectively known as "The Utica Artist"). See Paul D. Schweizer and Barbara C. Polowy, *"Utica Artist": Panoramas for the People* (Utica, N.Y., 1984), esp. no. 45 (*The Ruins at Pompeii with Tourists*) and no. 46 (*Eruption of Mount Vesuvius*).

31   On Daguerre's invention of the diorama, see Oettermann 1997 (note 29), 74–83; and Helmut Gernsheim and Alison Gernsheim, *L. J. M. Daguerre: The History of the Diorama and the Daguerreotype* (1956; New York, 1968). J. McNevin presented a "Magnificent Moving Diorama of Naples, Exhibiting the Grand Eruption of Vesuvius and Destruction of Pompeii" at London's Royal Cyclorama in Regent's Park in 1854; see his program, *Royal Cyclorama: A Description of the Colossal Dioramic Pictures of Naples, Vesuvius, and the Excavated City of Pompeii: The Eruption of Vesuvius, A.D. 79, Which Caused the Destruction of the City Is Represented in a Large Historical Picture, with the Aid of Mechanical Effects; The Drawings Were Made on the Spot in 1852, and the Original Pictures Painted by Mr. J. McNevin* (London, 1854).

32   Jeffrey Stanton, "Coney Island—Dreamland," http://naid.sppsr.ucla.edu/coneyisland/articles/dreamland.htm (accessed August 18, 2001).

33   The reference regarding accuracy of painting is to McNevin's diorama, cited in Dahl 1959 (note 29), 262; Catherwood himself served as the lecturer at these cycloramic events, drawing on "knowledge he had acquired on the actual sites" (ibid., 262).

34   Cyrus Cole, *The Auroraphone: A Romance* (Chicago, 1890), cited in Roemer 1976 (note 19), 138.

35   In some cities this connection was directly acknowledged in the naming of pyrodramatic exhibition buildings such as Boston's 1888 Pompeian Amphitheatre, on Huntington Avenue and Rogers Street, where a Pompeii reenactment (probably Pain's) was regularly exhibited (Will Holton, "Best of All Possible Worlds: A Historical View of Northeastern's Environs," in *Tra-*

dition and Innovation: Reflections on Northeastern University's First Century, ed. Brook K. Baker et al. [Boston, 1998]), 15–16. On the centrality of Pompeii's original amphitheater within the civic life of the town, its seating capacity, and its association with rioting audiences, see Richard Brilliant, *Pompeii A.D. 79: The Treasure of Rediscovery* (New York, 1979), 6.

36   For this turn-of-the-century debate about commercial amusement and its imbrication of race, technology, and the body, see Bill Brown, *The Material Unconscious: American Amusement, Stephen Crane, and the Economies of Play* (Cambridge, Mass., 1996). See also Lauren Rabinovitz, *Yesteryear's Wonderlands: Introducing Modernism to America. A CD-ROM* (Champaign, Ill., forthcoming).

37   On the influence of the Futurists on Stella and their mutual fascination with the synaesthetic merging of sound and sight, see Donna M. Cassidy, *Painting the Musical City: Jazz and Cultural Identity in American Art, 1910–1940* (Washington, D.C., 1997), 37–68. Joann Moser suggests that *Battle of Lights, Coney Island*, "might arguably be considered the most fully developed Futurist painting by an American artist" (*Visual Poetry: The Drawings of Joseph Stella* [Washington, D.C., 1990], 59). John Baur has drawn on Stella's autobiographical notes (1946) to dispel the "often published story" that *Battle of Lights* was exhibited at the 1913 Armory Show. In fact, it was begun after the show had closed and was first exhibited in 1914 at the Montross Gallery (John I. H. Baur, *Joseph Stella* [New York, 1971], 31–32).

38   Joseph Stella, autobiographical notes (1946), reprinted as "Discovery of America: Autobiographical Notes," *Art News* 59 (November 1960): 65.

39   Ibid.

40   "Sebastopol's First Fall: A Shivering Crowd Declare It Deeply Impressive," *New York Times*, June 12, 1887, 2. Other accounts in the *New York Times* confirm that Pain's show was typically the highlight of any visit to Coney Island; audiences would wait "impatient[ly]" for this event, not returning home until the finale was over ("A Saturday by the Sea" [note 1], 7).

41   Salatino 1997 (note 1); for fireworks in American painting from Whistler's *Nocturnes* onward, see *Fireworks: American Artists Celebrate the Eighth Art*, ed. Pamela Lawrentz (Youngstown, Ohio, 1986).

42   Maxim Gorky, "Boredom," *The Independent*, August 8, 1907, 309, 310.

43   James Huneker, "Coney Island," in idem, *New Cosmopolis* (New York, 1915), 152–54, 165–66. On Huneker's career as a critic, see Arnold T. Schwab, *James Gibbons Huneker: Critic of the Seven Arts* (Stanford, 1963).

44   Huneker 1915 (note 43), 154.

45   James Huneker, "In Praise of Fireworks," in idem, *The Pathos of Distance: A Book of a Thousand and One Moments* (New York, 1913), 345–46.

46   Ibid., 345.

47   On Pain's use of local actors and his efforts to "induc[e] local businessmen to venture into a profit-sharing arrangement," see Mayer 1994 (note 24), 92, 94.

48   Obituary 1935 (note 1), 19.

FIGURE 1
East wall, room 5, Villa of
the Mysteries, Pompeii, first
century B.C.

Photo: James Stanton-Abbott,
2002. Courtesy Ministero
per i Beni e le Attività Culturali,
Soprintendenza archeologica
di Pompei.

Replicating Roman Murals in Pompeii: Archaeology, Art, and Politics in Italy of the 1920s

Elaine K. Gazda

I N APRIL 1909 excavators working outside the walls of Pompeii discovered a room with walls that had been painted with monumental figures profiled against a vivid red background [FIG. 1].[1] These were the most extraordinary murals yet discovered at Pompeii and among the finest to have survived from classical antiquity.[2] Notices appeared in the press within weeks of the initial excavation. Scholarly articles appeared in rapid succession. By 1913 the murals had been published at least five times.[3]

Virtually from the moment of the murals' excavation, it was agreed that the god Dionysos, also known as Bacchus, was the central figure of the drama enacted on the four walls. In the intervening years many interpretations of that narrative have been put forward, and new ones continue to emerge. One long-established reading holds that the murals represent the initiation of a young woman into the cult of Dionysos in preparation for marriage.[4] The villa's ancient paintings and their meanings are, however, subjects unto themselves. Here I want to focus instead on a single episode of their afterlife, an episode that we can document in considerable and enlightening detail.

Bettina Bergmann's paper in this volume chronicles the vicissitudes of the murals from the time of their discovery. My study focuses on one episode of that narrative that began in 1924. In that year Francis Willey Kelsey, professor of Latin language and literature at the University of Michigan, commissioned Maria Barosso, head of archaeological drafting for excavations in the Roman Forum and on the Palatine Hill, to paint a full-scale replica of the murals in the Villa of the Mysteries. In this story, the agendas of Kelsey, the scholar; Barosso, the artist; and Mussolini, the most prominent political figure in Italy, intersect in complex and revealing ways. This essay explores that nexus to illuminate the kinds of relationships that developed among archaeologists, artists, and politicians in Italy during the 1920s, which in turn reveal the political exploitation of ancient Rome in Italy between the two world wars.[5]

Kelsey's Project

In 1924 Francis Kelsey wrote to his former student, Esther Van Deman, then residing in Rome, to ask for her help in identifying an artist who could make an accurate copy of the famous Bacchic murals in the Villa of the Mysteries in Pompeii. Van Deman, who had conducted extensive research on the House of the Vestal Virgins (Atrium Vestae) in the Roman Forum, knew of Maria Barosso and her work.[6] Barosso had made watercolor replicas of Roman murals found in the Forum and on the Palatine Hill, which Van Deman admired.[7] She recommended Barosso to Kelsey, and Barosso accepted the assignment with enthusiasm. Between 1925 and 1927, working largely on-site in Pompeii, Barosso produced a striking, nearly full-scale watercolor representation of the four walls of the famous room [FIG. 2].[8] Barosso's work was exhibited in Rome before being sent to Ann Arbor, where it has since resided at the University of Michigan.[9]

Kelsey's agenda in commissioning a replica of the Roman murals is not altogether certain, but from his diaries and memoranda, his correspondence with Barosso and Van Deman, and other sources the main lines are clear enough. Soon after his arrival in Ann Arbor in 1889, Kelsey energetically set about assembling an antiquities collection for the university to familiarize his Latin students with Roman material culture. He began making purchases in 1893 in Carthage and at various Italian sites but was especially drawn to Pompeii, where in 1883 he had studied briefly with the renowned scholar and director of the German Archaeological Institute in Rome, August Mau.[10] In the 1890s Kelsey collaborated with Mau on the English edition of Mau's great synthetic work, *Pompeii: Its Life and Art*.[11] Although Kelsey later turned to other parts of the Roman Empire, like many classicists, he maintained a lively interest in Pompeii throughout his career. In fact, at the time of his death in May 1927, Kelsey was at work on a large study of Pompeii.[12]

Following World War I, Kelsey embarked on his project to make a replica of the Villa of the Mysteries murals, which he intended to display in Ann Arbor for study by scholars and students.[13] While his principal goal was to foster research, he was also concerned about the deterioration of Pompeian paintings, which had been left exposed to the elements after their excavation. He saw replication as a means of preserving these precious ancient works.[14] In a letter of April 1925 to Amedeo Maiuri, the superintendent of antiquities of Pompeii, Kelsey first broached having a color copy made of "certain important frescoes in Pompeii," starting with a group from the "initiation scene" found in the Villa of the Mysteries.[15] A month later, Kelsey approached Maiuri about copying the entire room in the villa.[16]

Beyond replicating the Bacchic murals, Kelsey also wanted Barosso to make a detailed record of her observations of ancient painting techniques, which then, as now, were the subject of debate.[17] Unfortunately, Barosso's report, a copy of which Kelsey advised her to give to Maiuri, has not yet been located, and only a brief account of her views has been published.[18] For Kelsey, the Villa of the Mysteries project thus served multiple agendas: scholarly, preservationist, and political (in that it was part of a larger program of archaeological work in Pompeii for which he sought permission from the Italian authorities).

In commissioning a large-scale replica of the Bacchic room of the Villa of the Mysteries, Kelsey followed such patrons as Carl Jacobsen, who had underwritten a

FIGURE 2

Maria Barosso (Italian,
1879–1960), *Murals in
Room 5, Villa of the
Mysteries, Pompeii*, 1925.
View toward the east wall.
Watercolor on canvas-
backed paper. Ann Arbor,
University of Michigan,
Kelsey Museum of
Archaeology, 2000.2.3a–c.

Photo: Patrick Young, 2000.
Courtesy Kelsey Museum.

systematic campaign of copying Etruscan tomb paintings, at full scale, for his new
museum in Copenhagen between 1895 and 1913, but Kelsey's project also broke new
ground.[19] Apart from Antonio Niccolini's re-creation of a Pompeian house on one
of the Bourbon estates in 1827 and another made around 1839–40 by Friedrich von
Gärtner for Ludwig I of Bavaria at Aschaffenburg (loosely based on the House of the
Dioscuri) large-scale reproduction of Pompeian interiors had not been attempted.[20]
Since the eighteenth century artists had rendered substantially scaled-down reproductions of wall paintings and views of house interiors in Pompeii and Herculaneum,
an enterprise that in its early years often involved fanciful reconstruction of the presumed original appearance of the buildings and their decor. More rigorous standards
were introduced in the nineteenth century, but the images produced remained small,
intended mainly for publication.[21] Kelsey's commission thus extended the scope of
archaeological recording practices at Pompeii.

Like many of his contemporaries, Kelsey was drawn principally to the grand
mythological paintings of Pompeii and other Roman sites.[22] Among them, those of the
Villa of the Mysteries were in a class of their own by virtue of the unique content and
continuous composition of the main figural frieze. Moreover, their majestic Hellenistic
style marked them in Kelsey's mind as masterpieces worthy of accurate, "scientific"
reproduction.[23] But Kelsey's project for the Villa of the Mysteries went beyond the
central figural frieze. Perhaps inspired by Jacobsen's Etruscan tomb project, it included
the entire wall scheme—the lower faux-marble and upper faux-alabaster zones of
the walls as well as the delicate inhabited acanthus scroll that runs above the faux-
alabaster panels.[24] Apart from large-scale photographic replicas of the room made in
the latter part of the twentieth century, Barosso's replica provided as close to a "virtual

reality" experience of the villa's Bacchic murals as one could conjure in the era before computer-generated images.[25]

Barosso shared her patron's concern for accurate, scientific reproduction; she was, in fact, an archaeologist in her own right.[26] Yet, despite her repeated claims of objectivity in executing her replica of the Pompeian murals, during the course of her work she made some telling aesthetic judgments. Moreover, we can infer from her letters to Kelsey that her passionate pride in Italy's past and strong nationalistic leanings informed her work on the murals. Her role in the project, therefore, must be understood in relation to her personal artistic and ideological proclivities as well as to larger archaeological, artistic, and political developments of the mid-1920s in Italy.

The Artist

Born in Turin in 1879, Barosso studied classics in Milan, where she also attended the Accademia di belle arti.[27] In 1899 she moved to Rome and was hired by Giacomo Boni as the chief technical artist for his recently begun excavations in the Roman Forum, the first woman to hold such a post. Her work with Boni plunged her into a stimulating, formative environment, dominated by Boni's conviction that "the passionate evocation of ancient history and literature, [was] the ultimate aim of the material rediscovery of the past."[28] This belief, which influenced Barosso's approach to recording antiquities, presented both advantages and obstacles as she strove to achieve her own and her patron's goal of producing a fully accurate record of the Villa of the Mysteries murals.

By the time Barosso undertook Kelsey's commission in 1925, she was in her midforties, highly accomplished, and much in demand for her technical and artistic expertise.[29] Although she regularly received offers of work outside her official duties at the Office of the Forum and Palatine, the scale and travel inherent in the Michigan commission posed a number of potentially serious problems. Van Deman wrote to Kelsey asking him not to mention Barosso's name when speaking of the commission with Italian officials, "for she will meet with jealousy on Boni's part and he may try to block her way."[30] By June 1925, however, Barosso had obtained a temporary transfer from Rome to the Bay of Naples, and by late July or early August of that year she had set up shop in Pompeii.

Barosso's letters to Kelsey reveal her commitment to his dream of making the extraordinary murals in the Villa of the Mysteries available to scholars across the Atlantic. Although the task was enormous and difficult and the place and conditions miserable, she worked daily well into December, when it was especially cold and damp.[31] It was a physical and psychological trial, but, as she wrote to Kelsey, she persevered because of her dedication to art and *Italianità*. Indeed, she wrote to her patron periodically, and with palpable satisfaction, that the work was turning out splendidly.[32]

Barosso selected watercolor as the medium best able to capture the subtleties of color and tone of the ancient murals. She used high-quality Windsor & Newton paints and canvas-backed watercolor paper from Germany and France.[33] Her lightly penciled sketches of the figures are visible on many parts of the finished watercolors. Whether she made tracings of the Roman figures or referred to photographs in the course of her work is not known. She never mentions either procedure in her letters to Kelsey, yet other artists, such as those who had made full-scale replicas of Etruscan tomb paintings

for Jacobsen, had employed both techniques.[34] Perhaps the necessity of reducing the scale of the figures meant that Barosso had to rely wholly on her own measurements and observant eye.[35]

The fidelity of Barosso's colors is difficult to gauge from photographic comparisons, but, according to her letters to Kelsey, observers who made direct comparisons while the watercolors were in progress were struck by the degree of their faithfulness to the Roman paintings.[36] In June 2003, thanks to the cooperation of the Soprintendenza archeologica di Pompei and the Kelsey Museum of Archaeology, one of Barosso's works (the full-scale sample of the so-called Bride) traveled to Pompeii in order to make it possible once again to view the ancient and modern paintings side by side [FIG. 3].[37] At first the colors of the ancient mural appeared somewhat darker and more saturated than those of Barosso's watercolor. When, however, the conservators from the Superintendency cleaned small patches on the ancient walls, removing a thin layer of dust and modern wax that darkens the appearance of the Roman colors today, the cleaned areas presented a considerably brighter palette—one that is much closer to Barosso's own [FIG. 4].[38] Moreover, the surface of the cleaned patches appeared more matte than the areas that retained the modern wax coating. If Barosso saw this brighter, flatter surface in the mid-1920s, the medium of watercolor on matte paper would indeed have been her most suitable choice.

Whether the walls that are in better condition preserve ancient wax beneath the modern is not known at this stage of investigation. Barosso, however, thought wax had been used as a medium for the pigments, maintaining that the walls had been painted in

FIGURE 5
Detail of figure 1.

Photo: James Stanton-Abbott,
2002. Courtesy Ministero per
i Beni e le Attitivà Culturali,
Soprintendenza archeologica
di Pompei.

FIGURE 6
Detail of figure 2.

Photo: Patrick Young, 2000.
Courtesy Kelsey Museum.

encaustic, a medium that entails mixing pigments with wax.[39] We know from ancient authors that Roman mural painters employed encaustic at times and that when they used cinnabar they waxed the surfaces of their paintings.[40] The newly exposed patches of ancient wall surface on the panel of the Bride and on the adjacent wall, however, provide no obvious evidence of ancient waxing. It would require further cleaning, on the better-preserved walls of the room, to determine whether ancient wax is present beneath the modern.

Barosso's vivid colors, her effective trompe l'oeil representations of cracks in the wall plaster, and her brushwork, which mimics that of the ancient painter, seduce the

FIGURE 7

Area of discoloration, 1909,
north wall, room 5, Villa of
the Mysteries, Pompeii, first
century B.C.

Photo: Courtesy Ministero per
i Beni e le Attività Culturali,
Soprintendenza archeologica
di Pompei.

viewer into thinking that she represented every detail—even the damage—with careful precision. On closer inspection, however, it becomes clear that Barosso made her own artistic choices. While she faithfully portrayed the major cracks and patches of missing paint, she largely ignored the surface incrustations on the bodies and garments of the figures and only sketchily indicated minor damage such as the flakes of missing paint on the green borders of the architectural pilasters that segment the background of the main frieze [FIGS. 5–6]. The technical difficulty of rendering numerous minute traces of damage might in itself have inhibited Barosso from attempting to do more than suggest their presence. Her treatment of other damage, however, is harder to explain. The large, mottled, dark rings on the background of the north wall above the heads of a female attendant and Silenus, so visible today, are only barely discernible in Barosso's replica. Photographs taken in 1909 and soon thereafter show some traces of these stains [FIG. 7], but they do not seem nearly as prominent as they were in 1929 or 1930, when the color photographs that appear in Maiuri's publication of 1931 were taken.[41] Did these stains rapidly worsen after 1926, when Barosso worked on the north wall, or did she simply decide that they were too disfiguring to represent in detail? How scientifically accurate, in fact, are Barosso's reproductions?

While her letters to Kelsey make clear that Barosso strove to produce a scientific replica, they make equally clear that capturing the original aesthetic character of the murals was also of enormous importance. She wrote that she needed to work at certain times of day for the right lighting and particular atmospheric conditions that brought out the "true beauty" of the murals, for under some conditions the paintings appeared "more stained, ruined, or with softness and marvelous chromatic delicacies."[42] On the one hand, her highly illusionistic rendering of the cracks and the larger areas of loss lend an impression of veracity to her work and impart the look of age to the reproduced images. On the other hand, representing the smaller areas of flaked paint and the incrustations presented both technical and aesthetic problems. I suspect that in Barosso's judgment reproducing this type of damage would have added little

FIGURE 8

The Domina (detail), west wall, room 5, Villa of the Mysteries, Pompeii, first century B.C.

Photo: James Stanton-Abbott. Courtesy Ministero per i Beni e le Attività Culturali, Soprintendenza archeologica di Pompei.

FIGURE 9

Maria Barosso (Italian, 1879–1960), the Domina (detail) from *Murals in Room 5, Villa of the Mysteries, Pompeii*, 1926. Watercolor on canvas-backed paper. Ann Arbor, University of Michigan, Kelsey Museum of Archaeology, 2000.2.1a.

Photo: Patrick Young, 2000. Courtesy Kelsey Museum.

FIGURE 10

The Bride (detail), south wall, room 5, Villa of the Mysteries, Pompeii, first century B.C.

Photo: James Stanton-Abbott. Courtesy Ministero per i Beni e le Attività Culturali, Soprintendenza archeologica di Pompei.

FIGURE 11

Maria Barosso (Italian, 1879–1960), the Bride (detail) from *Murals in Room 5, Villa of the Mysteries, Pompeii*, 1925. Watercolor on canvas-backed paper. Ann Arbor, University of Michigan, Kelsey Museum of Archaeology, 2000.2.5a.

Photo: Patrick Young, 2000. Courtesy Kelsey Museum.

FIGURE 12

The Bride, south wall, room
5, Villa of the Mysteries,
Pompeii, first century B.C.

Photo: Courtesy Ministero per
i Beni e le Attività Culturali,
Soprintendenza archeologica di
Pompei. Fototeca Inv. C383.

in the way of scientific or "age value."[43] She must have realized, too, that showing
all the incrustations on the flesh and drapery would have undermined her attempt to
recover the original beauty of the figures. Such choices reveal her delicate balancing
of aesthetic and scientific priorities throughout the course of her work. In the process
she focused on what her contemporaries would have agreed were the most important
elements—the monumental figures themselves and the most obvious and artistically
appealing, as well as the least disfiguring, instances of damage that affected them.

Close comparison of the figures in Barosso's watercolors to their ancient models
further reinforces the impression that accuracy was not always the artist's main concern. Beyond omitting most of the incrustations on bodies and garments, she did not
consistently represent anatomy correctly. In some cases the ancient figures themselves
were painted awkwardly, and she copied them as they appeared, but in other cases
she misjudged the proportions. Comparative measurements show that the torso of the
Bride in the sample that Barosso painted at a scale of 1:1 is significantly broader than
that of the Roman version.[44] In addition, the face of the so-called Domina, which is
delicate in the Roman painting, appears coarse in Barosso's rendering, especially in
the area of the mouth [FIGS. 8–9]. Yet even when she portrayed faces, bodies, and
limbs elegantly, not all is necessarily correct. The face of the Bride, in the reduced
5:6 scale version, is exquisite, but, like its 1:1 counterpart, it does not reproduce the
proportions of the features accurately [FIGS. 10–11]. Moreover, both of Barosso's
versions of the Bride restore their model, as is clear from the amount of damage that
the Roman figure had sustained, which is well documented by photographs taken some
fifteen years before Barosso painted her copy [FIG. 12]. Once again, Barosso seems
to have struggled to fulfill her conflicting agendas. As an archaeologist, she wanted to

provide accurate, objective documents for scholars, but as an artist she wanted to capture—or, better, to recover—the original artistic power and subtlety of the Roman
walls.[45] Inevitably, her personal interpretation of the images emerges. Given her deep
feelings of *Italianità*, Barosso may well have thought of herself as a latter-day collaborator with her ancient professional counterparts, intuitively drawing out from
their timeworn works what the average viewer could no longer see. At the same time
it seems highly likely that her aesthetic choices were motivated in part by her desire to
present her nation's heritage in the best possible light, a desire that would have found
ample reinforcement in contemporary political and cultural ideology, which stressed
the spiritual affinity between ancient and modern Italy.[46]

The Fascist Context

Although Barosso was sympathetic to the Fascist government, it is not clear how
deeply committed she was to its emerging political agenda when she painted the
watercolors of the Villa of the Mysteries, nor is it certain whether she was a member
of the party at that time.[47] The Italian government, however, was involved in the project almost from its inception. Barosso was a ranking employee of the government's
archaeological service and both she and Kelsey had to secure permission from the
archaeological and ministerial authorities to carry out the plan. The negotiations took
some time and required delicate diplomacy. Barosso had to deal with potential resistance not only from Giacomo Boni but also from others in the administration. In a
letter of March 1925 Van Deman reported to Kelsey that Barosso's work had attracted
the attention of those in power and that the Michigan project might imperil her career
because "she has refused some very flattering appeals for her work from government
leaders." Van Deman continues: "I trust all may turn out well in the work for the U.
of M., which has an element of danger for her popularity in certain quarters—and
important ones since she is near her next promotion and must provoke no criticism."[48]

Kelsey, with characteristic diplomacy, offered the government the right to retain
Barosso's watercolors for one year after their completion and to publish them before
they were sent to Ann Arbor.[49] Barosso herself may have suggested the plan, for
she mentions those conditions several times in her letters, implying that they were
a requirement of her participation.[50] More than a decade later, in 1938, an article on
Barosso's work in a government-sponsored journal set the strategy adopted by Barosso
and Kelsey retrospectively, but squarely, in a political context. The fact that the artist had insisted that Italy retain the reproduction rights to her watercolors is cited as
evidence of her loyalty to the government.[51] Although it was not until the mid-
1930s that the regime demanded the loyalty of artists and other professionals to the
Fascist Party, even at the time that Kelsey was negotiating the agreement the government was making and unmaking appointments within the archaeological service based
on political considerations. In Pompeii, for example, Vittorio Spinazzola, director of
the Pompeii excavations since 1910, was removed from office in 1924 because of his
liberal views and affiliation with the anti-Fascist political factions. He was replaced by
Amedeo Maiuri, who remained director of excavations until 1962.[52]

Kelsey's first request to Maiuri, dated April 9, 1925, sought to replicate only one
wall, a request that Maiuri granted apparently without hesitation. The result was the
Bride, which Barosso painted at a scale of 1:1. When shortly thereafter Kelsey requested

permission to replicate the entire room, however, Maiuri did not immediately assent. Sensitive to the political situation, he was concerned that the Italian government take precedence in publishing the important murals. In a second appeal on May 26, 1925, Kelsey acknowledged Maiuri's concern and offered assurances. Both he and Barosso thought that it was only right that her work be published "first and foremost by the Italian government."[53]

Matteo Della Corte, then an inspector at Pompeii, supported Kelsey's proposal.[54] It also received the support of Pietro Fedele, minister of public instruction, whom Barosso had met in Pompeii in June. Barosso wrote to Kelsey about that meeting: "I, together with Prof. Maiuri and the inspectors, talked about your proposal. The superintendent [Maiuri] gave a worthy explanation [of the proposal]; the minister took a personal interest and promised to look into everything in Rome."[55] Following that meeting, Fedele, accompanied by the director general of higher education, visited Barosso's studio in Rome, where she had stored the completed full-scale panel of the Bride.[56] With evident pleasure and excitement, she wrote to Kelsey that Fedele had spoken knowledgeably about art and had praised the monumental watercolor as well as other works in her studio.[57] Not long after, Kelsey's proposal was accepted, and, after a short delay, Maiuri wrote to him on June 22 that the superior ministry had granted permission to proceed.[58]

Nearly a year and a half after Barosso had begun working in Pompeii, as she was nearing completion of the main frieze, she informed Kelsey that Fedele had arranged for an exhibition of her artwork, including the Pompeian watercolors, to take place from late November to early December 1926 at the Galleria Borghese, a prestigious Roman venue where the work of a modern artist had never before been shown.[59] Beyond Barosso's artistry and skill, Fedele may also have been attracted to the Bacchic subject matter of the Roman murals, since Dionysian elements played a significant part in the development of "aesthetic fascism."[60] Given his position in the Fascist government, however, the decision to organize an exhibition was surely not motivated solely by the visual power or iconographic content of Barosso's paintings. The exhibition also celebrated the project as a product of the regime and engaged the public with the regime's emerging ideology of *Romanità*. This facet of Fascist ideology was intended to stimulate the pride of Italians in their ancient imperial past and build a new Italian spirit. It also provided justification for a modern Italian empire based on forms and values derived from its ancient Roman predecessor. Some of these ideas were already being articulated and fostered in the 1920s and had appeared even earlier in the visual and archaeological rhetoric of pre-Fascist Italian nationalism.[61]

The exhibition of Barosso's work was an outstanding success [FIG. 13]. At the opening on November 26, Italian officials, Rome's intelligentsia—including artists and representatives from foreign academies—and the press gathered to admire Barosso's impressive achievement. Although Mussolini was unable to attend, he sent a senator to represent him. King Victor Emanuel III visited the show the next day in Barosso's company, followed two days later by the queen and her entourage. One reviewer, writing for *Roma fascista*, a government organ, proclaimed the show a "great Fascist triumph in the field of art."[62] Clearly the regime had appropriated Kelsey's project for its own ends. By now, if not earlier, Barosso herself was sympathetic to the regime and felt greatly honored by this official, public recognition of her work. She was no doubt pleased to be seen as publicly supportive of the Fascist cause as well.[63]

FIGURE 13

Maria Barosso (Italian, 1879–1960), *Murals in Room 5, Villa of the Mysteries, Pompeii*, 1925. Watercolor on canvas-backed paper. On exhibit at the Galleria Borghese, Rome, November–December 1926. Photo Archives of the Kelsey Museum of Archaeology, Bentley Historical Library, University of Michigan (Papers of the Kelsey Museum of Ancient and Mediaeval Archaeology and Francis W. Kelsey, Butler Papers, box 7).

Photo: Courtesy Kelsey Museum.

Barosso's exhibition incorporated both art and archaeology, two fundamental components of the many-faceted Fascist exhibition culture that had begun to emerge shortly after Mussolini's March on Rome on October 28, 1922. In the 1920s art exhibitions took the lead in this propaganda campaign. The artists of the Novecento group had been encouraged by Margherita Sarfatti, Mussolini's mistress and confidante, to draw inspiration from the historical past in creating a pure art worthy of the modern Italian state.[64] As early as March 1923, at the opening of the exhibition *Sette pitture del Novecento* in Milan, Mussolini expressed the view that it was the state's duty to encourage the arts, a notion he further articulated in 1926 at another exhibition of Novecento artists, where he publicly declared an intimate relationship between art and politics.[65] Although Barosso did not belong to the Novecento group or to any other artistic movement supported by the state in the mid-1920s, her watercolor representation of the murals in Pompeii was received by the public, including artists, as a modern and Fascist work of art in its own right, a fact that astonished Kelsey, who until then had regarded it only as a scientific copy.[66] Not long thereafter, Barosso began to be referred to as an "artist-archaeologist" in recognition of the dual nature of her artistic work. In 1938, reflecting back on Barosso's work at the Villa of the Mysteries, Maria Krasceninnicowa characterized the Michigan project as part of the regime's "first flowering of activity in the artistic-archaeological field in 1926."[67]

By highlighting a great work of ancient Roman art with a high-quality, large-scale reproduction of it, Barosso's exhibition, along with the *Mostra archeologica* of 1911, anticipated important developments in archaeological aspects of Fascist exhibition culture of the later 1920s and 1930s. Nationalist politics and archaeology had allied themselves in the *Mostra archeologica*, an exhibition organized by the prominent archaeologist Rodolfo Lanciani on the occasion of the fiftieth anniversary of national unity. This important exhibition made political use of Rome's former territorial reach by calling attention to the role of the provinces of the Roman Empire in the development of ancient Roman civilization. As Genevieve Gessert observed, "Objects and reproductions were donated to the show as a form of diplomatic currency, associating ancient cultural connections with modern political ones."[68] Following World War I, there were successive reinstallations of this exhibition in the complex that had once housed the Pastificio Pantanella in the ancient Forum Boarium, and in May 1929 it reopened in the new Museo dell'Impero in the same complex.[69] This iteration of the exhibition once again emphasized the former Roman provinces, but it now openly provided historical legitimacy for the Fascist government's colonial policy and imperialist ambitions.[70]

The use of reproductions of archaeological artifacts to draw connections between antiquity and the present would reach its apogee in the famed *Mostra Augustea della Romanità* of 1938–39. Because Barosso's exhibition, which centered on her reproduction of the Pompeian murals, received wide publicity and was likely intended by Pietro Fedele as a deliberate political statement, it should be regarded, along with Lanciani's exhibition, as a key forerunner of the *Mostra Augustea*.[71] By the 1930s Mussolini's regime had taken firm control of the visual arts as instruments of propaganda and had invested heavily in the work of archaeologists, whose special knowledge of the Roman past was also put to use in the service of the state.[72] The *Mostra Augustea della Romanità* celebrated the genius of the Italian race, tracing its roots to Roman antiquity. The extraordinary year-long exhibition opened on September 23, 1937, the two-thousandth birthday of the emperor Augustus, a figure with whom Mussolini identified. Notably, the exhibition relied extensively on copies of archaeological artifacts as well as models of Roman buildings, works of engineering, machinery, and other inventions based on archaeological finds from many sites in the territories of the former Roman Empire.[73] The copies and models, as works of the Fascist era, in effect presented the celebrated Roman achievements as products of the regime. The organizers of the *Mostra Augustea* included copies and models of Pompeian artifacts throughout the show, but they appeared most prominently in the section on houses and gardens. The highlight of this section, a life-size, fully furnished model of a typical Roman house of the Augustan period, based largely on the atrium type found in Pompeii and Herculaneum, was the "jewel of the exhibition."[74] In my view the notion of making a full-scale model of a house was prompted at least in part by Kelsey's project and the subsequent exhibition of Barosso's watercolors.

The highly publicized exhibition at the Borghese Gallery gained Barosso sudden notoriety. It also seems to have propelled her career in a direction more overtly allied with the developing Fascist agenda. In the following year, 1927, she was invited to participate in the exhibition *Roma sparita*, organized by the art historian Antonio Muñoz, then superintendent of the monuments of Lazio and director of the antiquities and fine arts of Rome. Barosso had long been in the habit of making sketches, etchings, and watercolors of the ruins of ancient and medieval Italy, some of which Muñoz could have seen in the Borghese exhibition.[75] After *Roma sparita* and well into the 1930s, perhaps inspired by Muñoz's encouragement of artists to record Rome's transformation under Mussolini, Barosso made many lively, colorful views of Rome that capture the frenetic pace of demolition, archaeological excavation, and urban renewal.[76] In 1933 about thirty other views of Rome undergoing renovation were exhibited at the Museo di Roma.[77] Although Barosso does not seem to have been a high-profile political activist, as an artist-archaeologist whose work was valued by the regime, she clearly contributed to the promulgation of Fascist ideology. In this she had much in common with many other artists of the 1920s and 1930s whose work was similarly appropriated by the state.

The Fate of Kelsey's Project

The Italian government retained Barosso's watercolors for one year after the exhibition, until December 1927, for the purpose of publishing them in full color. Ultimately, however, this official publication did not go forward. In a letter to Kelsey dated April 19, 1927, Van Deman cites "red tape" and "dirty politics," and she alludes to "the old row between Spinazzola and his rotten 'gang' & more decent men. For reasons of jealousy of the greenest type, the powers that ought not 'to be' are determined that the Barosso pieces shall not be published by the government."[78] The minister, apparently yielding to pressure, renounced the government's right to publish the watercolors and gave permission for them to be published by a private firm in Bergamo, the Istituto italiano d'arti grafiche. That arrangement, too, fell through, apparently for monetary reasons. Van Deman had informed Kelsey of the firm's need for assurance that it would not lose financially.[79] Kelsey would no doubt have secured the necessary funds for the project, but by the time he received Van Deman's letter he was gravely ill, and he died shortly thereafter.

The publication of Barosso's watercolors could have gone forward under another initiative, but for a variety of reasons it was abandoned. In 1929–30 Maiuri undertook large-scale excavations at the Villa of the Mysteries, which uncovered virtually the entire edifice, as if to assert the Italian claim to this important villa and its famous murals. Maiuri's publication of those excavations was a major state production. *La Villa dei Misteri*, issued by the Istituto poligrafico dello Stato in Rome in 1931, included the first color photographs of the murals. Printed at a folio scale, they have remained the standard published images of the ancient paintings. With these photographs of the Roman murals, there was no longer a pressing need to publish Barosso's watercolors.

In Ann Arbor Kelsey's project met with further adversity. Kelsey had intended Barosso's watercolors to be displayed at the University of Michigan as soon as they arrived in Ann Arbor. He had written to Barosso in March 1927 that she must quickly send him measurements and requirements for lighting so that he could make plans for their installation in the new museum that he envisioned. The Museum of Classical Archaeology (which would ultimately be known as the Kelsey Museum of Archaeology) was not, however, officially chartered by the regents of the university until 1928–29, well after Kelsey's death in 1927.[80]

Moreover, after Kelsey died other obstacles may have prevented his plan from being carried out. First, there was a question regarding the necessary funds to pay Barosso the remaining half of the honorarium of one hundred thousand lire that Kelsey had lately agreed to furnish in addition to the sums he originally committed and regularly sent to cover her wages and expenses in Pompeii. According to Orma Butler, first curator of the Museum of Classical Archaeology, Kelsey had kept the financing of the project in his own hands; and, as was his habit, he had been planning to approach potential donors in person for the outstanding funds.[81] Second, his illness in the spring of 1927 probably kept him from carrying forward plans for a new museum. Third, the project was Kelsey's own, and although Butler assumed responsibility for concluding the financial arrangements, she may well have been more concerned with the safety of the watercolors than with their exhibition. Butler notes in her first report to the university regents in 1929–30 that only those objects in the collection that could withstand fire were moved to Newberry Hall, adding that the space available was insufficient for exhibiting the collection properly.[82] Given these circumstances and the fact that Orma Butler and her sister, Nita, had struck up a cordial friendship with Barosso on their trips to Italy, it seems unlikely that the failure to display the watercolors in Ann Arbor was in any way due to purposeful neglect. Nor, I think, is it likely that anti-Fascist politics played a role. Kelsey himself seemed approving of Italy's Fascist government of the mid-1920s, and Butler's friendship with Barosso suggests that she, too, may have been sympathetic, at least during those early years of the regime.[83]

▣ ▣ ▣

The watercolors of the Villa of the Mysteries by Maria Barosso, once again brought to light at the Kelsey Museum of Archaeology, provide a sharply focused lens through which we can view the larger political and cultural fluctuations occurring in Italy during the 1920s. An artistic achievement in their own right, the watercolors of the grand murals in the Villa of the Mysteries testify to the delicate balancing act that "artist-archaeologists" like Barosso performed as they worked in the service of the Italian state.

The recovery of antiquity, in the case of Kelsey's project for the Villa of the Mysteries, played to contemporary aesthetic, scientific, and political agendas, which became inextricably entangled. That sort of entanglement, which for the study of the reception of classical antiquity is both intriguing and instructive, must surely have occurred many times over in the Fascist period as Mussolini forged his new Italy from the ruins of ancient Rome.

Notes

1   My research for this essay benefited from the assistance of Alessandra Capodiferro, Carol Finerman, Elizabeth de Grummond, Katherine Geffcken, Raymond Grew, Martha Hoppin, Jennifer Johnston, Rosella Leone, Jane Shepherd, and the persons acknowledged in the notes below.

2   See Bettina Bergmann's discussion in this volume of the "gold rush" of private excavations of Roman villas in Campania.

3   Paul Hartwig, *Neue freie Presse* (Vienna), May 27, 1910, 1–4; Giulio de Petra, "Villa Romana presso Pompei," *Notizie degli scavi* 7, fasc. 4 (1910): 139–45; Georges Nicole, "Les dernieres fouilles de Pompéi," *Gazette des Beaux-Arts* 53, no. 1 (1911): 21–33; Franz Winter, "Die Wandgemälde der Villa Item bei Pompeji," *Kunst und Künstler* 10, no. 11 (1912): 548–55; P. B. Mudie Cooke, "The Paintings of the Villa Item at Pompeii," *Journal of Roman Studies* 3 (1913): 157–74. Six shorter notices were also published. For this bibliography, see Mudie Cooke 1913, 157n. 1. The villa was originally called Item after the first excavator, Aurelio Item, who owned a hotel adjacent to the site. Bergmann in this volume provides additional notices and bibliography.

4   Jocelyn M. C. Toynbee, "The Villa Item and a Bride's Ordeal," *Journal of Roman Studies* 19 (1929): 67–87.

5   Correspondence between Kelsey and Barosso, which documents the commission and its execution in great detail, is contained in the Archives of the Kelsey Museum of Archaeology, Papers of the Kelsey Museum of Ancient and Mediaeval Archaeology and Francis W. Kelsey, Bentley Historical Library, University of Michigan; see Butler Papers, box 7, folders 18–20 (hereafter abbreviated as Papers). An essay by Elizabeth de Grummond, "Maria Barosso, Francis Kelsey,

and the Modern Representation of an Ancient Masterpiece," which appears in the exhibition catalogue, *The Villa of the Mysteries in Pompeii: Ancient Ritual, Modern Muse*, ed. Elaine K. Gazda (Ann Arbor, 2000), 129–37, provides an essential foundation for my ongoing work on this subject. For detailed measurements and a description of the general condition of Barosso's watercolors, see in the same catalogue nos. 69, 200–204. The present essay presents my work in progress, preliminary to a longer treatment of the subject. For that longer study de Grummond has prepared a translation of Barosso's letters. I use her translations in the present article.

6   Esther B. Van Deman, *The Atrium Vestae* (Washington, D.C., 1909). On Van Deman, see *Fotografia archeologica, 1865–1914*, ed. Karin Einaudi (Rome, 1979), 13–15; Karin Einaudi, "Esther Boise Van Deman: Un'archeologa americana," in *L'archeologia in Roma capitale tra sterro e scavo*, ed. Giuseppina Pisani Sartorio and Lorenzo Quilici (Venice, 1983), 41–47; Karin Einaudi, with contributions by Katherine A. Geffcken, *Esther B. Van Deman: Images from the Archive of an American Archaeologist in Italy at the Turn of the Century* (Rome, 1991); and de Grummond 2000 (note 5), 129–30.

7   Barosso also painted a replica of a large mosaic from Old Saint Peter's (Barosso to Kelsey, April 30, 1925, Papers).

8   Barosso painted a sample panel of the so-called Bride at a scale of 1:1, but, for reasons that remain obscure, she was told by Amedeo Maiuri, director of excavations of Pompeii from 1924 to 1962, that she could not make a full-scale replica of the whole room (Maiuri to Kelsey, June 22, 1925, Papers). Resigned to the new restriction, she began again, choosing a 5:6 scale, which best suited the size of the German paper she had obtained for the project (Barosso to Kelsey, June 23, 1925, and Francis W. Kelsey diary, May 23, 1925, Papers). See also de Grummond 2000 (note 5), 130, 131nn. 20–24. As Barosso's work progressed she assured her patron that the reduced format did not diminish the monumental effect (Barosso to Kelsey, April 30, 1925; November 15, 1925; August 8, 1926, Papers).

9   Kelsey died in May 1927, just a few months before the watercolors were completed. When Barosso's watercolors arrived some time later, they were put into storage and remained unaccessioned until 2000, when they were displayed in their entirety for the first time in the exhibition *The Villa of the Mysteries in Pompeii*.

10   Orma Fitch Butler, "Report of the Museum of Classical Archaeology," in *Reprint from the Report of the President of the University of Michigan, 1928–1929* (Ann Arbor, 1930), 3, describes Kelsey's earliest collecting. Carol Finerman, "Visions of Excellence: The Career of Francis W. Kelsey," *LSA Magazine* 10, no. 2 (1987): 12, notes Kelsey's early studies with Mau.

11   August Mau, *Pompeii: Its Life and Art*, trans. Francis W. Kelsey (1899; New York, 1902).

12   For reference to Kelsey's work on a "huge, detailed study of Pompeii," see Finerman 1987 (note 10), 12. Kelsey's interest in Pompeii was widely shared by professional and nonprofessional audiences, even in the days when the Greeks rather than the Romans dominated the archaeological agenda. See Steven L. Dyson, *Ancient Marbles to American Shores: Classical Archaeology in the United States* (Philadelphia, 1998).

13   The permit for the project specified that no commercial gain would be realized from them (Kelsey to Maiuri, May 25, 1925; see also Della Corte to Maiuri, May 24, 1925, Papers).

14   For the deterioration of Campanian wall paintings, see Eric M. Moormann, "Destruction and Restoration of Campanian Mural Paintings in the Eighteenth and Nineteenth Centuries," in *The Conservation of Wall Paintings: Proceedings of a Symposium Organized by the Courtauld Institute of Art and the Getty Conservation Institute, London, July 13–16, 1987*, ed. Sharon Cather (Los Angeles, 1991), 87–101.

15   Kelsey to Maiuri, April 9, 1925, and Kelsey to Barosso, May 15, 1926 (Papers).

16   Kelsey to Maiuri, May 26, 1925 (Papers). Although Kelsey first sought permission to copy only one panel, his intention from the start was to replicate the entire room (Barosso to Kelsey, October 18, 1924; Kelsey to Van Deman, December 31, 1924, Papers).

[17]   Kelsey's request for a technical study came after Barosso was well into the project, in January 1926 (Kelsey to Barosso, January 1 and 11, 1926; Barosso to Kelsey, February 1, 1926, Papers). He and she both knew that no one else had studied the paintings in as great detail as she and that as an artist she was uniquely qualified to carry out such a study. On the current debates, see, among others, Pamela Pratt, "Wall Painting," in *Roman Crafts*, ed. Donald Strong and David Brown (New York, 1976), 228–29; Umberto Pappalardo, "Beobachtungen am Fries der Mysterien-Villa in Pompeji," *Antike Welt* 13, no. 3 (1982): 10–20; Roger Ling, *Roman Painting* (Cambridge, 1991), 198–211, with earlier references.

[18]   One copy of the report was to go to Maiuri and another to Kelsey (Francis W. Kelsey diary, August 21, 1926; memorandum no. 16, October 1, 1926–December 31, 1926, Papers). Maria Barosso, "La datazione delle pitture della Villa dei Misteri di Pompei," in *6. Internationaler Kongress für Archäologie: Berlin 1939* (Berlin, 1940), 505–10. See also de Grummond 2000 (note 5), 130 and 135n. 15.

[19]   Mette Moltesen and Cornelia Weber-Lehmann, *Catalogue of the Copies of Etruscan Tomb Paintings in the Ny Carlsberg Glyptotek* (Copenhagen, 1991), 10–11. Full-scale replicas of Etruscan paintings had already been made for the Vatican and for Ludwig I of Bavaria by Carlo Ruspi in 1832–37. See ibid., 11, 24; also Horst Blanck and Cornelia Weber-Lehmann, *Malerei der Etrusker in Zeichnungen des 19. Jahrhunderts* (Mainz am Rhein, 1987), 16–40. Thirty-three reproductions made for Jacobsen are now in the Museum of Fine Arts, Boston (accession nos. 98.2–98.9, 05.44–46, 08.492–08.514), according to Christine Kondoleon, curator of Greek and Roman art (personal communication). For predecessors and successors to Jacobsen's project, which yielded facsimiles of the paintings in twenty-eight Etruscan tombs, see Moltesen and Weber-Lehmann 1991, 23–40. The Etruscan tomb paintings are notably smaller than the murals in the Villa of the Mysteries.

[20]   See Curtis Dahl, "A Quartet of Pompeian Pastiches," *Journal of the Society of Architectural Historians* 14, no. 3 (1955): 3–7. See also Richard Brilliant, *Pompeii A.D. 79: The Treasure of Rediscovery* (New York, 1979), 160.

[21]   The brothers Fausto and Felice Niccolini were among the most famous publishers of such images in the latter half of the nineteenth century. See Pier Luigi Ciapparelli, "The Editorial Adventures of the Niccolini Brothers," in Roberto Cassanelli et al., *Houses and Monuments of Pompeii: The Works of Fausto and Felice Niccolini*, trans. Thomas M. Hartmann (Los Angeles, 2002), 10–25. Such reproductions and reconstructions were essential for ongoing research on houses at the two Campanian sites.

[22]   Brilliant (1979 [note 20], 135, 138, 250) exempts Mau from this sort of thinking because he considered entire wall schemes rather than only the mythological panels that formed parts of those schemes. While this is true of Mau's work, Mau himself (and presumably his collaborator, Kelsey) clearly regarded the mythological panels as overwhelmingly the most important paintings on Pompeian walls (Mau 1902 [note 11], 474).

[23]   Barosso and Kelsey both used the term "scientific" to describe her facsimile of the Bacchic murals. I employ it in this essay to be consistent with their usage and also to underscore the level of precision that Kelsey and Barosso had in mind. Similarly, my use of the term "Hellenistic" to describe the style of the Roman murals accords with Kelsey's usage (Kelsey to Barosso, March 17, 1925, Papers).

[24]   The ancient scroll frieze does not survive on the west and south walls. Barosso reproduced in detail the two small portions of this frieze that survive on the east wall, but for the long north wall she completed only a black-and-white sketch of it. Her unfinished scroll frieze was exhibited at the Galleria Borghese. She continued to work on this frieze after the exhibition but never finished it, perhaps because she was concerned about receiving the final payment for the project (Barosso to Kelsey, January 1, 1927, Papers).

[25]   See, for example, the photographic replica of the room at the Ruhr University Museum in Bochum, Germany (Bettina Bergmann, personal communication, 2005).

[26]   Barosso assumed responsibility for some of Giacomo Boni's archaeological projects in the Roman Forum after his death in 1925. In 1935 she resumed his work on the structures that lie beneath the Basilica of Maxentius and Constantine in the Roman Forum, and the results of her studies received high praise from prominent scholars such as Giulio Quirino Giglioli. She wrote several papers and articles on the topography of the Roman Forum and on other structures on which she had worked, including the Villa of the Mysteries. For the latter, see note 18.

[27]   Bianca Maria Margarucci Italiani, "Maria Barosso, archeologa e pittrice di Roma," *Donne di ieri a Roma e nel Lazio* (Rome, 1978), 317, implies that Barosso studied at more than one academy in Milan but does not specify which ones. In contrast, a brief entry on Barosso in A. M. Comanducci, *Dizionario illustrato dei pittori, disegnatori e incisori italiani moderni e contemporanei*, 5th ed. (Milan, 1982), 1:248, claims that the artist studied at the Accademia Albertina. The *Allgemeines Künstler-Lexikon: Die bildenden Künstler aller Zeiten und Völker* (Munich, 1993), 7:136, adds that the Accademia Albertina in question was in Turin. Neither publication mentions Barosso's studies in Milan. That both lexicons mistakenly claim that Barosso was born in 1918 undermines their credibility. Margarucci Italiani knew Barosso personally and, therefore, is likely to be the more reliable source.

[28]   Rosella Leone, "Iconographie des démolitions à Rome: Les aquarelles d'une artiste archéologue et les albums photographiques du governatorato," in *École romaine, 1925–1945* (Paris, 1997), 129–38. Leone notes that Boni's circle included Rodolfo Lanciani, Christian Hülsen, Thomas Ashby, and Esther Van Deman, who debated the practice and theory of the archaeological excavations related to world-famous sites and monuments in Rome. Romke Visser, "Fascist Doctrine and the Cult of the *Romanità*," *Journal of Contemporary History* 27 (1992): 5–17, throws further light on Boni's own intellectual context. On Barosso's artistic development, see Margarucci Italiani 1978 (note 27).

[29]   Her calling card identifies her as "Prof. Maria Barosso del R. Ufficio del Palatino e Foro Romano." See also Van Deman to Kelsey, October 21, 1924, and Van Deman to Kelsey, undated letter written sometime in October 1924 (Papers).

[30]   Van Deman to Kelsey, October 21, 1924 (Papers).

[31]   Van Deman had reported to Kelsey on October 21, 1924, that Barosso was eager to make the exceptional Roman murals known to scholars in the United States (Papers).

[32]   Barosso wrote to Kelsey on May 28, 1926 (Papers). On the significance of *Italianità*, see Visser 1992 (note 28), 16–17. For the artist's pride in her results, see Barosso to Kelsey, October 18, 1925, and July 2, 1926, among other letters (Papers).

[33]   Of her choice of watercolor as the medium Barosso says, "only watercolors can give all of the delicate and intense shadings of the ancient fresco" (Barosso to Kelsey, October 16, 1924, Papers). On the paints and German paper, see Barosso to Kelsey, October 18, 1924 (Papers). Compare de Grummond 2000 (note 5), 131–32. For the long "back" (east) wall Barosso had found a single piece of canvas paper made in France (Barosso to Kelsey, November 15, 1925, Papers).

[34]   For the techniques and standards adopted for this sort of artistic work, see Moltesen and Weber-Lehmann 1991 (note 19), 12, 14.

[35]   Barosso to Kelsey, June 23, 1925 (Papers), mentions that she prepared drawings at a reduced scale while in Rome waiting for permission to go to Pompeii. See also de Grummond 2000 (note 5), 130–31. Standards varied widely among artists who engaged in reproducing ancient murals. Piet De Jong, who reproduced many Mycenaean wall paintings, apparently worked freehand. I am grateful to Carol Hershenson of the Department of Classics at the University of Cincinnati for sharing this observation.

[36]   Among the scholars whom Barosso mentions in her letters to Kelsey are Professor Franz Winter from the University of Bonn, September 21, 1925; Professor Arthur van Buren and his students from the American Academy in Rome, March 21, 1926; and Professor Albert von Ippel from Berlin and Professor Ludwig Curtius from Heidelberg, May 28, 1926 (Papers).

37 Because the image of the Bride is on the most damaged wall in room 5, its colors are now far less saturated than those on the better-preserved walls. I am grateful to Pietro Giovanni Guzzo, archaeological superintendent of Pompeii; Concetta Ossani, former secretary to the superintendent; Antonio D'Ambrosio, director of the excavations of Pompeii; Ernesto De Carolis, director of conservation; and my fellow curators at the Kelsey Museum. In the field I was superbly assisted by Bettina Bergmann, Barbara Kellum, Elizabeth Marlowe, and Patricia Simons, who lifted, carried, photographed, measured, and in many other ways supported my efforts to make as detailed a comparison as possible.

38 The cleaning of four patches, three on the panel of the Bride and one on the panel of the Eros, was done by the *capotecnico*, Stefano Vanacore, assisted by Vincenzo Serrapica, who also took samples for analysis. The routine upkeep of Pompeian paintings until about twenty years ago involved wiping the walls with a solution of wax apparently dissolved in *benzina*, a treatment recorded repeatedly in the archives of the excavations. For the practice of applying a coat of wax to the painted walls in Pompeii, see Ernesto De Carolis, "A City and Its Rediscovery," in *Pompeii: Life in a Roman Town*, ed. Annamaria Ciarallo and Ernesto De Carolis (Milan, 1999), 27, 39. Because the wall of the Bride had sustained the greatest amount of damage, its matte surface may be a result of its poor condition; yet the ancient wall surface of the Eros panel, which is not as badly damaged, is also rather matte. In 1913 Mudie Cooke (note 3), 171, observed that Petra 1910 (note 3) and Nicole 1911 (note 3) had criticized the paintings because "the tints are flatter and more monotonous than is usual in Pompeian art." Barosso, in contrast, observed that the walls' changing appearance depended on the lighting and atmospheric conditions (Barosso to Kelsey, February 1, 1926, Papers). How modern waxing may have affected these differing perceptions is difficult to determine.

39 Barosso 1940 (note 18), 507. See also Barosso to Kelsey, February 1, 1926 (Papers). Barosso never mentions the waxy sheen on the surface that one sees very clearly today in raking light, which reveals the broad, sweeping strokes of the polisher's cloth.

40 On the use of wax with cinnabar, see Vitruvius *On Architecture* 7.9.3; on encaustic, see Pliny the Elder *Natural History* 35.1.122–25, 149. It is often claimed that the red of the background of the Bacchic murals in the Villa of the Mysteries is cinnabar. See also Bergmann in this volume on the use of red ocher and vermilion for the paintings at Boscoreale.

41 Amedeo Maiuri, *La Villa dei Misteri* (Rome, 1931), colorplate 4. The condition of the walls as evidenced by the older black-and-white photographs is not always clear.

42 Barosso to Kelsey, February 1, 1926 (Papers). Perhaps Petra and Nicole saw the paintings under unfavorable atmospheric conditions or before they were fully cleaned. See notes 3 and 38.

43 On "age value," see Erika Naginski, "Riegl, Archaeology, and the Periodization of Culture," *Res* 40 (2001): 135–52, especially 150.

44 Other measurements of this figure show a similar tendency. I am grateful to Patricia Simons for suggesting that we measure the figures and to her and Barbara Kellum for helping in the process. I have not yet attempted to compare the 5:6 scale figures and all their Roman counterparts.

45 Barosso claimed in several letters that she studied all the details very closely and painted them as they should be seen (Barosso to Kelsey, February 1, 1926; July 2, 1926; August 8, 1926; November 12, 1926, and Barosso to H. Sanders, August 9, 1927, Papers).

46 On the ideology of the *Romanità* and the importance assigned by Fascist archaeologists and historians to intuition in the interpretation of Roman history and civilization—especially the intuition of scholars of Latin and particularly those of Italian ancestry (who, according to this view, possessed the quality of *Italianità*)—see Visser 1992 (note 28), 16–17. See also Marla Stone, "A Flexible Rome: Fascism and the Cult of *Romanità*," in *Roman Presences: Receptions of Rome in European Culture, 1789–1945*, ed. Catharine Edwards (Cambridge, 1999), 205–20.

47 I have not yet made a thorough search of the various Italian archives for membership lists maintained by the Fascist Party, but in a memorandum to the university's Near East Research

Committee, Kelsey states: "Signorina Barosso, as all other intelligent Italians whom Mr. Kelsey has met since the fascist party was organized, is sympathetic with the fascist regime" (memorandum no. 16, October 1–December 31, 1926, Papers). In her letters to Kelsey and Orma Butler, Barosso expresses patriotic feelings, often with religious overtones (Barosso to Kelsey, December 8, 1925, and July 2, 1926; see also Barosso to Butler, undated, Papers). She does not, however, present herself as someone personally involved in political affairs nor does she speak of them in her letters to Kelsey. She seems to have been concerned primarily with promoting Italy's ancient heritage and contributing to the nation's international reputation through her art (Barosso to Kelsey, August 4, 1925, Papers).

48   Van Deman to Kelsey, March 8, 1925 (Papers). See also de Grummond 2000 (note 5), 130 and 136n. 16. Another of Van Deman's letters, probably written in October 1924, underscores Barosso's growing prominence: "She has offers of work of a tempting kind, but your offer came first and she will, of course, keep her word—she had become rather famous lately & deservedly so" (Papers).

49   Kelsey to Maiuri, April 9, 1925, and May 26, 1925 (Papers).

50   Although arrangements for publication were apparently not part of the original agreement between Kelsey and Barosso (Barosso to Kelsey, October 18, 1924, Papers), they were an important factor in negotiations with the Italian authorities.

51   That the watercolors were intended for an American university and would not remain in Italy may well have raised some eyebrows within Mussolini's regime. For a discussion of Barosso's artistic works in the context of Mussolini's excavation and urban renewal program in Rome, see Maria Gibellino Krasceninnicowa, "Roma fascista attraverso l'arte di Maria Barosso," *Rassegna della istruzione artistica* 9 (1938): 347–57. In regard to the Villa of the Mysteries project, Krasceninnicowa asserts retrospectively that as a good Fascist Barosso had insisted on the Italian right to publish her work (347).

52   De Carolis 1999 (note 38), 29. Maiuri held multiple titles simultaneously—superintendent of the antiquities of Campania and Molise, director of the National Museum of Naples, and director of the excavations of Pompeii (Maiuri to Kelsey, June 22, 1926, Papers).

53   Kelsey to Maiuri, May 26, 1935 (Papers).

54   Della Corte's letter to Maiuri is dated May 24, 1925 (Papers).

55   In this letter Barosso praises Fedele as "professor at the Royal University of Rome, worthy Minister of National Culture, and a great lover of art and history" (Barosso to Kelsey, June 23, 1925, Papers).

56   Barosso to Kelsey, June 23, 1925 (Papers). Barosso does not give the name of the director general. She had painted the full-scale panel of the Bride in May and June 1925. For a brief biography of Fedele, see the entry "Pietro Fedele" by Monte S. Finkelstein in *Historical Dictionary of Fascist Italy*, ed. Philip V. Cannistraro (Westport, Conn., 1982), 219–20.

57   Barosso to Kelsey, August 4, 1925 (Papers). The date of Fedele's visit to Barosso's studio is unknown. It may well have occurred before permission for the project was granted, but it certainly took place sometime before Barosso sent the sample watercolor, which Fedele saw in her studio, to Ann Arbor before she moved to Pompeii in late July 1925.

58   Maiuri to Kelsey, June 22, 1925 (Papers). While waiting for the permit to come through, Barosso worked in Rome on calculating the reduced dimensions of the paintings (Barosso to Kelsey, June 23, 1925, Papers). See also de Grummond 2000 (note 5), 136n. 23. In the same letter she says that during this period she had finished the borders of the sample watercolor of the Bride in preparation for shipping it to Ann Arbor.

59   Barosso to Kelsey, November 12, 1926 (Papers). As early as March 1925 Kelsey had indicated his willingness to allow the government to exhibit Barosso's watercolor, but a show was not part of the official agreement concluded in June 1925 (Kelsey to Barosso, March 17, 1925, Papers).

60 Regarding the Dionysian element in what she calls "aesthetic fascism," Mary Ann Frese Witt, in *The Search for Modern Tragedy: Aesthetic Fascism in Italy and France* (Ithaca, 2001), x, claims: "Seminal to the aesthetic fascists in both Italy and France was their reading of the works of Nietzsche, in particular *The Birth of Tragedy*. The origins of tragedy in Mediterranean Dionysian sacrificial rapture justified its promotion in the literary and theatrical form most apt to fuse antiquity with the present, violence with beauty, and the individual with the totalitarian corporate body." Further, "In contrast to decadent individualism, Dionysian mass fervor brings each soul into contact with the universal soul, creating a true freedom of the will superior to rationalistic-individualistic illusory freedom" (10–11). According to Visser 1992 (note 28), 7, 14, the "(aesthetic) virtues of hellenistic culture" also had special resonance for Italian Fascism. On Fascist aesthetics (as distinct from aesthetic Fascism), see Marla Stone, *The Patron State: Culture and Politics in Fascist Italy* (Princeton, 1998), 23–94; see also *Fascism, Aesthetics, and Culture*, ed. Richard J. Golsan (Hanover, 1992), especially Golsan's introduction, ix–xvii, and the essay by Jeffrey T. Schnapp, "Epic Demonstrations: Fascist Modernity and the 1932 Exhibition of the Fascist Revolution," 1–5.

61 Emilio Gentile, "The Myth of National Regeneration in Italy: From Modernist Avant-Garde to Fascism," in *Fascist Visions: Art and Ideology in France and Italy*, ed. Matthew Affron and Mark Antliff (Princeton, 1997), 25–45. See also Visser 1992 (note 28) on *Romanità* as part of a pre-Fascist notion of nationhood, developed further, and for different ends, under Mussolini. Stone 1999 (note 46), 205–20, offers this definition: "*Romanità*, the quality of Romanness, for the Fascists, meant a profound spiritual and historical destiny to be made real through Fascism" (205). She presents a lucid analysis of the malleability of the construct of *Romanità*, how the ideology associated with it changed over time, and how those changes were reflected in art and architecture as well as in forms of popular culture such as films and exhibitions.

62 Memorandum no. 16, October 1–December 31, 1926 (Papers). See also de Grummond 2000 (note 5), 137n. 49. Other, apparently longer, notices appeared in the Italian press, but Kelsey had arrived in Italy too late to see them. He obtained copies, which he submitted with his memorandum to the Near East Research Committee (Kelsey to Frank E. Robbins, December 10, 1926, Papers). The archives of the committee have yet to be located. Kelsey later asked Barosso to obtain more copies for him, which he would "use . . . to advantage" (Kelsey to Barosso, February 7, 1927, Papers). These, too, have not been located.

63 Ten years later Barosso expressed her political sympathies in the obituary she wrote for Esther Van Deman, who likewise supported the Fascist cause (Maria Barosso, "Esther Boise Van Deman," *L'Urbe: Rivista romana* 2, pt. 1, no. 5 [1937]: 43–44).

64 Philip V. Cannistraro, "Mussolini's Cultural Revolution," *Journal of Contemporary History* 7 (1972): 122–24; see also Jean Henry, "Novecento Movement," in Cannistraro 1982 (note 56), 372–73. For a general account of the initial development of the Novecento movement and Sarfatti's leading role in it, see Philip V. Cannistraro and Brian R. Sullivan, *Il Duce's Other Woman* (New York, 1993), 277–85. For more recent commentary, see Emily Braun, *Mario Sironi and Italian Modernism: Art and Politics under Fascism* (Cambridge, 2000); and Stone 1999 (note 46), 211.

65 On Mussolini's speech at the exhibition opening in Milan in 1923, see Braun 2000 (note 64), 1. On his speech at the 1926 opening, a large part of which was surely written by Sarfatti, see Cannistraro and Sullivan 1993 (note 64), 313–14. See also Marla Stone, "The State as Patron: Making Official Culture in Fascist Italy," in Affron and Antliff 1997 (note 61), 205–38. Stone characterizes the period of political stabilization (1925–30) as one in which the regime took "administrative and bureaucratic control of the arts" and placed "the institutions of cultural display under official control" (209). One of those institutions of cultural display was the Galleria Borghese. For further analyses of Fascist exhibition culture, see Stone 1999 (note 46) and Stone 1998 (note 60).

66 Memorandum no. 16, October 1–December 31, 1926 (Papers). In fact, Barosso's watercolors of the Villa of the Mysteries murals bear considerable stylistic resemblance to the work of

some classicizing artists of this period, who may well have admired her representations of the ancient murals. See, for example, paintings by artists such as Ferruccio Ferrazzi and Giuseppe Capogrossi illustrated by Maurizio Fagiolo dell'Arco, *Scuola romana: Pitture e sculture a Roma dal 1919 al 1943* (Rome, 1986), 8, 60 (fig. b), 248. I owe this reference to Joan Mickelson.

[67] Krasceninnicowa 1938 (note 51), 347–48. See also Leone 1997 (note 28), 129, who also uses the term "artist-archaeologist" to refer to Barosso. The designation seems to have applied more generally to the artists whom Antonio Muñoz encouraged to document the progress of Mussolini's urban renewal program.

[68] Genevieve Gessert, "Ancient Art and Exhibition Culture under Mussolini: The *Mostra Augustea della Romanità*, 1937–38," 1–2, a paper delivered on May 8, 2004, at the annual meeting of the Association of Ancient Historians in Ann Arbor, Michigan. I thank Professor Gessert for allowing me to cite her unpublished paper and for providing me with additional references on the subject.

[69] Matilde Burri Rossi, *Museo della civiltà romana* (Rome, 1976), 5.

[70] According to Gessert 2004 (note 68), 2, "While the diplomatic value of the multi-national collection was still important in the Museo dell'Impero, the nationalistic value of such a unique assemblage was increasingly appreciated." Among archaeologists, such as Giulio Quirino Giglioli, a student of Lanciani's, the Museo dell'Impero was seen as "an opportunity to re-establish Rome as the center of Roman scholarship."

[71] That articles continued to be written about Barosso's show well into 1927 reinforces this proposition. Barosso wrote to Kelsey on February 12, 1927: "The impression made by my show at the Borghese Gallery is still very strong. The consensus was unanimous, beyond rare, a unique instance, not one voice of disagreement! It was considered an event of highest artistic and scientific interest, and various magazines are still writing about it" (Papers).

[72] Visser 1992 (note 28), 5–17, examines the central role of Italian classical historians and archaeologists in the formation of Fascist doctrine, particularly that of *Romanità*. Stone 1999 (note 46) focuses on the role of Rome in the development of Fascist ideology and exhibition culture.

[73] Giglioli's "prezentazione" in the exhibition catalogue notes that the show was "tutta costituita di riproduzioni" (*Mostra Augustea della Romanità*, ed. Giulio Quirino Giglioli, 2d ed. [Rome, 1937], xiv). In contrast, Anna Maria Liberati, "The Pompeian Collection in the Museo della civiltà romana," in Ciarallo and De Carolis 1999 (note 38), 17, claims that originals were also used in the show. According to Liberati, the reproductions of the furnishings were made under Maiuri's supervision.

[74] For the Augustan house, see Giglioli 1937, 152–58, pls. XXXVIII–XLI. None of the displays were limited to materials from Pompeii. All Roman Italy and the empire were represented in an obvious effort to highlight the extent of the territory under ancient Roman sway to support the claims of the Fascist government to be the rightful heir to the ancient empire. See, for example, section 26 of the exhibition, entitled "Immortalità dell'idea di Roma: La rinascita dell'Impero nell'Italia fascista," 79. For a detailed biographical profile of Muñoz's career and the numerous offices he held, see Calogero Bellanca, *Antonio Muñoz: La politica di tutela dei monumenti di Roma durante il governatorato* (Rome, 2003), 15–24. For the exhibition, see Leone 1997 (note 28), 129.

[75] The checklist for the exhibition has been lost, but Kelsey reported to the Near East Research Committee at the University of Michigan that a second room of the exhibition contained "examples of her other work, both as a painter and etcher" (memorandum no. 16, October 1– December 31, 1926, Papers).

[76] Krasceninnicowa 1938 (note 51), 347–56, and Leone 1997 (note 28) illustrate a number of Barosso's views of Rome. For Muñoz's encouragement of artists' recordings of the phases of transformation, see Bellanca 2003 (note 74), 230n. 23.

77   Krasceninnicowa 1938 (note 51), 349. In 1928, at the first Congresso di studi romani, Muñoz along with Ceccarius Paluzzi and Galassi Paluzzi proposed establishing a museum of the city of Rome. The Museo di Roma was inaugurated in April 1930 in the former Pantanella complex, which at that time occupied the space in the same complex as the Museo dell'Impero. Bellanca has suggested that the location may have been chosen strategically, because it was adjacent to the archaeological area of the Forum Boarium (Bellanca 2003 [note 74], 230–31).

78   Van Deman to Kelsey, April 19, 1927 (Papers). In a letter to H. Sanders at the University of Michigan, Van Deman offers a similar explanation of the situation (Van Deman to Sanders, June 18, 1927, Papers).

79   Van Deman to Kelsey, April 19, 1927 (Papers).

80   Butler 1930 (note 10), 11–12.

81   Butler to Barosso, August 10, 1927 (Papers).

82   Butler 1930 (note 10), 11. The new museum was assigned the first floor of Newberry Hall, a small Richardsonian Romanesque building built in 1888–91 to house the Student Christian Association. Because the building was not fireproof, only the sturdier objects in the collection were displayed there. The more vulnerable objects were stored in safer quarters in the Classical Seminary Room and Archaeological Laboratory in Angell Hall, a classroom building across the street. In addition, Butler faced the daunting task of accommodating finds and field records from the university's excavations at Karanis and Seleucia on the Tigris, which took precedence over exhibiting Barosso's watercolors.

83   Memorandum no. 16, October 1–December 31, 1926 (Papers). See also note 47, above.

FIGURE 1
Elaine Gazda and Bettina Bergmann taking infrared photographs of the north wall of room 5 in the Villa of the Mysteries, Pompeii, June 2003.

Photo: Patricia Simons. Courtesy Ministero per i Beni e le Attività Culturali, Soprintendenza archeologica di Pompei.

FIGURE 2
View into room 5 from west entrance, June 2002.

Photo: James Stanton-Abbott. Courtesy Ministero per i Beni e le Attività Culturali, Soprintendenza archeologica di Pompei.

Seeing Women in the Villa of the Mysteries: A Modern Excavation of the Dionysiac Murals

Bettina Bergmann

ARLY IN THE SUMMERS of 2002 and 2003 we returned, at different times of day and night, to stand among the ancient figures on Pompeian red walls. Coming at midday, *permesso* in hand, we stepped over the rope keeping out tourists, inciting glares and sometimes curses. Again and again we peered, from manifold angles, up close and from afar, with flashlights, through various shapes and thicknesses of lenses [FIG. 1]. What were we seeking? What mysteries did we, women scholars of various ages, perceive in our intense scrutiny of the painted wall surfaces? Each had her own questions, but the unspoken, collective goal was to see: to see more and to see more clearly, and through this enhanced seeing, to know the frescoes as they originally were and to solve the special mysteries they held for us. It was only later, in preparing this essay on the early discovery of the famous Dionysiac frescoes, that the central issue emerged to be the very desire and process of such a quest.

The reader might well ask how modern responses may add to our understanding of an ancient object. The Villa of the Mysteries frescoes present an especially compelling case for the need to consider their existence in recent history before one can try to make sense of their ancient past. Consider, for example, the common fantasy that the vivid red walls of the villa emerged from the ground miraculously well preserved and remain so today [FIG. 2]. The frescoes' ongoing life in photographic reproductions glosses over any breaks or discolorations resulting from nearly a century of exposure and thus perpetuates this misconception. That century included two world wars, earthquakes and volcanic eruptions, ongoing upheavals in local politics, and in more recent decades the daily onslaught of automobiles and tourists. As a result, the walls of the Villa of the Mysteries have amassed, from their excavation to the present, an accretion of surfaces, of layers applied to older surfaces, at times leaving visible traces beneath the new. In a parallel process of accrual, images of the frescoes continue to multiply. Floating apart from the physical context of the room, these reproductions and their attendant mythology have found their ways into our homes and memories.

How much of what we think we see in these images is actually ancient, and how much the impression of collective modern memories? Can one peel back the accumulated layers of matter and interpretation that have made this mysterious villa and the frescoes it contains into a cultural icon and understand how the modern Villa of the Mysteries came to be?

The following study undertakes a stratigraphic analysis that seeks to uncover, both physically and metaphorically, the famous room 5's thickest layers. This investigation brings to light the now largely forgotten discovery of the villa in 1909 and then traces some of the room's afterlives since that discovery to show how the formation and sequence of superimposed strata follow various movements in the twentieth century, specifically those of archaeology, art history, psychoanalysis, gender theory, and tourism.

My "excavation" begins with the layer that is highest in most scholars' perception: the extraordinary photographs that accompanied Amedeo Maiuri's glamorous 1931 publication, *La Villa dei Misteri*. The impression of fresh and brilliant red surface conveyed by Maiuri's pioneering colorplates, combined with the intriguingly psycho-erotic subject matter, made an indelible impression on the eager public that purchased his work. But how accurate are these reproductions compared to the frescoes' appearance when excavated some two decades earlier, let alone to their appearance on the night of the volcanic eruption in A.D. 79, when they already were well over a century old?

To try to answer these questions, we must dig deeper, back to the turn of the twentieth century, and revisit the dramatic discovery of the red walls in May 1909. This discovery effected a major change in Italian archaeology by bringing to a halt a gold rush of private excavations around Pompeii. The unpublished excavation logs of 1909 to 1912 housed in the archives of the Soprintendenza archeologica di Napoli reveal an intriguing back story of perilous incidents and physical intervention. These neglected episodes raise troubling questions and expose the abiding paradox of the frescoes as being at once fragile and yet fixed in their appearance. In a further attempt to establish the murals' state upon excavation, I then examine photographic images made in the initial months and years. This quest for the frescoes' state in 1909, however, is quickly thwarted by myriad disparities among the extant reproductions. Archaeological methods and forms of documentation have their own history and properties, from which the object of study cannot be detached. Indeed, to what degree have our mental images of the frescoes been shaped by surface restorations and by the vicissitudes of photographic reproductions?

At this juncture, I turn from a retrospective search for the "authentic" murals to their replication and afterlives within a broader cultural milieu. Since the early twentieth century the Dionysiac frieze has been made to cater to personal and collective desires as its parts have been recalled and reconstructed to different ends. Such reconstructions, by producing something entirely new, project the ancient images forward in time, and it is this tension—between purposeful hindsight and spontaneous, imaginative reuse—that both captures the room's endless fascination and makes it a provocative example of the archaeological metaphor in modern thought. Through its newer history, we can trace how theories of gender, and especially feminine sexuality, evolved in psychology and literature, how female spectatorship catapulted women into shaping archaeological method, how artists interacted with the ancient images, and how photography transformed certain parts of the murals into ubiquitous cultural symbols.

This exercise in the archaeology of interpretation unveils the superimposed strata —conceptual, historical, art-historical, psychoanalytic, and popular-cultural meaning—that overlie the Villa of the Mysteries. Due to the twentieth-century discovery of the villa's frescoes, their reputed high state of preservation, and their compelling subject matter, the cycle has been adopted as "almost...modern," as has no other monument from Pompeii. But this protomodernity comes at a cost. Because of the complexity of the nested historical and conceptual frameworks, the villa stands provocatively at the physical and theoretical intersection of desire and impossibility.

In undertaking a look at these separate strata, I offer an interpretive framework for questioning the basis of how we know this monument while underscoring its ultimate elusiveness and even the impossibility of ever fully knowing it. The modern story of the Villa of the Mysteries sheds light on the status of classical archaeology within the larger field of art history, particularly the ways in which the ancient is coded as "original" and "authentic," while simultaneously requiring us to confront the inviability of this very signification.

PART ONE

The Second Discovery: Maiuri's Reconstruction of 1929–31

The Villa of the Mysteries was first exposed to light in 1909, and I will return to this episode later. The villa's discovery entered public consciousness, however, some twenty years later with Amedeo Maiuri, a central figure in Italian archaeology, who alternately has been heralded as the most positive force in the excavations of Pompeii and condemned as the agent of its second destruction.[1] In 1929 Maiuri resumed unearthing the ruins at the end of the Street of the Tombs, recovered the perimeter of the building, and reconstructed the walls and roof, giving the villa a finished appearance (despite the fact that it lacks its original upper story).[2] Previously unpublished photographs of his excavation show workers wheeling soil in carts on rails near columns of the courtyard emerging from volcanic debris [FIG. 3].[3] Maiuri is often credited with discovering the Villa of the Mysteries because he published his reconstituted history of the building and its contents in a lavish, limited-edition, two-volume set, which remains the standard reference for the complex.[4] Intended to be a model of modern Italian publishing and the first in a projected series on Italian painting, the 1931 publication also affirmed the ascent of Maiuri, who retained power over much of Campanian archaeology for the next thirty years and gave Pompeii its contemporary reconstructed appearance.

La Villa dei Misteri offered the first full visual documentation of the villa and its finds and self-consciously far outstripped the poor, piecemeal reproductions of previous publications. Maiuri aimed to present the frescoes as they had once appeared within their physical context and raised ample funds for state-of-the-art photography. Images fill the volumes; drawings, plans, and photographs accompany text on the page; and photographs of the best-known walls, shot in natural light, appear in black-and-white plates at the back of the first volume. But the truly spectacular contribution was the

second volume of eighteen colorplates, made with the revolutionary trichrome technique then normally used for glossy magazine advertisements rather than scholarly documentation [FIG. 4]. Because the bright "Pompeian red" ground was such an integral part of the allure of the Villa of the Mysteries frescoes, these color reproductions had a special resonance. A 1934 review by Jocelyn Toynbee applauds the author and the Istituto poligrafico dello Stato: "This is the first time that the frescoes of the Villa Item have been photographed in color, and those who have visited the site will realize how admirably the plates reproduce the *freshness and vividness of the originals*. . . . Dr. Maiuri stresses the importance of studying these works of art in close relation with their provenance and setting, . . . that in interpreting the pictures the structural lay-out of the building should be kept clearly in view" (italics added).[5]

Maiuri's color reproductions of the Dionysiac frieze of room 5 had a dual aim. He claimed that painstaking color corrections were made by repeated reference to the actual frescoes not only to achieve fidelity to the original in A.D. 79 but also to record all current signs of damage.[6] Notably, just a few years earlier, Francis Kelsey of the University of Michigan had commissioned the Italian painter Maria Barosso to execute watercolor renderings of the frieze because photography was not capable of producing satisfactory color facsimiles. Although Maiuri overcame this obstacle, the logistics of book production could not entirely accommodate his vision, for textual and visual representations of the frescoes appear separated from their architectural context. Indeed, the painted room 5, at five by five meters, cannot be captured in any still photograph, but only as a spatial experience in time, and authors have been hard put to articulate in words what photographs fail to convey.

Nevertheless, Maiuri's text and illustrations represent a milestone in archaeological publishing. The complex formally received its name as the Villa of the Mysteries, and Maiuri established an enduring story of the villa. Noting the structural interconnection of room 5 with the sleeping alcove (room 4), he identifies the suite as the private apartments of master and mistress, made to the wishes of the domina [see p. 214, FIG. 8]. Maiuri populates the villa with living Romans, ascribing to them religious and gender roles. The domina was "a lady of enlightened artistic tastes, for the whole villa was decorated with great elegance...on the walls of her salon, paintings celebrate her wedding, creating a kind of domestic sanctuary in which the domina, herself an initiate and priestess, received friends." In this narrative the villa's glory days came to an end when, sometime between A.D. 14 and 63, the patrician owners apparently sold it to a freedman, who converted the residence into an agricultural factory, making drastic alterations with complete disregard for existing decoration: "some uncouth and ignorant owner, who, without having the slightest regard for the previous arrangement and decoration of the rooms had, just prior to the eruption, set to work to divide the rooms, to close old ways of communication and open new ones, and, what is even worse, to have the walls repainted." So slipshod was the remodeling that Maiuri concludes with hyperbolic flair: "The eruption was providential; it prevented the wall wreckers from accomplishing the most grievous crime by destroying the greatest monument of ancient painting."[7]

Maiuri's master narrative has persisted, with the elaborate rooms segregated both in time and ownership from the working parts of the villa. But lately it has become increasingly clear that even though the complex underwent major renovations, late republican villas of the first century B.C. often combined rustic working areas and richly embellished living rooms. In fact, such complexes seem to have been the norm and need not signal a change in ownership or function of the villa.[8] As for the most controversial aspect of the villa, the subject of the figural frescoes of room 5, Maiuri drew on hypotheses set forth in articles of the previous two decades by the female scholars P. B. Mudie Cooke, Jocelyn Toynbee, and Margarete Bieber.[9] These authors argued that the frieze depicts a female ritual, perhaps preparations for a wedding, and they found key iconographic comparisons in ancient art. Maiuri agreed with Bieber and Toynbee that the frescoes are Dionysiac in theme and portray scenes of a prenuptial initiation but differed by seeing the frieze as one single scene depicting several brides rather than a continuous narrative representing the same woman in sequential stages of a ritual. The latter theory that the walls depict one individual female's experience would find special resonance among feminists in the latter twentieth century.

The combination of color reproductions and Maiuri's contextual approach raised the bar for archaeological method. As study of Roman art has become increasingly specialized, however, scholars unfortunately have not always followed Maiuri's attention to context and focused on the finds alone, especially the frescoes. As for the "truth" of the color photographs, Toynbee makes a revealing remark. She disagrees with Maiuri's belief in the frieze as the simultaneous initiation of specific women, stating: "and a reexamination of the paintings in his excellent photographs and plates has done nothing to change the present reviewer's belief that all the figures...have a sufficiently close relationship to one another to justify" it as a continuous narrative. Toynbee's statement acknowledges the growing authority of photographic reproduction in scholarly arguments. Good photographs should sustain the observations made by the scholar, but while Maiuri's color reproductions facilitated closer looking and allowed scholars to see unknown details, they did not necessarily affect interpretations of the subject represented.[10] In this case the reviewer read and looked but did not see multiple women in the frieze.

Within a few years Maiuri's volumes themselves became an object of desire. One thousand published copies of *La Villa dei Misteri*, five hundred in Italian and five hundred in English, were not sufficient to satisfy demand, although the turmoil of World War II prevented a second edition until 1947. In the preface to the second edition Maiuri notes that so much had been discovered and debated in the sixteen years since the first edition that it was necessary to revise discussions of the villa's building phases, update the bibliography, and add a separate section on the various interpretations of the great frieze. He also substantially rewrote the treatment of ancient painting technique in light of new chemical analyses and other studies.[11]

Today Maiuri's book has assumed a dual status as both an "original" and a "reproduction" and functions as a souvenir and a miniaturized version of the Pompeian site. *La Villa dei Misteri* is the first source to which one turns for a richly documented and illustrated overall picture of the villa. Packaged in the cutting-edge photographic techniques of advertising, the murals resembled fantasy objects seen in magazines, just as they would later cater to dreams of travel in postcards. Yet in the book's synthesis, some of the villa's crucial history, namely, that of its initial discovery, disappears. A look at the now-forgotten evidence of that earlier history adds new dimensions to Maiuri's pictures and raises questions about the twenty years between 1909 and 1929. These questions challenge much of what we think we know about the Villa of the Mysteries.

Gold Rush, 1880–1909: Discovery and Deconstruction of Roman Villas

To imagine the Villa of the Mysteries as it emerged from the soil in 1909, we must look past the manufactured images of the 1930s to the late nineteenth century, a tumultuous period in Italian archaeology. Since the 1861 unification of Italy, the ancient sites on the Bay of Naples had ceased to be the stage for spectacles and a quarry of artifacts for foreign kings. They assumed a vital role in the construction of a national Italian heritage under the Neapolitan Giuseppe Fiorelli, appointed inspector of excavations at Pompeii and professor of archaeology at the University of Naples in 1860. In 1863 Fiorelli took over direction of the Museo nazionale in Naples and reorganized the collections, and in 1866 he established the Scuola di archeologia at Pompeii to train top Italian archaeologists.[12] Most importantly for this study, Fiorelli was among the first to adopt geological methods and examine the stratigraphy of a site. Reversing the earlier practice of clearing streets and excavating buildings from the ground floor up, he uncovered deposit layers from the top down, thereby preserving upper stories and their contents and allowing for more reliable restorations.[13]

Fiorelli's attention to the soil also intensified the mythology of Pompeii as the Lost City. Recognizing that the volcanic ash covering plants and human bodies had hardened and left cavities, he introduced the practice of pouring plaster into the holes to mold their forms. The results, with strikingly vivid facial expressions and bodily contortions frozen in white, deepened popular perceptions of Pompeii as a metaphor for instantaneous death and subsequent recovery. The German historian Ferdinand

Gregorovius, after being escorted by Fiorelli through the ruins in 1864, described what he saw: "The four figures—cast in plaster—of Pompeian fugitives, who were turned to stone (!), while in the very act of flight, make an indescribable impression: life incarnate in its most awful tragedy."[14] Fiorelli's poignant casts [see p. 179, FIGS. 3–5] inevitably affected responses to all human forms emerging from the ashes, and these included the lifelike painted women in the Villa of the Mysteries.

Meanwhile, during the second half of the nineteenth century, Pompeii became a transnational project as European intellectuals descended to plumb its archaeological remains for evidence of Roman daily life.[15] The still-influential August Mau established a chronology of Roman wall painting by combining the building phases distinguished by Fiorelli with the thematic categories of painting by Wolfgang Helbig. Mau's 1882 book provided a system of four consecutive Pompeian wall painting styles between roughly 300 B.C. and A.D. 79. It was immediately adopted and is still used today.[16] The study of Roman wall painting as an independent subject thus was instituted well before the Villa of the Mysteries frescoes came to light in 1909, the year Mau died.

Another significant development that would shape understanding of the Villa of the Mysteries was the crusade to return ancient buildings to their original state.[17] Figural scenes routinely had been cut from painted walls and along with mosaic floors, furniture, and other objects had been transported to the Naples museum. Now, restored roofs with wood beams and clay tiles were built to protect the surviving decor in situ. Giulio de Petra, who in 1910 would write the first scholarly analysis of the Villa of the Mysteries, finished such a restoration, the House of the Vettii, in 1895, which still gives the most complete impression of any structure in Pompeii.

As excavation and conservation at the site of Pompeii became ever more controlled, outside the city walls landowners began hunting for Roman treasures.[18] The impetus came from new museums in Europe and the United States, along with private collectors, who competed to replace their plaster casts and reproductions with original works. Meanwhile, an uncertain Italian bureaucracy struggled to gain control.[19] The controversy over archaeological finds is especially well documented for Boscoreale, a few miles north of the Villa of the Mysteries. In 1895 a Roman wine-producing *villa rustica* was discovered, initiating the first of several scandals involving Vincenzo Prisco.[20] A worker found a wine vat containing the stunning first-century Boscoreale treasure, a trove of 108 embossed silver vessels and 1,000 gold coins. Prisco quickly smuggled the collection of silver out of the country and sold it for five hundred thousand francs to the French banker Édouard von Rothschild, who in turn donated it to the Louvre.[21] This transaction proved a public humiliation for the Italians; how had they let these precious objects slip away and enrich French patrimony? Yet, astonishingly, Prisco's growing wealth and local influence enabled him to keep digging for nearly three decades. Early-twentieth-century guidebooks inform visitors that only by special permission of the proprietor, Signor De Prisco of Boscoreale, can they gain access to a Roman villa north of Pompeii.[22] The continuing power of this man over an archaeological site of this import, extending even to tourist access, exemplifies the situation in Campania in the decade before the discovery of the Villa of the Mysteries.

In 1899 Prisco hit upon another extraordinary villa, with the richest frescoes recovered to date. Several rooms were painted with superb examples of Mau's second style, notably the illusionary architecture in the famous cubiculum, now in the Metropolitan Museum of Art in New York, and the megalography in a nearby room, where life-

FIGURE 5
Seated woman playing
a kithara, from room H,
Villa of P. Fannius Synistor,
Boscoreale, first century B.C.
New York, The Metropolitan
Museum of Art, Rogers Fund,
1903 (03.14.5).

size legendary figures sit, stand, or move against a brilliant red background [a room to which the Villa of the Mysteries frieze would be closely related; FIG. 5].[23] Prisco immediately stopped the dig and went about removing "his" seventy-one fresco sections, claiming the urgent need for protection from rain before reburying the rooms.[24] The removal of such magnificent frescoes alarmed the authorities, who created a state commission in 1900 to prevent their exportation. In the end, however, only five sections remained in Italy; the rest found their way to museums in Europe and the United States. Their arrival excited the international community, now aware that such treasures could be exported. On September 28, 1902, the *New York Times* announced: "For the first time millionaire art collectors are to have an opportunity of buying treasures which were buried by the same eruption of Vesuvius that destroyed Pompeii. In the little village of Boscoreale, at the foot of Vesuvius, and between Naples and Pompeii, a wonderful find on private property has been made.... The law forbidding such treasures to be sold and sent out of the country has in this case been modified. The Italian Government will keep some of the paintings and the remainder will be allowed to be sold and exported."[25]

Despite the sensational Campanian gold rush of the late 1800s, only a few of the countless villas on the slopes of the volcano have subsequently been unearthed.[26] This halt in exploration is due in large part to the Villa of the Mysteries, whose discovery in 1909 prompted the authorities to create a law banning all private digs in the region.[27] A hiatus of twelve years followed, and although legitimate excavations of the countryside resumed in the 1920s, they lacked the drama of the earlier sensational finds.[28] The discovery and restoration of the Villa of the Mysteries were the climax of the gold rush. Following the Boscoreale treasures and the struggles between Vincenzo Prisco and the state, the discovery of the villa triggered a local preservation movement in Campania, but not before months of intense conflict. It is to those months, and the emergence of the red walls, that we now turn.

The Discovery of 1909:
Early Responses and Restorations

The building's first official name, Villa Item, refers to Aurelio Item, who owned the popular Hotel Suisse just west of the Pompeii excavations.[29] As early as 1902 Item began exploring the unexcavated area at the north end of the Street of the Tombs, where in antiquity two roads diverged, one linking Pompeii to the slopes of Vesuvius to the east and the other following the curving shoreline to Naples and beyond to the ports of Puteoli and Baiae.[30] Since the eighteenth century this evocative spot outside the Herculaneum Gate has been significant. Romantic watercolors depict travelers among the overgrown, ruined tombs, reminders of life's transience. In one rendering cows graze at the very place where the Villa of the Mysteries would emerge [FIG. 6]. The villa's discovery at this hallowed spot thus automatically imbued its remains with a special aura.[31]

The land belonged to Elisabetta Gargiulio, who allowed Item to intensify his search in 1908.[32] By January 1909 Item had obtained official permission from Naples to excavate. Exactly a year later, in January 1910, his permissions were revoked for although Item's work lasted only four months, his undertaking created enormous political upheaval. After just one week of probing, he made a discovery as stunning as that of Prisco at Boscoreale. Memories of the gold rush were fresh, and the private dig led to friction with the authorities, by now highly sensitized by earlier blunders.

What follows, briefly, is the sequence of events. Item began digging on April 29, 1909, at the south end of the villa and immediately hit upon columns of the courtyard adjacent to room 5. The next week, the painted rooms 4 and 5 came to light [FIG. 7, rooms 16 and 20 in the plan]. Response from the authorities in Naples was swift. On May 10 Matteo Della Corte visited the site and saw the expanse of red walls and nearly life-size figures rising from the piles of volcanic debris [FIG. 8]. Recognizing their

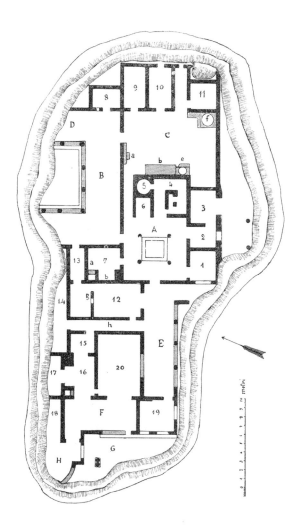

extraordinary importance, Della Corte alerted Naples that a private excavator had chanced upon a late republican villa of major importance. This site, he said, differed from others by its hillside location, multiple levels, and, above all, its extraordinary frescoes. He warned that exposure to the elements posed imminent danger to the precious red cinnabar and pressed for mature, trustworthy guards to protect the site from vandals.

Antonio Sogliano, then director of Pompeii, and others who followed compared the villa's architecture to the multilevel Villa of Diomedes, one hundred meters up the Street of the Tombs, which had been a popular tourist stop since the eighteenth century. But they noted that the Villa Item had something as yet never seen in Pompeii, namely, second-style paintings showing a "major advance" in megalography. This grandiose composition of animated, realistic figures, unified by a continuous red background on all four walls, recalled, as Sogliano wrote on May 24, the expansive painted murals described by Pausanias and Philostratus.[33]

Indeed, from the beginning, the figural frescoes were treated as a precious treasure. Their protection determined the course of the villa's modern history. Just three weeks after discovery, on May 16, excavation stopped, resuming only in spurts during the next two years in other parts of the villa. October and November 1909, for

FIGURE 7

Plan of Villa of the Mysteries, Pompeii (rooms 16 and 20 are today identified as rooms 4 and 5). From Giulio de Petra, *Descrizione della Villa romana* (1912), 140.

Photo: Courtesy Northampton, Mass., Smith College Libraries.

FIGURE 8

Villa of the Mysteries, Pompeii, room 5, north wall. Note lapilli at bottom and dripping water at left, suggesting that the wall has been dampened for photography.

Photo: Courtesy Ministero per i Beni e le Attività Culturali, Soprintendenza archeologica di Pompei. Fototeca Inv. C242.

example, saw the partial uncovering of rooms around the peristyle, of a tetrastyle atrium, and of "Egyptian" rooms painted in black and yellow. Nineteen years passed before Maiuri would clear the rest of the complex. Attention instead focused on conserving the frescoes. In Naples steps were taken to buy the land for the state. At the site guards blocked entry by tourists, potential robbers, and even interested scholars. This suburban villa, unlike those at Boscoreale and Boscotrecase, would not have its frescoes removed, carved up, and taken to Europe or the United States. The ruins were to be restored and transformed into the villa as it was at the moment of the eruption, a vision that would eventually be realized by Amedeo Maiuri.

The Villa of the Mysteries was thus the first suburban villa in which high-quality frescoes were left in situ. There do seem to have been problems with theft. In a May 19 letter addressed to Item, Sogliano stresses that everything, from the grand paintings to the smallest fallen fragment, absolutely must be kept in situ. Suspicion landed on Item; just twelve days later, on May 31, a memo signed by an august group that included Sogliano, Della Corte, and Giuseppe Spano asserts that small, nonfigural fresco fragments are missing from the back wall above Dionysos, probably having been removed for sale. Earlier entries in the daily logs claim that certain objects were being housed in the Hotel Suisse, and, indeed, the fragments in question were found in Item's rooms. The incident generated even greater suspicion of Item and urgency for the state to take control of the site, but the association with Item continued, by necessity, for at this point he was crucial for ongoing conservation. Growing apprehension about theft is conveyed in a June 6 memo from Petra admonishing Della Corte about a transgression of Petra's order not to let anyone gain access to the villa site without his personal, written permission; Della Corte must, he reiterates, strictly enforce this rule. But portable finds, it seems, were sold. Arnold Ruesch, for example, bought bronze bowls, an oil lamp, a pitcher, and a bracelet for his personal collection, apparently at the villa site itself.[34]

The other major concern in the first months of discovery was damage from the elements. That the paintings had not survived in perfect condition is clear from the few official photographs and the reports of May 1909, which record extensive damage upon excavation. This condition should not come as a surprise, for if we follow Mau's chronology the walls had stood for well more than a century before their violent burial in A.D. 79, and the earthquake of A.D. 62 certainly could have caused damage that necessitated ancient repairs. In addition, the effects of the scorching heat and volcanic fallout must have injured the painted plaster (because of the villa's location on a slope, its rooms filled to a higher level with soil and debris than most other Pompeian houses). Interment in humid soil for eighteen hundred years made things even worse, and since the villa lay beside the Sarno River canal, the frescoes were more affected by moisture than other walls in Pompeii.

But perhaps most injurious were substantial interventions by human agents. Repeated drastic and changing conservation efforts took place in 1909. The word *urgentissimo* recurs like a refrain in excavation logs citing dangers of humidity and lack of ventilation; problems with loosening, falling plaster; and the need for adequate covering to protect the frescoes from rain, fire, and earthquakes. The established practice of conserving murals, introduced under the directorship of Michele Ruggiero, was to detach and reattach the plaster either to the reinforced, ancient wall or to a rebuilt surface. According to excavation reports written in the months following May 1909, the east and north walls of room 5 were so rebuilt.[35] Ruggiero had also promoted the

FIGURE 9
East wall, room 5, Villa of
the Mysteries, Pompeii.
Note metal brace above and
incomplete restoration of
upper wall.

Photo: Courtesy Ministero per
i Beni e le Attività Culturali,
Soprintendenza archeologica di
Pompei. Fototeca Inv. 267.

Opposite page

FIGURE 10 [Top left]
East wall, room 5, Villa of the
Mysteries, Pompeii (detail).
Note repairs: three brackets
right of winged figure,
volcanic mud chipped away
at left; later cracks not yet
visible.

Photo: Courtesy Ministero per
i Beni e le Attività Culturali,
Soprintendenza archeologica di
Pompei. Fototeca Inv. 245.

FIGURE 11 [Bottom left]
South wall, room 5, Villa of
the Mysteries, Pompeii,
during excavation, probably
May or June 1909. The
window is visible at right.

Photo: Courtesy Ministero per
i Beni e le Attività Culturali,
Soprintendenza archeologica di
Pompei. Fototeca Inv. C243.

FIGURE 12 [Right]
North wall, room 5, Villa of
the Mysteries, Pompeii,
during excavation, 1909.
Note drips visible at sides,
indicating areas dampened
for photography. A nail or
bracket appears in the upper
right corner of the doorway
on the left.

Photo: Courtesy Ministero per
i Beni e le Attività Culturali,
Soprintendenza archeologica di
Pompei. Fototeca Inv. C240.

practice of applying a benzine-and-wax mixture to plaster surfaces to preserve the
ancient pigments. This technique continued under successive directors and accounts
for the waxy sheen on many walls.[36] From the first days the frescoes in room 5 were
cleaned and protected with this solution of *cera e benzina*. Fallen pieces of painted plaster were placed back on the walls "up to their full height," even though this procedure
was known to loosen plaster further, requiring yet more reinforcements. According to
a memo of May 17, such was the case with the north wall with Dionysos, which was
quickly fortified with an iron armature, the first of a series of metal braces used to
stabilize the plaster and masonry behind it [FIG. 9].

The biggest preservation problem was the presence of nitric salts, which rose up
from the ground, leached into the plaster, and created white patches on the top layer.
Between 1907 and 1908 Sogliano had introduced the use of lead strips that, when placed
into the walls or between the wall and floor, could keep water from seeping into the
plaster. In the Villa of the Mysteries, however, the lead did not fully block the seepage.[37]
To control the damaging effects of leaching, the surfaces were again cleaned repeatedly with the benzine-and-wax solution. Between May and October more drastic steps
of conservation were taken, when the masonry behind the walls was replaced with
"thirsty stones" to absorb the moisture. New, reinforced walls were constructed behind
the north wall and in the southeast and northwest corners (behind the twirling bacchante and behind the seated domina), but such an intervention was not possible
for the narrow north wall separating room 4 and room 5 because it bears frescoes on
either side.

The accounts written between May and October 1909 convey mounting anxiety
and exasperation. All measures were proceeding too slowly, including the state's purchase of land. On June 6 an earthquake shook the walls, loosening plaster above the
figure of Dionysos and bringing down antefixes and terracotta roof tiles of the portico
just outside. Most frustrating was Item's sluggish progress in fulfilling his promise to

build a protective roof for the paintings. It took him five months, during which time the rooms were alternately exposed and covered with cloth hangings, evident in early photographs [FIGS. 10–12]. On October 6 the minister wrote to the Soprintendenza that the pace of conservation was unacceptable and amounted to unjustified violence to and endangering of the precious works. Later that month the roof was completed, and a German team was brought in to conduct a thorough, professional restoration of the frescoes. Unfortunately, no details can be found in the records about this more extensive process and how it might have differed from the local methods of preceding months.

Given the anxieties reported between 1909 and 1912, it is surprising that already by 1912 the villa was accessible to visitors, if with some restrictions. Baedeker's *Southern Italy* directs the tourist to Aurelio Item's Hotel Suisse to obtain permission to see the room: "About 200 yards to the west a Villa with admirable frescoes of the Augustan period (recently purchased by the government) was unearthed in 1909, in the course of private excavations carried on by the proprietor of the Hotel Suisse...where permission to visit is obtained."[38] The itinerary leads visitors from the Herculaneum Gate down the Street of the Tombs to the end of the excavations, where, it is noted, the ancient suburbs began. Arriving at the villa, the high point in "the spacious triclinium ...is a continuous fresco, with 24 admirable figures, three-quarter lifesize, apparently representing the initiation of women into the Dionysiac mysteries." By the 1930 edition Item no longer held the key. Now the visitor requested permission at the photograph shop at the south end of the Strada del Foro, from whence a custodian would lead the way "in 6 minutes to the Villa dei Misteri Dionisiaci (or Villa Item) unearthed by Aurelio Item in 1909 with excellent frescoes...*remarkable for the freshness of their coloring*" (italics added).[39]

Such was the original discovery of the magnificent Pompeian red walls. Although it was customary in these years to remove vulnerable painted surfaces for protection, the Villa of the Mysteries frescoes were reattached to the walls, cleaned, waxed, and, when new damage occurred, repaired. They deteriorated, and eventually Maiuri's vibrant and unchanging photographic representations came to replace the altering and fragile walls themselves as documents of their true appearance.

Elusive Layers: Searching for a True Surface through Wax and Film

Fresco is an art of layering. After preparing a surface for adhesion, plaster underlayers are added and the design is sketched on a fresh coat, on top of which pigments mixed with limewater are brushed onto newer layers of fresh, damp plaster. The paint forms a chemical bond with the plaster as it dries, producing a durable surface. Since the lime plaster dries quickly, painters must continually apply new, damp plaster, so that a mural comprises a series of layers and patches created at different times. By its very nature, then, the Dionysiac frieze possesses no single original layer but is composed of multiples, made in subsequent stages during an initial campaign and probably again in later campaigns for renewal and repairs. By the time Vesuvius erupted, the walls of room 5 must have received many additions and cleanings over the previous century, long before it would see another century, the twentieth, and even more layers.

Nevertheless, the modern renown of the Villa of the Mysteries figural frieze owes much to the illusion of excellent preservation, particularly in the broad expanses of bright Pompeian red. The frescoes' legendary freshness, ironically perpetuated by cleaning and applications of wax but even more by elastic copyright laws, glosses the walls' physical history and charts a secondary life in reproductions. Maiuri's 1931 plates surpass most photographs made in the seventy-five years since; in them the frescoes certainly appear to be in a superior state of preservation to what we see in Pompeii today.

Might a closer examination of the photographs of the frieze made between 1909 and 1930 reveal some of its physical history during those two decades? At the very least the reproductions of the Villa of the Mysteries frescoes tell an important story about the role of photographs in twentieth-century scholarship, nationalism, and consumer-

FIGURE 13
Early-twentieth-century
souvenir book cover.

Photo: Courtesy Bettina Bergmann.

FIGURE 14
The Domina, west wall,
room 5, Villa of the
Mysteries, Pompeii, first
century B.C. Plate 20
from Guilio de Petra,
*Descrizione della Villa
romana* (1912).

Photo: Courtesy Northampton,
Mass., Smith College Libraries.

ism. In Pompeii that story began about the same time that Fiorelli established Pompeian archaeology as a disciplined science. In the mid-nineteenth century archaeologists began employing photography to illustrate and justify their discoveries using two standard types of documentary shots: landscape photographs recording the excavation in progress and close-ups of especially esteemed found objects, shot in isolation against a dark background.[40] (Because the primary goal of twentieth-century scholarship on the Villa of the Mysteries frieze has been to decode the meaning of the figures, photographic excerpts worked well for studies that looked to other media for iconographic parallels or prototypes. The spatial experience of the painted room was not as important in this quest for subject matter.) The archaeological photograph came to serve a more popular audience as well. By the 1870s tourists could purchase archaeological prints or customized souvenir albums with inserted shots of sites they had seen [FIG. 13]. For many these black-and-white photographs replaced the colorful, hand-painted watercolors so fashionable during the Grand Tour and later [see FIG. 6]. The scientific image of Pompeii thus developed a cachet among general consumers of travel.[41]

As soon as word spread about the discovery of the Villa of the Mysteries, several internationally distinguished scholars requested permission to photograph and publish the paintings.[42] By April 4, 1910, Petra had completed his own text, "Villa romana presso Pompei," and on June 24 the editor Francesco Gatti was given permission to print twenty plates within Petra's text in the June 1910 issue of *Notizie degli scavi degli antichità,* the official publication of the Soprintendenza. These, the first published photographic reproductions of the frescoes, were so important that Petra's article was republished separately in 1912 as *Descrizione della Villa Romana, detta Casa dei Flagellati*, by Detken and Rocholl in Naples.[43]

The black-and-white photographs accompanying Petra's short text [FIG. 14] show eye level, close-up shots of parts of painted walls, including three second-style architectural illusions of room 12, eight smaller figures on red ground in room 4, and nine figures of the Dionysiac frieze in room 5. Petra's division of figural groupings and their ordering into sequential segments that proceed clockwise around the room would become the standard treatment of the paintings.[44] The photographs focus on the figures and omit the lower and upper portions of the wall design, as do most subsequent reproductions. Although there are no views of entire rooms, Petra's photographs intentionally include corners, as well as door and window openings, giving the viewer a sense of the constructed interior. Unfortunately, the uneven quality of these early photographs makes the frescoes' state of preservation difficult to assess, but one can make out cracks, white surface blotches, and modern plaster repairs where fallen fragments have been pieced back together. Any effects of the repeated cleanings are difficult to detect.

Considering the formidable challenge of obtaining photographs for publication, one exception is of special interest. P. B. Mudie Cooke, apparently with the help of Eugenie Strong, director of the British School in Rome, was allowed to have prints made for her 1913 article. In the acknowledgments she thanks Corrado Ricci, director-general of antiquities and fine arts, for furnishing "new photographs from which the plates were prepared and for permission to publish them."[45] Yet it appears her photographs were not exactly new. Comparison with unpublished photographs in the Pompeii Fototeca, dated to 1909, as well as with Petra's 1910 illustrations, indicates that Mudie Cooke's must be among the earliest reproductions, probably made during the first weeks of excavation. The unpublished photographs show the walls still buried to the top of the socle; temporary cloth hangings gathered at the top of the wall indicate a hasty attempt at protection, and the south window remains to be fully excavated [FIGS. 8, 10–12, 15]. Some figural sections appear to have been dampened with water or benzine for the purpose of the photograph, for there are drips along the edges of the wet area, while the upper zone, left dry, is practically indecipherable. Signs of temporary interventions, such as a nail or hook in the doorframe to room 4, mark attempts to keep things in place [FIGS. 10, 12]. These same photos, it appears, were used for Mudie Cooke's article, but her publisher carefully masked the unexcavated soil and the rough edges of walls and doors, cropping the image to direct focus to the figural narrative at the expense of the surrounding decor, even to the point of erasing what little of that decor was visible at the time [FIG. 16].

Clearly at least two photo campaigns occurred between 1909 and 1910. Petra's images were made after more extensive excavation and the German team's October restoration, while Mudie Cooke received earlier excavation shots. All the photographs, of course, lack the most striking quality of the frescoes, namely, their color. Thus Francis Kelsey sought the help of Esther Van Deman to create a color facsimile and was led to the Italian artist and archaeologist Maria Barosso. Barosso's trompe l'oeil rendering of the frescoes with visible cracks and lacunae fulfilled Kelsey's wish to have the room remembered as it was in 1925, but as Elaine Gazda shows, even Barosso's scrupulous watercolor simulation could not elude the artist's subjective eye. Like Mudie Cooke's and Maiuri's doctored photographs, personal attitudes and selections

affected Barosso's manual process. In her watercolors Barosso "edited" and "cleaned" surfaces, altering the appearance of the "original" ruin [see p. 209, FIG. 2].

Any attempt to peel back the historical and physical layers of the frescoes clearly challenges the eye. The contradictory states of the walls in early reproductions reveal as much about the current state of photography and about the problematic ambient lighting of the villa as they do about the physical condition of the frieze. But they also show changes throughout the frieze that suggest damage or restoration. For example, two photographs of the southeast wall published in the 1938 volume by Pirro Marconi indicate loss to the upper layer of the kneeling woman's drapery. One, taken by Vittorio Spinazzola sometime before 1924, shows her billowing purple garment intact [FIG. 17]. The next plate, by Fratelli Alinari, reveals significant loss on the outer left edge, where pigment appears to have flaked off [FIG. 18].

Disparities between Maiuri's pristine photographs of 1931 and Barosso's 1926 watercolors thus raise the question of whether these differences betray alterations to the wall surface in the intervening few years. Or did different understandings of ancient painting affect the ways the images were reproduced? Confusion about how Roman muralists worked, it seems, has further complicated perception and treatment of the walls. In his 1910 article Petra states the prevailing view that the ancient painting technique at the villa was *tempera forte, non a buon fresco*, that is, made of powdered pigments mixed with water and some kind of binder like egg yolk or casein.[46] Twenty years later Maiuri instead argued for true, *buon fresco* without tempera.[47] Yet the person who spent the longest period looking closely at the walls, Maria Barosso, was convinced that the paintings were encaustic, with wax colors fused to the surface by heat.[48] Already in 1913 Mudie Cooke believed the walls to be of wax, and both Mudie Cooke and Barosso remarked that the murals appeared quite "flat," a curious statement considering the reflective sheen we see today but substantiated by a spot cleaning in 2003 [see p. 211, FIG. 4].[49] Were scholar and artist seeing ancient or early-twentieth-century wax layers? How much were they informed about the numerous treatments to the walls' surfaces done in the months and years following the first excavation? Not one comments on restorations. Unfortunately, these questions must remain unanswered. Since official photographs and reports cease with the growing tension of World War I, we will never know what transpired during the frescoes' first two decades above ground or among Mudie Cooke's 1909 photographs, Barosso's 1926 watercolors, and Maiuri's trichrome plates of 1930.[50]

Whatever the original technique, the twentieth-century protective layers gave the frescoes an altered, modern appearance. At the turn of the century and some places still today, wax was used as a panacea in conservation and thought to do no wrong. Applied to polish, brighten, or protect, the wax that is left behind (benzine eventually evaporates) can produce a hard, shiny surface, inclined to darken and collect dust. The dramatic alterations to a fresco's appearance was clear to the American scholar Nita Butler, who in 1933 examined Roman frescoes in the Naples museum just after they had been cleaned and their accreted layers removed: "Destruction and deterioration, continuing today despite all efforts to protect the walls, permit us to observe certain details that would otherwise have remained unseen. Among the most prolific causes of decay . . . [is the] too assiduous cleaning of the walls. . . . The preservative 'varnish' applied to the walls darkens and thickens with age. It has recently been removed from most of the paintings in the Naples Museum; the results at first seemed splendid, but the pictures now seem to be deteriorating even there."

As a result of this deterioration, and of the newly visible underlayers, Butler believed she could determine the ancient craftsman's process: "After observation and examination of the walls for many years I have come to the conclusion that the entire surface of the walls was painted in *buon fresco*, with the figures or pictures generally in tempera."[51] (Specialists still disagree about whether Roman fresco involved wax or tempera, but most now believe that walls are primarily *buon fresco*, with some details added *a secco*.)[52]

Brilliant crimson red—the boldest, most dramatic hue of the color spectrum—is the Mysteries frescoes' striking visual feature. Its chemical makeup has been another subject of debate. From the beginning, scholars saw the vivid red pigment as the valuable mineral ore of cinnabar so esteemed by ancient authors.[53] The aura of this luxury pigment added to the frescoes' and the villa's modern renown. But such intense color and luster can be achieved with the less expensive red ocher, a native clay containing iron oxide that was often used as a layer beneath cinnabar, just as it is still used as the underlayer for burnished gilding. As a topcoat, ocher can be polished to a high sheen and is difficult to distinguish from cinnabar. Ocher is also relatively permanent and able to withstand wind and rain. Other suggestions have been vermilion, made from mercuric sulfide, or hematite, an iron ore occurring in large deposits. Recent tests confirm the presence of cinnabar. In any case, the Pompeian red seen since 1909 is not the same as that seen by Romans in A.D. 79, as illustrated by the cleaning in 2003 [see p. 211, FIG. 4].[54]

The luminous color and apparent freshness of the frescoes have always amazed visitors to the room. It is curious that in his 1931 study Maiuri omitted mention of the repeated interventions to the surfaces of the first years, claiming that the frescoes were still in an excellent state of preservation, displaying *freschezza* and immediacy.[55] Yet the years of cleaning and restoration added to and subtracted from the frescoes, and these and other incidents of damage and loss have shaped our modern perception of the frieze. While wax offered protection and solidified the colors, with each new layer came visual alterations that can never be completely removed. Wax radically changed the matte quality the frescoes once had, thwarting any modern search for their original appearance.[56]

▣ ▣ ▣

The villa has a unique history, for its layers exist both as physical accretions and as intangible layers in photographs and other reproductions. This dual history is rooted in the moment of discovery, when a new technology was transforming the nature of the work of art and the "recuperative quest of the past."[57] Seemingly more accurate than the earlier, hand-drawn mementoes, the black-and-white photographic excerpt carried pleasurable associations with travel, high culture, and material possession. New photos of Fiorelli's human casts, for example, translated the odd and strange into familiar aesthetic formats, the same formats as those of reproductions of Vesuvius and the Dionysiac murals, and made them images a person could own [see p. 179, FIGS. 4–5]. If the ideas of Walter Benjamin come to mind, it is worth noting that in radio broadcasts to children made during the very years Maiuri excavated and published his opus on the villa, Benjamin compared the astonishing fidelity of human "imprints" captured by Vesuvius's ashes with the fraudulent copies of contemporary prints.[58]

Such comments speak as well to the seemingly miraculous preservation of certain parts of the frieze, for example, the pristine pale body of the kneeling, whipped woman as she appears in the very earliest photographs, taken when volcanic debris lay still unexcavated over the socle, appearing distinct from all around her, almost like a "human imprint" fully preserved [FIG. 17].

Benjamin claimed that the presence of the original is the prerequisite of authenticity.[59] Authenticity is a main goal of tourism. For visitors in the early twentieth century, the persuasive new medium of photographs offered the illusion of being there again or of possessing the archaeological artifact.[60] It was hardly a problem that the pictures captured entirely different aspects of the Dionysiac frescoes from those the tourist's eye could ever see. Reproductions enhanced the impact and memory of the frescoes and, by liberating them from the context of ruins, multiplied their function in unforeseen ways. It is these reproducible, mobile layers that have been the more powerful in perpetuating memories of room 5.

The reader may well ask what, so far, does this attempt to excavate the early written and visual records of the Villa of the Mysteries reveal, beyond a series of reactions and efforts to record? One important fact, I believe, becomes eminently clear, namely, how unattainable is the desired access to an original appearance of the Roman frescoes, for this quest is always mediated by a reflexive self-consciousness around the subsequent historical, environmental, and pictorial interventions that their surfaces have undergone.

In a speech about the Dionysiac frescoes delivered to the British Academy in 1963, G. Zuntz voiced the commonly held belief about the dangers of reproductions: "That inexhaustible essence of a great work of art is conveyed by the original, and only the original.... Our eyes and minds have been so corrupted by the incessant parade of mechanical replicas that we are liable to forget how essentially every photograph falsifies its model; the more dangerously so the more exquisite it be.... Our mind deceives our eyes even before the very originals, effacing them and putting in their place the familiar dead counterfeits, and a strenuous and ever-repeated effort is needed to rid ourselves of the corruption."[61]

As we strip the documentation layer from layer, we reach not a pure ancient surface but multiple levels of transformation, and from these new discoveries comes a more urgent question: Can the modern viewer, in fact, ever experience the authenticity of the villa in terms of (or despite) its multiplicity of photographic representations and historical meanings? And if so, how?[62]

PART TWO

The second part of this essay shifts the line of questioning from a study of surface to explore the frescoes' less visible, subterranean connections. It considers "the familiar dead counterfeits" so lamented by Zuntz, not as corrupting fakes but as creative responses essential to understanding how we see the ancient work. The many acts of recording and reconstruction, be they archaeological, psychoanalytic, or cinematic, have produced a history of accretion parallel to those surveyed in the previous sections of the essay, which, although not physically altering the wall surfaces, equally filters our perception of the frieze.

Archaeology of the Psyche:
Personal Discoveries and Erotic Narratives

The Villa of the Mysteries frieze has played a key role in twentieth-century debates about the psyche, religion, sexuality, and gender. What emerges from both the physical and metaphorical strata is the compunction of individuals to bore back in time, through acts of reconstruction, to connect with an original, whether it be an original appearance or an original meaning, and thereby come to terms with the contemporary self. These ever-multiplying creations endow the frescoes with their transhistorical, archetypal power. The following sections show how the Dionysiac frescoes lead in quite different directions but interconnect in the realms of allegory and fantasy about body and mind.

By the time the villa's frescoes came to light in 1909, Pompeii had penetrated into European consciousness from a century and a half of visits, images, literary musings, and spectacles. The naked, mysterious women on vivid red walls only amplified the sensationalism of the site. Consider the earliest public announcement of the frescoes' discovery to the American public, in 1911, which notes the figures' illusionism, their enigmatic poses and eroticism, highlighting the unusual

> detachment of the figures from their surroundings, in which almost the modern idea of perspective is maintained. This is particularly noticeable in a group of dancing girls, one of whom is to be beaten for some fault committed, or, more probably, in accordance with the Hellenic rite of flagellation. In other pictures unearthed in the same villa—evidently the summer abode of a Roman exquisite—this same detachment may be observed: in "A Virgin felling from an Orgie," "Women Indifferent to the Predictions of Silenus," and "A Woman Being Initiated into the Dionysian Mysteries."

And, of course, the excellent condition is emphasized: "This dwelling has been found to be one of the most *perfectly preserved*" (italics added).[63]

The erotic female of Pompeii was already the focus of several intersecting currents within intellectual circles in Europe and the United States. Ancient woman came to perform a central role in the first moving images of cinematic Pompeii, in drawings and paintings of contemporary artists, and in the practice of psychoanalysis. On the one hand, she inspired a retrospective nostalgia by embodying the memory of paganism and the coming of Christianity. On the other hand, as excavation became a metaphor for the personal quest, she became emblematic of modern woman and instrumental for her self-discovery.[64]

The myth of the ancient female was integral to the stratigraphic model of the psyche articulated by Sigmund Freud, an armchair archaeologist and collector who had visited Pompeii and climbed Vesuvius in 1902.[65] Comparing dreams to archaeological finds, Freud describes "how dreams sometimes bring to light, as it were, from beneath the deepest piles of debris under which the earliest experiences of youth are buried in later times, pictures of particular localities, things or people, completely intact and *with all their original freshness*" (italics added).[66] Although the villa frescoes were not Freud's direct concern, they appeared on the scene just as Pompeii and its excavation, female sexuality, and the individual psyche registered as interconnected symbols

FIGURE 19
Edmund Engelman (Austrian, 1907–2000), Sigmund Freud's study in Vienna with cast of Gradiva on wall at right, 1938.

Photo: © Edmund Engelman. Courtesy Freud Museum, London.

among European artists and intellectuals. The painted women would soon be adopted by Freud's followers, who both perpetuated and analyzed a tradition that had begun in the eighteenth century, namely, a male pursuit among Pompeii's ruins for a woman, true love, and, ultimately, the self.[67] Freud explored the theme in his essay about the 1903 novella by Wilhelm Jensen, *Gradiva: Ein pompejanisches Phantasiestück*, the story of a German archaeologist, Norbert Hanold, who returns from Rome with the cast of a marble relief depicting a dancing maiden.[68] In a dream the marble maiden awakens Hanold's desire. Envisioning her living in Pompeii, he goes to find her and, once there, stumbles on a female face imprinted in lava, whereupon he suddenly realizes that the dream's protagonist is a woman he once loved in his own past.[69] Not finding her (after looking, incidentally, at the Hotel Suisse), Hanold finally encounters his lost German love in the Villa of Diomedes, the popular tourist stop near our villa.

While Jensen's *Gradiva* follows the popular nineteenth-century theme of male infatuation with a female phantom, Freud linked the fantasy with the construction of the male ego. Pompeii is the site where man's erotic impulse combines with his fight against mortality to discover the original self. Key to this discovery in Freud's essay, "Delusions and Dreams in Jensen's *Gradiva*," is the sensual arousal induced by an ancient, fragmentary object.[70] So taken was Freud with the tale of Gradiva that he himself purchased a plaster copy of the relief on a trip to Rome in 1907 and hung it above the couch in his study [FIG. 19].[71] Thereafter Gradiva became an emblem of the therapeutic-psychoanalytic method, as Freud's followers dutifully purchased and hung the Pompeian muse on their office walls.[72]

Freud's views had a major impact on romantic attitudes about the erotics of excavation among an educated and well-traveled European elite. The eminent art historian and contemporary Aby Warburg, for example, followed Freud in seeking personal enlightenment through the artistic image of a female. Of his Nympha, another striding maiden with fluttering garments, Warburg asked: "Have I encountered her before?

I mean one and a half millennia earlier?"[73] The sexuality of the painted women in the Dionysiac frieze likewise inspired hyperbole. Amedeo Maiuri: "After 19 centuries of burial in volcanic lava, the modeling of the naked bodies still elicits a sensuous response.... A recent critic has commented: 'Who could fail to be fascinated by the voluptuous bodies of the woman brandishing the whip, the suffering girl, and the dancer, by the proudly out-thrust breasts, the trembling delicate shoulders, and the harmonious movement of her hips — three hallmarks of feminine grace, all magnificently depicted? There is no doubt that the paintings in the Villa of the Mysteries occupy a special place in the history of erotic art.'"[74]

Some twenty-four years after the publication of "Delusions and Dreams," Maiuri acknowledged Freud's Pompeian "excavation" and Gradiva's significance in an article for the Neapolitan press but voiced skepticism that a true archaeologist like Norbert Hanold (and by implication, Freud) should be taken by such a mediocre relief, in a plaster copy no less.[75] Nevertheless, Gradiva served to integrate psychoanalysis into extant paradigms and thereby transform them. Norbert Hanold's journey, it has been argued, can be seen as "the passing from a disenchantment with one system of knowledge to a recovery of fascination in another. Each system is represented by a woman and the transition is effected through a forgetting and subsequent remembering of language."[76]

Gradiva became a metaphor for transcendence through deep tunneling and excavation. By the 1930s the Villa of the Mysteries had assumed a direct role in the Gradiva phenomenon, whose afterlife revived with the translation of Jensen's novella into French in 1931, the same year that Maiuri's resplendent volume on the villa appeared. A cult of the ancient feminine was gaining momentum among the surrealists, and André Masson, Salvador Dalí, and André Breton envisioned Gradiva as a female personification of transition "from death to life, dream to wakefulness, unconsciousness to consciousness."[77] For his 1939 painting *Gradiva* Masson invoked the Dionysiac frieze, which he himself had sketched. Whitney Chadwick observes of the painting: "The compression of images, the type of condensation found in dream imagery, contributes to the painting's spatial dislocation. The background of the painted paneling suggests the interior of a Pompeian house."[78] That Gradiva possessed a superhuman spatial power for this artistic circle emerges from both Breton's and Dalí's descriptions of her as a "piercer of walls," able to intercede between the real and the surreal, not unlike the full-bodied women in the Villa of the Mysteries whose energy seems to be released from the deep red, so that they hover between our space and another.[79]

For some viewers it was not so much the erotic women but the mysterious vertical object about to be unveiled that mattered. As early as 1913 Mudie Cooke had identified the hidden object as a phallus. In 1958 Jacques Lacan made this scene central to his theory of the patriarchal law of the father. Critiquing Freud's analysis of female inspiration as an example of transference, Lacan saw the unveiling of the phallus and, to the right, the winged, female demon wielding the whip as symbolic of the true issues of psychoanalysis, namely, the sexual shame and castration anxiety that arise from any exposure of the genitals.[80] Taking Lacan's theory further, his follower Bice Benvenuto explains: "the ancient Mysteries and the unveiling of the Phallus prefigure discoveries in Lacanian psychoanalysis about the symbol, the feminine and the sacred.... Both the clinical and the symbolic threads together in a new theory of feminine sexuality which takes up where Lacan drew the veil."[81]

The Essential Female:
Modern and Ancient Women in the Red Room

Defining feminine sexuality became the major relevance of the Dionysiac frieze to the later twentieth century. The authors of these definitions, it is worth noting, range widely in discipline, academic stature, and influence, reaching diverse sectors of society. Since the 1960s, for example, female Jungian analysts have invested the Villa of the Mysteries frieze with a vital role. Seeing Dionysos as a woman's god and the source of her sensuality, Jung encouraged his female students to turn to the frieze and collaborate in his own fantasy of women, dreams, and images. Between the 1960s and the 1980s several women wrote books engaging with the frescoes. Cropped color photographs of individual scenes represent symbolic moments in a woman's life; seen as a sequence, the frieze charts a path for the female psyche moving through the painful process of self-knowledge. In 1957 Jung's close associate Linda Fierz-David wrote *Psychologische Betrachtungen zu der Freskenfolge der Villa der Misteri in Pompeii: Ein Versuch*, which reads the frieze as a dream sequence that offers a key to the mysteries of modern woman's midlife crises: "It is the typical primeval experience of a human being who, instead of looking at the frescoes in the Villa of the Mysteries esthetically or archaeologically, experiences the psychic reality radiating from them." For Fierz-David and her colleagues the frieze embodies an archetype of the female individuation process whereby the modern initiate engages in a concentrated experience that connects her with ancient initiates through a "communal ecstasy and exaltation."[82]

Reconstruction of the frieze could take the form of live performance. To partake in the experience firsthand, some women have traveled to Pompeii and physically inserted themselves into the space. By reenacting a cult drama handed down by tradition, they witness the divine reality itself, moment by moment. The frescoes mediate between the human and the divine in these transcendent rituals. Katherine Bradway described her thoughts in 1982: "Here I was, in a room to which women—two thousand years before me—had come in anticipation, apprehension, or even dread to experience something which they had been told would change them in an indescribable way. The quest of the Roman woman appears to be paralleled in many ways by that of the twentieth century woman, who has also experienced the unrest of significant social transitions."[83]

The "original" sought in these quests is not the Roman appearance of the murals, nor even their ancient meaning, but a universal and timeless female experience. Bradway recognizes a connection between the Roman and the twentieth-century woman, failing to note that the Roman women she sees are merely representations; through reenactment she can gain access to their ancient, long-dead counterparts. Indeed, in nearly all reconstructions of the Dionysiac frieze, photographs of the frescoes have guided the way to iconographic identifications, sometimes to the actual villa itself, other times inspiring a virtual visit.[84] Several artists, for example, re-created the frieze to place themselves graphically into the groupings [FIG. 20].[85] The painter Patricia Olson relates how the photographs in *Those Women* by Nor Hall (1988) inspired a series of oil paintings with herself as an initiate in the frieze. "In reflecting on the reproductions printed in *Those Women*, I resolved to follow this ritual inner journey myself, by retelling my story as a contemporary woman, using the murals of the Villa

of the Mysteries as touchstone and guide. Placing my body into the Roman initiation story, I claim a bond with the old mysteries."[86] Nor Hall herself, who wrote the introduction to Olson's exhibition catalogue, reaffirms the mystical connection between past and present made possible through artistic re-creation: "Perhaps because she is a painter, Olson goes directly to the imagistic core of the Mysteries without getting stopped by the conceptual question of who this Dionysos is."[87] The "imagistic core"— yet another kind of original—thus can be reached in a creative attempt to reanimate the ancient ritual.

Importantly in such narratives, the desire to reconnect ultimately succeeds where the use of logic or reason to decode meaning fails. The message is that women possess the instinctual means to re-enter their cyclical history. The identification of modern women with their perceived ancient counterparts finds its most theoretical and feminist champion in Hélène Cixous, whose concept of *l'écriture féminine*, articulated in the 1970s, focused on women's struggle for identity. Writing in 1980, Cixous considers the woman bearing the tray, seen by some as pregnant, and claims that it matters not whether she really is pregnant, for she is "psychologically and symbolically pregnant with herself." The enigma of the frieze, she explains, speaks to the universal riddle of the sexes: "life has traditionally been seen as the secret OF women, a secret FROM men." The indecipherability of the visual narrative is a language of women—mysterious, secret, contained—comprehensible only by a woman coming and going through the cycles of her life. In fact, the domina, with lips half open and chin on hand, looks out over the murals from near the doorway, as if from the outside [see FIG. 14]. Cixous argues that the whole narrative is, in fact, the domina's personal vision. Gazing absently into the middle distance and not taking any personal part, she sees "herself in years past entering, through marriage, into the realm of Dionysus...recalling her self-realization in devotion to her god."[88] The domina, in essence, symbolizes the viewer's own dialogical relation with the frescoes.

Both authors, inspired by Jungian doctrine and feminist theory, articulate a particularly female, intuitive attraction to the murals. It is interesting to note that even in the early modern history of the Dionysiac frescoes the most acute scholarly analyses were also by women: Mudie Cooke (1913), Barosso (1926), Bieber (1928), and Toynbee (1929). Each played a role in defining methods within the new academic disciplines of art history and classics. The connection between these twentieth-century academic women and later psychologists and writers is established by Nor Hall, a psychotherapist, scholar, and poet.[89] Building on Fierz-David and Bradway, Hall envisions a mystery chamber where ten scenes of dramatic initiation frame the experiences of death, maenadic madness, and the changes to women in midlife. But her scenario includes the analytical classicist's response along with the poetic and spiritual quest, as she invokes the great scholar Jane Harrison (who prefaced her *Epilegomena* on ancient religions by acknowledging her debt to Freud and Jung) and the poet H.D. (Hilda Doolittle), a patient of Freud's.[90] The line between analysis and creative response blurs. In fact, during one of her famous lectures Harrison performed the Villa of the Mysteries frieze by unveiling a liknon, the winnowing fan holding the phallic herm, fusing objective scholarship and intuitive response.[91]

The engagement with the frescoes by women throughout the century thus captured that tension between the analytical, "scientific" search for the ancient original and the personal, inspired search for the self that characterizes so many responses to the villa. To Cixous, as to Nor Hall and other female writers and artists, the woman's epiphany is the man's mystery. For Freud, Hanold, and others in the first half of the twentieth century, man resolves the mystery of the self through an epiphany of his female counterpart. The late twentieth century saw a twist to this essential gender duality when the frieze experienced a new afterlife in the spiritual and sexual quest of male artists. In his small watercolor *Turnstile* of 1994 [FIG. 21], Wes Christensen renders the whipping figure in black leather and places her in a domestic interior before a poster of the winged figure from Tony Kushner's *Angels in America*. Attracted to the "elusive meaning" of the ancient frieze, Christensen claims that it "plays right into our contemporary coæncerns with 'implied narrative' imagery, which purposely presents ambiguous scenarios to our audience in an attempt to engage viewers in a sort of conversation about what the meaning actually is." In another inversion, David Cannon Dashiell's *Queer Mysteries* (1993) renders the same scene to reflect the self, but sexual identities become complicated in this artist's autobiographical, cross-gender reconstruction.[92] One wonders whether the shock experienced by viewers of Dashiell's graphic sex scene is greater or less than the shock incited by the initial sight of naked women on red walls in 1909.

In their modern history the murals of room 5 operate on several levels of gender analysis. I began the essay with a distinctive tradition of female scholars pursuing meaning in the frescoes, from the early encounters of Mudie Cooke and Maria Barosso to the present author. There are the Pompeian phantoms of Freudian dreams, the pregnant feminine of Cixous's essentialist vision, and Jung's female followers seeking to connect with the ur-feminine. Artists re-create the murals and immerse themselves in the ancient mysteries, sometimes problematizing the very categories of male and female so embedded in traditional theories about the frieze. Then there are the women who are depicted on the walls themselves and the fantasies that they incite. If there is

FIGURE 21
Wes Christensen (American, b. 1949), *Turnstile*, 1994. Watercolor and pencil. Private collection.

Photo: Courtesy Koplin Del Rio Gallery, Los Angeles.

just one woman undergoing stages of a ritual, why is the winged female whipping a naked, kneeling woman and another having her hair braided before Eros? On every level the individual pursuit projects new fantasies and new layers of meaning onto the Roman frescoes.

The last section of the essay looks at judgments about pagan hedonism and sexuality embodied by the Dionysiac women and at the cinematic and artistic manifestations of those judgments in specific political climates.

Animating Pictures of Pagan Sex, Mysteries, and Political Decline

The Dionysiac murals, we should remember, were not conceived by their painters or patron to address a global audience in photographic excerpts as they do today. They were meant to be experienced in an enclosed room and from different viewpoints over time [see FIG. 2]. In a sustained encounter, the patient viewer who is allowed entry can observe a complex interplay of the figures in fluctuating light on four surrounding walls. As surfaces reflect, the inhabitant of the space never loses sight of the self as viewed and held within the room's visual field.[93] This theatrical inclusion of an observer is enhanced by the illusionistic stage-space on which the figures move, dramatically lit, and, above all, by the figures' interactions and glances exchanged across corners and between walls. The barrier between fictive and real dissolves, as the women and creatures consistently alert and engage us, inviting our participation. It should not surprise, then, that the liveliest responses to the frieze have involved performance and movement, both within the room and from afar.

At the time of the villa's discovery in the early 1900s, live performance was finding its most mimetic replication in history. The new technology of the moving image offered a startlingly realistic experience of the classical past, and the vibrant, painted figures in room 5 assumed a topical resonance.[94] Of course, a desire for immersion within a virtual Pompeii had stimulated theatrical reenactments since the first discoveries of the 1700s, but the Villa of the Mysteries frieze was discovered when cinema was developing a novel popular image of the Lost City. Key in the visual narrative of pagan and imperial decline were the 1908 and 1913 productions of *Gli ultimi giorni di Pompei*, films based on Edward Bulwer-Lytton's famous 1834 novel featuring the female love-object Ione, a prefiguration of Freudian phantoms ("Love her, and you entered into a new world, you passed from this trite and common-place earth"). The 1908 silent melodrama was one of the first grand film epics, re-creating the eruption of Vesuvius in an unprecedented spectacle by adapting the forms of pyrodramas, Victorian painting, and nineteenth-century stage designs. The recurring tableaux of figural scenes, not unlike those in the Dionysiac frieze, were reused again and again in remakes of the film through the 1920s.[95] A fundamental change came in 1924, the same year that Maiuri assumed power in Pompeii and two years after Mussolini formed L'unione cinematografia educativa. There followed a very different adaptation of *Gli ultimi giorni di Pompei* (1926): now, the camera tracks through the excavations just as they would have looked to a visitor in the 1920s, with dramatic displays of Roman women dancing and being flagellated, thus appealing to the current taste for archaeological exactitude, brutality, and sensuality.[96] The themes and scenes are familiar: a lost beloved among the ashes, frenzied women in sexual abandon, salvation with the coming of Christianity.

If the erotic violence and female nudity of the Villa of the Mysteries and early cinema personified the fall of Roman civilization, the eruption of Vesuvius signaled divine punishment for Pompeii's wayward pagan excesses. In creating their sets Italian filmmakers were fully aware of modern reconstructions and of the actual rebuilding at Pompeii, including Maiuri's completed Villa of the Mysteries. In turn, it is hard to believe that the master rebuilder Maiuri was not influenced by cinematic re-creations of Pompeii's fall, especially considering his own descriptions of Pompeii linking the uninhibited women in the Dionysiac frieze with the fall of paganism. Speaking of a visitor's day at the ruins, for example, he presents the itinerary as a dramatic historical narrative:

> Thus, after having walked amid streets, squares, temples, houses, works and shops, after having listened to the different multitudes in search of pleasure and wealth, the peace and silence of the [Street of the Tombs] have led us, by a strange fate, to the threshold of a house where the anxious fever of the spirit, human bounds, find their human and divine expression in the religion of the mysteries. Thus the last voice we are able to catch of the newly-risen Pompeii, is the profound and eternal one of a spiritual drama, a drama that tormented and comforted a few elect souls, whilst, little by little, the religion of their fathers was slowly dying out and the new faith from the east [Christianity] was beginning its victorious advance.[97]

In setting this scene the premier Italian archaeologist of the twentieth century gives the Dionysiac frescoes a starring role in Rome's degeneracy and fall. But Maiuri was not the first to see the painted room as containing the secrets of three-thousand-year-old pagan rituals, which contained the seeds of Christianity. In 1926 the *New York Times* reported that Vittorio Macchioro had "the distinction of being the discoverer of the key to the secret of the 'Mystery Villa,' an old orphic temple built outside the walls of Pompeii to avoid restrictions on the cult." In the article Macchioro is quoted as claiming that "this same idea of spiritual rebirth and regeneration lies at the bottom of the Christian rite of communion."[98]

The intertextual responses of cinema, archaeology, politics, and cultural history to the painted images in room 5 were undoubtedly influenced by the status of discourses on Dionysos and on sadomasochistic sexuality and derepression during the early part of the twentieth century. The critical text in these years about collective understandings of the Dionysiac, Friedrich Nietzsche's *Birth of Tragedy* (1872), was tremendously important in establishing a broader cultural discourse about the polarized qualities of Apollonian reason and rationality versus Dionysian sensuality, ecstasy, and mysticism. The Dionysiac signifier shaped art-historical, as well as archaeological, accounts of such themes produced during the period, especially with the popularization of Freudian discourse in the 1910s and 1920s. Calls for derepression around modernist abstract painting resemble those around the Pompeian frescoes, despite their completely distinctive formal and iconographic qualities.[99]

In following decades the Dionysiac features of the frieze inspired quotation for political purposes. Pablo Picasso, for example, visited the villa in 1917 and knew the frieze through its publication in books and popular magazines. In 1944, in the wake of French victory, Picasso evoked the communal Dionysiac promise of transcendence

and rebirth by celebrating the Parisian insurrection against Nazi Germany with a watercolor and gouache called *The Triumph of Pan* (location unknown), a reworking of Poussin's 1636 painting of the same title (National Gallery, London). In rendering the face of Pan, Picasso emulated the mask held by the satyr [see p. 212, FIG. 5], and in his 1960 lithograph *Hommage à Pan*, he returned to the scene to represent in reverse the same satyr gazing into the bowl beside the god Dionysos.[100]

But although certain features have been excerpted to specific ends, it is the erotic women of the Villa of the Mysteries frieze that continue to inspire and assume the most effective new lives. Especially since the explosion of widespread color reproduction in the 1970s, glossy red excerpts of the bold dancing and whipping figures lure visitors to the site, and as advertisements, book covers, and images on the Internet they serve to reinforce familiar notions of lurid, pagan eroticism. The nude female body twisting in wild abandon, her fluttering garment swinging around her exposed buttocks, especially signals Pompeii as "sin city" and hints at the titillating, frivolous energy of a less-repressive time. The nude women of the Dionysiac frieze have made cameo appearances in such fantastic re-creations and parodies of classical antiquity as Fellini's *Satyricon* (1970) and Monty Python's *Life of Brian* (1979) as well as in the television miniseries *The Last Days of Pompeii* (1984) and *Rome* (2005) [FIG. 22]. The frescoes' future afterlives in this twenty-first century are guaranteed to proliferate through film, whereby simulations engender ever-new fantasies and reconstructions.

The Modern Visit

For visitors to Pompeii the red room beckons from the moment they arrive at the train station. The villa still lies at the end of the tourist itinerary and is the goal of a day touring the ruined city, where at last one stands behind a rope and briefly glimpses the familiar, animated figures as cameras flash into the shuttered room. Yet despite their proximity, the figures' actions remain enigmatic. The faces display no emotions, with vacant expressions or averted eyes. Psychologically, the characters stay out of reach. Indeed, one could say that the entire viewing experience in the room is about looking while not being able to see. The scenes seem to play with us, offering up clues and then taking them away. Look, for example, at the seated woman holding her arm over the boy's shoulder and pointing with her pen at the roll from which he reads, presumably aloud [see FIG. 12]. She shows him what we cannot see and he says words we cannot hear. What of the two young satyrs, one looking out at us as does the animated mask he holds, while the other gazes into a bowl at something we cannot see [see FIG. 15]? Ancient viewers must have understood the rules of engagement and enjoyed the ongoing game of revelation and concealment, as figures obscure, unveil, or lift layers. What, for instance, lies beneath the cover being lifted from the table that is blocked by the woman sitting with her back to us [see FIG. 2, left]? And we remain in perpetual anticipation as the kneeling woman uncovers something—could it be, as scholars imagine, a sacred phallus [see FIG. 9]?

Viewers allowed beyond the rope and into the room can create a narrative sequence by moving in any direction. In this experience, the meaning of the ten separate scenes changes depending on which one comes into focus: from a bride's preparation for a wedding, to a satyr play or pantomime, or secret initiations into a cult. Indeed, the room speaks less to a rational, chronological reading and more to an associative, intuitive response.[101] Of one thing we can be fairly sure: ancient visitors did not stand behind a rope or walk around the room as in a picture gallery. If we can trust Romans' accounts of time spent in such villa spaces, a viewer approaching the entrance might well have witnessed a group of carousing, reclining diners seeming to mingle with the painted celebration going on behind them, where, at the axial center of the room, a woman lounges beside the god Dionysos, the only anthropomorphic figure among all twenty-nine that we can surely identify.

On leaving the villa, before memory can begin to fade, we are greeted with reproductions of the red walls at souvenir stands and restaurants on the road called the Via della Villa dei Misteri. The frieze is so embedded in the visitor's experience of Pompeii that one unconsciously experiences an initiation from the moment of arrival at this strange otherworld of the archaeological site.

IN SUM

The past century has been a story of the interplay among representations and changing modes of viewing. Photography, the medium through which we customarily see and know the world, can take us closer to the frescoes than can the naked eye. But the more we see, the more elusive is that layer the Roman eye might have seen. The Villa of the Mysteries frieze as we know it can never be an ancient original. It consists of multiple strata of matter as it does of the muffled interpretations of a long century.

A few central metaphors emerge from this historical excavation. Far from perpetually fresh, the frescoes emerge as eternally frail, delicate, almost lost. The very stability of the murals' instability resonates with a universal, human anxiety about the passage of time and with the collective urge, especially at the turn of the past century (and, it seems again, at present), to reexperience the past. Second, the frescoes are emblems of a tension that is pervasive in and formative of current culture, namely, the tension between highly motile images and their fixed contexts. Third, accounts of archaeological reconstruction, psychosexual interpretations of subjectivity, regenerations of selfhood in the wake of derepression, and the great cyclical narratives of the history of civilizations all turn to the Dionysiac murals for shared promises of self-knowledge, liberation, and rebirth. In attempting to historicize and reconstruct the recurrent manifestation of these transhistorical patterns, associative and intuitive responses ultimately trump rational ones. The Villa of the Mysteries then takes on a larger, timeless quality, serving as an allegory of the frailty of physical existence and the ephemerality of presence. What lies beneath the twentieth-century layers may well enlighten us about the materials and techniques of ancient painting. But, true to the nature of the frescoes, the painted inhabitants of room 5 will continue to equivocate, defer, and play their coy games with future generations of rapt viewers.

Should we conclude, then, that the search to understand how people in the days of the first century of the first millennium saw the murals ultimately is an exercise in futility? On the contrary, if one acknowledges that our version of the past must always be mediated, we may, through careful scrutiny of the history and forms of that mediation, better distinguish antiquity's own forms of mediation. The Dionysiac murals may themselves be a re-creation of a lost Greek original or of an earlier Roman copy of that Greek original. But that has been and will continue to be the subject of other studies.

Notes

I would like to thank Elaine Gazda for first inviting me to think about this topic for a keynote address in conjunction with the 2000 exhibition *The Villa of the Mysteries in Pompeii: Ancient Ritual, Modern Muse* at the University of Michigan, Ann Arbor, and for sharing many fascinating hours at the villa. The following people read and offered invaluable warnings and suggestions: Marcia Brennan, Richard Brilliant, Darcy Buerkle, Michael T. Davis, Barbara Kellum, Dana Leibsohn, Karen Remmler, Patricia Simons, and Elizabeth Young. I am, as always, extremely grateful to Dottore Stefano de Caro and Dottore Pietro Giovanni Guzzo for allowing me access to the villa, the Fototeca, and the archives in Naples and Pompeii. The editors of this volume have been exemplary in their encouragement and close attention.

[1] The same year that Mussolini visited Naples, Maiuri became director of the Museo archeologico di Napoli and replaced Vittorio Spinazzola as Soprintendente. Fausto Zevi, "La storia degli scavi e della documentazione," *Pompei, 1748–1980: I tempi della documentazione* (Rome, 1981), 11–21; Antonio Varone, *Pompei: I misteri di una città sepolta. Storia e segreti di un luogo in cui la vita di è fermata duemila anni fa* (Rome, 2000), 291–95. Amedeo Maiuri, *Mestiere d'archeologo: Antologia di scritti*, ed. Carlo Belli (Milan, 1978). For a bibliography of works about Maiuri and a list of his own publications, see Laurentino García y García, *Nova biblioteca pompeiana, 250 anni di bibliografia archeologia* (Rome, 1998), 747–66.

[2] Progress of the excavations could be followed in short reports in foreign journals: A. W. Van Buren, "Art and Activities in Italy," *Archaeological News* (1929): 439–40; idem, "Recent Art Activities in Rome," *Parnassus* (1931): 17–18.

[3] Many texts mistakenly date the discovery of the villa to Maiuri's time: Colin Amery and Brian Curran, Jr., *The Lost World of Pompeii* (Los Angeles, 2002), 187 ("1929–30: The Villa of the Mysteries is discovered"); Marcel Brion, *Pompeii: The Glory and the Grief* (New York, 1962), 151.

[4] Amedeo Maiuri, *La Villa dei Misteri* (1931; 2d ed., Rome, 1947).

5   Jocelyn M. C. Toynbee in *Journal of Roman Studies* 24 (1934): 236–39.

6   In the preface to the 1931 edition (note 4), Maiuri writes: "La tavole in tricromia sono il frutto di diligenti e ripetute correzioni fatte con la collazione delle bozze con gli originali, e nulla è stato risparmiato per ottenere la desiderata e raggiungibile perfezione di fedeltà dei toni di fondo e dei toni di colore delle figure quali attualmente sono, senza alcun tentative di integrazione o di restauro delle poche parti deteriorate o mancanti." Maiuri attributes the technical work to Prof. Cav. Pampaloni of the Istituto poligrafico dello Stato.

7   Maiuri 1931 (note 4), 121–22; idem 1947 (note 4), 171–73; idem, *Pompeii* (Novara, 1951), 79; idem, "Del mistero di Dioniso," in *Pompei ed Ercolano fra case ed abitanti*, ed. Guido Clemente (Florence, 1998), 103–15. Idem, *Passeggiate campane* (Milan, 1990), is a collection of essays on his discoveries, including the Villa of the Mysteries.

8   *Storie da un'eruzione: Pompei, Ercolano, Oplontis: Guida alla mostra*, ed. Pietro Giovanni Guzzo (Naples, 2003).

9   P. B. Mudie Cooke, "The Paintings of the Villa Item at Pompeii," *Journal of Roman Studies* 3 (1913): 157–74; Jocelyn Toynbee, "The Villa Item and a Bride's Ordeal," *Journal of Roman Studies* 19 (1929): 67–87; Margarete Bieber, "Der Mysteriensaal der Villa Item," *Jahrbuch des deutschen archäologischen Instituts* 43 (1928): 298–330. An English summary appeared in *American Journal of Archaeology* 34 (1930): 494.

10   Maiuri's photographs revealed details such as clothing textures and animal pelts; see Maiuri 1947 (note 4), 144, 218n. 48.

11   Ibid., 164–68. For bibliographies, see Reinhard Herbig, *Neue Beobachtungen am Fries der Mysterien-Villa in Pompeji* (Mainz, 1958), 70–77; Giles Sauron, *La grande fresque de la Villa des Mystères à Pompéi: Mémoires d'une dévote de Dionysos* (Paris, 1998), 157–58; *The Villa of the Mysteries in Pompeii: Ancient Ritual, Modern Muse*, ed. Elaine K. Gazda (Ann Arbor, 2000), 250–61.

12   Ernesto De Carolis, "A City and Its Rediscovery," in *Pompeii: Life in a Roman Town*, ed. Annamaria Ciarallo and Ernesto De Carolis (Milan, 1999), 23–30; *Pompei 79: Raccolta di studi per il decimonono centenario dell'eruzione Vesuviana*, ed. Fausto Zevi (Naples, 1979), 5–9; Alison E. Cooley, *Pompeii* (London, 2003), 83–96.

13   On the history of archaeological methods and current use of stratigraphic analysis in Pompeii, see Joanne Berry, *Unpeeling Pompeii: Studies in Region I of Pompeii* (Milan, 1998); Amedeo Maiuri, "Gli scavi di Pompei dal 1879 al 1948," in *Pompeiana: Raccolta di studi per il secondo centenario degli scavi di Pompei* (Naples, 1950), 9–40.

14   Ferdinand Gregorovius, *The Roman Journals of Ferdinand Gregorovius, 1852–1874*, ed. Friedrich Althaus, trans. Mrs. Gustavus W. Hamilton (London, 1911), 211–12.

15   August Mau, *Pompeji in Leben und Kunst* (Leipzig, 1889); idem, *Pompeii: Its Life and Art*, trans. Francis W. Kelsey (1899; New York, 1902).

16   August Mau, *Geschichte der decorativen Wandmalerei in Pompeji* (Berlin, 1882); Wolfgang Helbig, *Wandgemälde der vom Vesuv verschütteten Städte Campaniens* (Leipzig, 1868), catalogues by subject all paintings excavated up to 1867; Giuseppe Fiorelli, *Gli scavi di Pompei dal 1861 al 1872* (Naples, 1873); Umberto Pappalardo, *La descrizione di Pompei per Giuseppe Fiorelli. Con una cronistoria per immagini e la lettera di Giuseppe Fiorelli alla Guardia nazionale del distretto di Castellammare di Stabia* (Naples, 2001). Mau anticipated the shift from the search for lost Greek models to the consideration of entire wall designs within their architectural contexts, thus stressing their *Romanitas* some twenty years before Franz Wickhoff and Alois Riegl would articulate a distinctively "Roman" art and worldview. Franz Wickhoff, *Roman Art: Some of Its Principles and Their Application to Early Christian Painting*, trans. and ed. Mrs. S. Arthur Strong (London, 1900); idem, *Römische Kunst: Die wiener Genesis* (Berlin, 1912); Alois Riegl, *Die spätrömische Kunst-Industrie, nach den Funden in Österreich-Ungarn dargestellt von Alois Riegl* (Vienna, 1901–23).

17 Continuing Fiorelli's work as superintendents of the excavations were Michele Ruggiero (1875–93), Giulio de Petra (1893–1900), Ettore Pais (1900–1905), again Giulio de Petra (1906–10), and, as director of excavations and collaborator with Petra, Antonio Sogliano (1905–10). They were followed by Vittorio Spinazzola (1910–24), who abandoned the northern part of the city for the Via dell Abbondanza and undertook even more ambitious reconstructions of facades and upper stories. Spinazzola was replaced by Amedeo Maiuri in 1924 for political reasons (Varone 2000 [note 1]). For a brief history and the current state of management of Pompeii, see Pietro Giovanni Guzzo, *Pompei, Ercolano, Stabiae, Oplontis: Le città sepolte dal Vesuvio* (Naples, 2003), 6–21.

18 "Pompeii" in these years included the nearby sites of modern Torre Annunziata, Boscotrecase, Boscoreale, Scafati, and Gragnano, an area known in antiquity as the *pagus augustus felix suburbanus*. Andreas Oettel, *Fundkontexte römischer Vesuvvillen im Gebiet um Pompeji: Die Grabungen von 1894 bis 1908* (Mainz, 1996); Michael Rostovtzeff, *The Social and Economic History of the Roman Empire* (Oxford, 1957), 2:551n. 2, 564n. 23; Valentin Kockel, "Archäologische Funde und Forschungen in den Vesuvstädten I," *Archäologischer Anzeiger* (1985): 495–571, esp. 534, figs. 23–24; John H. D'Arms, *Romans on the Bay of Naples: A Social and Cultural Study of the Villas and Their Owners from 150 B.C. to A.D. 400* (Cambridge, Mass., 1970).

19 Stephen L. Dyson, *Ancient Marbles to American Shores: Classical Archaeology in the United States* (Philadelphia, 1998).

20 Egon Cesar Conte Corti, *The Destruction and Resurrection of Pompeii and Herculaneum*, trans. K. and R. Gregor Smith (London, 1951), 208. For Boscoreale's archaeological records, see *Pompei: I tesori di Boscoreale: Lettere e documenti*, ed. Paola Poli Capri, 5 vols. (Rome, 2001). On Prisco and the scandals, see Antonio Cirillo and Angelandrea Casale, *Il tesoro di Boscoreale e il suo scopritore: La vera storia ricostruita sui documenti dell'epoca* (Naples, 2004).

21 François Baratte, *Le trésor d'orfèverie romaine de Boscoreale* (Paris, 1986); Gina Carla Ascione, "Da Boscoreale al Louvre, la 'fuga' del tesoro," in *Il tesoro di Boscoreale: Una collezione di argenti da mensa tra cultura ellenistica e mondo romano. Pitture, suppellettili, oggetti vari della "Pisanella"* (Milan, 1988), 19–24.

22 Karl Baedeker, *Southern Italy and Sicily: Handbook for Travellers*, 16th ed. (Leipzig, 1912), 170; idem, *Southern Italy and Sicily: Handbook for Travellers*, 17th ed. (Leipzig, 1930), 172.

23 Megalography is a type of monumental figural painting mentioned by Vitruvius *On Architecture* 7.5.2.

24 On the paintings from the Villa of P. Fannius Synistor, see Phyllis William Lehmann, *Roman Wall Paintings from Boscoreale in the Metropolitan Museum of Art* (Cambridge, Mass., 1953).

25 "Big Find of Art Treasures," *New York Times*, September 28, 1902, 25. For further disputes about the Boscoreale excavations, see Poli Capri 2001 (note 20).

26 A villa at Boscotrecase with third-style paintings came to light in 1902. The owner immediately removed the frescoes and reburied the villa. In a prelude to the Mysteries frescoes, between 1903 and 1906 losses were filled with various plaster compounds, and oil paints were applied over large areas of original pigments. Peter H. von Blanckenhagen and Christine Alexander, *The Augustan Villa at Boscotrecase* (Mainz, 1990).

27 Oettel 1996 (note 18), 334; Guzzo 2003 (note 8), 200–223.

28 Maiuri 1947 (note 4), 23, places the discovery of the Villa of the Mysteries within the series of "humble" digs in the *agro pompeiano* between 1890 and 1923, thus implying that the law of 1909 did not entirely suppress private quarrying. Guzzo 2003 (note 8), 346–48.

29 Baedeker 1912 (note 22), 143.

30 A June 12, 1902, law gave license for independent excavation (Giulio de Petra in *Notizie degli scavi degli antichità* [June 1910]: 139–45).

31   The tombs were first discovered in the 1760s. Valentin Kockel, *Die Grabbauten vor dem Herku-laner Tor in Pompeji* (Mainz, 1983), 1–6. *Pompei: Pitture e mosaici*, ed. Giovanni Pugliese Carratelli, vol. 10, *La documentazione nell'opera di disegnatori e pittori dei secoli XVIII e XIX* (Rome, 1995), 1–16, 939–1023. Amedeo Maiuri, *Bollettino d'arte*, n.s. 7 (1927–28): 377. Maiuri rhapsodized about this zone in describing the walk beyond the city walls to villas and tombs: "The unearthed town, with its miraculous re-birth and with the breath of new life wafting through it, reawakening our never-flagging admiration at every turn, causes us to lose all sense of time and death; and, possibly, because of this, the unexpected sight of the tombs lined along the Via Sepolcri stirs us to our inmost depths" (Maiuri 1951 [note 7], 69).

32   Aurelio Item was not alone in exploring this area. In 1907 and 1908 Antonio Sogliano and Giuseppe Spano officially investigated the northwest end of the Street of the Tombs and found Samnite burials under the Villa of the Mosaic Columns.

33   The following account of events is based on excavation reports in the archives of the Soprin-tendenza archeologica di Napoli.

34   "Auf dem Bauerngute selbst erworben, wo die Villa steht," in A. Ruesch, *Sammlung A. Ruesch Zürich. Griechische, etruskische und römische Altertümer* (Lucerne, 1936), 14, 124–28; Andreas Oettel, *Bronzen aus Boscoreale in Berlin* (Berlin, 1991); Guzzo 2003 (note 8), 252–54, 350–51.

35   On the completion of the rebuilding of the east and north walls, see unpublished archaeological records of September 9–October 3. Previous entries state that the rebuilding of the other walls was suspended: "La prima porzione di parete, quella all'angolo SO ha già a terzo un solido muro moderno che è sostituto all'antico, altrettanto di casi per le altre porzione agli angoli SE e NE. Con tali lavori sono assicurati definitivamente: Il gruppo di 4 figure muliebri fra cui e la baccante nuda danzante è scena di toilette ed è quasi completato e domina seduta" (excavation reports in the archives of the Soprintendenza archeologica di Napoli, August 30–September 9).

36   De Carolis 1999 (note 12); Paolo Mora, Laura Mora, and Paul Philippot, *Conservation of Wall Paintings* (London, 1984), 67, 89–104, 295, 297; *Roman Wall Painting: Materials, Techniques, Analysis, and Conservation*, ed. H. Béarat et al. (Fribourg, 1997).

37   De Carolis 1999 (note 12); Roberto Cassanelli et al., *Houses and Monuments of Pompeii: The Works of Fausto and Felice Niccolini*, trans. Thomas M. Hartmann (Los Angeles, 2002).

38   Baedeker 1912 (note 22).

39   Baedeker 1930 (note 22), 169.

40   W. M. Flinders Petrie, *Methods and Aims of Archaeology* (London, 1904); Henry Parker in 1879 first codified archaeological photography (Bruno Brizzi, *Roma: Cento anni fa nelle fotografie della raccolta Parker* [Rome, 1975]); *A New History of Photography*, ed. Michel Frizot (Cologne, 1998), 377–85; Michael Shanks, "Photography and Archaeology," in *The Cultural Life of Images: Visual Representation in Archaeology*, ed. Brian Molyneaux (London, 1997), 73–107.

41   Roberto Cassanelli, "L'image de Pompéi: De la gravure à la photographie," in Roberto Cas-sanelli et al., *Le case e i monumenti di Pompei nell'opera di Fausto e Felice Niccolini* (Novara, 1997), 48; *Alinari Brothers' Museum of the History of Photography. Special Albums, Souvenir de Pompeii; Alinari Archives* (Florence, 1993); Pugliese Carratelli 1995 (note 31).

42   But, in an echo of the Accademia ercolanese, Petra supported his own, state-sanctioned publica-tion, and on June 18, 1909, the French art historian Theodore Reinach was denied permission to illustrate the frescoes for the *Gazette des Beaux-Arts*. On June 20, 1909, Petra gave Paul Herrmann permission to see the frescoes but not to make visual recordings of any kind. In January 1910 Petra expressed alarm about the rumor of a large-scale study of the frescoes by Maurizio Rizzo of Turin. When Rizzo requested photographs, Petra politely acknowledged his scholarly stature but suggested that Rizzo write an article for a journal, which he did, publish-ing four images in a two-part article that did not appear until 1914 and 1918: Maurizio Rizzo, "Dionysos Mystos, Part II: Le pitture della Villa pompeiana nel fondo Gargiulio," *Memorie della Reale accademia di archeologia, lettere, e belle arti di Napoli* 3 (1918): 63–102.

43 Petra 1910 (note 30). The foreign press had picked up the discovery by May 1910: Paul Hartwig, *Neue freie Presse* (Vienna), May 27, 1910; Salomon Reinach, "Une grand décoration murale à Pompéi," *Revue archéologique* 4, ser. 16 (1910): 430–31; seven photographs of excerpts of the frieze accompanied Georges Nicole, "Les derniers fouilles de Pompéi," *Gazette des Beaux-Arts* 53, no. 1 (1911): 21–33; and Franz Winter, "Die Wandgemälde der Villa Item bei Pompeji," *Kunst und Künstler* 10, no. 11 (1912): 548–55.

44 Petra's order of the figural units, beginning in the west end of the north wall (here paraphrased): (1) the first of the women striding from the door toward the young boy reading beside a seated woman to the wreathed woman; (2) the figures around the table and Silenus; (3) the goats and satyrs and running figure with billowing mantle; (4) next, east wall: the seated Silenus and satyrs with bowl and mask, and Bacchus, with his female companion oddly cropped down the middle; (5) left knee of Bacchus's female companion, the revelation of the "phallus" and winged woman with whip; (6) next, south wall (with corner visible) of kneeling woman with head on lap of seated woman and whirling dancer (to whose right one can glimpse a view through the window to an unexcavated embankment); (7) (right of window) bride and Eros; (8) Eros on next, west wall (including corner); (9) domina (with corner and edge of door).

45 Mudie Cooke 1913 (note 9), 159n. 1.

46 Petra 1910 (note 30), 144.

47 On ancient fresco technique Maiuri cites Otto Donner, "Die antiken Wandmalereien in technischer Beziehung," in Helbig 1868 (note 16), 1–CXXVII; and A. Eibner, *Entwicklung und Werkstoffe der Wandmalerei von Altertum bis zur Neuzeit* (Munich, 1926).

48 Maria Barosso, "La datazione della pittura della Villa dei Misteri a Pompei," in *6. internationaler Kongress für Archäologie: Berlin 1939* (Berlin, 1940), 505–10.

49 Mudie Cooke 1913 (note 9), 171; Barosso stated firmly that the walls were not fresco. Apparently the frieze was covered with wax as recently as the 1980s.

50 A thorough study of all the reproductions of the frieze between 1909 and 1935 would need to include those by Alinari made for Ludwig Curtius, *Die Wandmalerei Pompejis* (Leipzig, 1929), 343–76; Pirro Marconi, *Il fregio dionisiaco della Villa dei Misteri* (Bergamo, 1938), with forty plates, including stunning details attributed to Vittorio Spinazzola, Maiuri's predecessor.

51 Nita Butler, "The Destruction of Pompeian Wall Paintings," *American Journal of Archaeology* 38 (1934): 182–83. See Christel Faltermeier, "Technical Observations on the Wall Paintings from Boscotrecase in the Metropolitan Museum of Art," in Blanckenhagen and Alexander 1990 (note 26), 65–73. I am grateful to Joan Mertens for permission to observe the current conservation of the Boscoreale frescoes at the Metropolitan Museum of Art. Christel Faltermeier, Rudolf Meyer, and Hubert von Sonnenburg offered expert opinions. On the painter's process in the Dionysiac frieze, see Umberto Pappalardo, "Nuove osservazione sul fregio della 'Villa dei Misteri' a Pompei," in *La regione sotterata del Vesuvius: Studi e prospettive* (Naples, 1982), 599–633; idem, "Beobachtungen am Fries der Mysterien-Villa in Pompeji," *Antike Welt* 13, no. 3 (1982): 10–20.

52 Leonetti Tintori and Millard Meiss recognized a combination of *buon fresco* and *fresco secco*, "Additional Observations on Italian Mural Technique," *Art Bulletin* 46, no. 3 (1964): 377–80, which is substantiated by more recent discoveries of Roman walls. In Ciarallo and De Carolis 1999 (note 12), 237, Bernardo Marchese, citing Vitruvius *On Architecture* 7.8–9.3, contends that "workers used Punic wax in a liquid form mixed with oil" to polish the final surface and thus prevent alterations.

53 Vitruvius *On Architecture* 7.8–9; Pliny the Elder *Natural History* 33.36.

54 A recent microscopic analysis by Daniela Daniele, a researcher at Berlin's Staatliche Museum, apparently revealed a very finely processed cinnabar powder in the villa frescoes (http://www.dsc.discovery.com/news/briefs/20041101/pompeiired.html). Results of an analysis of the sample taken during the cleaning of several patches for Elaine Gazda in June 2003 are not avail-

able. Vitruvius *On Architecture* 7.9.3; and Pliny the Elder *Natural History* 33.118–20; Roger Ling, *Roman Painting* (New York, 1991), 209; *Pigments et colorants d l'antiquité et du moyen âge* (Paris, 1990), 245–71.

55   Maiuri 1931 (note 4), 116, 208. Toynbee in her review of Maiuri similarly acknowledges the "freshness and vividness of the originals" twenty-five years after their exposure: *Journal of Roman Studies* 24 (1934): 236. Maiuri expressed concern about the conservation of the walls when beginning his excavation in 1928, noting the need for ventilation and protection from the elements: "Richiede per le condizioni precarie in cui trovasi quello scavo interrotto e non più ripreso dal 1909–1910 speciali provvidenze preservative e continua ed oculata sovreglianza fino a che completato lo scavo di tutto l'edificio e liberato dal terrapieno che incombe da ogni lato, la maggiore aerazione e ventilazione degli ambienti non costitiuiscano gia di per se la più efficace difesa contro la insidiosa e deleteria azione" (*Bollettino d'arte* 7, no. 2 [1928]: 374–77).

56   I am grateful to Jack Soultanian of the Conservation Department at the Metropolitan Museum of Art, New York, for his assistance on this matter in 2002. While both are solvents, benzine (*benzina*) is very different from benzene. The *benzina* recorded in the logs must surely refer to the mild benzine. Although benzine could be used alone as a mild cleaning solvent, it is more likely that it was added to the wax to create a paste (solid wax is very hard), which might be applied cold, or, if carefully heated, by brush. In its paste form the mixture could also be used as a cleaning agent or just as a coating.

57   Erika Naginski, "Riegl, Archaeology, and the Periodization of Culture," *Res* 40 (Autumn 2001): 135–52, esp. 144.

58   Jeffrey Mehlman, *Walter Benjamin for Children: An Essay on His Radio Years* (Chicago, 1993), 23–28.

59   Walter Benjamin, "The Work of Art in the Age of Mechanical Reproduction," in idem, *Illuminations*, ed. Hannah Arendt (New York, 1968), 1.

60   Victor Burgin, "Looking at Photographs," in *Thinking Photography*, ed. Victor Burgin (London, 1982), 142; Alan Sekula, "On the Invention of Photographic Meaning," in Burgin 1982, 84–109; see also the essays in *Classic Essays on Photography*, ed. Alan Trachtenberg (New Haven, 1980).

61   Günther Zuntz, "On the Dionysiac Fresco in the Villa dei Misteri at Pompeii," *Proceedings of the British Academy* 49 (1963): 177–202.

62   Christopher Tilley, *Metaphor and Material Culture* (Oxford, 1999).

63   "Fine Pompeiian Paintings: Mural Decorations of a Villa Reveal Singular Detached Perspective," *New York Times*, January 1, 1911, C2. On flagellation rituals, see Mario Praz, *The Romantic Agony* (London, 1933). On the feminist response to these themes, see Mari Jo Bulhle, *Feminism and Its Discontents: A Century of Struggle with Psychoanalysis* (Cambridge, Mass., 1998).

64   On stratigraphy as a historical method whereby time is defined as a series of superimposed layers, see the articles in *Res* 40 (Autumn 2001): especially Naginski 2001 (note 57); Matthew Biro, "History at a Standstill: Walter Benjamin, Otto Dix, and the Question of Stratigraphy," 153–76; and Robert Bork, "The Pros and Cons of Stratigraphic Models in Art History," 177–87. Jennifer Wallace, *Digging the Dirt: The Archaeological Imagination* (London, 2004), appeared as I was completing this essay and addresses similar issues.

65   His case study "The Rat Man" (1909), published the same year the Villa of the Mysteries frescoes came to light, invoked Pompeii's burial as emblematic for psychic repression. Pointing to ancient sculptures in his study, he commented that "their burial had been their preservation: the destruction of Pompeii was only beginning now that it had been dug up" (Sigmund Freud, "Notes upon a Case of Obsessional Neurosis," in *The Standard Edition of the Complete Psychological Works of Sigmund Freud*, trans. and ed. James Strachey (London, 1953), 10:19; Wolfgang Mertens and Rolf Haubl, *Der Psychoanalytiker als Archäologie: Eine Einführung in die Methode*

der Rekonstruktion. Psychoanalytische Behandlung (Stuttgart, 1996); Suzanne Cassirer-Bernfeld, "Freud and Archaeology," *American Imago* 8 (1951): 107–28. On modern scholars' tendency to simplify the archaeological metaphor, see Kenneth Reinhard, "The Freudian Things: Construction and the Archaeological Metaphor," in *Excavations and Their Objects: Freud's Collection of Antiquities*, ed. Stephen Barker (New York, 1996), 57–79.

66 *The Standard Edition of the Complete Psychological Works of Sigmund Freud* 1953 (note 65), 4:15; Sabine Hake, "*Saxa loquuntur:* Freud's Archaeology of the Text," *boundary 2* 20, no. 1 (1993): 164n. 18.

67 On the feminization of the ruins during the Grand Tour, see Chloe Chard, *Pleasure and Guilt on the Grand Tour: Travel Writing and Imaginative Geography, 1600–1830* (Manchester, 1999).

68 Wilhelm Jensen, *Gradiva: Ein pompejanisches Phantasiestück* (Dresden, 1903); idem, *Gradiva: A Pompeiian Fancy*, trans. Helen M. Downey (New York, 1918). On the novella as part of the literary tradition, see Wolfgang Leppmann, *Pompeii in Fact and Fiction* (London, 1966), 145–54.

69 The imprint of the elusive beloved in Vesuvius's lava was a trope long before Jensen envisioned the ideal female, considering Fiorelli's dramatic plaster casts of the victims. Also Théophile Gautier's *Arria Marcella: Souvenir de Pompéi* (Paris, 1852) describes "salles peintes en rouge antique"; Leppmann 1966 (note 68), 136–44; Christiane Zintzen, "Wilhelm Jensen's *Gradiva* im Kontext: Archäologische, touristische und populäre Pompejana im 18. und 19. Jahrhundert," in Michael Rohrwasser et al., *Freuds pompejanische Muse: Beiträge zu Wilhelm Jensens Novelle "Gradiva"* (Vienna, 1996), 66–67. For recent imaginary visits to Pompeii using the same tropes, see Keith Hopkins, *A World Full of God: The Strange Triumph of Christianity* (London, 2001); and Robert Harris, *Pompeii* (London, 2003). On the history of skeletons and plaster casts, see Guzzo 2003 (note 8).

70 Carl Jung had introduced *Gradiva* to Freud. Sigmund Freud, *Der Wahn und die Träume in Wilhelm Jensens Gradiva* (Vienna, 1907); the second edition (Vienna, 1912) includes a proper archaeological identification of the relief as a fragment of a multifigural frieze. *The Freud/Jung Letters: The Correspondence between Sigmund Freud and C. G. Jung*, ed. William McGuire; trans. Ralph Manheim and R. F. C. Hull (Princeton, 1974), 49–55. On May 24, 1907, Jung writes, "Your *Gradiva* is magnificent." Freud's essay comes up repeatedly in letters through November 1907, at times with comments about its mixed reception.

71 Christfried Tögel, *Berggasse-Pompeji und Zurück: Sigmund Freuds Reisen in die Vergangenheit* (Tübingen, 1989), 154; Rohrwasser 1996 (note 69); Yael Levin, "Conrad, Freud, and Derrida on Pompeii: A Paradigm of Disappearance," *Partial Answers: Journal of Literature and the History of Ideas* 3, no. 1 (January 2005): 81–99; Rachel Bowlby, "One Foot in the Grave: Freud on Jensen's *Gradiva*," in *Still Crazy after All These Years: Women, Writing, and Psychoanalysis* (London, 1992), 157–82; Hake 1993 (note 66), 146–73.

72 In 1938 Freud took the relief into exile with him to London. Martin Bergmann, "Science and Art in Freud's Life and Work," in *Sigmund Freud and Art: His Personal Collection of Antiquities*, ed. Lynn Gamwell and Richard Wells (Binghamton, 1989), 176–77. Leopold Feiler, *Mysterion: Gedanken vor den dionysischen Fresken der Mysterienvilla in Pompeji* (Vienna, 1946), is a small book written by a doctor who was affected by seeing the frescoes and contains valuable insights; Joan Copjec, "Transference: Letters and the Unknown Woman," *October* 28 (Spring 1984): 60–90, esp. 85.

73 Ernst Gombrich, *Aby Warburg* (London, 1970), 106; Jack Spector, "The State of Psychoanalytic Research in Art History," *Art Bulletin* 70, no. 1 (March 1988): 66–67.

74 Maiuri 1951 (note 7).

75 Amedeo Maiuri, "Freud à Pompei," *Il mattino*, October 18, 1962, n.p.

76 Copjec 1984 (note 72), 89.

77   Whitney Chadwick, "Masson's *Gradiva*: The Metamorphosis of a Surrealist Myth," *Art Bulletin* 52, no. 2 (1970): 422; idem, *Myth in Surrealist Painting, 1929–39* (Ann Arbor, 1980); Gisela Steinlechner, "Fundsache Gradiva: Auftritt der pompejanischen Muse im Surrealismus," in Rohrwasser 1996 (note 69), 122–55; Spector 1988 (note 73), 53–54.

78   André Masson, *Gradiva (Metamorphoses of Gradiva)*, 1939, oil on canvas (Knokke, Belgium, formerly Nellens Collection). Max Ernst's *Premier mot limpide (At the First Limpid Word)*, 1923 (Düsseldorf, Kunstsammlung Nordhein-Westfalen), was based on Freud's analysis of *Gradiva*. Salvador Dalí conflated his wife, Gala, with Gradiva in *Gradiva Finds Anthropomorphic Ruins*, 1931 (Madrid, Foundation Thyssen-Bornemisza, Museo Thyssen). Also inspired by Jensen's and Freud's treatments of *Gradiva* was André Breton's gallery in Paris, called "Gradiva." Marcel Duchamp's 1937 photograph of its facade became a symbol that lasted through the 1960s, and he also designed the cover of the first issue of *Le surréalisme même*, which featured a long article on *Gradiva*: Thomas Girst, "Duchamp's Window Display for André Breton's *Le surréalisme et la peinture* (1945)," *Tout fait: The Marcel Duchamp Studies Online Journal*, issue 4 (2002): 4–5. For a discussion of *Gradiva*'s importance for surrealist artists, see Antje von Graevenitz, "Duchamp's Tür Gradiva: Eine literarische Figur und ihr Surrealistenkreis," *Avantgarde* 2 (1989): 63–96.

79   Martin Ries, "André Masson: Surrealism and Its Discontents," *Art Journal* 61, no. 4 (Winter 2002): 74–85.

80   Jacques Lacan, "The Signification of the Phallus," in *Écrits: A Selection*, trans. Alan Sheridan (New York, 1977); Michael Payne, *Reading Theory: An Introduction to Lacan, Derrida, and Kristeva* (Cambridge, Mass., 1993), 85–91; Patricia Simons, "*Whose* 'Mysteries'? The Ancient Phallus and Women's Sexuality at Pompeii's 'Villa of the Mysteries'" (unpublished manuscript, Ann Arbor), 17; Spector 1988 (note 73), 60.

81   Bice Benvenuto, *Concerning the Rites of Psychoanalysis; or, the Villa of the Mysteries* (Cambridge, 1994).

82   Linda Fierz-David, *Psychologische Betrachtungen zu der Freskenfolge der Villa der Misteri in Pompeii: Ein Versuch* (Zurich, 1957); Linda Fierz-David, *Women's Dionysian Initiation: The Villa of Mysteries in Pompeii*, trans. Gladys Phelan (Dallas, 1988); R. S. Kraemer, "Ecstasy and Possession: The Attraction of Women to the Cult of Dionysos," *Harvard Theological Review* 72 (1979): 55–80; Patricia Reis, "The Villa of the Mysteries: Initiation into Woman's Midlife Passage," *Continuum* 1, no. 3 (1991): 64–91. Linda Fierz-David and Nor Hall's *Dreaming in Red: The Women's Dionysian Initiation Chamber in Pompeii* (Putnam, Conn., 2005), combines revisions of Fierz-David 1988, and Nor Hall, *Those Women* (Dallas, 1988).

83   Katherine Bradway, *Villa of Mysteries: Pompeian Initiation Rites of Women* (San Francisco, 1982). Women's groups still make the journey: Shakira Khan, "Midlife in the Villa of the Mysteries," *Power Trips* (December–January 1999): 10–13.

84   Gregg M. Horowitz, *Sustaining Loss: Art and Mournful Life* (Palo Alto, 2001).

85   Diane Kirkpatrick, "Ancient Mysteries, Modern Meanings," in Gazda 2000 (note 11), 139–49; on Olson, see 138, 141–42, 244–45.

86   Patricia Olson, "The Mysteries," in *The Mysteries: Patricia Olson, 18 September–27 October, 1999* (Saint Paul, 1999), 6. The installation consisted of seven sets of oil paintings on board, ranging from 152.4 to 243.8 centimeters in height.

87   Nor Hall, "Woman Lost and Woman Found: Images of an Ancient Passage," in *Mysteries* 1999 (note 86), 4.

88   Hélène Cixous, "Arrive le chapitre qui vient (Come the following chapter)," *Enclitic* 4, no. 2 (Fall 1980): 44–58. That the frieze is the vision of the domina has also been proposed by art historians Günther Zuntz (1963 [note 61]) and Gilles Sauron (*La grande fresque de la Villa des Mystères à Pompéi: Mémoires d'une dévote de Dionysos* [Paris, 1998]).

89 Hall 1988 (note 82); see also Fierz-David and Hall 2005 (note 82).

90 Bergmann 1989 (note 72), 173–83; on Gradiva and H.D., see esp. 176–79. On Freud's *Totem and Taboo*, the Fascist myth of the Mother, and Jane Harrison, see Elizabeth Abel, *Virginia Woolf and the Fictions of Psychoanalysis* (Chicago, 1989), 25–29.

91 Annabel Robinson, *The Life and Work of Jane Ellen Harrison* (Oxford, 2002); Mary Beard, *The Invention of Jane Harrison* (Cambridge, Mass., 2000).

92 Alison Syme, "Love among the Ruins: David Cannon Dashiell's *Queer Mysteries*," *Art Journal* (Winter 2004): 81–95; Wes Christensen's *Turnstile*, 1995 (Santa Ynez, Calif., private collection), is discussed in Gazda 2000 (note 85), 243–44. The nonnarrative, abstract qualities of the villa walls inspired Mark Rothko during a 1959 visit. His gouache for Mies Van der Rohe's Seagram Building in New York, made in 1958–59, renders great sheets of a saturated red from floor to ceiling. See Stephen Polcari, "Mark Rothko: Heritage, Environment, and Tradition," *Smithsonian Studies in American Art* 2, no. 2 (Spring 1988): 32–63.

93 John Gage, *Color and Culture: Practice and Meaning from Antiquity to Abstraction* (Boston, 1993), 25, 26, 337n. 107.

94 Zintzen 1996 (note 69), 42–89.

95 Productions of *The Last Days of Pompeii*: Luigi Magi, 1908, Italy; Mario Caserini, 1913, Italy; Camine Gallone, 1926, Italy; Ernest B. Schoedsack, 1935, United States. Maria Wyke, "Cinema and the City of the Dead: Reel Histories of Pompei," in *New Scholarship from British Film Institue Research* (London, 1996), 140–56; idem, *Projecting the Past: Ancient Rome, Cinema and History* (London, 1997).

96 The 1908 film combines stage sets with location shots, captures vast crowds at the arena in breathtaking scope, and in the final twenty minutes, after an hour of silver-toned film, at the very instant the eruption begins, transforms from black-and-white into red-tinted chaos. The 1913 film was produced by the prolific director Mario Caserini, who used a completely static camera, turning each shot into a living tableau.

97 Maiuri 1951 (note 7), 83.

98 Vittorio Macchioro quoted in Edwin Hullinger, "New Beauties Found in Pompeii; Decorated Facades Made Picture Galleries of the Streets; Temple Ruins Disclose Story of Secret Rites," *New York Times*, August 22, 1926, xx4.

99 As expressed, for example, in Alfred H. Barr, Jr.'s, reconception of modern art in his famous exhibition at the Museum of Modern Art in New York in 1936: Alfred H. Barr, Jr., *Cubism and Abstract Art* (1936; New York, 1974).

100 Picasso owned illustrated volumes about Pompeii (Victoria Beck Newman, "'The Triumph of Pan': Picasso and the Liberation," *Zeitschrift für Kunstgeschichte* 62 [1999]: 106–22, esp. 113).

101 James Elkins, "On the Impossibility of Stories: The Anti-narrative and Non-narrative Impulse in Modern Painting," *Word and Image* 7 (October–December 1991): 348–64.

Odysseys of Life and Death in the Bay of Naples: Roberto Rossellini's *Voyage in Italy* and Jean-Luc Godard's *Contempt*

Jennie Hirsh

Rome is the modern world, the West; Capri, the ancient world, nature before civilization and its neuroses.[1]

Jean-Luc Godard

THE BAY OF NAPLES, like other prominent antique sites, has attracted innumerable spectators through the mediating powers of the literary and visual arts for more than two millennia. Most recently, the region has figured prominently as the dramatic setting for cinematic productions ranging from early, silent films to more recent, feature films and even popular television miniseries that have memorialized "the last days of Pompeii."[2] For more than a century, the archaeological excavations at Pompeii and Herculaneum and their surrounding landscape have served as a prefabricated microcosm of antiquity onto which directors have projected their narrative fantasies. Replete with petrified specters of everyday life, these sites appear as seemingly abandoned, ready-made theatrical sets that grant access to the inner workings of antique society at the moment of the fatal eruption of Mount Vesuvius in A.D. 79.[3]

Roberto Rossellini's *Voyage in Italy* (1953) and Jean-Luc Godard's *Contempt* (1963) are two interconnected, postwar films that constitute a nostalgic return to this geographical region, where images of instantaneous, apocalyptic death continue to haunt spectators through ashen remains and formidable ruins. This essay will focus on how these two films function as striking filmic meditations on the role of Campagna in the modern cultural imagination preoccupied with the simultaneous persistence and inaccessibility of antiquity in the present, that is, in *their* present. Unlike both their cinematic predecessors and contemporary "sword-and-sandals" productions concerned with re-creating life in antiquity, these films encounter the past with the self-conscious distance of their own postwar moment.[4]

In what follows, I argue for the particularity of these two films' use of the Bay of Naples as a vehicle through which to address limitations of the past's stability in the present, a motivating factor for modernism's self-conscious break with the past. Rossellini and Godard similarly address this quandry through a return to—rather than abandonment of—the burden of tradition as embodied in the remains of Pompeii and Herculaneum, the cities we have come to know as the eternal homes of the spectral remains of those buried alive in A.D. 79. Aside from their common setting in the Bay of Naples, these two films also have additional affinities. Most notably, *Voyage in Italy* and *Contempt* invoke Homer's *Odyssey*, as both directors incorporate the ancient epic into their narratives of deteriorating romantic relationships.[5]

I will also highlight how these two films come to terms with intimate conflicts inherent in human relationships by contrasting the palpable mortality preserved in the remains of antiquity with the tragically dead emotions that often constitute love for the living. But, whereas revisiting death creates a sentimental crisis that ultimately—at least temporarily—redeems a marriage on the verge of divorce in *Voyage in Italy*, a similar confrontation with the burden of the past in *Contempt* fuels an irreversible devolution of love. Rossellini and Godard similarly enlist the diachronic nature of this landscape not only as an emotional catalyst for their characters but also as the device through which they remove their narratives from traditional temporal logic. By highlighting communication gaps and failures, both directors reveal how Campagna's enigmatic physical remains pose unanswerable questions about the past that undermine the characters' understanding of their present (and of each other). The Bay of Naples similarly thrusts each film's narrative out of time. Once the characters are dislocated physically and temporally from their perfunctory, modern urban environments, they evolve emotionally in unique narrative spaces, at once ancient and modern, past and present. Transcending their modern, socially prescribed circumstances leaves the characters susceptible to archetypal emotions.[6] Thus, by juxtaposing the mysteries of historical, cultural, and linguistic multiplicities frozen in Campagna's simultaneously perfect and imperfect temporalities with more banal instances of the modern failures of communication, Rossellini and Godard trap their characters in concurrent chronologies, so that they are unable to face their futures. My essay will focus on how visual and literary works of art are presented through acts of pictorial and verbal mistranslation, strategies through which these directors cinematically underscore antiquity's failure *to mean* in the present.

The Films

Voyage in Italy begins with Katherine and Alexander Joyce (Ingrid Bergman and George Sanders) at the end of a journey from London to Naples, where they will sell a villa recently willed to them by Alex's late, eccentric "Uncle Homer." Their claustrophobic car ride to southern Italy—a kind of modern odyssey—sparks light disagreements that escalate sharply as their trip progresses. Once in Campagna, Katherine and Alex grow conscious of the emptiness of their union and spend their trip exploring the region separately: Katherine visits local tourist attractions, including the Museo archeologico nazionale in Naples, the Cave of the Sibyl at Cumae, and a Neapolitan crypt, while Alex flirts ineffectually with other women, numbing his painful boredom with drink in Capri and Naples. In particular, Alex cannot bear Katherine's eruptive recollections of a former admirer, Charles Lewington, a deceased poet whose work was inspired by his deployment in the Bay of Naples during the Second World War. Katherine's memories thus serve as a double past: first, the real, historical past indexed by the modern trauma of war and, second, the more mythical, imaginative past of Naples lingering in the present. Katherine's spontaneous recitations of Charles's long-forgotten stanzas trigger memories of his unrequited love prior to her marriage to Alex, who resents this unexpected rival.[7] Their mutual frustration and jealousy culminate in a call for divorce, though this decision is quickly abandoned in the film's final moments as their now habitual bickering is interrupted by the chaos of a local religious festival whose linguistic and cultural incomprehensibility resurrects their need for one another.[8]

Based on Alberto Moravia's 1954 novel *Il disprezzo*, *Contempt* tells the story of a frustrated playwright, Paul Javal (Michel Piccoli), who prostitutes himself by writing commercial screenplays in order to support his beautiful wife, Camille (Brigitte Bardot).[9] The film opens as American producer Jeremiah (Jerry) Prokosch (Jack Palance) hires Paul to rewrite the script for a cinematic adaptation of Homer's *Odyssey*, which is being filmed under the direction of a stubborn Fritz Lang (who plays himself).[10] Although the film begins with Paul and Camille as a seemingly happy couple, their love degenerates quickly into contempt as Camille cannot forgive Paul for what she sees as his encouragement of Prokosch's sexual advances toward her, which marks a second instance of Paul's prostitution.[11] The narrative unfolds first in Rome—at the seemingly abandoned studios of Cinecittà, Prokosch's villa, and the couple's unfinished modern apartment—and then moves to the on-location shooting of the film-within-the-film in Capri, where various strains of antiquity converge as this romance meets its demise. Although the story line closely follows Moravia's novel, Godard introduces the role of Francesca Vanini (Giorgia Moll), who, in addition to serving as Prokosch's ill-treated lover and assistant, works as a parrotlike, polyglot translator among the principal characters of the cast. *Contempt* concludes in Capri during the shooting of Ulysses' first glance on Ithaca, just after Paul learns that Camille, who has left him, has been killed in a car crash with Prokosch.

Through bearing witness to the pleasure playgrounds of the petrified dead dispersed throughout the Bay of Naples, the couples in both films are shocked out of their paralyzed marriages—which represent an emotional death—into living chaos where they can express their true sentiments. *Voyage in Italy* and *Contempt* isolate the diachronic nature of Campagna's cultural graveyards to illustrate how the simultaneous persistence of different historical moments (classical, early Christian, and beyond) renders each temporality visible only in the muddled company of its imperfect disjunction from what either precedes or follows. These relics of the past seem to promise their viewers the lessons of history, whether real or mythologized, but the journeys of both couples through time and across cultures complicate the recovery of these various temporalities, which are discrete and yet intermingled, instants in time that are simultaneously singular and multiple.

Rossellini's *Voyage in Italy* relies on cultural miscommunications that are augmented by the enigmatic qualities of the Bay of Naples; the film's poignant setting forces its characters to see otherwise invisible shortcomings in their relationships.[12] In

FIGURE 1
Brigitte Bardot, Fritz Lang,
Giorgia Moll, Jack Palance,
and Michel Piccoli leave a
movie theater beneath a sign
that reads *Viaggio in Italia*
in a scene from *Contempt*.

Photo: Courtesy Criterion Films.

contrast, Godard self-consciously expands verbally and visually the various forms of historical, cultural, and linguistic foreignness and incommunicability compressed into Rossellini's film to foreground and explore more deeply the universal inevitability of communicative disjunctions. As I will show in what follows, while Rossellini maintains a touristic lens through which his characters fail to understand the relics of the past and the alien Neapolitan present, Godard complicates that project by interweaving a multitude of chronologies, artistic media, and languages. Together, Godard's cinematic strategies and classical motifs highlight not only the failure of the past to speak to the present but also the present's more tragic incapacity to grasp the lessons of the past, a failure that continues into the present, which in turn fails to communicate with itself and its audience. Thus, Godard implicates the film's spectators as much as the actors, who are themselves spectators of *The Odyssey*. Although both films and, by extension, their touristic spectators "travel" to witness the supposedly static remains of antiquity, in *Contempt* spectatorship itself is disoriented chronologically, as the viewer is assaulted by the continuous insertion of the film-about-antiquity within the film. By presenting self-conscious gaps between the past and the present, both directors insist on modernism's self-proclaimed break from the past and so the destabilized and fragmented nature of modernity itself.

Both Rossellini and Godard thus dramatize a melancholic relationship to the irretrievable past(s) through seemingly tangible physical remains whose meaning and function remain opaque and inaccessible. Rossellini grounds his narrative in differences between northern and southern European culture through a modern British couple's awkward visit to an antique past, foreign both chronologically and geographically. Godard pushes this premise further by intertwining real and self-consciously synthetic images of antiquity. Godard thereby undermines the possibility of authentic experience in terms of communicating via either a work of art or a person, and critiques modernism's preoccupation with authenticity and originality. Mistranslation confirms the instability and multiplicity of meaning in all texts, pictorial or verbal.

Much ink has been spilled on the relationship between these two films, especially given Godard's inclusion of Rossellini's film as the feature advertised at the movie theater that is the site of the audition for the part of Nausicaa in *Contempt*. The lit signage grabs the spectator's attention; as Bardot, Lang, Moll, Palance, and Piccoli leave the cinema, their lingering affords the spectator enough time to make sense of the numerous posters and film stills filling the windows and plastered to the walls of the cinema, inside and out [FIG. 1]. While it is well known that Rossellini served as both a hero and a father figure for many practitioners of the *nouvelle vague*, it seems that Godard had something specific to gain by juxtaposing the reality of the landscape found in *Voyage in Italy* with the artificiality of antiquity in *Contempt*. I will therefore examine how these films invoke and appropriate ultimately untranslatable antique themes, subjects, and strategies and also what was at stake for Godard in his return to the landscape of Campagna that had already played host to Rossellini's vision. For whereas Rossellini's travels include Capri as the present site of cocktails and recreation, Godard chooses Capri to reconstruct a modernized version of the past.

Pictorial Predicaments: Voyage in Italy

Voyage in Italy thematizes works of art and other sculptural bodies, whether fabricated or fossilized, by repeatedly inserting them into Katherine's emotional exploration of the self. Katherine's confrontations with relics and other specimens of the living dead ignite a number of emotional crises. To start, when Katherine and Alex arrive at the villa, Uncle Homer's British caretaker, Tony Burton, introduces them to the splendors of the house, which include a painting by Palizzi, whom he describes as a "famous nineteenth-century Neapolitan painter," yet who is clearly unknown to Katherine and Alex, thus marking the first object of bewilderment.[13] Katherine seems far more interested in the carvings of a large wooden chest, which features intarsia recalling Pompeian wall painting, thus foreshadowing her upcoming voyages back in time.

Katherine's sojourn in Campagna unfolds as a series of pilgrimages to modern art collections and key sites of antiquity. Her first solo exploration of Neapolitan culture is a visit to the Museo archeologico nazionale, where she confronts a panoply of sculptural specters of the past. Katherine's English-speaking guide describes works of art with a combination of historical information and personal anecdotes, both of which seem inaccurate. He starts with an introduction to the museum structure's complicated history as a cavalry barracks, then property of Charles VII, and finally home to archaeological treasures from the region, including secret works of art, whose nature he fails to describe.[14] He then presents *The Dancing Girls*, five sculptures discovered in the Villa dei Papiri in Herculaneum. Rossellini's score underlines Katherine's discomfort with these mystical and incomprehensible ancient objects; the disorienting, eerie, high-pitched music more accurately echoes the effects of these objects on Katherine. The guide personalizes his lecture by unconvincingly comparing the fourth sculpture to his own daughter, just one instance of his poor attempts to enliven his descriptions with anecdotal banter that he assumes will appeal to a woman. Likewise, he later points out that the sculpture of an aging Venus is his favorite—"she's the Venus I like most. She's not as young as the others...more mature"—using the sculpture to flatter his guest by implying that although Katherine is no longer youthful, being "more mature" is actually more beautiful. This comment startles Katherine, who realizes that she has moved past her youth and is therefore no longer a prime specimen of femininity, having aged over the course of her eight-year marriage.

As the uncanny music continues to reflect her bewilderment, the guide comments on sculptures that depict a satyr (described as a thankfully obsolete dangerous figure), a drunken faun (whose sleepy habits are praised by the Neapolitan guide, echoing Alex's comment on their first morning in Naples, "One certainly does sleep well in this country"), and a young discus thrower ("a Greek!"). The tour guide's heavy accent emphasizes the inadequacy and incommunicability of his verbal descriptions of these works of art whose world is long past, despite their pristine condition. Katherine's perusal of antiquities continues with a survey of ancient imperial portrait busts. Again, her guide's shallow analysis is overshadowed by the visual emphasis on Katherine's fascination, underscored by the unnatural musical accompaniment.

As Katherine enters the grand galleries housing the marble *Farnese Hercules* and the *Farnese Bull* [FIGS. 2–3], Rossellini conveys the awesome scale of these sculptures with the camera's slow, upward movement, a gesture that magnifies their overwhelming stature. After observing the gigantic representation of Hercules, whose bulging muscles and overt physicality embarrass a prudish Katherine, her guide explains that the ancient works were found in the Baths of Caracalla in Rome, further heightening the reaction of a naive Katherine to the mention of the fearsome emperor's name. Even more impressive to Katherine, however, is the description of the *Farnese Bull*, "carved out of a single block of marble and restored by Michelangelo." This work is not only a Roman copy of a Greek sculpture but also an inanimate object whose subsequent history is itself disjointed; though carved out of a single block, the work was clearly carved by more than a single artist.[15] The mention of Michelangelo as sculptor ensures the continued master status of a work that was not, in fact, rendered by his hand alone. What arrests Katherine is not simply the magnificent size of the object (which also impresses the viewer of the film) but also its diachronic history, one that remains dynamically provocative and elusive because of the ongoing chain of creation embedded in its unoriginal nature as an original copy.

Upon returning to Uncle Homer's villa, Katherine describes to Alex the power of the imperial portraits to convey their subjects in an exchange that marks a hiatus in their constant bickering. She tells him "to think that those men lived thousands of years ago and you feel that they are men of today. It's amazing! It is as if Nero or Caracalla, Caesar or Tiberius would suddenly tell you what they felt and you could understand what they were." Katherine's animated report demonstrates her burning desire to resuscitate the words of these lost souls whose lives have been preserved in dead objects. Alex's response returns, however, to a conflict at hand. Recalling Katherine's former admirer, he retorts, "Then they're not 'ascetic' figures after all," turning Katherine's words into a verbal assault on her own earlier nostalgic recollections of Charles Lewington's poetic memories of sites scattered throughout the Bay of Naples.

Shortly thereafter, Alex abandons his wife in search of an escape from their marital problems with frivolous flirtations in Capri (the site, as Katherine has recently learned from her museum guide, of the emperor Tiberius's far more lascivious pursuits two millennia earlier). Frustrated, Katherine nevertheless continues her exploration of the region, determined to continue her tourist experience. She travels to the landscape itself, the seemingly endless plains at the foot of Mount Vesuvius, where she witnesses the strange natural phenomenon of ionization. Katherine's next guide explains to her the volcano's volatile nature, highlighting the unstable subterranean vapors, which one can ignite by simply lighting a cigarette. Katherine is delighted by this geological

FIGURE 2

Ingrid Bergman beholds the *Farnese Hercules* in the Museo archeologico nazionale in Naples, in a scene from *Voyage in Italy*.

Photo: Courtesy British Film Institute.

FIGURE 3

Image of the *Farnese Bull* in the Museo archeologico nazionale in Naples in a scene from *Voyage in Italy*.

Photo: Courtesy British Film Institute.

wonder and captivated by the smoke escaping the earth, which suggests the uncannily warm and bodiless breath of a ghostly presence. Katherine insists on photographing the phenomenon for her absent husband in order to capture her experience: in this landscape history oscillates paradoxically between fixed instants of life and perpetual periods of death. Rossellini insists on photography's inherently stunning qualities; moreover, by including still photography within his motion picture, he confronts the viewer with temporal aspects that are simultaneously singular and multiple. In other words, Rossellini underscores the passage of time by inserting into film (a time-based medium) the action of photography, whose result is an inactive product that limits an act in an instant. Rossellini thus preserves his meditation on the paradoxical status of time within cinema, since film's representation of motion is really the suturing together of multiple fixed images.

Accompanied by Natalie Burton, the Italian wife of Uncle Homer's British caretaker, Katherine next visits a crypt in Naples. Mrs. Burton describes this place as one of her favorites, since she regularly pays homage to her dead brother there. The collections of anonymous skulls and skeletons deeply upset Katherine and emphasize her discomfort with bodies. This episode recalls a similar reaction earlier in the film, when Katherine first beholds various ancient sculptures; now her response is more deeply felt, since she is confronted with actual remains rather than representations of dead bodies. The scene at the crypt brings into focus the emotional disparity between Katherine's discomfort with death and Mrs. Burton's solace for the loss of her brother, further underscoring Rossellini's juxtapositions of English and Italian, that is, northern and southern (or Protestant as opposed to Catholic) cultures.

Perhaps the most hauntingly silent sculptural bodies are those that Katherine encounters when she and Alex accompany caretaker Burton to visit Pompeii in the hope of finding a body in "the moment he was surprised by death" [FIG. 4]. Once they arrive, Burton explains the process of recovering fossilized bodies incinerated by the eruption. The day of their visit is particularly productive, with the discovery of several hollowed-out areas into which archaeologists will pour plaster to re-create the shape of the suffocated bodies. Burton indicates the individual body parts until enough have been recast to discern a pair of human bodies, a man and a woman, clinging to each other. As these hollow bodies become plastic, their reunited limbs suggest a narrative of their final moments. Rossellini's powerful image of the fossil made visible when filled with plaster is singular: this delicate hollowness is a metaphor for the past as a necessary absence that we can only reconstitute artificially. Confronting these

two lovers, whose renewed tangibility solidifies both their fate and their eternal devotion, forces Katherine to see the hollowness of her own detached union with Alex, an empty emotional engagement completely divested of physical passion. The dramatic disjunction between the anonymous lovers' bond and Katherine and Alex's mutually repellent physical selves shocks Katherine so deeply that she bursts into tears and flees this site of unbearable archaeological and personal discovery. These bodies recall the dead souls who seemed to breathe life the day before during Katherine's observation of the volcanic emissions. Alex attempts to soothe his wife, but she cannot be consoled, insisting that they leave Pompeii at once. Rossellini's camera tracks their departure, slowly passing through the excavations, highlighting their traversal through the public and private spaces of the silent dead for whom these remains now speak. As the lens passes through ruined homes and abandoned streets littered with ancient amphorae, the camera pauses to focus on a wall painting from the House of the Ephebe [FIG. 5]. This depiction of Mars and Venus comes alive, as the divine lovers' passion contrasts with the chilling distance between Katherine and Alex.[16]

Pictorial Predicaments: Contempt

Godard, like Rossellini, includes structures, paintings, and sculptures that draw on antique subjects in his film, though most of these insertions are self-consciously artificial. Indeed, his film begins as a self-reflexive meditation on cinema's artifice, with a voice-over spelling out the fact that the film is a constructed work of art. As the first shots pan the abandoned streets of Cinecittà, Godard represents the abandoned heart of cinematic creation and then turns to capture the viewer in its frame. The second scene features an intimate exchange of words between Paul and Camille in an apparently postcoital moment. This tender shot of lovers has a prelapsarian innocence, as Camille slowly and deliberately asks her husband to catalogue the parts of her body, words that fail to match the images offered by Godard. By persistently shifting to the wrong body part, the director announces the failure of language to describe what should be experienced properly through vision. Through his disjointed combination of verbal and pictorial language, Godard transforms the living Camille into a dead, fragmentary statue.

The film then cuts to the deserted studios of Cinecittà, transporting the viewer to a modern ruin. This classicizing aspect of the abandoned studios is quickly confirmed

FIGURE 4

An archaeologist uncovers cast bodies in a scene from *Voyage in Italy*.

Photo: Courtesy British Film Institute.

FIGURE 5

Ingrid Bergman and George Sanders pass through the House of Ephebe in a scene from *Voyage in Italy*.

Photo: Courtesy British Film Institute.

FIGURE 6

Jack Palance hurls a film canister inside the Cinecittà film studios in a scene from *Contempt*.

Photo: Criterion Films.

when Paul arrives for a meeting with Prokosch in time to witness the obnoxious American producer's rejection of Fritz Lang's latest footage for his version of *The Odyssey*. Standing before a projection screen (thus starring in his own private show), Prokosch throws a film canister in an impromptu performance as a modern-day Discobolos [FIG. 6]. (This action elicits one of Lang's wittiest remarks: "Well, Jerry, you finally get the idea of Greek culture.") Whereas *Voyage in Italy* visits antique culture through a sculpture of a discus thrower—called "a Greek" by Katherine's guide—*Contempt* instead impersonates the antique figure, confronting the viewer with a dynamic work of art whose effect is predicated on its own pronounced artificiality. Both versions of the discus thrower acknowledge the impossibility of recuperating the impact of the original sculpture: Rossellini lingers on the arresting quality of the ancient figure's foreignness, while Godard reveals its incompatibility with modern culture by expressing its absurdity in the here and now.

Once Paul agrees to rewrite the script, Prokosch insists that the couple accompany him back to his Roman villa so that he can continue to gawk at Paul's attractive young wife. In two subsequent scenes Godard inserts self-consciously fake reproductions of art. First, when Paul arrives at the villa late, he finds Camille flipping through a book—Prokosch's seduction includes a coffee-table volume of pornographic paintings from Pompeii.[17] The sexually explicit images, derived at least in part from brothels, are multivalent metaphors for prostitution. In accepting Prokosch's offer to rewrite the script, Paul sells his intellect to the decadent film industry critiqued in *Contempt*. But when Paul realizes the power of his wife's sexuality, he sells her as well, manipulating her body for his own professional goals. Godard could easily have returned to film *Contempt* in either Pompeii or Herculaneum; instead, he emphasizes the deceptive conceits inherent in our revisiting the forbidden paintings as copies. For Godard, the paintings as reproductions extend visually the acts performed in these images of sex-for-sale, adding another layer to the commodification of bodies within this cinematic work that itself sold tickets precisely because of its female star.[18]

Paul and Camille, along with the volume of ancient paintings, return to their apartment, an unfinished, modernist stage set where they debate whether to travel with Prokosch to film in Capri. In between the scene in which the characters perambulate

the templelike ruins of Cinecittà (complete with their own metopes in the form of de-caying film posters) and the couple's arrival at Prokosch's villa, Godard splices into the film a shot of a bronze sculpture of Neptune, under whose gaze (and evil eye), Paul—a modern surrogate for Odysseus—has fallen. Whereas earlier, we saw antique sculpture awkwardly included in the scenes of *The Odyssey* already filmed under Lang's direction, now we find the same gods manipulating the lives of Paul and Camille. Godard uses Prokosch's brief reviewing of the clips as an opportunity to explain to his own audience how the gods make pawns of men, ancient or modern, within both films. Thus the reflexive gesture of the film-within-the-film serves as a grammatical tool through which the viewer experiences the temporal flexibility of Godard's classically inflected cinematic language.

Once in the apartment—the financial drain that impels Paul's prostitution—Godard underscores the tragic nature of Paul and Camille's relationship through their antique costumes. Camille—in a thick, red towel—and Paul—in a carefully knot-ted sheet-as-toga—move about the spaces of their apartment as if classical players in an abstracted theatrical stage set that is host to their private tragedy [FIG. 7]. Godard underscores the theatricality of this scene by substituting a short, black wig for Bardot's dyed blonde hair—itself a prop. The couple bicker about their relationship in this domestic scene, but, whereas in *Voyage in Italy* Katherine and Alex argue about their lack of anything in common, Camille and Paul's spat centers on the physicality of their relationship. If the couple are interpreted as Odysseus and Penelope, then Camille serves as a Penelope who yearns for her husband to leave without her. Camille picks up on Godard's larger theme of prostitution, pronouncing a list of profane words, includ-ing "putaine." Having failed to understand his wife in the flesh, Paul turns his attention to a bronze female sculpture, tapping different parts of her body, recalling the cata-loguing in the opening scene. Paul listens to the effects of his strokes, as if to determine if the exterior reflects the interior, a question he attempts to answer in this inanimate body since he has failed to answer it in the live body of his wife.

The scene featuring auditions for the part of Nausicaa further substantiates Godard's persistence in creating modern visions of antiquity. These tryouts do not include women made up in antique costumes reciting lines of epic poetry; rather, what we see resembles a 1960s dance party with a crowd of men dancing with women in knee-length, pleated skirts and loose knit pullovers—emphatically modern rather than Homeric—all following a young woman singing Adriano Celentano's song *Venti-quattromila baci* (Twenty-four thousand kisses), a popular Italian hit presented at San Remo in 1961. Immediately after this scene the relationship between the two films is made explicit as the main cast exits beneath the lit awning that reads *Viaggio in Italia*. Godard proclaims to both internal and external spectators that his film will make its own "voyage in Italy," although his move south to the Bay of Naples will be self-conscious. The fact that we see this announcement in bright lights installed across the ultimate temple of modern artifice, the cinema, declares Godard's unabashed enthu-siasm for ersatz culture's failed recuperations of antiquity. Godard stands in stark contrast with—and indeed suggests a way of avoiding cinematically—what Roland Barthes describes in his analysis of the persistence of mythologies in modern culture.[19] In "Romans in Films," Barthes laments how blockbuster, sword-and-sandal films try to convince viewers of their antique legitimacy through visual cues associated with ancient Rome. Godard instead makes a film within his film that is self-consciously fake, replete with exaggerated makeup; overlit scenes; supersaturated, primary colors; and

FIGURE 7

Clad in makeshift togas, Brigitte Bardot and Michel Piccoli become animated statues as they move through their apartment in a scene from *Contempt*.

Photo: Courtesy Criterion Films.

FIGURE 8

Artificial, classical sculptures stand awkwardly in a wild landscape in a scene from *Contempt*.

Photo: Courtesy Criterion Films.

awkwardly rendered imitations of classical sculptures. Even when Godard includes shots of archaic bronze sculptures, he disrupts their expected effect by inelegantly coloring the figures' eyes. I argue that the scenes of *The Odyssey* that we witness being filmed within the film (and, thankfully, they are few) are horribly rendered, not only as an assault on Hollywood but also as an insistence that these failed renditions of antiquity are the most valid or authentic possibility of perceiving the past left open to modern interpretations.

Godard assaults the viewer by simultaneously presenting antiquity in various synthetic forms, suggesting that its meaning can only be synthetic at best, a copy of an absent and inaccessible original. And yet he moves to a real site of antiquity, Capri, to film his tacky living sculptures—actors ridiculously made up and clad in pseudo-antique costumes as well as shoddy plaster casts of archaic and classical figures gone awry with absurd, brightly colored surfaces—who, set against the unadulterated landscape, function as ironically staged tableaux vivants [FIG. 8].[20] By casting together simulated bodies and the real landscape, Godard authenticates his own work of art as he articulates the failure of modernism to constitute a break from the past or, perhaps more pointedly, the symptomatic break within the present, which translates into its own failure to understand itself. Godard mis-places the modern actors in antique roles to underscore the failed marriage of past to present. The resulting disruptive images of the present's vision of the past sustain Godard's larger project of destabilizing the possibility of securing meaning.

When Prokosch-as-Discobolos berates Lang for his initial footage—"You've cheated me, Fritz. That's not what is in that script."—Godard comments on the failure of words to translate into images—even cinematic images—as Lang retorts, "It is!" and Prokosch must concede, "Yes, it's in the script. But it's not what you have on that screen." And Lang agrees, "Naturally, because in the script it is written, and on the screen it's pictures. Motion picture, it's called." But for Lang and Godard, these modern attempts to resurrect antiquity are destined to fail, since Cinemascope cannot accommodate the human form, ancient or modern, since, as Lang tells us, its horizontal format is more appropriate for snakes and coffins than for vertically oriented, mobile human beings. And thus Godard once again dooms the possibility of classical aesthetics in the modern moment; the inevitable crisis of representation encountered when moving between words and images is a crisis renewed and aggravated by the conditions (and possibilities) of cinema itself. In writing about the film years later, Godard said, "whereas the Odyssey of Ulysses was a physical phenomenon, I filmed a spiritual odyssey: the eye of the camera watching these characters in search of Homer replaces that of the gods watching over Ulysses and his companions."[21]

Cinema allows these directors to stage how we experience the actual landscape. In *Voyage in Italy* we first encounter the vastness of the Bay of Naples from the terrace at Uncle Homer's villa, where Katherine returns when she wants to explore her emotional predicament. There she enjoys magnificent views of Vesuvius, Pompeii, Castellammare, Torre Annunziata, Resonne, Naples, Ischia, Capri, and the Sorrento Peninsula, among which she finds the ruins where she retraces Charles's lost tracks. But when Godard descends to Capri, he replaces Uncle Homer's neoclassical villa with Adalberto Libera's Casa Malaparte, one of the most stunning examples of Italian modernist architecture [FIG. 9]. Set in an inlet among the island's cliffs, this 1937 modern ziggurat features views that fit Godard's emphatically modernist vision of the landscape. When filming inside the house, Godard focuses on the picture windows in order

to present the antique landscape in modern picture frames, much like the shots Lang will capture in his nearby filming of the story. Whereas Cinecittà provides the ruined modern temple, the Casa Malaparte reopens the possibility for sacred aesthetics in the contemporary moment through its unadulterated connections to the landscape enabled by its transparent features.[22]

Language or the Myth(s) of Echo

Rossellini marks *Voyage in Italy* with linguistic traces of local dialect and vernacular music. The soundtrack includes songs written in Neapolitan dialect (and performed by Rossellini's brother Renzo), often centered on the theme of jealousy. Rossellini insists on a trilingual (English, Italian, and Neapolitan dialect) environment, never compromising the foreignness of his characters with dubbing or subtitles. Thus, Rossellini challenges his audience by retaining what would have been for most viewers an unlikely combination of languages.

One of the film's most striking linguistic breakdowns occurs early on when Alex and Katherine have just arrived at Uncle Homer's villa and are relaxing on the terrace after lunch. The failure of the Joyces to comprehend Burton and each other is illustrated by their inability to understand Neapolitan culinary codes: their spastic consumption of pasta, a task particularly challenging to Katherine, who cannot manage the spaghetti with her fork, and Alex's excessive midday consumption of wine.[23] The postprandial siesta of the villa's staff (including Burton), a concept utterly foreign to Alex, thwarts his search for a second carafe of wine. Deeply irritated, Alex awakens the kitchen staff for a colorful exchange with one of the cooks, who cannot understand Alex's request in English. When his attempts to communicate fail, Alex speaks more loudly, ultimately abandoning spoken language and resorting to what he hopes is a universal language of gesture. The frustrated duo eventually enlists Burton and his Italian wife for translation when the servant finally exclaims, "Noi non ci capiamo! Vieni con me." The linguistic breakdown between Alex and the cook continues the film's thematization of failed translations and meaning, this time pointing to differences in culture and social class. Rossellini's incorporation of verbal and gestural communication breakdown is appropriate, since he shows that the words of Neapolitan dialect cannot be divorced from their accompanying gestures, an integral part of the language itself.[24]

Katherine and Alex attend an elegant cocktail party held in their honor in Naples at the home of the duke of Lipoli, one of Uncle Homer's best friends. In a powerful exchange about the differences between northern and southern European culture, one of the guests tries to explain to Katherine the concept of *dolce far niente*. In an effort to explain Neapolitan culture to Katherine, the duke emphatically asks, "How do you say in English *dolce far niente*?" to which another Italian guest replies, "It is impossible to say it in English. Perhaps I could translate it, 'how sweet it is to do nothing.'" Katherine politely replies, "Oh, I understand," although the words clearly remain meaningless to her since what is impossible to understand are not the words *dolce far niente* but rather the concept of pleasure in rest, a Neapolitan notion which makes Alex, a professed workaholic, uncomfortable throughout the film.[25]

Rossellini underscores the power of (mis)communication through linguistic games of repetition. Katherine's guides constantly repeat themselves; this continual failure to convey meaning is staged most dramatically in her visit to the Cave of the Sibyl. Here, Katherine's guide explains not only the ancient tradition of visiting the Cumaean Sibyl to hear her prophecies (especially about love) but also the more recent history associated with the site through the landing of the British troops toward the end of the Second World War. In an effort to flirt (or perhaps extract a tip), Katherine's guide personalizes her tour, shouting out sounds as they pass through the ancient corridor and explaining how much louder his echoes would have been if the halls had still been lined with bronze as they were in "ancient times." Her guide's performative echo anticipates the metaphorical echoes of Charles's poetry, whose strongest recollections by Katherine occur when she ventures above the cave to the Temple of Apollo, which she associates with the "Temple of the Spirits" in her lover's verses.

Godard's exploration of the impossibility of translation goes beyond the gaps between words and images; he includes interlinguistic investigations as well, most conspicuously fleshed out by his creation of Francesca, Prokosch's professional translator and unappreciated lover, who ensures that social and professional matters run smoothly. On a practical level Francesca's translations upset the possibility of dubbing, since a dubbed version would result in nonsensical repetitions of lines.[26] Francesca's Echo-like presence underscores the incommunicability of Godard's characters' emotions through their awkward linguistic discord as well as the inevitable losses in translation. Even the expert Francesca fails to provide exact meanings on occasion; she defies her lot as Echo, since sometimes she translates accurately, sometimes not, occasionally inflecting her repetitions of others' speech with personal commentary. Francesca's skills enable Prokosch, who defiantly speaks only English, to communicate with the French-speaking Camille and Paul Javal, Mr. Lang (who fluently moves among French, German, and English), and various members of the Italian-speaking staff and crew.[27] Yet Prokosch's brash and unsophisticated comments are perfectly clear, even to those unfamiliar with the English language. And if Francesca stands in for Echo, then Prokosch's limits can be read through his playing the role of her partner, Narcissus.

The emptiness of Prokosch's speech emerges as he recites from a tiny red book of famous quotations; he never cites their sources or explains their meanings. Godard thus makes explicit how words gain and lose meaning through their contexts. Through Prokosch's glaringly absurd misuse of phrases, the spectator witnesses, yet again,

Godard's hyperbolic exemplification of the instability of linguistic (and other) signs. Prokosch further misquotes Hermann Göring when he demands an answer from Paul about rewriting the screenplay. "Whenever I hear the word culture, I bring out my checkbook" is quickly recognized by Fritz Lang—who had fled Nazi Germany in 1933 upon being offered the position of official state filmmaker—as a sloppy and dangerous mistake. Lang corrects him in French, substituting the word "revolver," but when he points out Prokosch's misquotation of Göring, we understand the hidden menace of Prokosch's earlier comment to Paul in reference to Lang "but this is '63, not '33, Fritz" and thus also Godard's recalibration of the chronology of the film to point out different, more recent cultural horrors.

Cast as himself, a German director, Lang serves as an intellectual resource whose virtues would be wasted on (and hence should not be translated for) Prokosch. Lang's heritage is not accidental, since Prokosch reminds everyone that only a German could have discovered Troy. Thus Godard suggests that in the modern world only through cinema can the excavation of the past be made meaningful, since cinema, unlike archaeology and its endless quest for answers to questions about the past, is art rather than science. For Godard, cinema represents a last hope for asking rather than answering enduring questions about the past. Much of the dialogue between Lang and Javal remains untranslated for Prokosch, including discussions of literary figures such as Dante and commentary on the art of cinema itself, such as Paul's comment on Cinemascope: "J'aime beaucoup le Cinemascope," to which Lang responds, "N'est pas fait pour les hommes. C'est pour les serpentes ou les enterrements." Occasionally even Lang, who seems to have mastered all the languages in the film, asks for help with translation: "How do you say *étrange* en italienne?" Francesca replies, "Strano." When the main cast of characters later attends the auditions for Nausicaa, Godard notes the arbitrariness of linguistic signs through Lang's reference to Bertolt Brecht. In defending his position as a director engaged with a soulless producer, Lang quotes Brecht's comparison of selling one's wares at market each day to working in the film industry. When Paul recognizes the citation as Brecht's commentary on Hollywood, Lang confirms his assignment of the words to "B.B." In 1963 most spectators would have immediately understood the pun, since as we hear "B.B.," Brigitte Bardot, who was often referred to by her initials, struts across the screen.[28] Thus, for Godard, language fails to translate both interlinguistically and intralinguistically, as the arbitrary and coincidental assignments and relationships in language make clear.

(In)visible Texts

*V*oyage in Italy and *Contempt* include different forms of letters that I classify as (in)visible texts. Early in her trip to Campagna, Katherine recalls melancholically the poetic words of Charles Lewington. During her explorations of the region, Charles's phrase "Temple of the Spirits, no longer bodies but pure ascetic images compared to which mere thought seems flesh, heavy, dim" echoes in the powerful landscape that unfolds around her. Katherine tries to locate the inspirations for Charles's poetry as she visits sites to reactivate not only what she can remember of his words but also their unfulfilled feelings for one another. The impact of Charles's remembered love potently emerges as part of this palpitating landscape, since during his lifetime his words failed to express what they now elucidate for Katherine, now returned to their proper source. This reconnection of poetry to the landscape whose history far precedes its mistranslation into Charles's language is Katherine's own exploitation of language as a tool through which to gain access to her own and Charles's past. This reunion of the old text with her new experience of the ancient sites allows for an emotional journey across time despite absence and death.

Both films project handwritten letters across the screen, granting the written word the status of a visual artifact-in-the-making. When Alex runs off to escape their bickering, he writes (rather than speaks) to Katherine and informs her, "I'm going to Capri. To have a little fun, as you said. Museums bore me. You'll have more time for your pilgrimages this way. Alex." Alex thus differentiates himself from the deceased, yet increasingly present, Charles. Rossellini artfully films this slip of paper so that we (as audience) read it along with Katherine and thereby enter it into our growing log of ancient objects and more recent cultural oddities that we as cinematic tourists are by now well trained to recognize. By removing Alex's person from his message, Rossellini anticipates and illustrates the now familiar French poststructuralist critique of the modernist notion of authorship. The cleavage of Alex as subject from his text allows Rossellini to immerse the viewer more fully in Katherine's interpretive processing of that letter in light of the emphatic absence of its writer. Deprived of Alex's tone of voice, body language, and cadence, the text remains just what it is, words on paper that seem arbitrarily trite and hollow, unable to convey anything substantive, let alone personal. Thus Katherine fails to excavate any meaning from them other than what she wants to find as she runs the words over again in her head later that day.

In *Contempt*, Camille leaves a note for Paul, explaining that "since he will not leave Capri," she has taken a ride back to Rome with Prokosch, with whom she now seems to be involved, if only in response to her prostitution by Paul. She too could have spoken her plans to her partner, but like Alex she chooses instead a form of absent communication, an announcement whose receipt confirms her departure. Upon reading Alex's and Camille's notes, Katherine and Paul fulfill their prescription. In *Voyage in Italy* we see the complete text of Alex's letter, as if the totality of its presence can offer a complete message. In *Contempt*, however, we see only a fragment of Camille's final words to Paul. "Je t'embrasse. Adieu. Camille." And though written only hours before, these words are already an impossible part of an irrecuperable whole. The letter allegorically represents one limb of the shattered physical and emotional selves of Camille and Paul; indeed, it confirms that they will not have a chance to try to understand one another, although Camille's actual presence would not guarantee more meaningful communication with body or soul.

Both directors notably film the signatures of these letters. Jacques Derrida reminds us that the signature is just an element on which we rely to try to fix meaning, which, ultimately, remains unstable, even in the presence of context, here partially constructed by the trace of the writers of the notes. The signature has no meaning in its initial articulation but it later assumes significance when used to assign value to the text to which it is attached—the signature is one instance of "context" in the Derridean sense.[29] While signatures also assign authenticity to letters, documents, and other texts, they also confirm their own reproducibility, since the signature is meaningful only if recognized as a copy of a known entity. Much like the many layers of artistic copies embedded in these films, the signatures confirm not only their failures as originals but also their inadequacy to convey meaning. Instead, although the signatures suggest a context for the notes, they also expose the limitations of language, strings of words that can be used and reused to no avail. And letters, of course, remind us of the mutual absence of writer and reader, joined by the text that exists precisely because of their separation.

◙ ◙ ◙

In both films the failure of the past to have meaning in the present is expressed through unsuccessful communications, as texts fail not only as themselves but again when translated into pictorial surrogates. As films set firmly in the present, both foreground the spectator's painful predicament of being trapped in a place from which the past's significance remains inevitably inaccessible. Through their poignant portrayals of their characters' resulting contempt for one another, Rossellini and Godard unearth the ghosts of the past lingering in the Bay of Naples. As a modernist, Godard already anticipates postmodernism by showing sensitivity to the cyclical nature of historicity through his traditional iconography and insisting on history's inevitable self-repetition rather than by presenting the modernist vision of innovation and progress. If Rossellini is a modernist for highlighting our failure to read the past due to a modern alienation from it, then Godard is a postmodernist in his insistence on the movement possible across time through the art of self and others. While Rossellini is interested in the incommunicability of northern and southern European sensibilities, in a certain way, Godard finds enough material to focus his critique of failed meanings within Italy itself, since for him "Rome is the modern world, the West; Capri, the ancient world, nature before civilization and its neuroses." But Godard brings modern neuroses to the landscape and expresses them through failed communications of the past projected onto the hopelessly obtuse present.

Notes

Thanks are due to Allison Levy, Kevin Lubrano, Elias Markolefas, Glenn W. Most, Alexander Nehamas, Lisa Silverman, Isabelle Wallace, and students in "The Classical Tradition" at Oberlin College (2005). The Program in Hellenic Studies at Princeton University supported the final stages of this project. My love of these films grows out of conversations with Steven Levine and David Cast, Bryn Mawr College, whose visions animate static and motion pictures alike.

1   Jean-Luc Godard, *Godard on Godard*, trans. and ed. Tom Milne (New York, 1986), 200.

2   Fabrizio Pesardo, "Shadows of Light: Cinema, *Peplum*, and Pompeii," in *Tales from an Eruption: Pompeii, Herculaneum, Oplontis: Guide to the Exhibition*, ed. Pietro Giovanni Guzzo, trans. Jo Wallace-Hadrill (Milan, 2003), 34–35. Pesardo surveys cinematic productions set in antiquity, noting the popularity of two narratives: adaptations of Edward Bulwer-Lytton's *Last Days of Pompeii* and renditions of Nero's reign, such as *Quo Vadis*. He counts four adaptations of *The Last Days of Pompeii* and six of *Quo Vadis* before 1926. For an overview of literature set in Pompeii, see Eric Moormann, "Literary Evocations of Ancient Pompeii," in Guzzo 2003, 14–33. In particular, Moormann links interest in the gruesome aspects of volcanic eruption to the rise of the gothic novel in the eighteenth and nineteenth centuries. For theatrical and cinematic productions that revolve around stories set in antiquity, see also *Playing out the Empire: Ben-Hur and Other Toga Plays and Films, 1883–1908: A Critical Anthology*, ed. David Mayer (Oxford, 1994), esp. James Pain, "The Last Days of Pompeii," 90–103; as well as Maria Wyke, *Projecting the Past: Ancient Rome, Cinema, and History* (New York, 1997), esp. "Pompeii: Purging the Sins of the City," 147–82.

3   Filming on-location in Pompeii and Herculaneum was less expensive than building outrageously elaborate Hollywood sets at Cinecittà.

4   Wyke 1997 (note 2), 183–84, argues that *Contempt*'s self-conscious critique of the Hollywood film industry signifies the end of the postwar blockbuster films whose narratives draw on classical antiquity. Moreover, Wyke not only sees *Contempt* as emblematic of Godard's own contempt for the Hollywood film industry but also notes that its release coincides with *Cleopatra*, starring Elizabeth Taylor and Richard Burton.

5   Kaja Silverman and Harun Farocki, "In Search of Homer," in *Speaking about Godard* (New York, 1998), 56–57.

6   Several critics have written about *Voyage in Italy* in terms of its staging of the conflicts between the north and south; though the film inserts a British couple into the Italian landscape, the resulting cultural clash can be seen as an allegory of the tension between northern and southern Italy itself. See, for example, Mira Liehm, *Passion and Defiance: Films in Italy from 1942 to the Present* (Berkeley, 1984), 109.

7   As Laura Mulvey points out in her commentary on *Voyage in Italy*, this aspect of the story is loosely based on James Joyce's short story "The Dead." See *The Portable James Joyce*, ed. Harry Levin (New York, 1983), 190–242, esp. 236ff. Although the names and circumstances are altered, Rossellini borrows a woman's mournful recollection of a lost love, which preceded her marriage to another man.

8   Angela dalla Vacche, *The Body in the Mirror* (Princeton, 1992), 180–89, interprets this final scene as emblematic of Katherine Joyce's rejection of the Neapolitan body culture.

9   Alberto Moravia, *Il disprezzo*, trans. Angus Davidson (1954; London, 1999).

10 Colin MacCabe, *Godard: A Portrait of the Artist at Seventy* (New York, 2004), 157, points out that the Greek *Odyssey* appears in its Latinized version.

11 Paul's most recent creative compromise mirrors Godard's own struggles with his American producer Joe Levine and the commercial pressures of cinema. See ibid., 153–56.

12 Giuliana Bruno includes *Voyage in Italy* in her analysis of Naples and New York as "intrinsically filmic" cities. Citing Jean-Paul Sartre's invocation of Matilde Serao's coined phrase "the belly of Naples," Bruno traces the history of this dystopian city's key role in cinema, arguing that Naples as an ideally cinematic city is the direct inheritance of its central importance in the tradition of the Grand Tour. See Giuliana Bruno, "City Views: The Voyage of Film Images," in *The Cinematic City*, ed. David Clarke (London, 1997), 46–58; for her discussion of Rossellini's film, see esp. 47–48.

13 Of course, naming the caretaker of Uncle Homer's home "Burton" cannot be accidental and alludes to Robert Burton and his work on melancholy, what I see as an underlying structural element of the film.

14 Katherine's guide denies her a description of pornographic works removed from the sites of Pompeii and Herculaneum as he considers such sexually explicit content inappropriate for a prim female visitor on her own.

15 Christian Kunze, "Dall'originale greco alla copia romana," 13–42; Paul Zanker, "Collocazione ed effetto nelle Terme di Caracalla," 43–46; Gabriella Prisco, "Dalle Terme al Museo di Napoli," 47–68; and Ciro Piccioli, "Il restauro. Metodologia," 69–77, in *Il toro Farnese: La "montagna di marmo" tra Roma e Napoli* (Naples, 1991).

16 Alix Berbet, *La peinture murale romaine: Les styles décoratifs pompéiens* (Paris, 1985); and *Pompei: Pitture e mosaici*, ed. Giovanni Pugliese Carratelli, vol. 1 (Rome, 1990).

17 Although unidentifiable from the shots in the film, the book recalls numerous commercial publications marketing ancient taboo images. See, for example, Jean Marcadé, *Roma Amor: Essay on Erotic Elements in Etruscan and Roman Art* (Geneva, 1961); Antonia Mulas, *Eros in Antiquity*

(New York, 1978); Antonio Varone, *Eroticism in Pompeii*, trans. Maureen Fant (Los Angeles, 2001). For a scholarly treatment of prostitution in Pompeii, see Thomas A. J. McGinn, "Pompeian Brothels," in *Journal of Roman Archaeology*, suppl. no. 47 (2002): 7–46. See also John R. Clarke, *Looking at Lovemaking: Constructions of Sexuality in Roman Art, 100 B.C. to A.D. 250* (Berkeley, 1998).

18 By the time of *Contempt*'s release, Bardot's stardom had been well established by Roger Vadim's 1956 *And God Created Woman*.

19 Roland Barthes, *Mythologies*, trans. Annette Levers (1957; New York, 1998), 26–29.

20 The plaster casts included in *Contempt*, replete with unrealistically painted features, are absurdly whimsical when compared to the somber objects cast from the remains of the dead at Pompeii in *Voyage in Italy*.

21 Godard 1986 (note 1), 201.

22 Marida Talmonda, *Casa Malaparte* (New York, 1992). For an exploration of the literal and metaphorical significance of the transparency of glass, see Colin Rowe and Robert Slutzky, "Transparency: Literal and Phenomenal," in *The Mathematics of the Ideal Villa and Other Essays* (Cambridge, Mass., 1976), 160ff.

23 As a native speaker of Swedish, Ingrid Bergman spoke English with a certain awkwardness that occasionally slips into her performance, further underscoring the disjunctive nature of her communications throughout the film.

24 The full scene proceeds as follows:
    ALEX JOYCE. Excuse me, I'm sorry to trouble you. / SERVANT. Eh? /
    ALEX JOYCE. Well, I'm terribly thirsty, it's this food, you know. I'm not used to all those sauces. / SERVANT. Ma che volete? / ALEX JOYCE. Something to drink. / SERVANT. Ah. Fate meglio con una bicarbonata. / ALEX JOYCE. Well, I just want you to fill it up. / SERVANT. Capito. State ubriaco. Ma che succede dopo? / ALEX JOYCE. This wine is excellent, you know. (*He gestures with finger into bottle.*) / SERVANT. Non volete carbonata? / ALEX JOYCE. But you misunderstand me. I want you to fill it up. / SERVANT. Va bene. Noi non ci capiamo! Vieni con me. Vieni. Vieni. Vieni! Vieni! VIENI! / ALEX JOYCE. How dare you speak to me like that! / SERVANT. Andiamo dalla Signora. Vieni con me che' io non voglio risponsabilità. / MRS. BURTON. Si. Che c'è? / SERVANT. Scusa. Ma questo signore non vuol capi. Si sente male. / ALEX JOYCE. Oh. (*He covers his eyes when he realizes that Mrs. Burton is dressed only in her slip.*) / MRS. BURTON. To fill up a bottle of water you should do like this (*makes gesture with thumb and not index finger*). Il signore vuole anche una bottiglia di acqua minerale. / SERVANT. Oh. Chiudo io.

25 For an exploration of stereotypical descriptions of southern Italian behavior, see Nelson Moe, *The View from Vesuvius: Italian Culture and the Southern Question* (Berkeley, 2002).

26 Francesca's presence also thwarted efforts to dub Godard's film, a preventative strategy effective in both the French and American releases. The Italian producer Carlo Ponti, however, went ahead with the dubbing, which makes the entire film, and especially Francesca's character, seem absurd, since the same lines are unnecessarily repeated. See Wheeler Winston Dixon, *The Films of Jean-Luc Godard* (Albany, 1997), 44.

27 Although the addition of Francesca is Godard's most notable departure from Moravia's novel, it is not the only change in the story; see Silverman and Farocki 1998 (note 5).

28 MacCabe 2004 (note 10), 151, mentions this pun as well.

29 See Jacques Derrida, "Signature, Event, Context," in *The Margins of Philosophy*, trans. Alan Bass (Chicago, 1982), 307–30.

Index

Note: *Italic* page numbers indicate illustrations.